Business Information Management II:
Texas Edition

Andrea Mehaffie

Amy Reyes

Catherine Skintik

Teri Watanabe

Boston • Columbus • Indianapolis • New York • San Francisco
Amsterdam • Cape Town • Dubai • London • Madrid • Milan • Munich • Paris • Montréal • Toronto
Delhi • Mexico City • São Paulo • Sydney • Hong Kong • Seoul • Singapore • Taipei • Tokyo

Pearson

Copyright © 2017. Pearson Education, Inc. All Rights Reserved.

Printed in the United States of America. This publication is protected by copyright, and permission should be obtained from the publisher prior to any prohibited reproduction, storage in a retrieval system, or transmission in any form or by any means, electronic, mechanical, photocopying, recording, or otherwise. For information regarding permissions, request forms and the appropriate contacts, please visit www.pearsoned.com/permissions to contact the Pearson Education Rights and Permissions Department.

Unless otherwise indicated herein, any third party trademarks that may appear in this work are the property of their respective owners and any references to third party trademarks, logos or other trade dress are for demonstrative or descriptive purposes only. Such references are not intended to imply any sponsorship, endorsement, authorization, or promotion of Pearson Education Inc. products by the owners of such marks, or any relationship between the owner and Pearson Education Inc. or its affiliates, authors, licensees or distributors.

Credits and acknowledgments borrowed from other sources and reproduced, with permission, in this textbook appear on the appropriate page within text. Microsoft and/or its respective suppliers make no representations about the suitability of the information contained in the documents and related graphics published as part of the services for any purpose. All such documents and related graphics are provided "as is" without warranty of any kind.

Microsoft and/or its respective suppliers hereby disclaim all warranties and conditions with regard to this information, including all warranties and conditions of merchantability, whether express, implied or statutory, fitness for a particular purpose, title and non-infringement. In no event shall Microsoft and/or its respective suppliers be liable for any special, indirect or consequential damages or any damages whatsoever resulting from loss of use, data or profits, whether in an action of contract, negligence or other tortious action, arising out of or in connection with the use or performance of information available from the services.

The documents and related graphics contained herein could include technical inaccuracies or typographical errors. Changes are periodically added to the information herein. Microsoft and/or its respective suppliers may make improvements and/or changes in the product(s) and/or the program(s) described herein at any time. Partial screen shots may be viewed in full within the software version specified.

Microsoft® and Windows® are registered trademarks of the Microsoft Corporation in the U.S.A. and other countries. This book is not sponsored or endorsed by or affiliated with the Microsoft Corporation.

330 Hudson Street, New York, NY 10013

Hardcover ISBN 10: 0-13-444682-8
Hardcover ISBN 13: 978-0-13-444682-0

Table of Contents

Introduction vii

Navigating the Textbook ix

Microsoft Word 2013

Chapter 5
Using Advanced Formatting, Lists, and Charts 2

Lesson 36 – Inserting Text Files and Blank Pages..... 4
Lesson 37 – Creating and Editing Styles 10
Lesson 38 – Managing Style Formatting 18
Lesson 39 – Working with Multilevel Lists 29
Lesson 40 – Inserting Charts 35
End-of-Chapter Activities 42

Chapter 6
Using Reusable Content and Markup Tools.......... 46

Lesson 41 – Customizing Language and Word Options 48
Lesson 42 – Using Advanced Find and Replace 58
Lesson 43 – Using Building Blocks 67
Lesson 44 – Inserting Fields from Quick Parts 73
Lesson 45 – Creating Custom Templates, Themes, and Style Sets................... 79
Lesson 46 – Tracking Changes 91
Lesson 47 – Comparing Documents 98
Lesson 48 – Restricting Access to Documents..... 107
End-of-Chapter Activities 112

Chapter 7
Using Advanced Tables and Graphics 116

Lesson 49 – Customizing Table Styles 118
Lesson 50 – Using Advanced Table Features 126
Lesson 51 – Using Advanced Graphics 137
Lesson 52 – Linking Text Boxes 146
Lesson 53 – Creating WordArt and Watermarks.... 155
End-of-Chapter Activities 161

Chapter 8
Working with Long Documents................ 166

Lesson 54 – Working with Outlines............. 168
Lesson 55 – Advanced Layout Options 176
Lesson 56 – Working with Master Documents 184
Lesson 57 – Creating Custom Headers and Footers, Bookmarks, and Cross-References.... 191
Lesson 58 – Creating an Index 200
Lesson 59 – Managing Source Information and Generating Special Tables 208
End-of-Chapter Activities 220

Chapter 9
Embedding and Linking Objects, Using Mail Merge, and Creating Macros....... 226

Lesson 60 – Copying, Moving, and Embedding Data and Objects 228
Lesson 61 – Linking Files and Objects........... 237
Lesson 62 – Integrating Word and PowerPoint..... 243

Table of Contents

Lesson 63 – Using Merge to Create Letters, Envelopes, Labels, and E-mail 248
Lesson 64 – Creating a Directory with Mail Merge . . . 260
Lesson 65 – Working with Macros. 269
End-of-Chapter Activities 281

Microsoft Excel 2013

Chapter 6
Managing Large Workbooks 286

Lesson 49 – Customizing the Excel Interface and Converting Text 288
Lesson 50 – Formatting Cells 296
Lesson 51 – Hiding and Formatting Workbook Elements 304
Lesson 52 – Customizing Styles and Themes. 312
Lesson 53 – Customizing Data Entry 322
Lesson 54 – Formatting and Replacing Data Using Functions 329
Lesson 55 – Working with Subtotals 337
End-of-Chapter Activities 347

Chapter 7
Creating Charts, Shapes, and Templates 352

Lesson 56 – Formatting Chart Elements 354
Lesson 57 – Formatting the Value Axis 361
Lesson 58 – Creating Stacked Area Charts 370
Lesson 59 – Working with Sparklines and Trendlines. 378
Lesson 60 – Drawing and Positioning Shapes 385
Lesson 61 – Formatting Shapes 391
Lesson 62 – Enhancing Shapes with Text and Effects. 396
Lesson 63 – Working with Templates. 403
End-of-Chapter Activities 413

Chapter 8
Creating Macros and Using Data Analysis Tools 418

Lesson 64 – Recording a Macro 420
Lesson 65 – Using Functions 430
Lesson 66 – Working with Absolute References and Using Financial Functions 439
Lesson 67 – Creating and Interpreting Financial Statements. 446
Lesson 68 – Creating Scenarios and Naming Ranges. 453
Lesson 69 – Finding and Fixing Errors in Formulas 460
End-of-Chapter Activities 468

Chapter 9
Importing and Analyzing Database Data. 472

Lesson 70 – Importing Data into Excel. 474
Lesson 71 – Working with Excel Tables 480
Lesson 72 – Using Advanced Filters, Slicers, and Database Functions 488
Lesson 73 – Using Flash Fill and Data Consolidation 499
Lesson 74 – Linking Workbooks 507
Lesson 75 – Using PivotTables 514
Lesson 76 – Using PivotCharts 522
Lesson 77 – Using PowerPivot and Power View 530
End-of-Chapter Activities 539

Chapter 10
Collaborating with Others and Preparing a Final Workbook for Distribution 542

Lesson 78 – Tracking Changes 544
Lesson 79 – Ensuring Data Integrity 554
Lesson 80 – Protecting Data. 563

Lesson 81 – Securing a Workbook 570
Lesson 82 – Finalizing a Workbook 576
Lesson 83 – Sharing a Workbook 581
End-of-Chapter Activities 587

Microsoft Access 2013

Chapter 4
Customizing Tables and Databases 590

Lesson 26 – Normalizing and Analyzing Tables 592
Lesson 27 – Using Advanced Field and Table Properties 602
Lesson 28 – Formatting and Correcting Tables 610
Lesson 29 – Creating Macros 614
End-of-Chapter Activities 621

Chapter 5
Developing Advanced Queries 624

Lesson 31 – Creating Crosstab Queries 626
Lesson 32 – Creating Queries That Find Unmatched or Duplicate Records 633
Lesson 33 – Creating Queries That Prompt for Input 637
Lesson 34 – Creating Action Queries 644
Lesson 35 – Working with Advanced Query Options . . 647
End-of-Chapter Activities 653

Chapter 6
Customizing Forms and Reports 656

Lesson 36 – Working with Report Layouts 658
Lesson 37 – Working with Controls 668
Lesson 38 – Formatting Controls 677
Lesson 39 – Creating Special Forms 684

Lesson 40 – Working with Subforms and Subreports 689
Lesson 41 – Working with Charts 698
Lesson 42 – Creating Switchboards 705
Lesson 43 – Creating Navigation Forms 712
End-of-Chapter Activities 718

Chapter 7
Securing, Integrating, and Maintaining Data 720

Lesson 44 – Converting and Securing Data 722
Lesson 45 – Sharing Data with Word and Other Text Applications 728
Lesson 46 – Sharing Data with Excel and Access . . . 733
Lesson 47 – Linking to Data Sources 740
Lesson 48 – Customizing Access 744
End-of-Chapter Activities 750

Microsoft PowerPoint 2013

Chapter 5
Working with Masters, Handouts, and Text 752

Lesson 32 – Working with Advanced Slide Master Features 754
Lesson 33 – Customizing Themes and Effects 761
Lesson 34 – Working with Notes and Handouts 766
Lesson 35 – Integrating PowerPoint with Word 775
Lesson 36 – Fine-Tuning Text Formats 782
Lesson 37 – Using Research Tools 790
End-of-Chapter Activities 796

Chapter 6
Working with Graphic Objects and Media.........800

Lesson 38 – Applying Advanced Picture Formatting..................... 802
Lesson 39 – Working with Advanced Multimedia Features...................... 810
Lesson 40 – Applying Advanced Animations 815
Lesson 41 – Drawing and Adjusting Tables 824
Lesson 42 – Formatting Tables 833
Lesson 43 – Formatting Charts................ 841
End-of-Chapter Activities 850

Chapter 7
Finalizing and Sharing a Presentation.............854

Lesson 44 – Making a Presentation Accessible to Everyone 856
Lesson 45 – Saving a Presentation in Other Formats 861
Lesson 46 – Working with Links and Actions 868
Lesson 47 – Working with Online Presentations.... 875
End-of-Chapter Activities 886

Index 891

Introduction

Microsoft Office 2013 is Microsoft's suite of application software. The Standard version includes Word, Excel, Outlook, and PowerPoint. Other editions may also include Access, Publisher, OneNote, and InfoPath. This book covers Word (the word processing tool), Excel (the spreadsheet tool), PowerPoint (the presentation tool), and Access (the database tool). Because Microsoft Office is an integrated suite, the components can all be used separately or together to create professional-looking documents and to manage data.

How the Book Is Organized

Business Information Management II continues building on the skills introduced in ***Business Information Management I***. The book is made up of four sections:

- **Word 2013.** With Word you can create letters, memos, Web pages, newsletters, and more.
- **Excel 2013.** Excel, Microsoft's spreadsheet component, is used to organize and calculate data, track financial data, and create charts and graphs.
- **Access 2013.** Access is Microsoft's powerful database tool. Using Access you will learn to store, retrieve, and report on information.
- **PowerPoint 2013.** Create dynamic onscreen presentations with PowerPoint, the presentation graphics tool.

Chapters are comprised of short lessons designed for using Microsoft Office 2013 in real-life business settings. Each lesson is made up of six key elements:

- **What You Will Learn.** Each lesson starts with an overview of the learning objectives covered in the lesson.

- **Words to Know.** Key terms are included and defined at the start of each lesson, so you can quickly refer back to them. The terms are then highlighted in the text.
- **What You Can Do.** Concise notes for learning the computer concepts.
- **Try It.** Hands-on practice activities provide brief procedures to teach all necessary skills.
- **Practice.** These projects give students a chance to create documents, spreadsheets, database objects, and presentations by entering information. Steps provide all the how-to information needed to complete a project.
- **Apply.** Each lesson concludes with a project that challenges students to apply what they have learned through steps that tell them what to do, without all the how-to information. In the Apply projects, students must show they have mastered each skill set.
- Each chapter ends with two assessment projects: **Critical Thinking** and **Portfolio Builder**, which incorporate all the skills covered throughout the chapter.

Working with Data and Solution Files

As you work through the projects in this book, you'll be creating, opening, and saving files. You should keep the following instructions in mind:

- For many of the projects, you will use data files. Other projects will ask you to create new documents and files and then enter text and data into them, so you can master creating documents from scratch.
- The data files are used so that you can focus on the skills being introduced—not on keyboarding lengthy documents.
- The data files can be accessed from the Navigate IT Web site (www.pearsonhighered.com/navigateit). Select "Student" and browse for "Business Information Management II: 2013."
- When the project steps tell you to open a file name, you open the data file provided.
- All the projects instruct you to save the files created or to save the project files under a new name. This is to make the project file your own and to avoid overwriting the data file in the storage location. Throughout this book, when naming files and folders, replace *xx* with your name or initials as instructed by your teacher.
- Follow your instructor's directions for where to access and save the files on a network, local computer hard drive, or portable storage device such as a USB drive.
- Many of the projects also provide instructions for including your name in a header or footer. Again, this is to identify the project work as your own for grading and assessment purposes.
- Unless the book instructs otherwise, use the default settings for text size, margin size, and so on when creating a file. If someone has changed the default software settings for the computer you're using, your exercise files may not look the same as those shown in this book. In addition, the appearance of your files may look different if the system is set to a screen resolution other than 1024 × 768.

Navigating the Textbook

Software Skills
Each lesson begins with an introduction to the computer skills that will be covered in the lesson.

Words to Know
Vocabulary terms are listed at the start of each lesson for easy reference and appear in bold in the text on first use.

What You Can Do
The technology concepts are introduced and explained.

---

168 | Chapter 8 | Word | Business Information Management II

Lesson 54

Working with Outlines

> **What You Will Learn**
> Creating an Outline
> Managing an Outline
> Numbering an Outline

WORDS TO KNOW

Body text
Outline text that is not formatted with a heading-level style.

Collapse
To hide subtopics in an outline.

Demote
To move down one level in an outline.

Expand
To show subtopics in an outline.

Outline
A document that lists levels of topics.

Promote
To move up one level in an outline.

Software Skills Create an outline to organize ideas for any document that covers more than one topic, such as an article, a report, a presentation, or a speech. For example, you might create an outline to list the chapters or headings in a report or to arrange main subjects for a presentation. The outline serves as a map you can follow as you complete the entire document.

What You Can Do

Creating an Outline

- Use Outline view to create and edit an **outline**.
- When you switch to Outline view, the OUTLINING tab becomes available on the Ribbon.
- An outline is similar to a multilevel list (refer to Word, Lesson 7). Outline topics are formatted in levels, which may be called headings: Level 1 is a main heading, Level 2 is a subheading, Level 3 is a sub-subheading, and so on up to 9 heading levels.
- By default, text you type in an outline is formatted as **Body Text**. You use the tools in the Outline Tools group on the OUTLINING tab of the Ribbon to **promote** or **demote** paragraphs to different levels.
- Headings in an outline are preceded by one of three outline symbols:
  - Levels that have sublevels under them are preceded by a circle with a plus sign in it ⊕.
  - Levels that do not have sublevels are preceded by a circle with a minus sign in it ⊖.
  - Body Text that is not formatted as a heading level is preceded by a small circle ○.
- Note that although outline levels print as expected, they do not appear onscreen in Print Layout view or on the Print tab in the Backstage view.

Navigating the Textbook

Try It!
Short, hands-on activities give students the opportunity to practice the software features in a sample document.

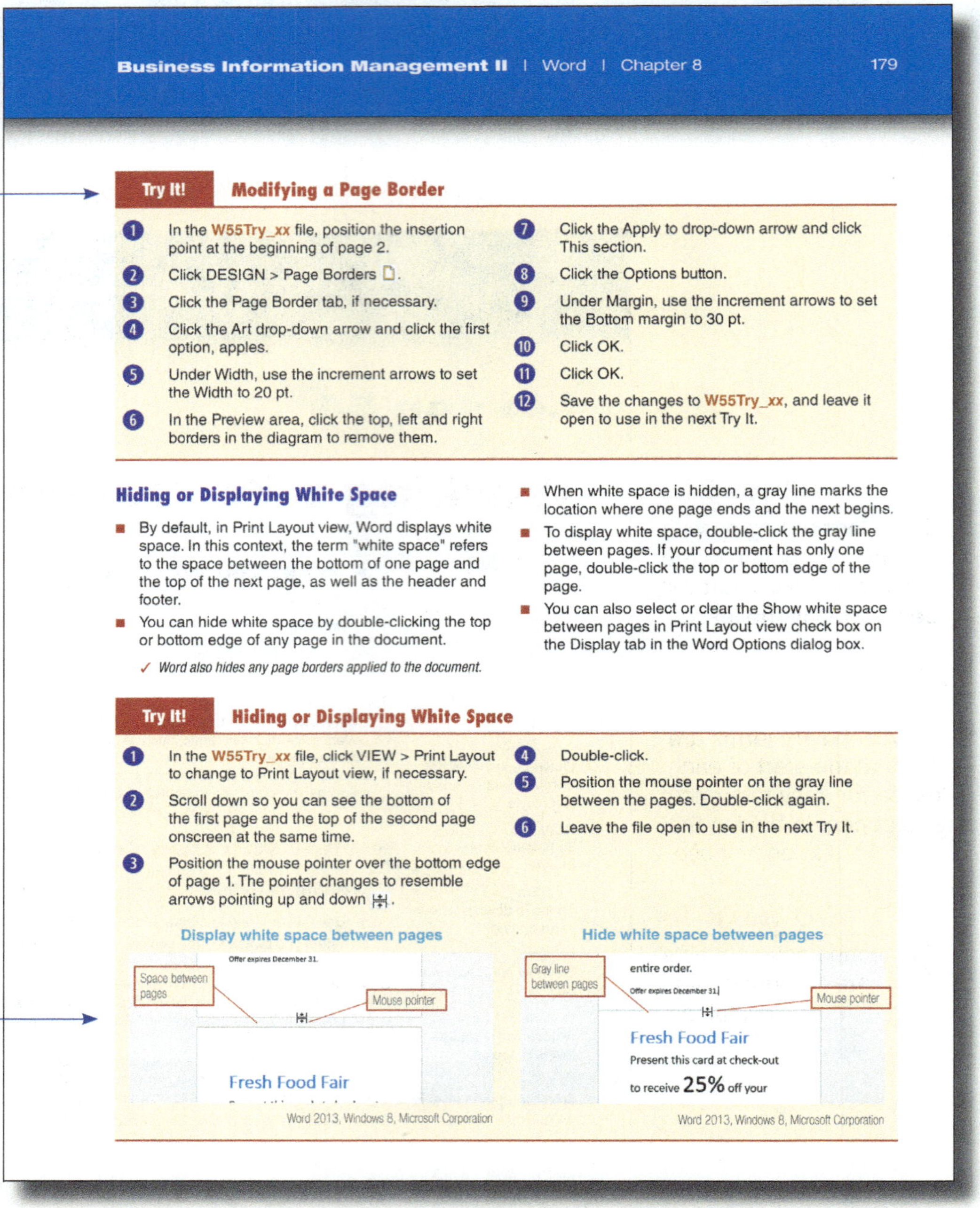

Business Information Management II | Word | Chapter 8 179

Try It! Modifying a Page Border

1. In the **W55Try_xx** file, position the insertion point at the beginning of page 2.
2. Click DESIGN > Page Borders.
3. Click the Page Border tab, if necessary.
4. Click the Art drop-down arrow and click the first option, apples.
5. Under Width, use the increment arrows to set the Width to 20 pt.
6. In the Preview area, click the top, left and right borders in the diagram to remove them.
7. Click the Apply to drop-down arrow and click This section.
8. Click the Options button.
9. Under Margin, use the increment arrows to set the Bottom margin to 30 pt.
10. Click OK.
11. Click OK.
12. Save the changes to **W55Try_xx**, and leave it open to use in the next Try It.

Hiding or Displaying White Space

- By default, in Print Layout view, Word displays white space. In this context, the term "white space" refers to the space between the bottom of one page and the top of the next page, as well as the header and footer.
- You can hide white space by double-clicking the top or bottom edge of any page in the document.
  ✓ *Word also hides any page borders applied to the document.*
- When white space is hidden, a gray line marks the location where one page ends and the next begins.
- To display white space, double-click the gray line between pages. If your document has only one page, double-click the top or bottom edge of the page.
- You can also select or clear the Show white space between pages in Print Layout view check box on the Display tab in the Word Options dialog box.

Try It! Hiding or Displaying White Space

1. In the **W55Try_xx** file, click VIEW > Print Layout to change to Print Layout view, if necessary.
2. Scroll down so you can see the bottom of the first page and the top of the second page onscreen at the same time.
3. Position the mouse pointer over the bottom edge of page 1. The pointer changes to resemble arrows pointing up and down.
4. Double-click.
5. Position the mouse pointer on the gray line between the pages. Double-click again.
6. Leave the file open to use in the next Try It.

Display white space between pages | Hide white space between pages

Word 2013, Windows 8, Microsoft Corporation

Illustrations
Illustrations throughout the text can be used as guidelines for visual learners.

Navigating the Textbook xi

Business Information Management II | PowerPoint | Chapter 5   793

Lesson 37—Practice

The Clifton Community Center (CCC) runs a presentation on a screen in the lobby to keep community members up to date with the latest events in the community and at the center for a given month. The CCC is committed to serving a diverse population with information for and about different cultures. In this project, you begin work on the November presentation. You use the Translator and the Research task pane to locate information about a November event and define a word.

DIRECTIONS

1. Start PowerPoint, if necessary, and open **P37Practice** from the data files for this lesson.
2. Save the presentation as **P37Practice_xx** in the location where your teacher instructs you to store the files for this lesson.
3. Display slide 2.
4. Click at the end of the bullet item, press ENTER, and type **The dictionary defines mincemeat as follows:**
5. Double-click the word *mincemeat* that you just typed, and then click **REVIEW** > **Research** to open the Research task pane with the word *mincemeat* already shown in the Search for box.
6. Click the drop-down arrow for the reference tools list and select **Encarta Dictionary**. Definitions display in the task pane.
    ✓ *Use an online dictionary if you do not have access to Encarta in the Research task pane.*
7. Under the heading *1. fruit and spice mixture*, drag over the definition (*a mixture of spiced . . .*), right-click, and click **Copy**.
8. On the slide, press ENTER at the end of the second bullet item, press TAB, and then press CTRL + V to paste the definition.
9. Remove the bullet formatting from the definition, change the first letter to a capital *A*, and then drag the left indent marker on the ruler to create a **1"** left indent. Your slide should look similar to Figure 37-1.

Figure 37-1

Word for the Month

○ Mincemeat pies are a traditional accompaniment to American Thanksgiving dinners, but what in the world is mincemeat?
○ The dictionary defines mincemeat as follows:
    A mixture of spiced and finely chopped fruits such as apples and raisins, usually cooked in pies

End-of-Lesson Projects
Each lesson includes two hands-on projects where students can use all of the skills that they have learned in the lesson.

End-Result Solutions
Students can refer to solution illustrations to make sure that his or her work is on track.

Business Information Management II | Word | Chapter 5 39

Lesson 40—Practice

You are investigating the possibility of home delivery service for Fresh Food Fair, a natural food store. In this project you will create a chart to illustrate the results of a customer survey.

DIRECTIONS

1. Start Word, click **Blank document**, and save the document as **W40Practice_xx** in the location where your teacher instructs you to store the files for this lesson.
2. Double-click in the header, and type your full name and today's date. Click **Close Header and Footer**.
3. Position the insertion point on the first line of the document.
4. Click **INSERT** > **Chart**.
5. Verify that the selected chart type is **Column** and the subtype is **Clustered Column**, and click **OK**.
6. Replace the sample data in the worksheet with the following survey results:

	Responses
No	10
Maybe	38
Yes	49
Don't Know	3

7. Select columns C and D headers, right-click, and click **Delete**.
8. Resize the data range to include only the cells that contain data (A1:B5), if necessary.
9. Close the Excel window.
10. Click **CHART TOOLS DESIGN** > **Change Chart Type** > **Pie** > **3-D Pie** subtype > **OK**.
11. Double-click the chart title text **Responses** and change the font size to **12 points**.
12. With the chart title still selected, type **Likely to Purchase Home Delivery**.
13. Click the selection frame around the chart to select it > **Chart Elements** > **Legend** to hide the chart legend.
14. In the Chart Elements shortcut menu, hover the mouse pointer over **Data Labels**, click the arrow, and click **Outside End** to display the data labels outside the chart.
15. Click **CHART TOOLS FORMAT** > **Chart Elements** drop-down arrow and click **Series "Responses" Data Labels**.
16. Click **Format Selection** to display the Format Data Labels task pane.
17. Click to select the **Category Name** and **Percentage** check boxes, and, if necessary, click to clear the **Series Name** and **Value** check boxes. Close the **Format Data Labels** task pane.
18. Click **CHART TOOLS DESIGN** > **Edit Data** to display the worksheet. Click cell **B3**, and type **30**. Click cell **B4**, type **57**, and click [ENTER].
19. Close the Excel window.
20. Click the selection frame around the chart to select it, click **CHART TOOLS FORMAT**, change the value in the **Shape Height** box to **2.5"** and the value in the **Shape Width** box to **4"**.
21. Check and correct the spelling and grammar in the document, and save the document.
22. **With your teacher's permission**, print the document. It should look similar to Figure 40-1 on the next page.
23. Save and close the document, and exit Word.

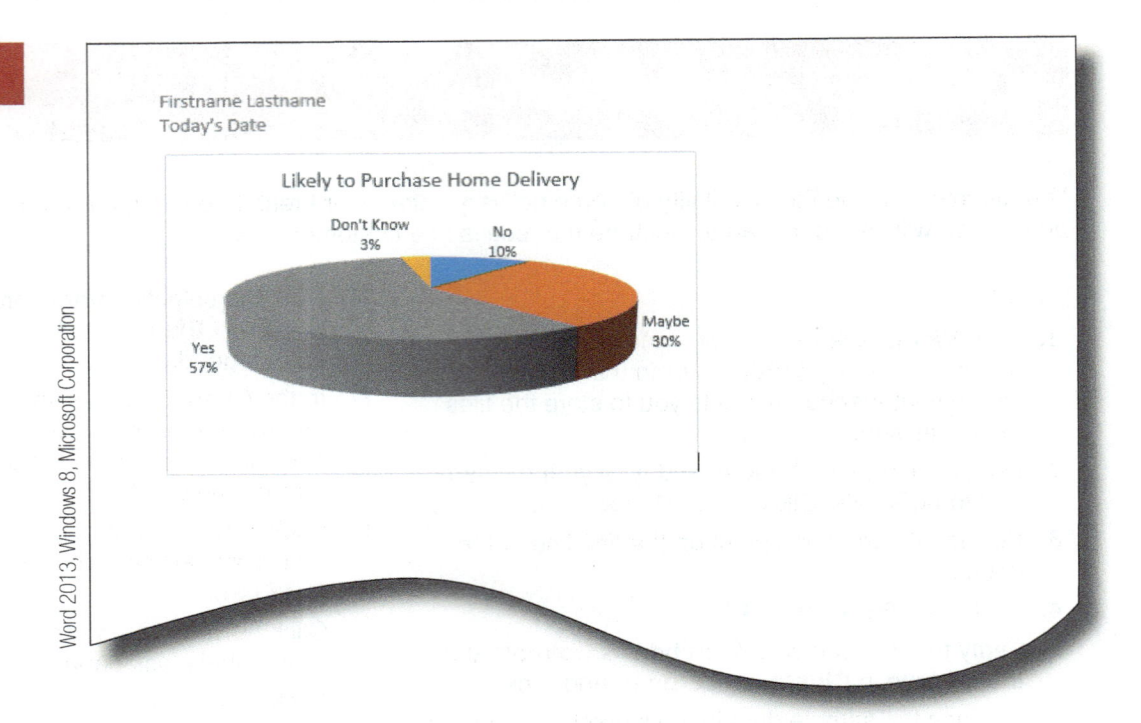

Figure 40-1

Firstname Lastname
Today's Date

Likely to Purchase Home Delivery
- Don't Know 3%
- No 10%
- Maybe 30%
- Yes 57%

Word 2013, Windows 8, Microsoft Corporation

Lesson 40—Apply

You are continuing to investigate the possibility of home delivery service for Fresh Food Fair. In this project, you will create charts illustrating the results of two customer surveys and include them in a memo to the company owner.

DIRECTIONS

1. Start Word, and open **W40ApplyA** from the data files for this lesson.
2. Save the file as **W40ApplyA_xx** in the location where your teacher instructs you to store the files for this lesson.
3. Replace the sample text *Student's Name* with your own name and *Today's Date* with today's date.
4. Position the insertion point on the last line of the document.
5. Insert a **Clustered Column** chart.
6. Start Excel and open the workbook file **W4ApplyB** from the data files for this lesson.
7. Copy the data in cells **A4:E8** to the Clipboard, anhd exit Excel without saving any changes.
    - ✓ To copy the data, click cell A4, press and hold Shift, click cell E8, and click Copy.
8. Click cell **A1** in the Chart in the Microsoft Word worksheet, and paste the data from the Clipboard.
    - ✓ To paste the data, press and hold Ctrl, and click V.
9. Close the workbook.
10. Resize the chart to **2.5"** high by **4"** wide.
11. Apply **Chart Layout 3**.
12. Change the chart title to **Product Preferences by Area**.
13. Apply **Chart Style 8** to the clustered column chart.
14. Apply **Chart Style 7** to the pie chart.
15. Change the font size of the chart titles of both charts to **12 points**.
16. Reposition the chart title of the pie chart higher in the chart area.
    - ✓ Click the chart title to select it, press and hold the mouse pointer, and drag the chart title up slightly.

17. Change the Chart Area color of both charts to a **solid fill Blue, Accent 5, Darker 50%**.
18. Check and correct the spelling and grammar in the document, and save the document.
19. **With your teacher's permission**, print the document. It should look similar to Figure 40-2.
20. Save and close the document, and exit Word.

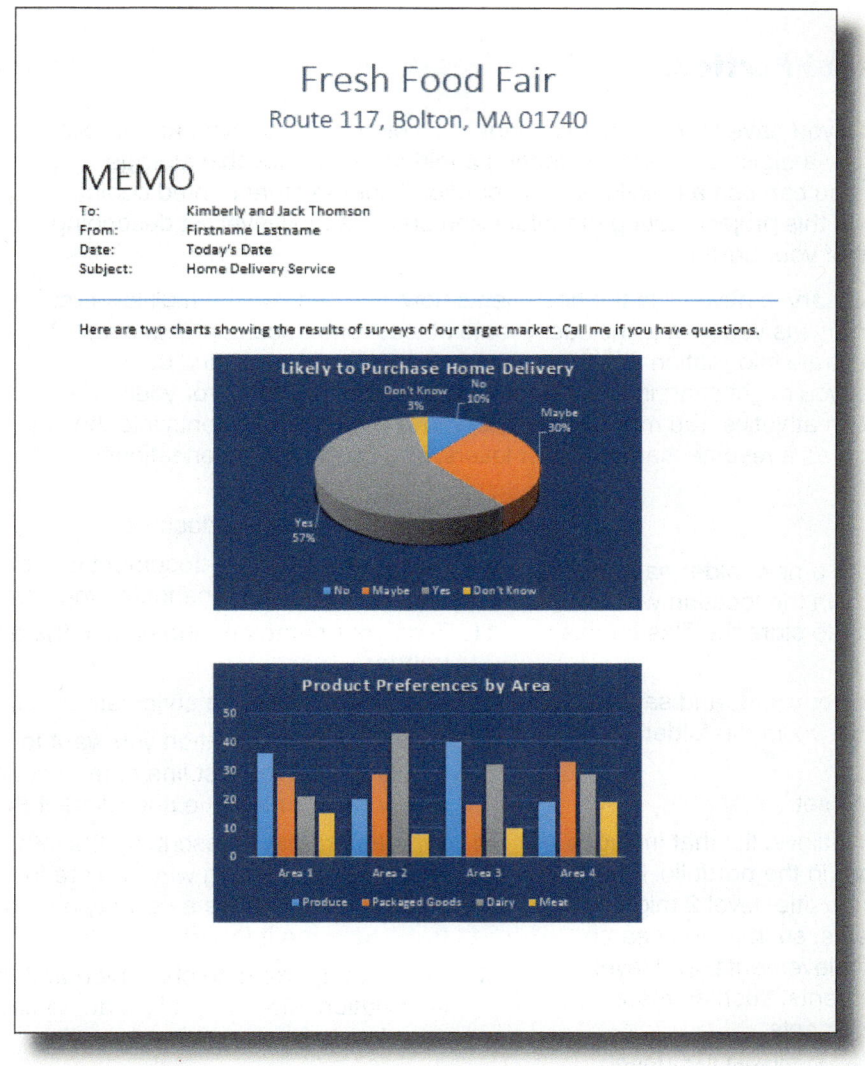

Figure 40-2

End-of-Chapter Activities

▶ Word Chapter 5—Critical Thinking

Employment Portfolio

Use the skills you have learned in this chapter to set up an employment portfolio. You can create a digital portfolio by creating a folder on a removable storage device, and you can use a manila or an accordion folder to store printed copies of documents. In this project, set up the folder and create a multilevel list describing the contents of your portfolio.

It is not necessary to have all of the documents now; you can use the multilevel list as a guide for items you plan to include. Create at least one document that uses a chart to illustrate information you think a potential employer might find useful. For example, you might chart improvement in your grades over time, or your performance in athletics. You may also copy or move existing documents into the portfolio, such as a resume, sample cover letters, or a list of recommendations.

DIRECTIONS

1. Use File Explorer to create a new folder named **WChapter5_portfolio_xx** in the location where your teacher instructs you to store the files for this chapter.
2. Start Word, click **Blank document**, and save the document as **WCT05A_xx** in the folder you created in step 1.
3. Apply a theme and a style set.
4. Set up an outline-style multilevel list that includes the items you plan to store in the portfolio. For example, level 1 might be a title, level 2 might be main categories of items, such as job search materials or academic achievements, and level 3 might be specific documents, such as resume, references, or school transcripts.
5. Choose one of the built-in multilevel list styles, or define your own for use in this document only. Use direct formatting to indicate documents you have already created and added to the portfolio compared to documents you plan to create in the future.
6. Insert a cover page for the outline, and include a title, your name, and the date.
7. Check and correct the spelling and grammar in the document, and save the document.
8. **With your teacher's permission**, print the document, and put the printed document in your portfolio.
9. Save and close the document.
10. Create a new, blank document in Word and save it as **WCT05B_xx**, in the folder you created in step 1.
11. Type your name and the date in the document header.
12. Apply a theme and a style set.
13. Decide what information you want to chart, and type a title on the first line of the document. Create a new style for the title and name it **Portfolio Title**.
14. Type a paragraph describing the information in the chart, and explaining why you are including it in your portfolio. Create a new style for the paragraph text and name it **Portfolio Text**.
15. Insert an appropriate chart type and enter the information. Modify and format the chart to make it easy to read and visually appealing.
16. Check and correct the spelling and grammar in the document, and save the document.
17. When you are satisfied with the document, ask a classmate to review it and make comments or suggestions that will help you improve it.
18. Make changes and corrections, as necessary.
19. **With your teacher's permission**, print the document, and put the printed document in your portfolio.
20. Save and close the document, and exit Word.

Word Chapter 5—Portfolio Builder

Expansion Proposal

In response to a customer survey, Liberty Blooms flower shop has asked you to draft a proposal for expanding the business. In this project you will create an outline for the proposal, which you will format as a multilevel list. You will insert text from an existing file, create a style, and include a chart illustrating the results of the survey and a cover page. If time allows, compile your portfolio information into a presentation and present it to all interested stakeholders.

DIRECTIONS

1. Start Word, click **Blank document**, and save the document as **WPB05A_xx** in the location where your teacher instructs you to store the files.
2. Apply the **Organic** theme and the **Basic (Elegant)** style set.
3. Type your name and the date in the document header.
4. Set Word to track formatting inconsistencies.
5. Define a new multilevel list using the following formatting for each level:
   - Level 1   None (with no punctuation)
   - Level 2   Uppercase letters followed by a period
   - Level 3   Arabic numbers followed by a period
   - Level 4   Lowercase letters followed by a close parenthesis
6. On the first line of the document, press SHIFT + TAB to make the line level 1, type **Liberty Blooms Flower Shop Proposal Outline**, and press ENTER.
7. Press TAB, and type **Introduction**.
8. Press ENTER, and type **Background**.
9. Continue applying indents and typing to create the outline shown in Illustration A on the next page.
10. Select the first line of the text, increase the font size to **18 points**, and apply a solid underline.
11. Create a new Quick Style with the name **Proposal Title**. Set the **Style for following paragraph** to **Normal**.
12. Insert a new page at the end of the document.
13. Type **Customer Survey Results**, and format it with the **Proposal Title** style.
14. Reveal the style formatting, and examine it closely. Note that it includes list formatting.
15. Remove the list formatting, and update the style to match the selection.
    - ✓ Hint: Click Multilevel List, and select None from the List Library.
16. Close all open task panes.
17. Position the insertion point on the line below the second page heading, and clear all formatting.
18. Insert the text from the **WPB05B** file from the data files for this chapter, and apply the **Normal** style.
19. Apply bold to the text *Most Favorable* and *Least Favorable*.
20. On a line below the inserted paragraph, insert a pie chart using the following data:

	Average Rank
Expand the current store	3.2
Open a new store downtown	9.3
Open a new store at the mall	1.6
Open a new store in the next town	7.8
Don't change a thing	6.6

21. Apply the **Chart Layout 6** and the **Chart Style 3**.
22. Change the chart subtype to **3-D Pie**.
23. Format the Chart Area fill to a solid **Blue-Gray, Accent 3, Lighter 60%**.
24. Edit the Chart Title to **Average Customer Rankings**.
25. Center the chart object on the page horizontally.
26. Set Word to not track formatting.
27. Insert the **Austin** style Cover Page. Replace the content controls as follows:
    - Abstract: **This proposal examines the pros and cons of expanding the Liberty Blooms flower shop business.**
    - Document title: **Liberty Blooms Expansion Proposal**
    - Subtitle: *Today's date*
    - Author: *Your full name*

28. Check and correct the spelling and grammar in the document, and save the document.
29. **With your instructor's permission**, print the document. Page 2 should look similar to Illustration 5A, and page 3 should look similar to Illustration 5B on the next page.
30. Save and close the document, and exit Word.

Illustration 5A

Firstname Lastname
Today's Date

<u>Liberty Blooms Flower Shop Proposal Outline</u>

A. Introduction
B. Background
   1. History of Liberty Blooms
   2. Description of Business
   3. Description of Neighborhood
C. Growth Opportunities
   1. Expansion of Current Location
      a) Pros
      b) Cons
   2. Expansion into New Territory
      a) Pros
      b) Cons
D. Customer Survey
   1. Methodology
   2. Summary of Results

Word 2013, Windows 8, Microsoft Corporation

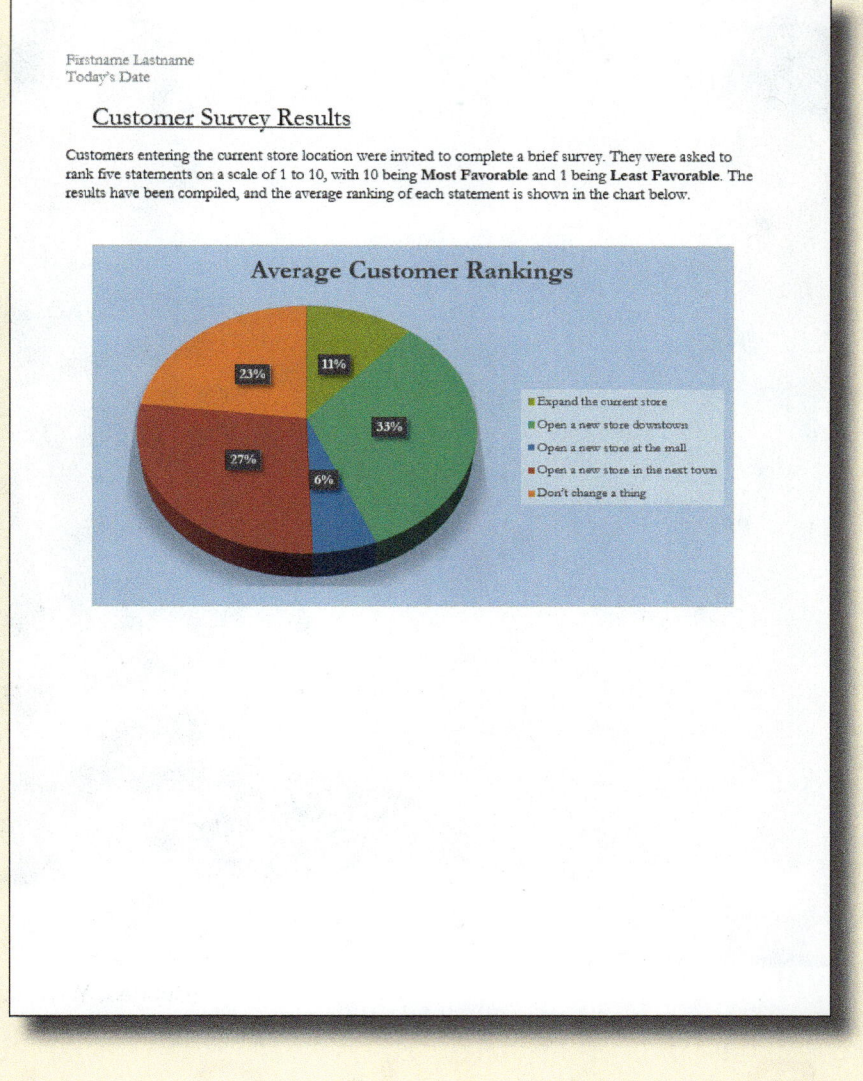

Business Information Management II | Word | Chapter 5

Illustration 5B

Firstname Lastname
Today's Date

Customer Survey Results

Customers entering the current store location were invited to complete a brief survey. They were asked to rank five statements on a scale of 1 to 10, with 10 being **Most Favorable** and 1 being **Least Favorable**. The results have been compiled, and the average ranking of each statement is shown in the chart below.

Average Customer Rankings

- 11% — Expand the current store
- 33% — Open a new store downtown
- 6% — Open a new store at the mall
- 27% — Open a new store in the next town
- 23% — Don't change a thing

Word 2013, Windows 8, Microsoft Corporation

Chapter 6

(Courtesy Yuri Arcurs/Shutterstock)

Using Reusable Content and Markup Tools

Lesson 41
Customizing Language and Word Options

- Analyzing Effective Communication
- Translating Text
- Using Accessibility Features
- Customizing the Quick Access Toolbar
- Customizing the Ribbon
- Locating the Default Save Options
- Personalizing Your User Name and Initials
- Adding and Removing Document Metadata
- Customizing the View for Opening E-Mail Attachments

Lesson 42
Using Advanced Find and Replace

- Analyzing Conflict
- Collecting Images and Text from Multiple Documents
- Using the Navigation Task Pane
- Finding and Replacing Formatting
- Using Wildcard Characters in Find and Replace
- Understanding Projects and Project Management

Lesson 43
Using Building Blocks

- Inserting a Built-In Building Block
- Creating a Custom Building Block
- Using the Building Blocks Organizer

Lesson 44
Inserting Fields from Quick Parts

- Inserting a Field from Quick Parts
- Setting Field Display Options
- Analyzing Employment Packages

Lesson 45
Creating Custom Templates, Themes, and Style Sets

- Creating and Saving a Custom Template
- Modifying a Custom Template
- Creating a New Document from a Custom Template
- Deleting a Custom Template
- Creating a Custom Theme
- Applying, Resetting, and Deleting a Theme
- Creating a Style Set
- Applying, Resetting, and Deleting a Style Set
- Demonstrating Professional Standards of Behavior

Lesson 46
Tracking Changes

- Tracking Changes
- Customizing Revision Marks
- Accepting and Rejecting Changes

Lesson 47
Comparing Documents

- Viewing Documents Side by Side
- Comparing Documents
- Combining Documents

Lesson 48
Restricting Access to Documents

- Setting and Removing Restrictions in a Document
- Changing a Password in a Protected, Encrypted Document
- Using Online Word Processing Technologies

End-of-Chapter Activities

47

Lesson 41

Customizing Language and Word Options

➤ What You Will Learn

Analyzing Effective Communication
Translating Text
Using Accessibility Features
Customizing the Quick Access Toolbar
Customizing the Ribbon
Locating the Default Save Options
Personalizing Your User Name and Initials
Adding and Removing Document Metadata
Customizing the View for Opening E-Mail Attachments

WORDS TO KNOW

Accessibility
The ability to make documents easier for people with disabilities to use.

Accessibility Checker
A feature in Word that checks for and displays issues in a document that might be challenging for a user with a disability.

Active listening
Paying attention to a message, hearing it, and interpreting it correctly.

Alternative text (alt text)
Text that appears when you move the mouse pointer over a picture or object.

Software Skills   Effective communication skills are essential for succeeding in any business or career. Microsoft Word 2013 provides tools to help you get your message across, including the ability to translate text to and from English. Customize Word Options, the Ribbon, and the Quick Access Toolbar so you have easy access to the tools and features you use most often.

What You Can Do

Analyzing Effective Communication

- In business, it is important to make sure all **communication** is clear and effective in speeches, e-mails, blogs, and Web posts, as well as more traditional letters, memos, and reports.
- Effective communication is when the receiver interprets the message the way the sender intended.
- Ineffective communication is when the receiver misinterprets the message.
- Talking is usually a very effective form of **verbal communication**. When you write, you lose some of the context, which can make the communication less effective.
- **Nonverbal communication** includes visual messages that the receiver can see, such as a smile. It also includes physical messages, such as a pat on the back, and aural, or sound, messages, such as your tone of voice.

- Nonverbal communication also includes the use of visual aids, such as pictures and charts, which can help clarify your message and put it in context.
- **Active listening** is a sign of respect. It shows you are willing to communicate and that you care about the speaker and the message. When you listen actively, the other person is more likely to listen when you speak, too.
- It is also important that a communicator considers his or her audience and that global content standards are considered so that the material is accessible to the audience.

Translating Text

- You can use Microsoft Word 2013 to **translate** document text from one language to another.
- Right-click a word and click Translate on the shortcut menu to display the translation in the Research task pane.
- Use the Translate button in the Language group on the REVIEW tab of the Ribbon to display all translation commands or to set translation options.
  - Use the Translate Selected Text command to display the translation in the Research task pane. You can select the languages you want to translate from and to.
  - Use the Mini Translator to display a pop-up translation. The Mini Translator also includes buttons for opening the Research task pane, copying the text, playing an audio file of the text in its current language, or displaying help.
  - If you have access to an online translation service, you can select the Translate Document command to transmit the entire document to the service.
- By default, Word uses the online dictionary if there is a connection to the Internet. Otherwise, only the languages for which you have bilingual dictionaries installed will be available for translation.
- Translation options are not the same as Office Language Preferences.
- You can customize the Office Language Preferences on the Language tab of the Word Options dialog box to set the default language of text entry and editing and for displaying Help and ScreenTips.
  - For example, you can set the default language for editing and for displaying Help and ScreenTips.
  - Office Language Preferences affect all Word documents globally, so be sure that you want any customization to apply to all your documents.

Communication
The exchange of information between a sender and a receiver.

Document properties
Details about a document, such as author, subject, and title.

Nonverbal communication
The exchange of information without using words.

Translate
To change text from one language into another.

User name
A name assigned to someone who uses a computer system or program that identifies the user to the system.

Verbal communication
The exchange of information by speaking.

Try It! Translating Text

1. Start Word, and open **W41Try** from the data files for this lesson.
2. Save the file as **W41Try_xx** in the location where your teacher instructs you to store the files for this lesson.
3. Select the sentence **My mother went home.**, right-click, and click Translate to display the Research task pane.
4. In the Research task pane, click the To drop-down arrow and click Italian (Italy). The English to Italian translation displays in the Research task pane.
5. Click the REVIEW tab, and in the Language group, click Translate.
6. Click Choose Translation Language to display the Translation Language Options dialog box.

(continued)

Try It! Translating Text (continued)

Translation in the Research task pane

⑦ Under Choose Mini Translator language, click the Translate to: drop-down arrow, click French (France), and click OK.

⑧ On the REVIEW tab, click the Translate button and click Mini Translator. This toggles the feature on; it remains on until you toggle it off.

⑨ Rest the mouse pointer on the word *mother*. A dim Mini Translator displays.

⑩ Move the mouse pointer over the Mini Translator to make it display clearly.

✓ *The options may differ depending on whether you are working from an online or an installed dictionary.*

⑪ On the REVIEW tab, click Translate > Mini Translator to toggle the feature off.

⑫ Close the Research task pane.

⑬ Save the changes to **W41Try_xx**, and leave it open to use in the next Try It.

The MiniTranslator

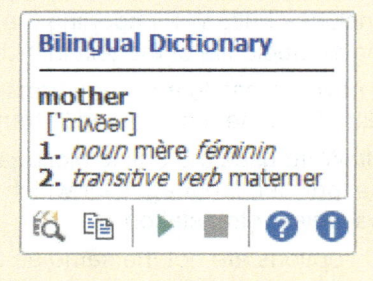

Using Accessibility Features

- You can use **accessibility** features in Word 2013 to make documents more accessible to users with disabilities.
- **Alternative text**, or **alt text**, is an accessibility feature that helps people who use screen readers to understand the content of a picture in a document.

  ✓ *Alt text may not work with touch-screen or mobile devices.*

- When making a document accessible, you should include alt text for objects such as pictures, embedded objects, charts, and tables.
- You can add alt text from the Layout & Properties group of the Format Picture task pane.
- When you use a screen reader to view a document, or save it to a file format such as HTML, alt text appears in most browsers when the picture doesn't display.

  ✓ *You may have to adjust the computer's browser settings to display alt text.*

- Screen readers and other assistive technologies read the tab order of objects from left to right starting at the top of the page and moving down to the bottom of the page.
- You can change the tab order by moving and reordering the text, pictures, and graphics on the page.
- You can use the **Accessibility Checker** to check and correct a document for possible issues that might make it hard for a user with a disability to read and interpret the content.
- You access the Accessibility Checker from the Info tab on the FILE tab.

Business Information Management II | Word | Chapter 6   51

Try It! Using Accessibility Features

1. In the **W41Try_xx** file, click FILE.
2. On the Info tab, click Check for Issues > Check Accessibility. Note the Missing Alt Text error in the Accessibility Checker task pane.
3. Right-click the picture of the globe, and click Format Picture to display the Format Picture task pane.
4. Click Layout & Properties > ALT TEXT.
5. In the Title box, type **Globe**.
6. In the Description box, type **A picture of planet earth**. The Accessibility Checker Inspection Results now finds no accessibility issues.
7. Close the Format Picture and Accessibility task panes.
8. Save the changes to **W41Try_xx**, and leave it open to use in the next Try It.

Customizing the Quick Access Toolbar

- By default, there are three buttons on the Quick Access Toolbar: Save, Undo, and Repeat.
  ✓ *The Repeat button changes to Redo once you use the Undo command.*
- Use the Customize Quick Access Toolbar button to display a menu of common commands to add or remove from the toolbar, or to choose to display the Quick Access Toolbar below the Ribbon.
- To add a command to the Quick Access Toolbar, locate the command on the Ribbon, right-click it, and select Add to Quick Access Toolbar.
- You can also select any command from a list of all available commands using the Quick Access Toolbar tab in the Word Options dialog box.
- You can rearrange the order of buttons on the Quick Access Toolbar, and you can reset the Quick Access Toolbar to its default configuration.

Try It! Customizing the Quick Access Toolbar

1. In the **W41Try_xx** document, click the Customize Quick Access Toolbar button to display a menu of common commands.
   ✓ *A check mark indicates the command is already on the Quick Access Toolbar.*
2. Click Quick Print on the menu. The Quick Print button is added to the Quick Access Toolbar.
3. Click Customize Quick Access Toolbar > Show Below the Ribbon.
4. Click Customize Quick Access Toolbar > Show Above the Ribbon.
5. Click HOME, right-click the Bold button, and click Add to Quick Access Toolbar.
6. Click Customize Quick Access Toolbar, and click More Commands to display the Quick Access Toolbar tab in the Word Options dialog box.
7. Click the Choose commands from drop-down arrow > FILE tab.
8. In the list of commands, click Close, and click the Add button.
9. In the list of commands on the Quick Access Toolbar, click Bold, and click the Remove button.
10. In the list of commands on the Quick Access Toolbar, click Close, and click Move Up twice.
11. In the list of commands on the Quick Access Toolbar, click the Redo button > Move Down > OK.
12. Click Customize Quick Access Toolbar > More Commands.

(continued)

Try It! Customizing the Quick Access Toolbar (continued)

13. Click Reset `Reset ▼` > Reset only Quick Access Toolbar.
14. Click Yes in the confirmation dialog box > OK.
15. If necessary, click Customize Quick Access Toolbar `▼` > Show Above the Ribbon.
16. Save the changes to **W41Try_xx**, and leave it open to use in the next Try It.

Customized Quick Access Toolbar

Word 2013, Windows 8, Microsoft Corporation

Customizing the Ribbon

- In Word 2013 you can customize the Ribbon by adding commands you use frequently or removing commands you rarely use.
- You can create new groups on a Ribbon tab, and you can create a new tab with new groups.
- Commands for customizing the Ribbon are on the Customize Ribbon tab of the Word Options dialog box.

Try It! Customizing the Ribbon

1. In the **W41Try_xx** document, right-click the Ribbon, and click Customize the Ribbon.
2. On the right side of the Word Options dialog box, under Main Tabs, click to clear the check mark to the left of Insert, and click OK. Notice that the Ribbon no longer displays the INSERT tab.
3. Right-click the Ribbon, and click Customize the Ribbon.
4. Under Main Tabs, click Home to deselect the check box, and click New Tab `New Tab`. Word creates a new tab with one new group.
5. Click New Tab (Custom) > Rename `Rename...` > type **Documents** > OK.
6. Click New Group (Custom) > Rename `Rename...` > type **Management** > OK.
7. Click the Choose commands from: drop-down arrow > File Tab.
8. In the list of commands, click Close > Add `Add >>`.
9. In the list of commands, click New > Add `Add >>`.
10. In the list of commands, click Save As > Add `Add >>`.
11. Click OK, and click the Documents tab on the Ribbon to view the new group of commands.
12. Right-click on the Ribbon > Customize the Ribbon.
13. Click Reset `Reset ▼` > Reset all customizations.
14. Click Yes in the confirmation dialog box > OK.
15. Save the changes to **W41Try_xx**, and leave it open to use in the next Try It.

Customized tab on the Ribbon

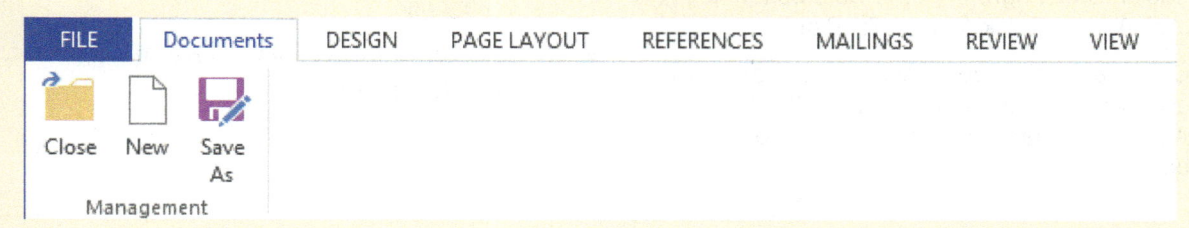

Word 2013, Windows 8, Microsoft Corporation

Locating the Default Save Options

- Word 2013 is set to save files using default options.
- By default, Word 2013 saves documents in the Word Document (*.docx) format, in the Documents folder.
- Word saves AutoRecover information every 10 minutes.
- You can change the default save options on the Save tab in the Word Options dialog box.
- Additional save options are available on the Advanced tab in the Word Options dialog box. For example, you can select a default folder for storing specific file types, such as clip art pictures and templates.
- Your system may have been customized to use different save options. For example, files may be saved on a network.

Try It! Locating the Default Save Options

1. In the **W41Try_xx** document, click FILE > Options to display the Word Options dialog box.
2. In the left pane, click Save.
3. Examine the Save options.
4. In the left pane, click Advanced, and scroll down to the General group in the dialog box.
5. Click the File Locations button to view the storage locations for specific file types.
6. Click Close.
7. Click Cancel to close the Word Options dialog box without making any changes.
8. Save the changes to **W41Try_xx**, and leave it open to use in the next Try It.

Personalizing Your User Name and Initials

- When you set up Microsoft Word 2013 on your computer, you enter a **user name** and initials.
- Word uses this information to identify you as the author of new documents that you create and save, and as the editor of existing documents that you open, modify, and save.
- In addition, your user name is associated with revisions that you make when you use the Track Changes features, and the initials are associated with comments that you insert.
- You can change the user name and initials using options in the General group in the Word Options dialog box.

Try It! Personalizing Your User Name and Initials

1. In the **W41Try_xx** document, click FILE > Options to display the Word Options dialog box.
2. Under Personalize your copy of Microsoft Office, view the current User name and Initials.
3. Click Cancel to close the Word Options dialog box without making any changes.
4. Save the changes to **W41Try_xx**, and leave it open to use in the next Try It.

Adding and Removing Document Metadata

- You can add information, such as a title and subject, to the document properties of your document.
- Document properties can also include information that is automatically maintained by Office programs, such as the name of the person who authored a document, the date when a document was created, and the document location.
- You can access the document properties from the Properties drop-down menu on the Info tab of the FILE tab.
- You can use the Document Panel to add or edit **document properties**. From the Properties drop-down menu, click Show Document Panel.
- When active, the Document Panel will appear below the Ribbon.
- You can also use the Advanced Properties button to add and edit additional properties.

Try It! Adding and Removing Metadata

1. In the **W41Try_xx** file, click FILE > Info.
2. On the right side of the Info tab, click Properties > Show Document Panel. The Document Panel appears. Notice that Word automatically entered the file location in the Location box.
3. In the Author box, type your name.
4. Click the Close button ✘ of the Document Panel.
5. Save the changes to **W41Try_xx**, and leave it open to use in the next Try It.

Customizing the View for Opening E-Mail Attachments

- By default, when you open a document that you receive as an attachment to an e-mail message, it displays in Full Screen Reading view.
- You can use the Word Options dialog box to disable the feature so that the document opens in Print Layout view.

Try It! Customizing the View for Opening E-Mail Attachments

1. In the **W41Try_xx** document, click FILE > Options to display the Word Options dialog box.
2. Under Start up options, click to clear the **Open e-mail attachments and other uneditable files in reading view** check box.
3. Click **Cancel** to close the Word Options dialog box without making any changes.
4. Save and close the file, and exit Word.

Lesson 41—Practice

A Fresh Food Fair store wants to post a sign with the company slogan in Spanish. In this project, you will translate the slogan from English to Spanish to create the sign. You will also practice customizing and personalizing Word 2013 options.

DIRECTIONS

1. Start Word, if necessary, click **Blank document**, and save the document as **W41Practice_xx** in the location where your teacher instructs you to store the files for this lesson.
2. Double-click in the header, and type your full name and today's date. Click **Close Header and Footer**.
3. Apply the **Slice** theme and the **Shaded** style set.
4. Click **Customize Quick Access Toolbar** ⋎ > **Spelling & Grammar** to add the button to the Quick Access Toolbar.
5. Click **INSERT** > right-click **Online Pictures** > **Add to Quick Access Toolbar**.
6. Click **PAGE LAYOUT** > **Orientation** > **Landscape**.
7. Click **VIEW** > **Page Width**.
8. On the first line of the document, type **Fresh Food Fair**, and format it with the **Title** style. Select the text, click in the **Font Size** box, and type **50** to increase the font size to **50 points**.
9. Press ENTER, type **Organic and Locally Grown for You**, and format it with the **Heading 1** style. Increase the font size to **16 points**.
10. Press ENTER to start a new line at the end of the document.
11. Select the text Organic and Locally Grown for You.
12. Right-click the selection > **Translate**.
13. In the Research task pane, click the To drop-down arrow, and click Spanish (Spain). The text is translated to *Orgánicos y cultivados localmente para usted*.
14. Position the mouse pointer on the blank line at the end of the document, and click the Insert button below the translated text.

    ✓ *To insert the á character, click INSERT > Symbol > More Symbols, click the character, click the Insert button, and click Close.*

15. Format the Spanish text with the **Heading 2** style.
16. Close the Research task pane.
17. Reposition the mouse pointer at the top of the document, and on the Quick Access Toolbar, click **Online Pictures**. Use the Insert Pictures dialog box to search for a photograph of vegetables, such as the one shown in Figure 41-1, and insert it into the document.

    ✓ *If you cannot find a suitable online picture, insert the file W41Practice_picture.jpg from the data files for this lesson.*

18. Click the picture to select it, click **PICTURE TOOLS FORMAT**, and resize it to **3"** high. The width should adjust automatically.
19. On the PICTURE TOOLS FORMAT tab, click **Position**, and click **Position in Top Left with Square Text Wrapping** (the first item in the first row of the With Text Wrapping group).
20. Open the Document Properties task pane, and add your full name to the Author box and **Fresh Food Fair** to the Title box.
21. On the Quick Access Toolbar, click the **Spelling & Grammar** button. Check and correct the spelling and grammar in the document—ignoring the errors in the Spanish, and save the document.
22. **With your teacher's permission,** print the document. It should look similar to Figure 41-1 on the next page.
23. Click **Customize Quick Access Toolbar** ⋎ > **More Commands**.
24. In the Word Options dialog box, click **Reset** > **Reset only Quick Access Toolbar**.
25. Click **Yes** in the Reset Customizations confirmation dialog box, and click **OK**.
26. Save and close the document, and exit Word.

Figure 41-1

Lesson 41—Apply

A Fresh Food Fair store wants to post signs with the company slogan in English, Spanish, and Brazilian Portuguese. In this project, you will translate the slogan from English to Spanish and from English to Portuguese to create the signs. You will also practice customizing and personalizing Word 2013 options.

DIRECTIONS

1. Start Word, if necessary, and open **W41Apply** from the data files for this lesson.
2. Save the document as **W41Apply_xx** in the location where your teacher instructs you to store the files for this lesson.
3. Double-click in the header, and type your full name and today's date. Click **Close Header and Footer**.
4. Apply the **Wisp** theme and the **Shaded** style set to the document.
5. Add the **Print Preview and Print** button to the Quick Access Toolbar.
6. Customize the Ribbon to create a new Ribbon tab named **Photos**, with a group named **Formatting**.
7. Add the following buttons for working with pictures to the new group: **Picture**, **Position**, **Wrap Text**, **Shape Height**, and **Shape Width**.
8. Change the page orientation to **Landscape**, and set the zoom to **Page Width**.
9. Format the first line of text in the **Title** style, increase the Font Size to **50 points**, and center it horizontally.
10. Format the second line of text in the **Heading 1** style, increase the Font Size to **22 points**, and center it horizontally.
11. Format the third line of text in the **Heading 3** style, increase the Font Size to **22 points**, and center it horizontally.
12. Insert a new line at the end of the document.
13. Set the Mini Translator to translate to **Portuguese (Brazil)**, and toggle the Mini Translator feature on.
14. Select the text **Organic and Locally Grown for You**, and rest the mouse pointer over the selection.
15. Move the mouse pointer over the Mini Translator so you can see the translation, and on the Mini Translator, click **Copy**.
16. Position the insertion point on the last line of the document, and click **HOME > Paste**.

Lesson 46—Practice

The Director of Training at Restoration Architecture has asked you to review a document listing in-house training courses. In this project, you will use the Track Changes feature while you review and edit the document. You will then update the document by accepting or rejecting the changes.

DIRECTIONS

1. Start Word, if necessary, and open **W46Practice** from the data files for this lesson.
2. Save the document as **W46Practice_xx** in the location where your teacher instructs you to store the files for this lesson.
3. Double-click in the header, and type your full name and today's date. Click **Close Header and Footer**.
4. Click **REVIEW** > **Track Changes** to turn on the track changes feature. Click the **Display for Review** drop-down arrow > **Simple Markup**, if necessary.
5. Click the **Track Changes dialog box** launcher, and click **Advanced Options**.
6. Under Markup, click the **Insertions** drop-down arrow and click **Bold**, then click the **Insertions Color** drop-down arrow and click **Red**.
7. Click the **Deletions Color** drop-down arrow, and click **Blue**.
8. Under Balloons, click the **Margin** drop-down arrow, and click **Left**.
9. Click **OK** > **OK** to apply the changes and close the dialog boxes.
10. Click the Display for Review drop-down arrow, and click All Markup.
11. On the REVIEW tab, in the Tracking group, click **Show Markup** > **Balloons** > **Show Revisions in Balloons**.
12. In the document, on the address line, select one of the diamond symbols, and click **HOME** > **Copy** to copy it to the Clipboard.
13. Position the insertion point at the end of the address line, press SPACE, click **HOME** > **Paste**, press SPACE, and type **www.rarc.net**.
14. Select the entire address line and decrease the font size to **10 pt**.
15. In the description of the Microsoft Word 1 course, select the text *will cover*, and type **covers**.
16. In the same sentence, select the text *2007* and type **2013**.
17. In the description of the Microsoft Word 2 course, select the text *2007*, and type **2013**.
18. At the end of the description of the Microsoft Word 3 course, type the following sentence: **Open only to those who have completed the Word 1 and Word 2 courses.**
19. Select the last line in the document, and remove the italic formatting. Your document should look similar to Figure 46-1 on the next page.
20. Click **FILE** > **Print** to display the Print tab in the Backstage view.
21. Click the **Print All Pages** drop-down arrow, and check that **List of Markup** is selected.
22. **With your teacher's permission,** print the document with the markup.
23. Press CTRL + HOME to move the insertion point to the beginning of the document.
24. Click **REVIEW** > **Next Change**.
25. Click **Reject** to reject the formatting change and move to the next change.
26. Click **Reject** to reject the insertion of the Internet address and move to the next change.
27. Click **Reject** twice to reject the change to *will cover*.
28. Click the **Accept** drop-down arrow > **Accept All Changes and Stop Tracking**.
29. Check and correct the spelling and grammar in the document, and save the document.
30. **With your teacher's permission,** print the document.
31. Save and close the document, and exit Word.

Figure 46-1

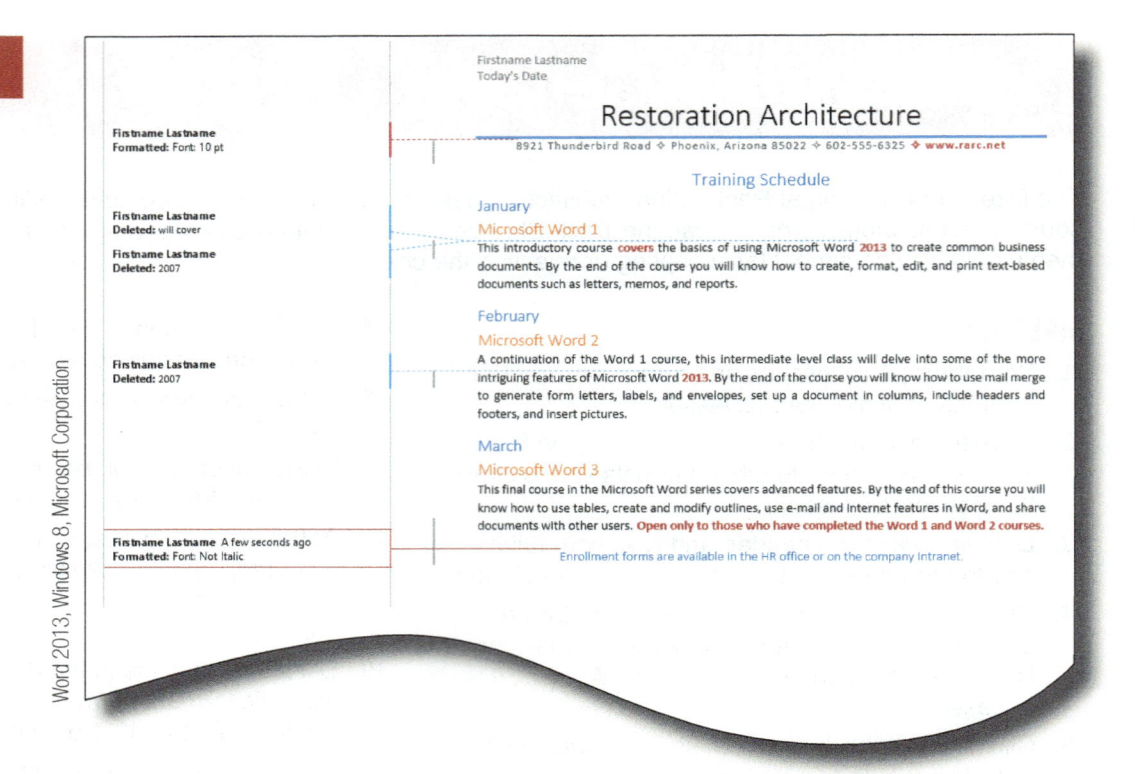

Lesson 46—Apply

The Director of Training at Restoration Architecture has asked you to update the in-house training document you previously revised. In this project, you will use the Track Changes feature while you review and edit the document. You will then update the document by accepting or rejecting the changes.

DIRECTIONS

1. Start Word, if necessary, and open **W46Apply** from the data files for this lesson.
2. Save the file as **W46Apply_xx** in the location where your teacher instructs you to store the files for this lesson.
3. Type your full name and today's date in the document header. Click **Close Header and Footer**.
4. Turn on the track changes features, and set tracking options to display insertions underlined in pink and deletions with a strikethrough in bright green. Display balloons in the markup area along the right margin of the page.
5. Show only comments and formatting in balloons, and set the display for review to **Simple Markup**.
6. Change the font of the address line to **Times New Roman**.
7. Replace the text *January* with **June**, *February* with **July**, and *March* with **August**.
8. Add the following sentence to the end of the Microsoft Word 2 course description: **If there is enough time, the course will also include basic desktop publishing concepts.**
9. Display the Reviewing pane vertically.
10. **With your teacher's permission,** print the document with the markup. It should look similar to Figure 46-2 on the next page.

11. Change the display for review to **All Markup**.
12. Accept the formatting changes in the document.
13. Accept the changes to the names of the months.
14. Reject all remaining changes in the document, and turn off the track changes feature.
15. Close the Reviewing pane.
16. Set the insertion and deletion colors to **By author**.
17. Check and correct the spelling and grammar in the document, and save the document.
18. **With your teacher's permission,** print the document.
19. Save and close the document, and exit Word.

Figure 46-2

Lesson 47

Comparing Documents

> ### ➤ What You Will Learn
> **Viewing Documents Side by Side**
> **Comparing Documents**
> **Combining Documents**

WORDS TO KNOW

Independent scrolling
The ability to scroll a window without affecting the display in other open windows.

Synchronous scrolling
A feature that links the scroll bars in two windows so that when you scroll in one window the other window scrolls as well.

Software Skills View documents side by side to compare the differences between similar versions. When you compare and combine documents, differences between the two are marked as revisions. You can accept or reject changes to incorporate revisions.

What You Can Do

Viewing Documents Side by Side

- You can select to view two open documents side by side so you can compare them to each other.
- Each document displays in a separate window; the active document displays on the left side of the desktop and the second document displays on the right.
- If your desktop is not wide enough, or if the monitor is not high enough, Word condenses the Ribbon commands into groups.
  - For example, on the HOME tab, paragraph formatting commands are condensed to the Paragraph group. Click the group drop-down arrow to display the commands.
- By default, both windows are set to use **synchronous scrolling**, which means that when you scroll in one document, the other document scrolls in the same direction by the same amount.
- You can turn off synchronous scrolling to use **independent scrolling**.
- Changes you make to the view in one window affect the other window as well.
  - For example, if you zoom in on one document, the other document zooms in by the same amount.
- The View Side by Side command is in the Window group on the VIEW tab of the Ribbon.
- You can only view two documents side by side at a time. If more than two documents are open in Word when you select the View Side by Side command, the Compare Side by Side dialog box displays so you can select the second document to view.

Try It! **Viewing Documents Side by Side**

1. Start Word, and open **W47TryA** from the data files for this lesson.

2. Save the file as **W47TryA_xx** in the location where your teacher instructs you to store the files for this lesson.

3. Open **W47TryB** from the data files for this lesson.

4. Save the file as **W47TryB_xx** in the location where your teacher instructs you to store the files for this lesson.

5. Click the VIEW tab.

6. In the Window group, click the View Side by Side button. Word arranges the document windows side by side, and turns synchronous scrolling on.

7. In the **W47TryA_xx** document window, click the scroll down arrow three times. Notice that the other document scrolls down as well.

8. Press CTRL + END. Both documents scroll down to the end of the document.

9. Click in the **W47TryB_xx** window, and click the Zoom In button on the status bar. Notice that the other document zooms in as well.

10. In the **W47TryB_xx** window, on the VIEW tab, click the Synchronous Scrolling button to toggle the feature off.

11. Press CTRL + HOME. Only the active document scrolls.

12. In the **W47TryB_xx** window, on the VIEW tab, click the View Side by Side button. Both windows are restored; the active window displays on top.

13. Close both **W47TryB_xx** and **W47TryA_xx**, and leave Word open to use in the next Try It.

View documents side by side with synchronous scrolling

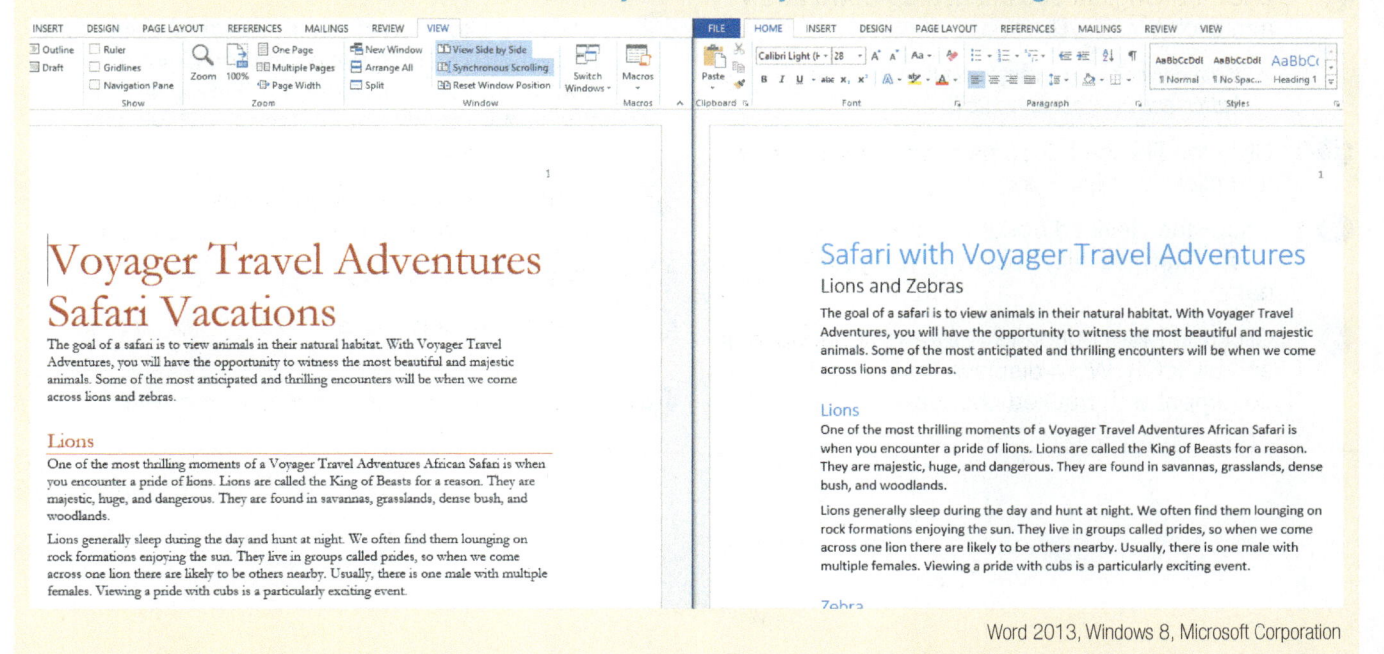

Word 2013, Windows 8, Microsoft Corporation

Comparing Documents

- You can compare two documents to mark the differences between them.
- To compare documents, you select the original document and the revised document; Word displays the original document with revision marks showing the differences between the two.
- You can choose to show the original document with tracked changes, the revised document with tracked changes, or both. Word creates a new document named Compare Result 1 and uses revision marks to indicate the differences between the original and revised documents.
- If you show both, Word displays all three documents onscreen, along with the Reviewing pane.
- By default, the user name of the author of the revised document is used to mark the revisions, but you can use different initials or text.
- Comparing documents is useful if you have more than one version of a document and need to see what changes have been made, or if someone has edited a document without using the track changes features.
- You can modify the way Word displays differences between the documents. For example, you can choose to display the revision marks in the original document or the revised document instead of in a new document.
- You can also select the types of differences to compare. For example, you can choose to compare formatting, but not headers and footers.

Try It!   Comparing Documents

1. In Word, click the REVIEW tab, click the Compare button, and click Compare.
2. Click the Original document drop-down arrow and click **W47TryB_xx**.
   - ✓ If the document you want is not listed, click the Browse button and navigate to locate it.
3. Click the Revised document drop-down arrow and click **W47TryA_xx**.
4. Under the Revised document box, click in the Label changes with box, and type your full name.
5. Click the More button to view additional options, and click OK. Word displays the original document with tracked changes.
6. Click the Compare button, click Show Source Documents, and click Show Both. Word displays all three documents and the Reviewing pane.
7. Click the Close button in the Original document, and click the Close button in the Revised document. Only the Compare Result 1 document remains open, with the Reviewing pane displayed.
8. Click the Accept drop-down arrow, and click Accept All Changes and Stop Tracking.
9. Close the Revisions task pane.
10. Save the document as **W47TryC_xx**, and close it.
11. Leave Word open to use in the next Try It.

(continued)

Business Information Management II | Word | Chapter 6   101

Try It! Comparing Documents (continued)

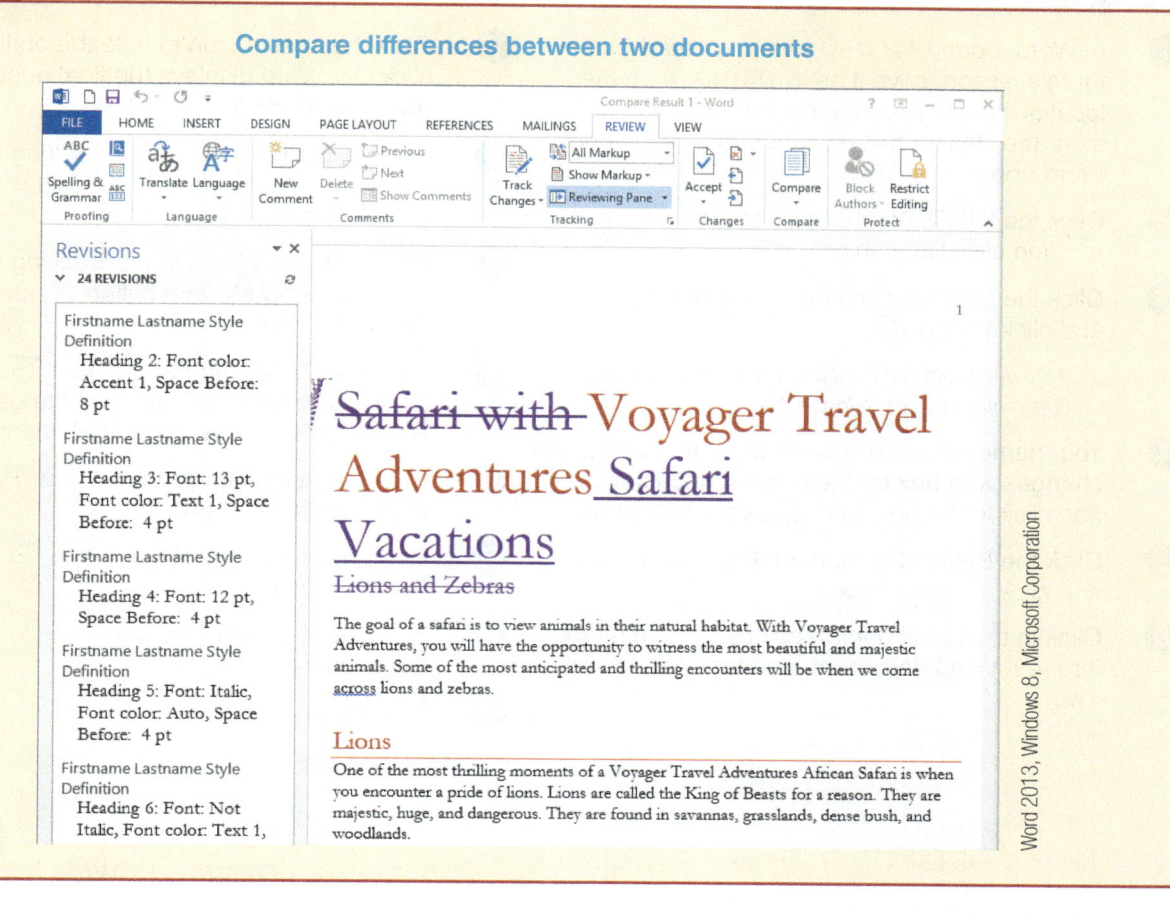

Compare differences between two documents

Combining Documents

- Use the Combine feature to combine revisions made by more than one reviewer into a single document.
- Word merges the two documents into a final document.
- Word can only store one set of formatting changes in the final document. If necessary, it prompts you to select which formatting changes to keep.
- By default, Word marks the changes made in the combined document with the user name of the document author.
- You can manage draft versions of the documents by changing the names of the document authors.

Try It! Combining Documents

1. In Word, open **W47TryD** from the data files for this lesson, save it as **W47TryD_xx** in the location where your teacher instructs you to store the files for this lesson, and close it. Leave Word open.

2. Click the REVIEW tab, click the Compare button, and click Combine.

3. Click the Original document drop-down arrow, and click **W47TryC_xx**.

   ✓ If the document you want is not listed, click the Browse button and navigate to locate it.

4. Your name should display in the Label unmarked changes with box for the original document. If not, click in the box, and type your full name.

5. Click the Revised document drop-down arrow, and click **W47TryD_xx**.

6. Click in the Label unmarked changes with box for the revised document, and type **Reviewer Two**.

7. Click the Less button to hide the options, and click OK. Word displays the final document with revisions marked.

8. On the REVIEW tab, in the Tracking group, click the Display for Review drop-down arrow, and click All Markup, if necessary.

9. On the REVIEW tab, in the Tracking group, click the Show Markup button, and click Formatting to deselect it.

10. Click the Reviewing Pane button. The marked changes indicate the changes made by Reviewer Two in the combined document.

11. Click the Accept drop-down arrow, and click Accept All Changes.

12. Click the Reviewing Pane button to close the Revisions task pane.

13. Save the document as **W47TryE_xx**, and close the document.

14. Exit Word.

Combine two versions of a document

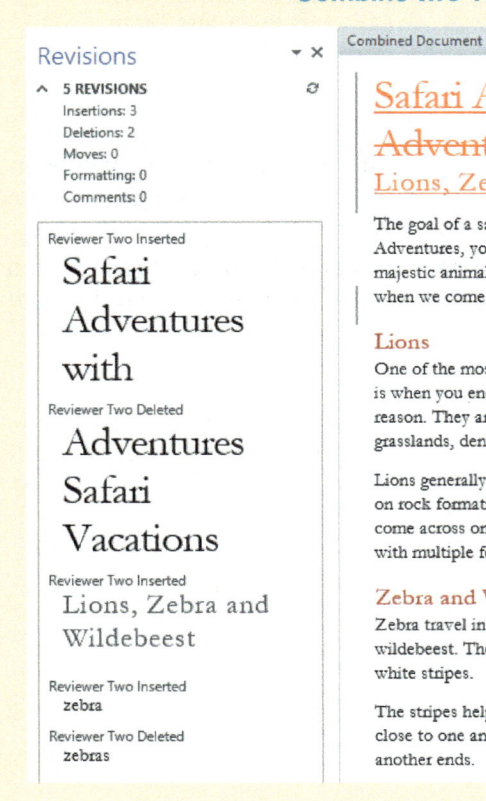

Lesson 47—Practice

You have been working on a newsletter about the value of employment benefits for Executive Recruitment Resources, Inc., a job search and recruitment agency. You will create the newsletter for your manager to review. Your manager sends you a version of the newsletter which she edited without using revision marks. You will view the two documents side by side to verify that they are not the same. You will then compare the documents and highlight the differences.

DIRECTIONS

1. Start Word, if necessary, and open **W47PracticeA** from the data files for this lesson.
2. Save the file as **W47PracticeA_xx** in the location where your teacher instructs you to store the files for this lesson.
3. Double-click in the header, type your full name and today's date, and close the header.
4. On the first line of the document, type the following headings and paragraphs:

   Career Planning

   An important aspect of career planning is identifying career opportunities that meet your needs and fit your skills, interests, and abilities. Here at Executive Recruitment Resources, we provide access to many job search resources, which are tools designed to help you find career opportunities. We also provide training and support to help you build your own job search resources.

   Occupational Outlook Handbook

   The U.S. Bureau of Labor Statistics (BLS) is a government agency that tracks information about jobs and workers. BLS publishes the Occupational Outlook Handbook in printed and online editions. The Handbook describes more than 200 occupations, including responsibilities, working conditions, education requirements, salary ranges, and job outlook.

   Networking

   Employers like to hire people who come with a recommendation from someone they know and trust. That's why networking is one of the best ways to find a job. Networking is when you share information about yourself and your career goals with people you know already or new people you meet. One of these contacts might know of a job opening, or be able to introduce you to someone in a field that interests you.

   Networking is more than just chatting with others. It requires you to be focused and organized. It works best if you keep track of all the people you meet and talk to, and if you follow up by e-mail or phone.

5. With the insertion point in the second section of the document, click **PAGE LAYOUT** > **Columns** > **Two** to format the text in two newsletter-style columns.
6. Position the insertion point at the beginning of the heading Networking, and click **PAGE LAYOUT** > **Breaks** > **Column** to insert a column break.
7. Apply the **Heading 1** style to the three headings (Career Planning, Occupational Outlook Handbook, and Networking).
8. Change the spacing before the Networking heading to **22 pt** so it visually aligns with the Career Planning heading.
9. Check and correct the spelling and grammar in the document, and save the document.
10. Open **W47PracticeB** from the data files for this lesson.
11. Save the file as **W47PracticeB_xx** in the location where your teacher instructs you to store the files for this lesson, type your full name and today's date in the header, and close the header.
12. Click **VIEW** > **View Side by Side** to arrange the documents side by side with synchronous scrolling.
13. Adjust the view using the zoom and scroll controls so you can easily see the left column in both documents.
14. Compare the text in the left column of each document.
15. Highlight in yellow the differences in the **W47PracticeB_xx** document.

   ✓ *To highlight text, select the text, click HOME > Text Highlight Color .*

16. Adjust the view using the zoom and scroll controls so you can easily see the right columns of each document.
17. Compare the text in the right column of each document, and highlight in yellow the differences you find in **W47PracticeB_xx**.
18. In **W47PracticeB_xx**, click **VIEW** > **View Side by Side**.
19. Save and close **W47PracticeB_xx**, and save and close **W47PracticeA_xx**. Leave Word open.
20. In Word, click **REVIEW** > **Compare** > **Compare**.
21. Click the **Original document** drop-down arrow, and click **W47PracticeB_xx**.
    ✓ If the document you want is not listed, click the Browse button and navigate Windows Explorer to locate it.
22. Click the **Revised document** drop-down arrow, and click **W47PracticeA_xx**.
23. Click in the **Label changes with** box, and type your full name, if necessary.
24. Click **OK**.
25. Click **REVIEW** > **Display for Review** drop-down arrow > **All Markup**.
26. Save the Compare Result document as **W47PracticeC_xx** in the location where your teacher instructs you to store the files for this lesson.
27. **With your teacher's permission,** print the document with markup. It should look similar to Figure 47-1.
28. Save and close the document, and exit Word.

Figure 47-1

Firstname Lastname
Today's Date

EXECUTIVE RECRUITMENT RESOURCES, INC.
8921 Thunderbird Road ❖ Phoenix ❖ Arizona ❖ 85022
Phone: 602-555-6325 ❖ Fax: 602-555-6325 ❖ www.errinc.net

Career Planning
An important aspect of career planning is identifying career opportunities that meet your needs and fit your skills, interests, and abilities. Here at Executive Recruitment Resources, we provide access to many job search resources, which are tools designed to help you find career opportunities. We also provide training and support to help you build your own job search resources.

Occupational Outlook Handbook
The U.S. Bureau of Labor Statistics (BLS) is a government agency that tracks information about jobs and workers. BLS publishes the Occupational Outlook Handbook (OOH) in printed and online editions. The OOH Handbook describes more than 200 occupations, including responsibilities, working conditions, education requirements, salary ranges, and job outlook.

Networking
Employers like to hire people who come with a recommendation from someone they know and trust. That's why networking is one of the best ways to find a job. Networking is when you share information about yourself and your career goals with people you know already or new people you meet. One of these contacts might know of a job opening, or be able to introduce you to someone in a field that interests you. Employers like to hire people who come with a recommendation from someone they know and trust. That's why networking is one of the best ways to find a job.

Networking is more than just chatting with others. It requires you to be focused and organized. It works best if you keep track of all the people you meet and talk to, and if you follow up by e-mail or phone.

Take Action!
These and other resources are available to all of our clients. Make an appointment today. Our career counselors are waiting for the chance to help you make your career dreams reality.

Lesson 47—Apply

You work in the publications department of Executive Recruitment Resources, Inc. Your manager sent you a copy of the newsletter that she edited without using revision marks. You will compare your manager's copy of the newsletter and the one on which you are working. In this project, you will combine the revisions and create a final newsletter.

DIRECTIONS

1. Start Word, if necessary, and open **W47ApplyA** from the data files for this lesson.
2. Save the file as **W47ApplyA_xx** in the location where your teacher instructs you to store the files for this lesson.
3. Type your full name and today's date in the header, and close the header.
4. Open **W47ApplyB** from the data files for this lesson.
5. Save the file as **W47ApplyB_xx** in the location where your teacher instructs you to store the files for this lesson.
6. Type your full name and today's date in the header, and close the header.
7. View the documents side by side and use synchronous scrolling to compare the content to identify differences.
8. Remove the side-by-side display, then save and close both documents. Leave Word open.
9. Combine the two documents, using the following options:
   a. Use **W47ApplyA_xx** as the original document.
   b. Use **W47ApplyB_xx** as the revised document.
   c. Label unmarked changes in the original document with your full name, and unmarked changes in the revised document with your initials.
   d. Choose to show the changes in the revised document.
   ✓ *Click the More button in the Combine Documents dialog box and, under Show changes in, click the Revised document option button.*
10. If necessary, click **REVIEW** > **Display for Review** drop-down arrow > **All Markup**.
11. Check and correct the spelling and grammar in the document.
12. Save the changes to **W47ApplyB_xx**.
13. **With your teacher's permission,** print the document with markup. It should look similar to Figure 47-2 on the next page.
14. Close the Revisions task pane.
15. Save and close the document, and exit Word.

Figure 47-2

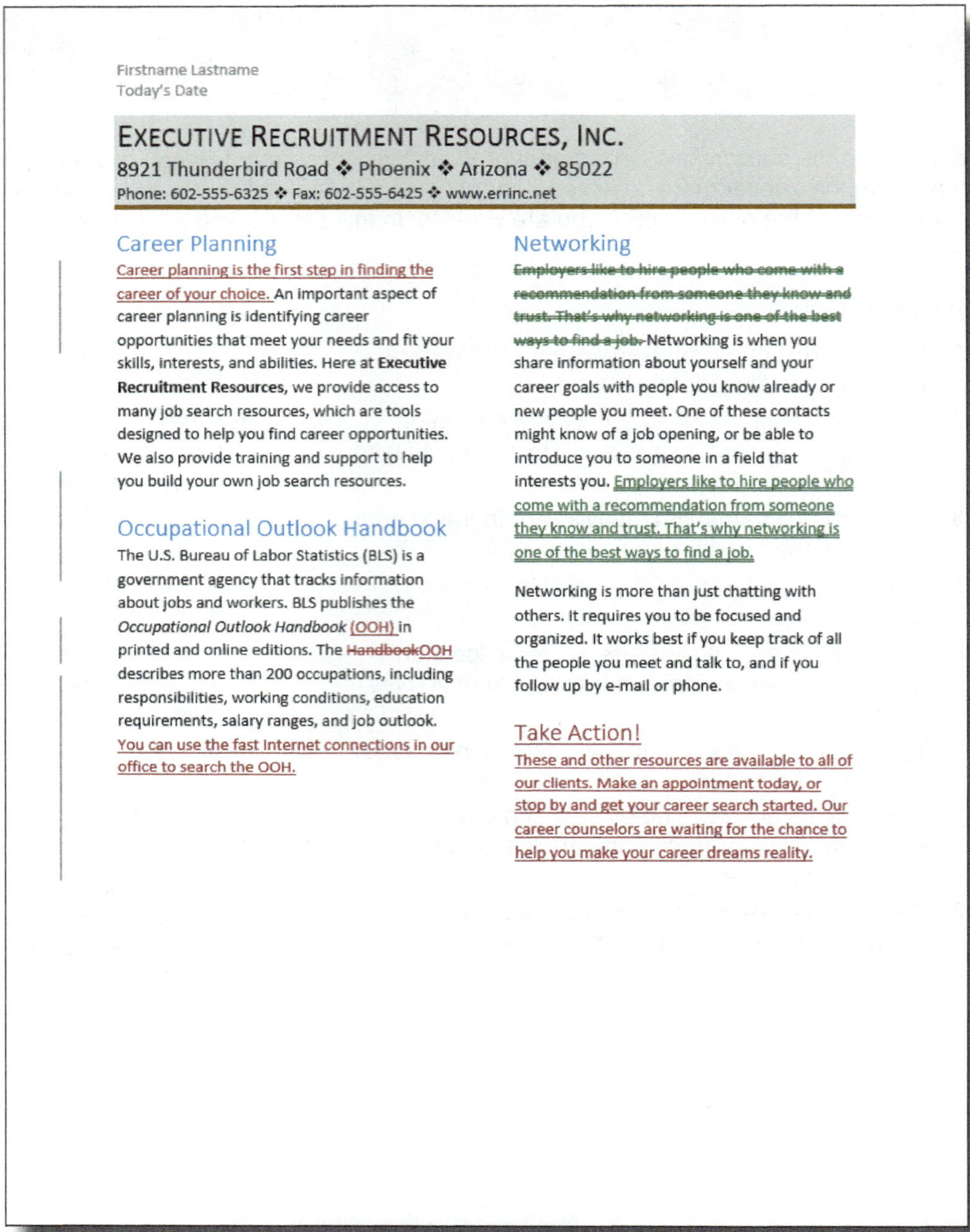

Firstname Lastname
Today's Date

EXECUTIVE RECRUITMENT RESOURCES, INC.
8921 Thunderbird Road ❖ Phoenix ❖ Arizona ❖ 85022
Phone: 602-555-6325 ❖ Fax: 602-555-6425 ❖ www.errinc.net

Career Planning
<u>Career planning is the first step in finding the career of your choice.</u> An important aspect of career planning is identifying career opportunities that meet your needs and fit your skills, interests, and abilities. Here at **Executive Recruitment Resources**, we provide access to many job search resources, which are tools designed to help you find career opportunities. We also provide training and support to help you build your own job search resources.

Occupational Outlook Handbook
The U.S. Bureau of Labor Statistics (BLS) is a government agency that tracks information about jobs and workers. BLS publishes the *Occupational Outlook Handbook* <u>(OOH)</u> in printed and online editions. The ~~Handbook~~<u>OOH</u> describes more than 200 occupations, including responsibilities, working conditions, education requirements, salary ranges, and job outlook. <u>You can use the fast Internet connections in our office to search the OOH.</u>

Networking
~~Employers like to hire people who come with a recommendation from someone they know and trust. That's why networking is one of the best ways to find a job.~~ Networking is when you share information about yourself and your career goals with people you know already or new people you meet. One of these contacts might know of a job opening, or be able to introduce you to someone in a field that interests you. <u>Employers like to hire people who come with a recommendation from someone they know and trust. That's why networking is one of the best ways to find a job.</u>

Networking is more than just chatting with others. It requires you to be focused and organized. It works best if you keep track of all the people you meet and talk to, and if you follow up by e-mail or phone.

Take Action!
<u>These and other resources are available to all of our clients. Make an appointment today, or stop by and get your career search started. Our career counselors are waiting for the chance to help you make your career dreams reality.</u>

Lesson 48

Restricting Access to Documents

➤ What You Will Learn

Setting and Removing Restrictions in a Document
Changing a Password in a Protected, Encrypted Document
Using Online Word Processing Technologies

Software Skills In Word, you can restrict the ability of authors to format, edit, or digitally sign a document. You can limit the number of authors that can revise a document. You can protect and encrypt a document with a password to limit unauthorized access to a document.

What You Can Do

Setting and Removing Restrictions in a Document

- You can restrict another author's ability to format and edit a document.
   - ✓ *You learned about protecting documents and restricting editing in Word, Lesson 28.*
- You can restrict whether an author can apply a different theme or style set to a document.
- Use the Formatting Restrictions dialog box to block authors from switching the document's contents to a different format.
- Recall that you can set formatting, read only, or comments restrictions, and that you can specify exceptions to allow access to all or parts of the document.
- When you mark a document as final, you can restrict another author's ability to edit the document. For example, you can restrict an author from inserting a **digital signature**.
   - ✓ *You learned about marking a document as final and digital signatures in Word, Lesson 30.*
- You can use a Windows Live ID to restrict permissions for specific users.
   - You can add permissions with the Restrict Access feature.
   - You can apply permissions using a template used by your organization.
- You must protect a document to enforce restrictions.
- Remove restrictions and protection to enable unlimited editing.
- Recall that restrictions apply to documents even when they are copied or saved with a new name.

WORDS TO KNOW

Authenticated
Checked and verified as real or legitimate.

Digital signature
An electronic, encryption-based, secure stamp of authentication on a macro or document.

Encryption
Scrambling so as to be indecipherable.

Password
A string of characters used to authenticate the identity of a user, and to limit unauthorized access.

Try It! Setting and Removing Restrictions in a Document

1. Start Word, and open **W48Try** from the data files for this lesson.
2. In the Password box, type **Try?W?48!**, and click OK.
3. Save the file as **W48Try_xx** in the location where your teacher instructs you to store the files for this lesson.
4. Click REVIEW > Restrict Editing.
5. In the Restrict Editing task pane, click Stop Protection, and in the Unprotect Document dialog box type **Try?W?48!**. Click OK.
6. In the Restrict Editing pane, under Formatting restrictions, click to select the Limit formatting to a selection of styles check box, and click Settings to display the Formatting Restrictions dialog box.
7. In the Formatting Restrictions dialog box, under Formatting, click the Block Theme or Scheme switching and the Block Quick Style Set switching check boxes, and click OK.
8. In the warning dialog box, click No.
9. In the Restrict Editing pane, under Editing restrictions, click to uncheck the Allow only this type of editing in the document check box.
10. In the warning dialog box, click Yes to remove the ignored exceptions.
11. Under Start enforcement click Yes, Start Enforcing Protection, and click OK without entering a password.
12. Click FILE > Protect Document > Mark as Final.
13. Click OK > OK.
14. Click the Back button. Notice that the editing options, including the ability to insert a digital signature, are disabled.
15. Close the document. Leave Word open to use in the Try It.

Restricted formatting

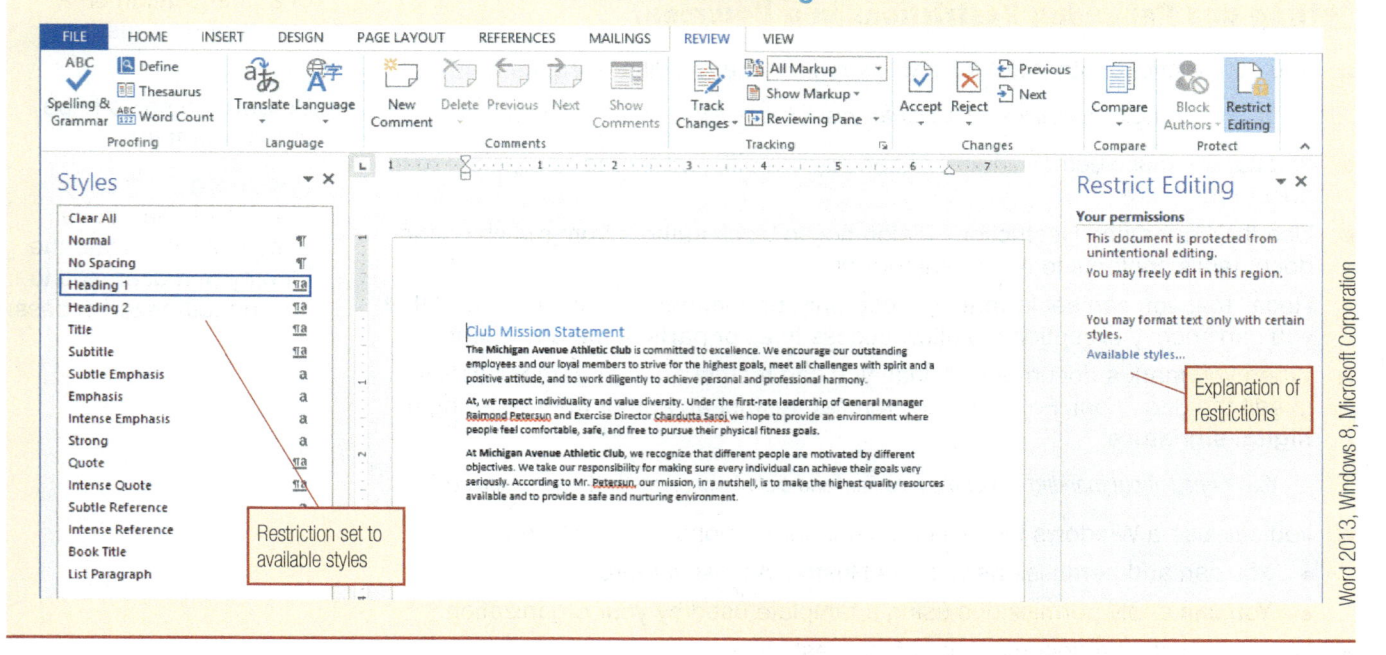

Restriction set to available styles

Explanation of restrictions

Business Information Management II | Word | Chapter 6

Changing a Password in a Protected, Encrypted Document

- You can use a **password** and **encryption** to ensure that users cannot remove or change restriction settings.
    - ✓ *You learned about password protection and encryption in Word, Lesson 28.*
- If you are an **authenticated** owner of the document, you can remove the document's protection and change the assigned password.
- You must know the current password and remove the document protection before you can change the password.
- You can reassign a password and re-encrypt a document at the same time using options on the Info tab in the Backstage view.
- Be careful to select a password you can remember. If you do not enter the correct password, you will not be able to access the document.
- Recall that the password protection applies to documents even when they are copied or saved with a new name.

Try It! Changing a Password in a Protected, Encrypted Document

1. Open the **W48Try_xx** file from the location where your teacher instructs you to store the files for this lesson.
2. In the Password dialog box, type **Try?W?48!**, and click OK.
3. In the MARKED AS FINAL bar, click Edit Anyway.
4. Click FILE > Protect Document > Encrypt with Password.
5. In the Password box, delete the existing password, and type **Try?W?48!New**. Click OK.
6. In the Reenter Password dialog box, click in the Enter new password box, and type **Try?W?48!New**. Click OK.
7. Click the Back button.
8. Save and close the document, and exit Word.

Using Online Word Processing Technologies

- Word Online is a free version of Microsoft Word available to anyone with a Microsoft or a school account.
- You can log in from any device with an Internet connection.
- Word Online does not include all the features of the desktop version of Microsoft Word or Word 365, which is the online app available to subscribers who pay a yearly fee.
- You can save documents created with Word Online on OneDrive or you can download them to a storage device connected to your computer.

Try It! Using Word Online

1. Go to https://office.live.com/start/Word.aspx and sign in with a Microsoft or school account. Word Online opens in your browser.
2. Click New blank document.
3. Type your name and today's date.
4. Click File > Save As > Download a Copy.
5. Click *Click here* to download your document. Your browser downloads the document.
6. Open the downloaded document and save it as **W48Try2_xx** in the location where your teacher instructs you to store the files for this lesson.
7. Close the document, exit Word, and exit your browser.

Lesson 48—Practice

The research and development department at Long Shot, Inc., is working on an exciting new product. It is important that all information related to the product remain confidential and out of the hands of business competitors. The department manager has asked you to generate a memo to all team members explaining the importance of confidentiality with regard to this project, and what problems might arise from a breach of confidentiality. In this project, you will create the document and set restrictions so that it cannot be changed.

DIRECTIONS

1. Start Word, if necessary.
2. Create a new blank document and save it as **W48Practice_xx** in the location where your teacher instructs you to store the files for this lesson.
3. Display the rulers and nonprinting characters, if necessary.
4. Set paragraph spacing **Before** to **24** points and paragraph spacing **After** to **36** points.
5. Set the line spacing at **Single**.
6. Type **MEMO**, and press ENTER.
7. Apply the **No Spacing** style, and set a left tab stop at **0.75"** on the horizontal ruler.
8. Type **To:**, press TAB, and type **Team Members**. Press ENTER.
9. Type **From:**, press TAB, and type your own name. Press ENTER.
10. Type **Date:**, press TAB, and type or insert today's date. Press ENTER.
11. Type **Subject:**, press TAB, and type **Confidentiality**. Press ENTER twice.
12. Apply the **Normal** style and type the following paragraphs.

    As you all know, we are working on a new and exciting product which the company expects will completely revolutionize the golf equipment industry. This memo is simply a reminder of the Long Shot, Inc., corporate policy on confidentiality and ethical behavior.

    Confidentiality in business refers to the protection of proprietary and secret information. In some businesses, the information belongs to a client, and it is the responsibility of the business to make sure no one else can access the information. In our case, the information belongs to the corporation, and it is our responsibility to make sure no one outside the company gains access.

13. Check and correct the spelling and grammar in the document, and save the changes.
14. Click **REVIEW** > **Restrict Editing**.
15. In the Restrict Editing pane, under *Formatting restrictions*, click to select the **Limit formatting to a selection of styles** check box, and click **Settings**.
16. In the Formatting Restrictions dialog box, click **Recommended Minimum** > **OK**.
17. If necessary, in the warning dialog box, click **No**.
18. In the Restrict Editing pane, under *Editing restrictions*, click to select the **Allow only this type of editing in the document** check box, click the drop-down arrow, and click **Comments**.
19. In the document, select the last paragraph.
20. In the task pane, under *Exceptions (optional)*, click to select the **Everyone** check box.
21. Under *Start enforcement* click **Yes, Start Enforcing Protection**.
22. In the Start Enforcing Protection dialog box, in the Enter new password (optional) box, type **!48?Project&**.
23. In the Reenter password to confirm box, type **!48?Project&**, and click **OK**.
24. Select the text *MEMO*, and try to apply the Title style.
25. Select the first paragraph, and press DEL.
26. Click **REVIEW** > **New Comment** and type **What about the code of conduct?**
27. Click outside the comment balloon, then in the task pane, click **Find Next Region I Can Edit** to select the last paragraph, and apply the **No Spacing** style.
28. Save the document.

Business Information Management II | Word | Chapter 6

29. **With your teacher's permission**, print the document. It should look similar to Figure 48-1.

30. Save and close the document, and exit Word.

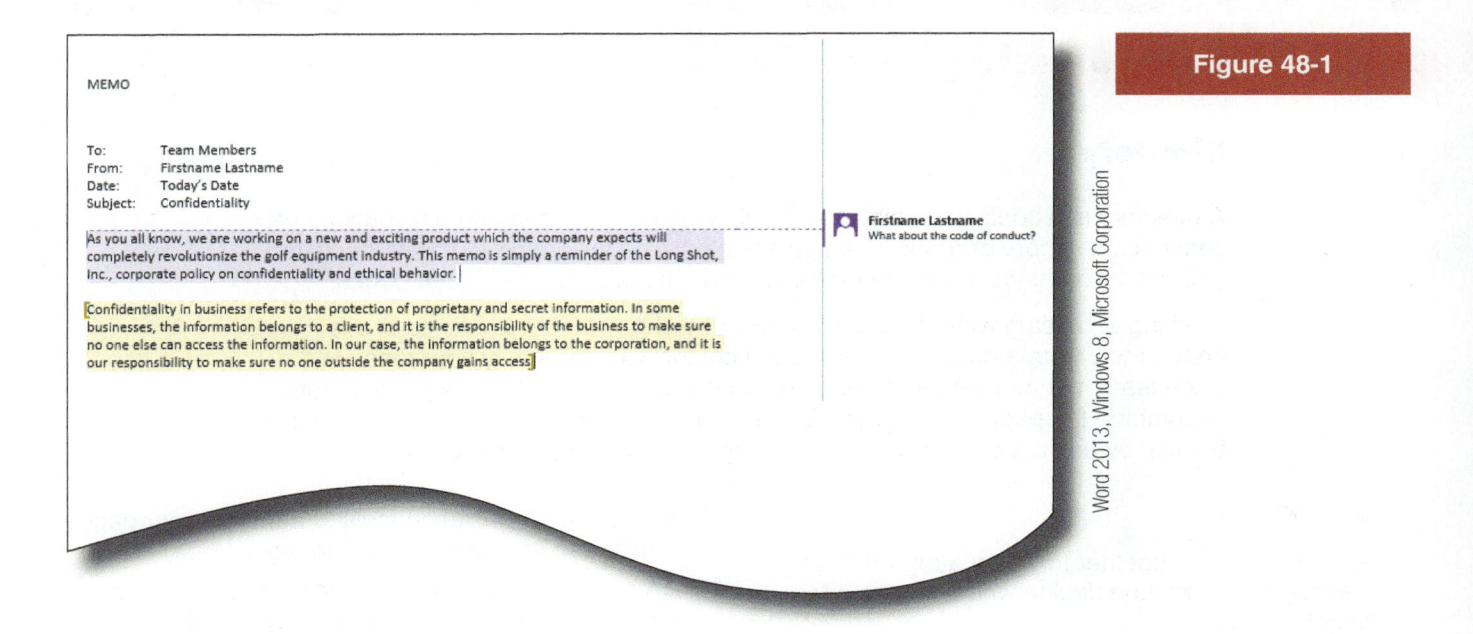

Figure 48-1

```
MEMO

To:        Team Members
From:      Firstname Lastname
Date:      Today's Date
Subject:   Confidentiality

As you all know, we are working on a new and exciting product which the company expects will
completely revolutionize the golf equipment industry. This memo is simply a reminder of the Long Shot,
Inc., corporate policy on confidentiality and ethical behavior.

Confidentiality in business refers to the protection of proprietary and secret information. In some
businesses, the information belongs to a client, and it is the responsibility of the business to make sure
no one else can access the information. In our case, the information belongs to the corporation, and it is
our responsibility to make sure no one outside the company gains access.
```

Firstname Lastname
What about the code of conduct?

Word 2013, Windows 8, Microsoft Corporation

Lesson 48—Apply

You have created a restricted document for Long Shot, Inc. so that product information will remain confidential. Your department manager has approved the memo and asked you to prepare the document so that the legal department can review and revise. In this project, you will restrict editing in the document to track changes and encrypt the document.

DIRECTIONS

1. Start Word, if necessary, and open **W48Apply** from the data files for this lesson.
2. Save it as **W48Apply_xx** in the location where your teacher instructs you to store the files for this lesson.
3. Replace the sample text *Student's Name* with your own name, and *Today's Date* with the actual date.
4. In the last line of the document, insert a signature line with the following instructions to the signer: **Before signing this document, verify that you have read the content you are signing.**
   - ✓ *You learned about digital signatures in Word, Lesson 30.*
   - ✓ *Hint: Click INSERT > Signature Line.*
5. Set options so users cannot apply any styles to the document, but do not remove existing styles.
6. Restrict editing to tracked changes, and start enforcement. Do not apply a password.
7. Close the Restrict Editing task pane.
8. Use the Info tab in Backstage view to encrypt the document with the password **&LSI?48**.
9. Save and close the document. Leave Word open.
10. Open the document using the correct password.
11. **With your teacher's permission,** print the document.
12. Save and close the document, and exit Word.

End-of-Chapter Activities

▶ Word Chapter 6 — Critical Thinking

Directory

A directory is a book containing an alphabetical list of names and descriptions of items in a category or group. The items might be people, such as the students in your class, or things, such as companies, countries, sports teams, or books.

Working as a team with other classmates, use skills you have learned in this chapter to create a directory of items in a category approved by your teacher. Each team member will write one page for the directory, and you will collaborate to combine the pages into a professional-quality, multi-page booklet. Enhance the booklet by using a custom theme and a logo saved as a building block.

DIRECTIONS

1. As a team, work together to select a topic that your teacher approves, and decide who will write each page.
2. Collaborate by designing a custom theme that will give your directory a unique look.
3. Also work together to design a logo you can use on each page, and then save the logo as a building block that you can all access.
4. Design a cover page for your directory using the theme and the building block. Enter all team members' names and the current date on the cover.
5. Individually, start Word, click **Blank document**, and save as **WCT06_xx** in the location where your teacher instructs you to store the files for this chapter.
6. Apply the custom theme your team designed, and insert the logo building block somewhere on the page.
7. In the footer, insert the user name and date fields from Quick Parts.
8. Write your directory page. It should have a title, be at least two paragraphs long, and may include a picture or other type of illustration.
9. Use Word's Translation tools to translate your page title into at least one other language.
10. Exchange documents with a teammate and use revision marks and comments to review the document and make suggestions for improvement.
11. When you receive your own document back, accept and reject changes, or compare and combine the documents to create the final.
12. Check and correct the spelling and grammar in the document, and save the document.
13. When you are satisfied with the document, ask a classmate to review it and make comments or suggestions that will help you improve it.
14. Make changes and corrections, as necessary.
15. **With your teacher's permission,** print the document.
16. Restore all default settings, and delete custom themes and building blocks you will no longer need.
17. Save and close the document.
18. Arrange the printed documents in alphabetical order, and staple them together with the cover page to create the booklet.

Word Chapter 6—Portfolio Builder

Information Sheet

You and a co-worker at Fresh Food Fair have been collaborating on a document explaining the benefits of organic farming. In this project, you will start by comparing and combining the two versions of the document. You will then use the skills you have learned in this chapter including translating text, advanced find and replace, building blocks, Quick Parts, comments, and revision marks to complete the document. You will also save the finished document as a template.

Design a Building Block and a Custom Theme

1. Start Word, click **Blank document**, and save as **WPB06_xx** in the location where your teacher instructs you to store the files for this chapter.
2. In the header, type **Fresh Food Fair** and format it in **48 point Times New Roman**. Select the text, and draw a text box around it.
3. Format the text box to have no fill or outline, and resize it to **1"** high by **4.5"** wide. Align the text box with the top of the page and with the left margin.
4. To the right of the text box, insert a clip art image of vegetables. If you cannot find a suitable image, insert **WPB06_picture** from the data files for this chapter.
5. Size the image to **0.8"** high and **1.18"** wide, and align it with the text box and the right margin.
6. Select the text box and the image and then save the selection as a building block in the Headers Gallery with the name **WPB06 Header** and the description **Header for Fresh Food Fair**.
7. Customize the theme with the **Green** theme colors and the **Cambria** theme fonts.
8. Save the custom theme with the name **WPB06 Theme**.
9. Close the document without saving changes. Leave Word open.

Compare and Combine Documents

1. In Word, open **WPB06A** from the data files for this chapter. This is the original document.
2. Save the file as **WPB06A_xx** in the location where your teacher instructs you to store the files for this chapter.
3. Type your full name and today's date in the footer, close the footer, and scroll to the top of the document.
4. Open **WPB06B** from the data files for this chapter. This is the revised document.
5. Save the file as **WPB06B_xx** in the location where your teacher instructs you to store the files for this chapter.
6. Type your full name and today's date in the footer, close the footer, and scroll back to the top of the document.
7. View the documents side by side, and use synchronous scrolling to compare the content to identify differences.
8. When you identify a difference, insert a comment in the revised document (**WPB06B_xx**) describing the difference. For example, insert a comment to identify the different title, and to note that terms beginning with the word organic are italicized.
9. When you complete the comparison, remove the side-by-side display, and save and close both documents. Leave Word open.
10. Combine the two documents, using the following options:
    - Use **WPB06A_xx** as the original document.
    - Use **WPB06B_xx** as the revised document.
    - Label unmarked changes in the original document with your full name, and unmarked changes in the revised document with your initials.
    - Choose to show the changes in the original document.
    - Unselect the Formatting option to keep formatting changes from the revised document.
11. Save the changes to **WPB06A_xx**.
12. Save the document as **WPB06C_xx** in the location where your teacher instructs you to store the files for this chapter.

Finalize the Document

1. In the **WPB06C_xx** document, delete all comments.
2. Show all revisions inline, and display the Reviewing pane vertically.
3. Accept the changes to the title.
4. Reject the changes to the first heading.
5. Reject the changes to the first sentence.
6. Accept all the remaining changes in the document.
7. Close the Reviewing pane, and set Word to Show Only Comments and Formatting in Balloons.
8. Save the changes to the document.
9. Use Find and Replace to find and match the case of **ly-** in the document, and replace with **ly** —with a space after the letters.
   ✓ *Hint: Click More > Match case.*
10. Clear the match case formatting options, and close the Find and Replace dialog box.
11. Insert the **WPB06 Header** building block.
12. Apply the **WPB06 Theme** custom theme.
    ✓ *If necessary, adjust the indent of the title line so it fits on one line, as shown in Illustration 6A.*
13. Use Word's translation features to translate the last line of text into Spanish, then insert a new line at the end of the document, and type the translated text. Format both lines with the **Heading 3** style, centered.
    ✓ *Remove hyperlink formatting, if necessary.*
14. Flush right in the footer, insert the **UserInitials** field with **Uppercase** format and the **Time** field in **HH:mm:ss** format.
15. Check and correct the spelling and grammar in the document, and save the document.
16. **With your teacher's permission,** print the document with markup. It should look similar to Illustration 6A on the next page.
17. Delete the **WPB06 Header** building block, and the **WPB06 Theme** custom theme.
18. Save the document, and exit Word. Save the building blocks template.
19. Start Word, and open **WPB06C_xx**.
20. Save the **WPB06C_xx** document as a Word Template with the file name **WPB06C_Template_xx** in the location where your teacher instructs you to store the files for this chapter.
21. Close the **WPB06C_Template_xx** template, and exit Word.

Fresh Food Fair

Organic Farming Information Sheet

What Is Organic Farming?
Organic farming is an ecological management system that promotes and enhances biodiversity, biological cycles, and soil biological activity. This system is based on management practices that restore, maintain, and enhance biological harmony. Organic farmers fertilize and build healthy soils by using compost and other biologically based soil modifications. This produces healthy plants which are better able to resist disease and insects.

Standards of Quality
Organic farmers follow a set of strict standards set by the U.S. Department of Agriculture (USDA). Essentially, the organic standards offer a national definition for the term "organic." The standards also state that all agricultural products labeled "organic" must originate from farms or handling operations certified by a state or private agency accredited by the USDA.

For products to carry the label "Made with Organic Ingredients," at least 70% of their ingredients must be organic. Furthermore, the standards provide information for consumers by requiring manufacturers to state the exact percentage of organic ingredients on the chief display panel of the product.

Benefits and Drawbacks
Because organic farming systems do not use toxic chemical pesticides or fertilizers, organic foods are not exposed to these toxins. Organic foods are also minimally processed to maintain the integrity of the food without artificial ingredients, preservatives, or irradiation, which some people believe makes them taste better.

Generally, organic foods cost more than conventional foods. This is because the prices for organic foods reflect many of the same costs as conventional foods in terms of growing, harvesting, transportation, and storage, but there are added costs as well. Organically produced foods must meet stricter regulations so the process is often more labor and management intensive, which costs more. Also, organic farms tend to be smaller, which increases costs.

Where to Find Organic Foods
Organic foods can be found at natural food stores, organic farm stands, as well as in the health food and produce departments of most supermarkets. Many restaurant chefs are using organic products because of its growing popularity, as well as its reputation for having superior quality and taste.

Available in Spanish at www.freshfoodfair.org
Disponible en español en www.freshfoodfair.org

Firstname Lastname
Today's Date

FL
13:49:10

Chapter 7

(Courtesy auremar/Shutterstock)

Using Advanced Tables and Graphics

Lesson 49
Customizing Table Styles

- Creating a Custom Table Style
- Modifying and Deleting a Table Style
- Adding a Caption to a Table

Lesson 50
Using Advanced Table Features

- Inserting Graphics in a Table Cell
- Inserting a Nested Table
- Creating a Repeating Header Row
- Splitting a Table
- Inserting an Excel Worksheet in a Word Document
- Copying Excel Data to Word and Converting a Table to Text

Lesson 51
Using Advanced Graphics

- Using Document Gridlines
- Using Advanced Sizing Features
- Using Advanced Position Features
- Adjusting Objects
- Cropping a Picture

Lesson 52
Linking Text Boxes

- Aligning an Object with Another Object
- Linking Text Boxes
- Compressing a Picture
- Removing a Picture Background

Lesson 53
Creating WordArt and Watermarks

- Creating WordArt
- Creating a Watermark

End-of-Chapter Activities

Lesson 49

Customizing Table Styles

> ## ➤ What You Will Learn
> **Creating a Custom Table Style**
> **Modifying and Deleting a Table Style**
> **Adding a Caption to a Table**

WORDS TO KNOW

Caption
A text label that identifies an illustration such as a figure, table, or picture.

Software Skills You can create a table style when none of the built-in table styles are suitable for your document. Add a caption to a table to help readers identify the table you are referring to in the document text.

What You Can Do

Creating a Custom Table Style

- Use the options in the Create New Style from Formatting dialog box to create and save a custom table style.
- As you select formatting, you can specify whether the formatting should apply to the whole table or to parts of the table.
- You can choose to include formatting for Table Style Options, such as a header row, banded rows, or banded columns.
- You can select to make the style available in all new documents based on the current template or only in the current document.
- The style becomes available in the Table Styles gallery so you can use it to format other tables.

Business Information Management II | Word | Chapter 7   119

Try It! Creating a Custom Table Style

1. Start Word, and open **W49Try** from the data files for this lesson.

2. Save the document as **W49Try_xx** in the location where your teacher instructs you to store the files for this lesson.

3. Click anywhere in the table. Click the TABLE TOOLS DESIGN tab, click the Table Styles More button, and click New Table Style to open the Create New Style from Formatting dialog box.

4. In the Name text box, type **W49Try**.

5. Click the Border Style drop-down arrow, and click the triple line style.

6. Click the Borders drop-down arrow, and click Outside Borders.

7. Click the Fill Color drop-down arrow and click Blue, Accent 1, Lighter 80%.

8. Verify that the Only in this document option button is selected, and click OK.

9. Click the Table Styles More button. Under Custom, click the W49Try table style to apply it to the table in the document.

10. Save the changes to **W49Try_xx**, and leave it open to use in the next Try It.

Create New Style from Formatting dialog box

Create New Style from Formatting

Properties
- Name: Style1
- Style type: Table
- Style based on: Table Normal

Formatting
- Apply formatting to: Whole table
- Calibri (Body) 11 B I U Automatic — *Font formatting options*
- ½ pt — Automatic — No Color — *Fill Color*

Border Style
Border Weight
Border Color

	Jan	Feb	Mar	Total
East	7	7	5	19
West	6	4	7	17
South	8	7	9	24
Total	21	18	21	60

Preview

Line spacing: single, Space After: 0 pt, Priority: 100
Based on: Table Normal

● Only in this document   ○ New documents based on this template

Format ▼   OK   Cancel

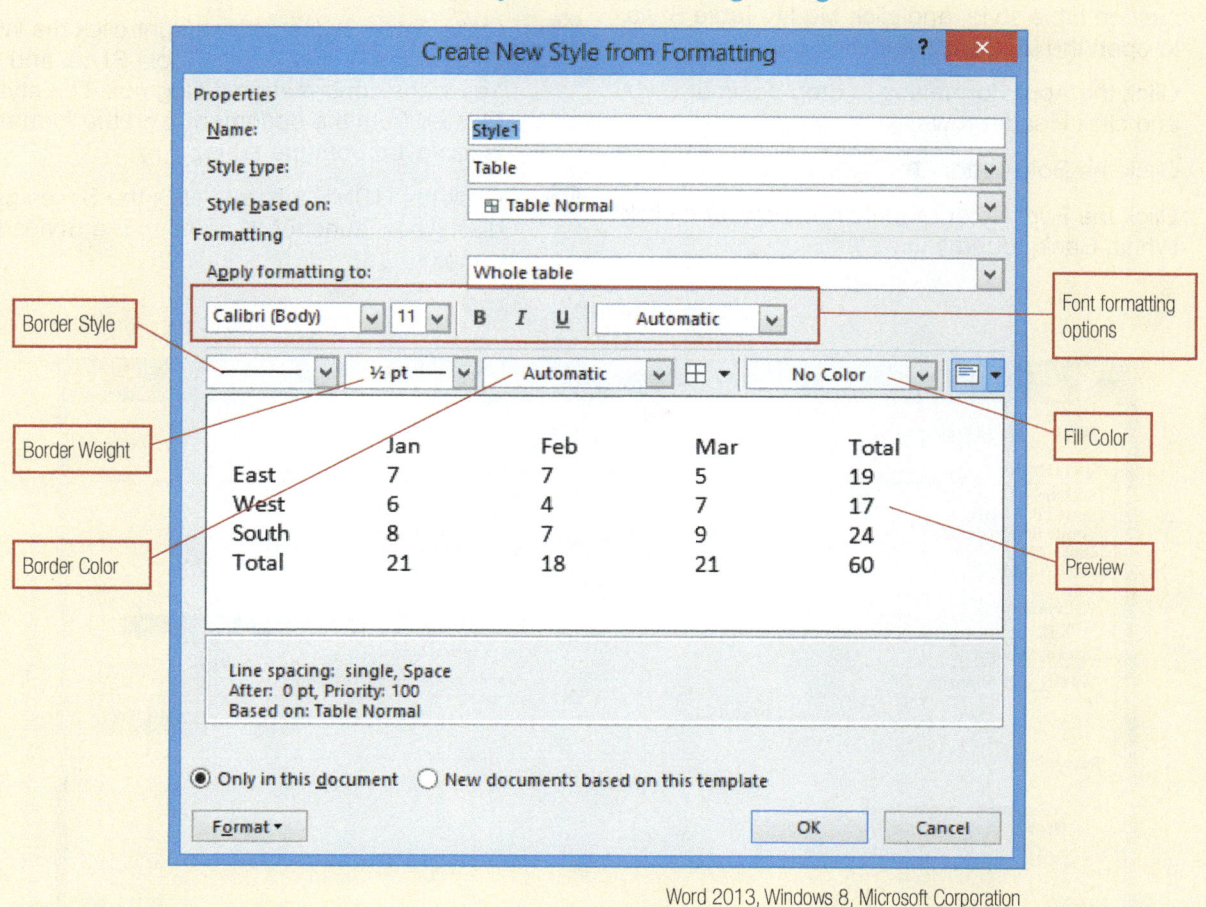

Word 2013, Windows 8, Microsoft Corporation

Lesson 52—Apply

You work in the publicity department of New Media Designs, a Web site design and management company. You are in charge of a campaign to inspire local students to pursue careers in computer information systems and technology. In this project, you will create a flier to advertise a contest for high school students. You will use pictures and text boxes to make the flier visually appealing and informative.

DIRECTIONS

1. Start Word, if necessary, and open **W52Apply** from the data files for this lesson.
2. Save the file as **W52Apply_xx** in the location where your teacher instructs you to store the files for this lesson.
3. Double-click in the header, type your full name and today's date, and close the header.
4. Insert an **Explosion 2** shape. Size it to **2"** high by **2.5"** wide, and add the text **High School Division!** in **14 point Arial**.
5. Position the object in the top left part of the document relative to the margins, and set the text wrapping to **Behind Text**.
6. Insert an **Explosion 1** shape. Size it to **2.5"** high by **2.5"** wide, and add the text **Winners announced June 1!** in **14 point Arial**.
7. Set the text wrapping to **Behind Text**, and align it with the Right margin.
8. Apply the **Subtle Effect - Black, Dark 1** shape style to both shapes.
9. Use the Selection Pane to select the objects, and align the middles of the shapes relative to each other.
10. Position the insertion point in the left text box, set the style to **No Spacing**, set the font size to **14 points**, and set the alignment to **Center**.
11. Type the following six lines:

    Category 1

    Video Presentation

    Category 2

    Web Page Design

    Category 3

    Essay Writing

12. Link the left text box to the middle text box, and the middle text box to the right text box.
13. Format the text boxes on the left and right with the **Moderate Effect - Blue, Accent 1** shape style and the text box in the middle with the **Moderate Effect - Orange, Accent 2** shape style.
14. Insert a blank line at the end of the document (remove the hyperlink from the URL, if necessary), and insert **W52Apply_picture**.
15. Set text wrapping to **Square**, resize the picture to **1.5"** wide, center the picture horizontally, and position it **0.25"** below the blank line.
16. Add a caption below the picture using the label Figure and Arabic numbers.
17. Compress the picture, and remove its background and other areas as necessary so it looks similar to the picture in Figure 52-2 on the next page.
18. Check and correct the spelling and grammar, and save the document.
19. **With your teacher's permission**, print the document.
20. Save and close the document, and exit Word.

Figure 52-2

Lesson 53

Creating WordArt and Watermarks

➤ What You Will Learn
Creating WordArt
Creating a Watermark

Software Skills Use WordArt to transform text into artwork for letterheads, logos, brochures, and other documents. WordArt lets you create special effects using any text that you type. You can stretch characters, rotate them, reverse direction, and even arrange the text in shapes such as circles, waves, or arcs. Place a watermark on a document to make an impression on readers, convey an idea, or provide a consistent theme. For example, a watermark on corporate stationery can communicate a corporate identity.

WORDS TO KNOW

Watermark
A pale or semitransparent graphics object positioned behind text in a document.

WordArt
A feature of Word used to transform text into a drawing object.

What You Can Do

Creating WordArt

- **WordArt** is an Office feature similar to text effects that you use to transform text into a drawing object.
- You create WordArt by selecting a style from the WordArt gallery.
- The WordArt text is inserted in a text box which you can size and position on the page.
- Use the tools in the WordArt Styles group on the DRAWING TOOLS FORMAT tab to customize the WordArt text.
- For example, you can apply text effects to transform the shape of the text, or to add a glow, reflection, or 3-D effect.
- You can also use the standard tools for formatting the text box, such as fill, outline, text wrapping, size, position, and alignment.
- The command for creating WordArt is in the Text group on the INSERT tab of the Ribbon.

Try It! Creating WordArt

1. Start Word, click Blank document, and save the document as **W53Try_xx** in the location where your teacher instructs you to store the files for this lesson.

2. Click INSERT, and in the Text group click the WordArt button to display the WordArt gallery.

3. Click the fourth style in the first row—Gradient Fill - White Outline - Accent 1, Shadow. Word creates the WordArt in a text box using sample text.

4. Type **Adventure!** to replace the sample text.

5. On the DRAWING TOOLS FORMAT tab, in the WordArt Styles group, click the Text Effects button to display a menu of text effects options.

6. Point to Transform to display a gallery of transform styles. Under Warp, point to the first option in the fourth row—Curve Up—to see how it affects the WordArt.

7. Scroll down to the bottom of the Transform gallery and click the first style in the last row—Slant Up.

8. In the WordArt Style group, click the Text Fill drop-down arrow, and click Gold, Accent 4.

9. In the Arrange group, click Position, and click Position in Top Center with Square Text Wrapping.

10. Save the changes to **W53Try_xx**, and leave it open to use in the next Try It.

WordArt

Word 2013, Windows 8, Microsoft Corporation

Creating a Watermark

- Insert text or graphics objects as a **watermark** to provide a background image for text-based documents.
- Word 2013 comes with built-in watermark styles that you can select from the Watermark gallery in the Page Background group on the DESIGN tab.
- You can also create a custom watermark using the options in the Printed Watermark dialog box.
- A watermark may be a graphics object, such as clip art, a text box, WordArt, or a shape.
- You can also create a watermark from text.
- Watermarks are usually inserted into the document header so that they automatically appear on every page, and so that they are not affected by changes made to the document content.
- To remove a watermark, click the Watermark button and click Remove Watermark, or make the header active, select the watermark, and press DEL.
- You can add a watermark to a template so that every document based on the template will display the same watermark.

Business Information Management II | Word | Chapter 7   157

Try It! Creating a Watermark

1. In the **W53Try_xx** file, adjust the zoom to display the entire page.
2. Click DESIGN, and in the Page Background group click Watermark to display the Watermark gallery.
3. Click the CONFIDENTIAL 1 style. Word inserts the watermark on the page.
4. Click the Undo button on the Quick Access Toolbar to remove the watermark.
5. Click Watermark, and click Custom Watermark to display the Printed Watermark dialog box.
6. Click the Picture watermark option button, and click Select Picture.
7. In the Insert Pictures dialog box, click From a file, navigate to the location where the data files for this lesson are stored, and insert **W53Try_picture**.
8. In the Printed Watermark dialog box, click OK.
9. Click Undo on the Quick Access Toolbar to remove the watermark, click Watermark, and click Custom Watermark to display the Printed Watermark dialog box.
10. Click the Text watermark option button, select the text in the Text box, type **Adventure!**, and click OK.
11. Save and close the document, and exit Word.

Lesson 53—Practice

Long Shot, Inc. is growing by leaps and bounds. To fill job vacancies, it is hosting an open house and career fair. In this project, you will use WordArt and a watermark to create a notice to announce the event.

DIRECTIONS

1. Start Word, if necessary, click **Blank document**, and save the document as **W53Practice_xx** in the location where your teacher instructs you to store the files for this lesson.
2. Double-click in the header, and type your full name and today's date. Click **Close Header and Footer**.
3. Position the insertion point on the first line of the document, set the font to **72 point Arial**, and type **SOAR**. Center the line horizontally.
4. Press ENTER, decrease the font size to **20 points**, type **to new heights with**, and press ENTER.
5. Click **INSERT**, and in the Text group click **WordArt**.
6. Click the **Gradient Fill - Blue, Accent 1, Reflection** style (second style in the second column).
7. In the WordArt text box, type **Long Shot, Inc.**
8. On the DRAWING TOOLS FORMAT tab, in the WordArt Styles group, click **Text Effects**, point to **Transform**, and under Warp, click **Inflate** (first style in the sixth row).
9. With the WordArt text box selected, click **Wrap Text** > **Top and Bottom**.
10. Click **Position** > **More Layout Options**.
11. Under Horizontal, click the **Alignment** option, click the **Alignment** drop-down arrow, click **Centered**, click the **relative to** drop-down arrow, and click **Margin**.
12. Under Vertical, click the **Absolute position** option, in the **Absolute position** box enter **3.25"**, click the **relative to** drop-down arrow, and click **Page**.
13. Click to select the **Lock Anchor** check box, and click **OK**.

14. Position the insertion point on the last line of the document, set the spacing before to **132 pt**, and press ENTER.
15. Set the spacing to before to **0 pt**, and type the following six lines, pressing ENTER between each line:
    Please Come to Our
    Open House and Career Fair
    Saturday, April 15th and Sunday, April 16th
    10:00 a.m. – 3:00 p.m.
    234 Simsbury Drive
    Ithaca, NY 14850
16. Click **DESIGN** > **Watermark**.
17. Click **Custom Watermark** to open the Printed Watermark dialog box.
18. Click the **Picture watermark** option, click **Select Picture**, click **Browse**, browse to the location where the data files for this lesson are stored, and insert **W53Practice_picture**.
19. In the Printed Watermark dialog box, click **OK**.
20. Check and correct the spelling and grammar, and save the document.
21. **With your teacher's permission**, print the document. It should look similar to Figure 53-1.
22. Save and close the document, and exit Word.

Figure 53-1

Lesson 53—Apply

You work for the publicity department of Long Shot, Inc. You are in charge of the publications for an open house and career fair. In this project, you will use WordArt and a watermark to create a handout for attendees.

DIRECTIONS

1. Start Word, if necessary, and open **W53Apply** from the data files for this lesson.
2. Save the file as **W53Apply_xx** in the location where your teacher instructs you to store the files for this lesson.
3. Double-click in the header, and type your full name and today's date. Click **Close Header and Footer**.
4. Insert a WordArt object using the **Fill - Gold, Accent 4, Soft Bevel** style.
5. In the WordArt text box, type **234 Simsbury Drive**, press ENTER, type **Long Shot, Inc.**, press ENTER, and type **Ithaca, NY**.
6. Resize the WordArt text box to **3.5"** high by **4.5"** wide.
7. Click **Text Effects** > **Transform**, and under Follow Path click **Button**.
8. Set the word wrap for the WordArt object to **Top and Bottom**, position it horizontally centered on the page and **3"** below the page, and lock the anchor.
9. Create a picture watermark using the **W53Apply_picture** file from the data files for this lesson.
10. Check and correct the spelling and grammar, and save the document.
11. **With your teacher's permission**, print the document. It should look similar to Figure 53-2 on the next page.
12. Save and close the document, and exit Word.

Figure 53-2

Firstname Lastname
Today's Date

Welcome

to our Open House and Career Fair

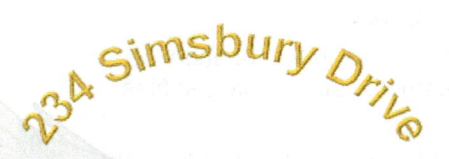

234 Simsbury Drive

Long Shot, Inc.

Ithaca, NY

Career Opportunities are available in:
- ✓ Manufacturing
- ✓ Marketing
- ✓ Design

Department managers are stationed in the cafeteria to provide additional information. Please complete a job application to submit along with your resume, letter of introduction, and list of references. We appreciate your interest in working at Long Shot.

Business Information Management II | Word | Chapter 7

End-of-Chapter Activities

► Word Chapter 7—Critical Thinking

Travel Itinerary

In this project, create an itinerary for yourself and three or four traveling companions. They might be your friends, family, or a club or organization to which you belong. You might start by looking up sample itineraries online, or searching online for itinerary templates to use to create the document.

Include the following information:

- The names of everyone who will be traveling.
- The locations, dates, and times of departure and arrival for all legs of the trip.
- The method of transportation, including schedule and flight, train, or bus numbers. You may choose to include the cost information, as well.
- Information about accommodations at the destination, such as hotel name, address, and telephone number, and the number of nights.
- A schedule of activities or sightseeing options.

Create the itinerary using the advanced tables and graphics skills you have learned in this chapter, including table styles, nested tables, advanced graphics sizing and positioning, captions, WordArt, and watermarks.

DIRECTIONS

1. Start Word, if necessary, and save a new, blank document or the itinerary template of your choice as **WCT07_xx** in the location where your teacher instructs you to store the files for this chapter.
2. Type your name and today's date in the document header, and apply a theme and style set.
3. Design the itinerary using tables and graphics. For example, you might use a large table to organize the page into columns, then insert a graphic image of your destination in one of the table cells. You might insert a nested table in a cell to enter the names of the travelers and the travel information.
4. Design and save a custom table style to give your tables a unique look.
5. Embellish and enhance the document by including shapes and pictures, and format the objects using advanced graphics features. Use document gridlines to help you make sure objects are aligned evenly on the page, and with each other.
6. When you have completed a first draft, exchange documents with a classmate, make suggestions for improvement, and then exchange back.
7. Make the improvements to your document.
8. Check and correct the spelling and grammar, and save the document.
9. **With your teacher's permission**, print the document.
10. When you are satisfied with the document, ask a classmate to review it and make comments or suggestions that will help you improve it.
11. Make changes and corrections, as necessary.
12. Restore all default settings, and delete custom styles.
13. Save and close the document, and exit Word.

► Word Chapter 7—Portfolio Builder

Invitation

You have been asked to design an invitation to a luncheon honoring the winners of New Media Design's Communications contest. You will use tables, graphics objects, WordArt, and a watermark to create an effective, eye-catching document.

DIRECTIONS

1. Start Word, if necessary, and save a new, blank document as **WPB07_xx** in the location where your teacher instructs you to store the files for this chapter.
2. Insert your name and today's date in the document header, and apply the **Integral** theme.
3. Use the following steps to create the document shown in Illustration 7A.
4. Insert a WordArt object using the **Fill - Turquoise, Accent 3, Sharp Bevel** style.
5. Type the text **New Media Designs**, and apply the **Chevron Up** transform text effect.
6. Resize the WordArt text box to **1"** high by **5"** wide, set the text wrapping to **Top and Bottom**, center it horizontally on the page, and position it along the top margin.
7. Insert a text box sized to **1"** high by **3"** wide. Position it horizontally aligned with the left margin and vertically **3"** below the page.
8. Set the style to **No Spacing**, set the font size to **16 points**, and type the following seven lines:
   You are invited to celebrate the winners of our first ever Communications Contest!
   Please join us for lunch.
   Friday, October 19
   12:30 p.m.
   New Media Designs
   Highway 73
   Cambridge, WA 53523
9. Draw a second text box of the same size. Position it centered horizontally and vertically **4"** below the page.
10. Draw a third text box of the same size. Position it horizontally aligned with the right margin and vertically **5"** below the page.
11. Link the left text box to the middle box and the middle box to the right box.
12. Apply the **Subtle Effect - Turquoise, Accent 3** shape style to the left text box, the **Subtle Effect - Blue, Accent 2** shape style to the middle text box, and the **Subtle Effect - Green, Accent 4** shape style to the right text box.
13. Insert a table with four columns and five rows, and drag it down near the bottom of the page (refer to Illustration 7A). Merge the cells in the top row. Enter the following data in the first two rows:

Communications Contest Winners			
Middle (5–8)	Category 1	Category 2	Category 3

14. In the second cell of the third row, insert a nested table with two columns and three rows and enter the following data:

1st	Alex Grogan
2nd	Michaela Jackson
3rd	Jaclyn Brown

15. In the third cell of the third row, insert a nested table with two columns and three rows and enter the following data:

1st	Jill Kline
2nd	Sam Lapp
3rd	Dinesh Patel

16. In the fourth cell of the third row, insert a nested table with two columns and three rows and enter the following data:

1st	Matt O'Toole
2nd	Chris White
3rd	Liz Jones

17. In the fourth row, enter the following data:

High School	Category 1	Category 2	Category 3

18. In the second cell of the fifth row, insert a nested table with two columns and three rows and enter the following data:

1st	Keith Feeney
2nd	Brady Kim
3rd	Olivia Tombola

19. In the third cell of the fifth row, insert a nested table with two columns and three rows and enter the following data:

1st	June Tsai
2nd	Leah Gold
3rd	George Wei

20. In the fourth cell of the fifth row, insert a nested table with two columns and three rows and enter the following data:

1st	Jen LeBlanc
2nd	Robbie Maltz
3rd	Jim Shepard

21. Apply the **List Table 3** table style to the main table. Increase the font size in the first row to **14 points**, and center the text horizontally and vertically.
22. Apply the **Grid Table 5 Dark - Accent 2** table style to all six nested tables. Adjust the column widths, as needed.
23. Click outside the table, and insert **WPB07_picture1** from the data files for this chapter.
24. Crop about **1.75"** from the right side and about **0.25"** from the left side.
25. Set the text wrapping to **In Front of Text**, and position the picture **4"** to the right of the margin horizontally and **1"** below the margin vertically.
26. Insert a caption below the picture that says: **1 Grand Prize Winner, Middle School**.
27. Insert **WPB07_picture2** from the data files for this chapter, and resize it to **2.5"** high.
28. Set the text wrapping to **In Front of Text**, and position it **0.5"** to the right of the margin horizontally, and **4"** below the margin vertically.
29. Insert a caption below the picture that says: **2 Grand Prize Winner, High School**. Adjust caption width, as needed.
30. Compress all of the pictures in the document, and remove the backgrounds.
31. Create a picture watermark using the file **WPPB07_picture3** from the data files for this chapter.
32. Check and correct the spelling and grammar, and save the document.
33. **With your teacher's permission**, print the document.
34. Restore all default settings, and delete custom styles.
35. Save and close the document, and exit Word.

Illustration 7A

New Media Designs

You are invited to celebrate the winners of our first ever Communications Contest!

Please join us for lunch.
Friday, October 19
12:30 p.m.

1 Grand Prize Winner, Middle School

New Media Designs
Highway 73
Cambridge, WA 53523

2 Grand Prize Winner, High School

	Communications Contest Winner				
Middle (5–8)	Category 1		Category 2		Category 3
	1st Alex Grogan	1st	Jill Kline	1st	Matt O'Toole
	2nd Michaela Jackson	2nd	Sam Lapp	2nd	Chris White
	3rd Jaclyn Brown	3rd	Dinesh Patel	3rd	Liz Jones
High School	Category 1		Category 2		Category 3
	1st Keith Feeney	1st	June Tsai	1st	Jen LeBlanc
	2nd Brady Kim	2nd	Leah Gold	2nd	Robbie Maltz
	3rd Olivia Tombola	3rd	George Wei	3rd	Jim Shepard

Chapter 8

(Courtesy lightpoet/Shutterstock)

Working with Long Documents

Lesson 54
Working with Outlines
- Creating an Outline
- Managing an Outline
- Numbering an Outline

Lesson 55
Advanced Layout Options
- Setting Paper Size
- Creating and Modifying a Page Border
- Hiding or Displaying White Space
- Adjusting Character Spacing
- Inserting a Non-Breaking Space

Lesson 56
Working with Master Documents
- Creating a Master Document
- Managing a Master Document
- Revising a Master Document

Lesson 57
Creating Custom Headers and Footers, Bookmarks, and Cross-References
- Customizing Headers and Footers
- Inserting Bookmarks
- Inserting a Cross-Reference

Lesson 58
Creating an Index
- Marking Index Entries
- Using an Index AutoMark File
- Generating an Index
- Modifying an Index

Lesson 59
Managing Source Information and Generating Special Tables
- Using the Research Task Pane
- Sharing Sources Between Documents
- Editing Shared Sources
- Using Multiple Footnote Formats in a Document
- Adding Styles to a Table of Contents
- Creating a Table of Figures
- Creating a Table of Authorities

End-of-Chapter Activities

Lesson 54

Working with Outlines

> ### What You Will Learn
> Creating an Outline
> Managing an Outline
> Numbering an Outline

WORDS TO KNOW

Body text
Outline text that is not formatted with a heading-level style.

Collapse
To hide subtopics in an outline.

Demote
To move down one level in an outline.

Expand
To show subtopics in an outline.

Outline
A document that lists levels of topics.

Promote
To move up one level in an outline.

Software Skills Create an outline to organize ideas for any document that covers more than one topic, such as an article, a report, a presentation, or a speech. For example, you might create an outline to list the chapters or headings in a report or to arrange main subjects for a presentation. The outline serves as a map you can follow as you complete the entire document.

What You Can Do

Creating an Outline

- Use Outline view to create and edit an **outline**.
- When you switch to Outline view, the OUTLINING tab becomes available on the Ribbon.
- An outline is similar to a multilevel list (refer to Word, Lesson 7). Outline topics are formatted in levels, which may be called headings: Level 1 is a main heading, Level 2 is a subheading, Level 3 is a sub-subheading, and so on up to 9 heading levels.
- By default, text you type in an outline is formatted as **Body Text**. You use the tools in the Outline Tools group on the OUTLINING tab of the Ribbon to **promote** or **demote** paragraphs to different levels.
- Headings in an outline are preceded by one of three outline symbols:
  - Levels that have sublevels under them are preceded by a circle with a plus sign in it ⊕.
  - Levels that do not have sublevels are preceded by a circle with a minus sign in it ⊖.
  - Body Text that is not formatted as a heading level is preceded by a small circle ○.
- Note that although outline levels print as expected, they do not appear onscreen in Print Layout view or on the Print tab in the Backstage view.

Business Information Management II | Word | Chapter 8   169

Try It! Creating an Outline

1 Start Word, and save a new blank document as **W54Try_xx** in the location where your teacher instructs you to store the files for this lesson.

2 On the VIEW tab, in the Views group, click the Outline button to change to Outline view.

3 On the first line of the document, type **Packing for International Travel** and press [ENTER].

4 In the Outline Tools group, click the Demote button, type **Travel Documents**, and press [ENTER].

✓ You can also press [TAB] to demote a paragraph.

5 Click the Demote button, type **Itinerary**, press [ENTER], type **Passport**, and press [ENTER].

6 In the Outline Tools group, click the Promote button, type **Boarding Documents**, and press [ENTER].

✓ You can also press [SHIFT] + [TAB] to promote a paragraph.

7 Click the Demote button, type **ID**, press [ENTER], type **Airline tickets**, press [ENTER], type **Boarding pass**, and press [ENTER].

8 Click the Demote to Body Text button and type **Print boarding pass 24 hours in advance**.

9 Save the changes to **W54Try_xx**, and leave it open to use in the next Try It.

An outline in Outline view

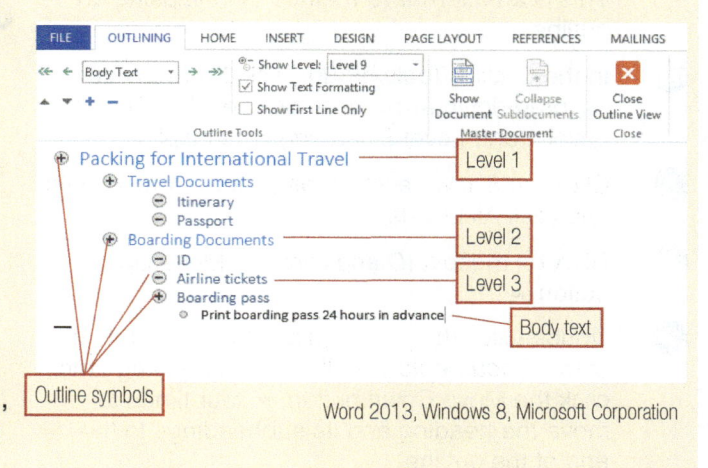

Word 2013, Windows 8, Microsoft Corporation

Managing an Outline

- When you want to work with only some heading levels at a time, you can **collapse** the outline.
- Collapsing an outline hides lower-level headings.
- A gray line appears under a collapsed heading to indicate that there are subheadings that are not displayed.
- You can also select to show only headings above a certain level in the outline, hiding the lower-level headings.
- To see hidden or collapsed levels, you can **expand** the outline.
- You can also move headings and subheadings up or down to reorganize the outline.
- You can edit an outline using the same techniques you use to edit regular document text. For example, you can insert and delete text at any location.
- Word automatically applies different styles to different levels in an outline. By default, Word displays the formatting in the document, but you can toggle it off.
- By default, Word displays all body text that you type in the document. If you have multiple lines of body text, you can select to show only the first line. An ellipsis at the end of the line indicates the remaining lines are hidden.

Try It! Managing an Outline

1. In the **W54Try_xx** file, double-click the plus sign symbol to the left of *Boarding Documents*. This collapses—or hides—the levels below.
2. Double-click the symbol again to expand the outline.
3. Click on the text *Boarding pass* and click the Collapse button ▬ in the Outline Tools group. This is an alternative method of collapsing an outline.
4. In the Outline Tools group, click the Show Level drop-down arrow and click Level 2. Only the Level 1 and Level 2 headings are displayed.
5. Click the Show Level drop-down arrow again, and click All Levels.
6. Click on the text *ID* and click the Move Up button ▲.
7. Double-click the plus sign symbol to the left of *Travel Documents* to collapse the heading, and click the Move Down button ▼ four times to move the heading and its subheadings to the end of the outline.
8. Position the insertion point after the Body Text *Print boarding pass 24 hours in advance*, press SPACE , and type **and verify seating as well as special meals**.
9. In the Outline Tools group, click to select the Show First Line Only check box.
10. Click to clear the Show Text Formatting check box.
11. Click to select the Show Text Formatting check box and to clear the Show First Line Only check box.
12. Save the changes to **W54Try_xx**, and leave it open to use in the next Try It.

An outline with no style formatting

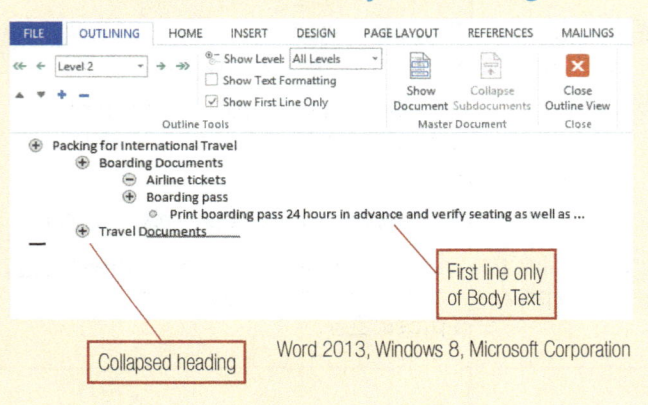

Word 2013, Windows 8, Microsoft Corporation

Collapsed heading

First line only of Body Text

Numbering an Outline

- Use a multilevel list to number an outline.
  - ✓ *Refer to Word, Lesson 7 for more on multilevel lists.*
- Traditionally, outlines are numbered using a I., A., 1., a) numbering style.
- You can apply numbering to an outline before you start typing the text, or you can apply numbering to an existing outline.
- Work in Print Layout view to select multilevel list formatting, then return to Outline view to view or edit the outline.
- Once you number an outline, the outline levels appear in Print Layout view and on the Print tab in the Backstage view.

Business Information Management II | Word | Chapter 8 171

Try It! Numbering an Outline

1. In the **W54Try_xx** file, on the OUTLINING tab, in the Close group, click the Close Outline View button ☒ .
2. Click in the text *Packing for International Travel*.
3. On the HOME tab, in the Paragraph group, click the Multilevel List button to display the gallery of multilevel list styles.
4. Under List Library, click the style on the left end of the bottom row.
5. Save and close the file, and exit Word.

Use a multilevel list style to number an outline

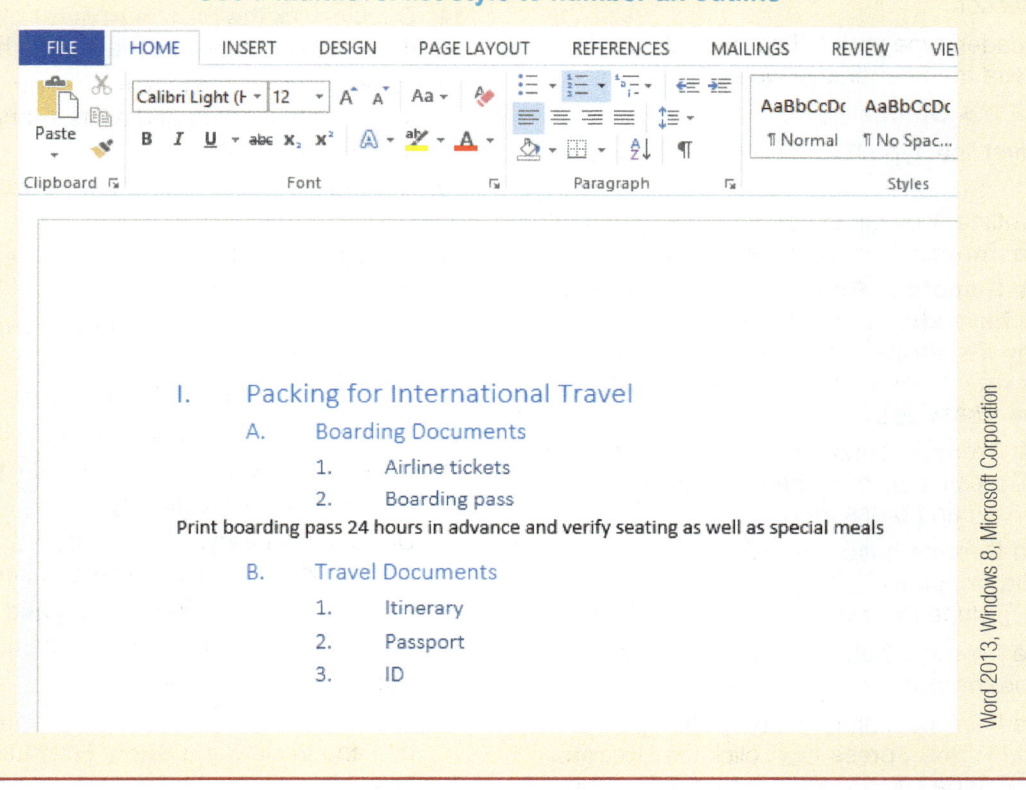

I. Packing for International Travel
    A. Boarding Documents
        1. Airline tickets
        2. Boarding pass
Print boarding pass 24 hours in advance and verify seating as well as special meals
    B. Travel Documents
        1. Itinerary
        2. Passport
        3. ID

Word 2013, Windows 8, Microsoft Corporation

Lesson 54—Practice

You work in the publishing department of the Michigan Avenue Athletic Club and want to publish a document describing some of the benefits of regular exercise. In this project, you will create an outline for that document.

DIRECTIONS

1. Start Word, if necessary, and save a new blank document as **W54Practice_xx** in the location where your teacher instructs you to store the files for this lesson.
2. In the header, type your full name and today's date. Close the header and footer.
3. Click **VIEW > Outline**.
4. On the first line, type **Exercise for Life** and press [ENTER].
5. In the Outline Tools group, click the **Demote** button →, type **Introduction**, and press [ENTER].
6. Click the **Demote to Body Text** button ⇒, type **Studies have shown that people who exercise regularly live longer, are healthier, and enjoy a better quality of life than those who do not exercise.** Press [ENTER].
7. Click the **Promote** button ←, type **Getting Started**, press [ENTER], click the **Demote** button →, type **Safety**, and press [ENTER].
8. Click the **Demote** button →, type **Doctor Supervision**, press [ENTER], type **Proper Equipment**, press [ENTER], type **Preparation**, and press [ENTER].
9. Click the **Promote** button ←, type **Tips**, press [ENTER], type **Instruction**, and press [ENTER].
10. Click the **Demote** button →, type **Using a Personal Trainer**, press [ENTER], click the **Demote** button →, type **Certification**, press [ENTER], type **References**, and press [ENTER].
11. Click the **Promote** button ← three times and type **Conclusion**.
12. Click the **Show Level** drop-down arrow and click **Level 2**.
13. Double-click the **plus sign symbol** to the left of the text *Getting Started* to expand the heading.
14. Double-click the **plus sign symbol** to the left of the text *Instruction* to collapse the heading.
15. Click the **Move Up** button ▲ to move the *Instruction* heading and all its subheadings above the heading *Tips*.
16. Click to clear the **Show Text Formatting** check box.
17. Click to select the **Show First Line Only** check box.
18. Click the **Show Level** drop-down arrow and click **All Levels**.
19. Click **OUTLINING > Close Outline View** ✖.
20. Click in the text *Exercise for Life*.
21. Click **HOME > Multilevel List** to display the gallery of multilevel list styles.
22. Under List Library, click the style on the left end of the bottom row to number the outline.
23. Check and correct the spelling and grammar in the document, and save the document.
24. Click **VIEW > Outline**.
25. Click to select the **Show Text Formatting** check box and to clear the **Show First Line Only** check box.
26. **With your teacher's permission**, print the document. It should look similar to Figure 54-1 on the next page.
27. Save and close the document, and exit Word.

Figure 54-1

> I. Exercise for Life
>   A. Introduction
> Studies have shown that people who exercise regularly live longer, are healthier, and enjoy a better quality of life than those who do not exercise
>   B. Getting Started
>   1. Safety
>   a) Doctor Supervision
>   b) Proper Equipment
>   c) Preparation
>   2. Instruction
>   a) Using a Personal Trainer
>   (1) Certification
>   (2) References
>   3. Tips
>   C. Conclusion

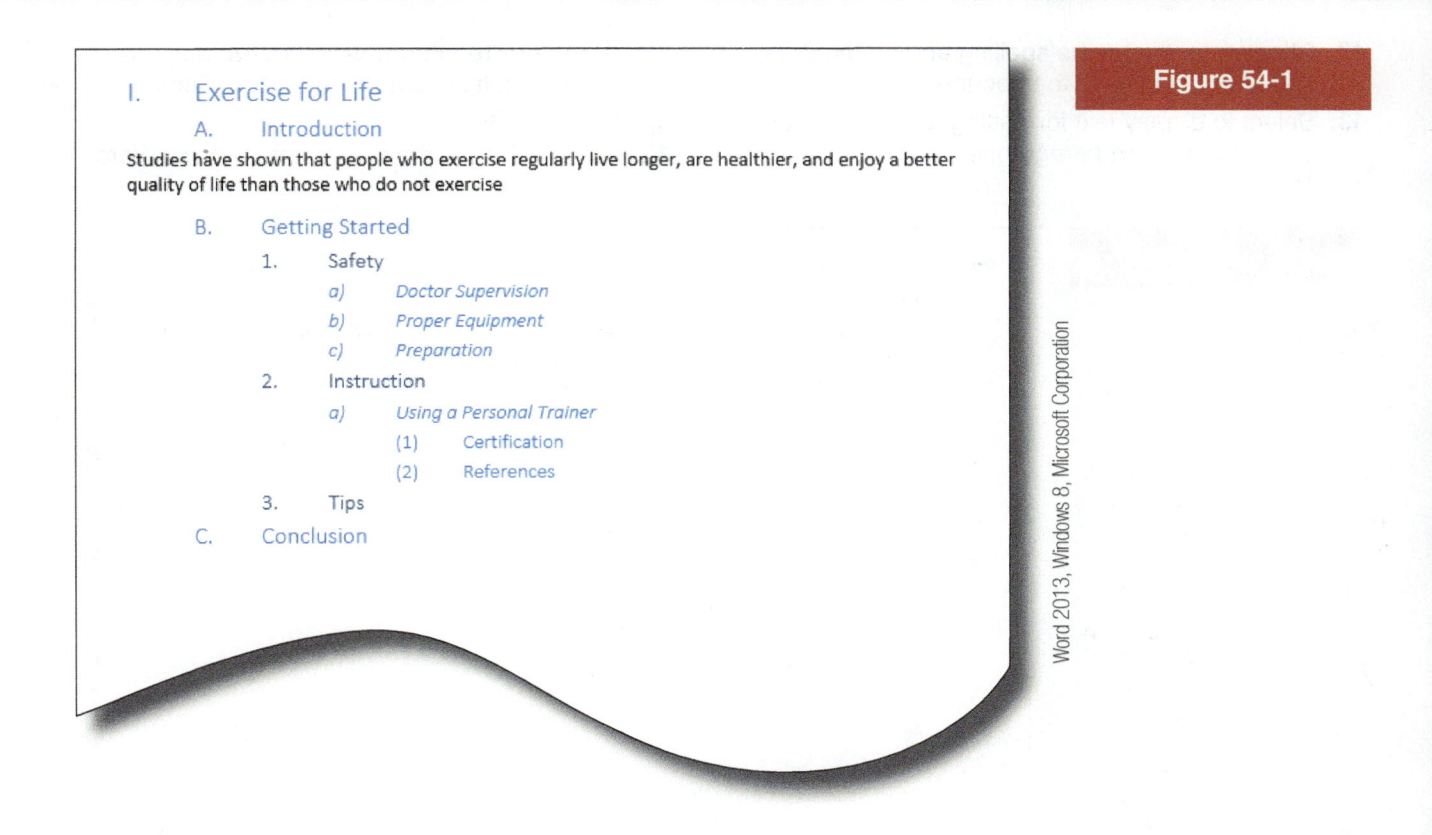

Lesson 54—Apply

You hold a brainstorming session with your colleagues, which results in an expanded list of topics for your document about exercise. In this project, you will turn the list into an outline, reorganize some of the topics, and add a new topic.

DIRECTIONS

1. Start Word, if necessary, and open **W54Apply** from the data files for this lesson.
2. Save the file as **W54Apply_xx** in the location where your teacher instructs you to store the files for this lesson.
3. In the header, type your full name and today's date. Close the header and footer.
4. Change to **Outline** view.
5. Promote and demote headings to create the outline shown in Figure 54-2 on the next page.
6. Hide text formatting and show the first line of Body Text only.
7. Move the Level 2 heading *Getting Started* and all of its subheadings above the Level 2 heading *Health Benefits*.
8. Promote the Level 3 heading *Tips* to Level 2, and move it down after the last subheading in the *Health Benefits* section, above the Level 2 heading *Conclusion*.
9. Add a new Level 4 heading, **Heart Disease**, between *Diabetes* and *Osteoporosis* under *Reduce Symptoms of Existing Conditions*.
10. Apply the **I., A., 1., a), (1)** multilevel list numbering style to the outline.
11. Set the spacing before and after all paragraphs to **0**.

12. Check and correct the spelling and grammar in the document, and save the document.
13. Select to display text formatting and to show all lines of Body Text paragraphs.
14. **With your teacher's permission**, print the document. It should look similar to Figure 54-3 on the next page.
15. Save and close the document, and exit Word.

Figure 54-2

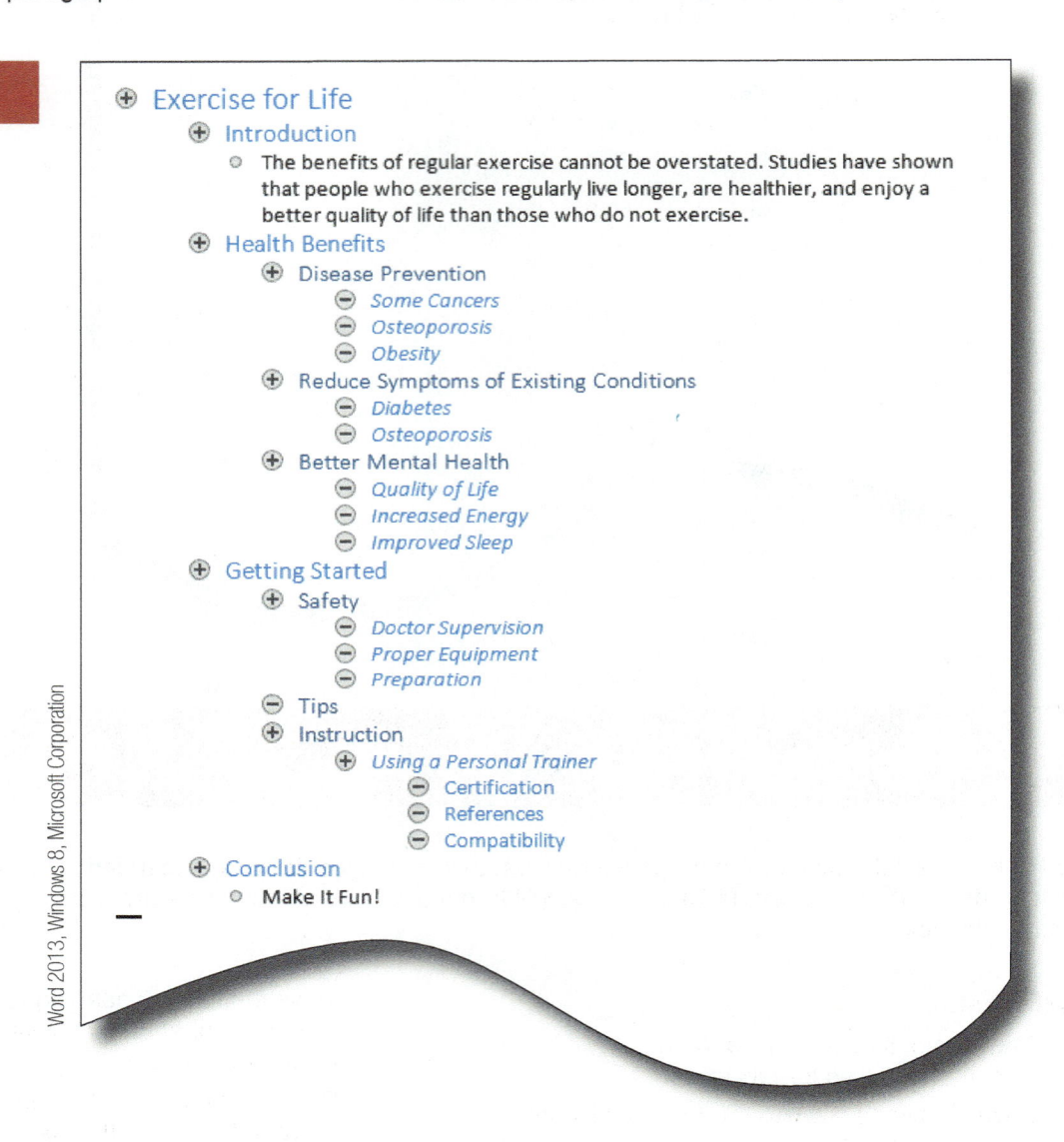

- Exercise for Life
  - Introduction
    - The benefits of regular exercise cannot be overstated. Studies have shown that people who exercise regularly live longer, are healthier, and enjoy a better quality of life than those who do not exercise.
  - Health Benefits
    - Disease Prevention
      - Some Cancers
      - Osteoporosis
      - Obesity
    - Reduce Symptoms of Existing Conditions
      - Diabetes
      - Osteoporosis
    - Better Mental Health
      - Quality of Life
      - Increased Energy
      - Improved Sleep
  - Getting Started
    - Safety
      - Doctor Supervision
      - Proper Equipment
      - Preparation
    - Tips
    - Instruction
      - Using a Personal Trainer
        - Certification
        - References
        - Compatibility
  - Conclusion
    - Make It Fun!

Figure 54-3

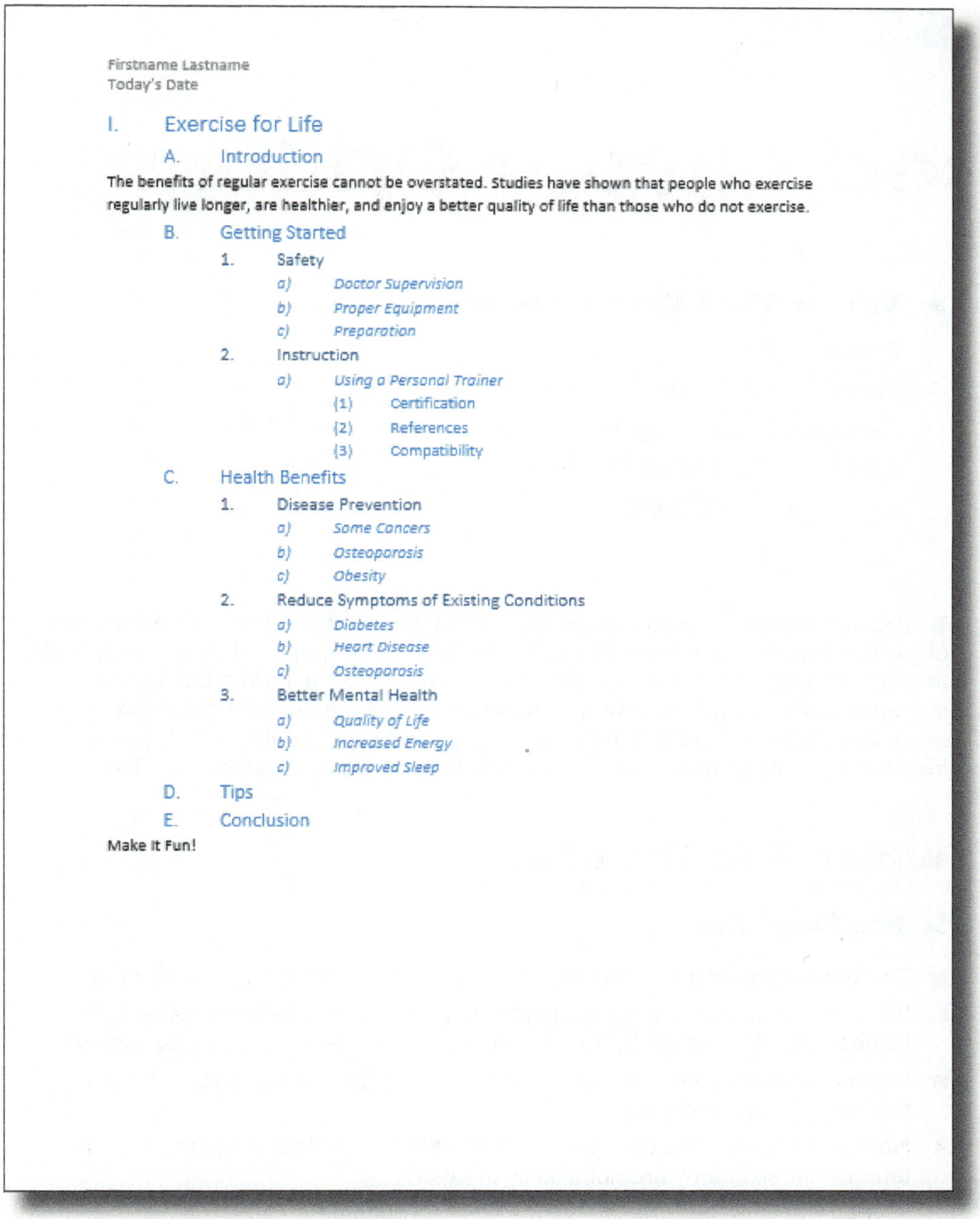

Firstname Lastname
Today's Date

I. Exercise for Life
    A. Introduction
The benefits of regular exercise cannot be overstated. Studies have shown that people who exercise regularly live longer, are healthier, and enjoy a better quality of life than those who do not exercise.
    B. Getting Started
        1. Safety
            a) Doctor Supervision
            b) Proper Equipment
            c) Preparation
        2. Instruction
            a) Using a Personal Trainer
                (1) Certification
                (2) References
                (3) Compatibility
    C. Health Benefits
        1. Disease Prevention
            a) Some Cancers
            b) Osteoporosis
            c) Obesity
        2. Reduce Symptoms of Existing Conditions
            a) Diabetes
            b) Heart Disease
            c) Osteoporosis
        3. Better Mental Health
            a) Quality of Life
            b) Increased Energy
            c) Improved Sleep
    D. Tips
    E. Conclusion
Make It Fun!

Lesson 55

Advanced Layout Options

> ## What You Will Learn
>
> Setting Paper Size
> Creating and Modifying a Page Border
> Hiding or Displaying White Space
> Adjusting Character Spacing
> Inserting a Non-Breaking Space

WORDS TO KNOW

Kerning
Spacing between pairs of characters.

Page size
The dimensions of a finished document page.

Paper size
The dimensions of the sheet of paper on which a document is printed. Also called sheet size.

Software Skills Select a paper size when you want to print on a specific piece of paper. Create a page border to add visual interest to graphical documents, such as marketing and promotional materials. Hide white space in Print Layout view to see more of the content of your document on the screen. Set character spacing to make text easier to read and improve the appearance of a published document. Insert non-breaking spaces when you want to keep words together on a line.

What You Can Do

Setting Paper Size

- The default **paper size** in Word 2013 is Letter, which is 8.5 inches by 11 inches.
- You can select from a list of different sizes such as A5 (5.83 inches by 8.27 inches), B5 (7.17 inches by 10.12 inches), or Legal (8.5 inches by 14 inches).
- You can also set your own custom size by using the options on the Paper tab of the Page Setup dialog box.
- Note that although the term *page size* is often used interchangeably with the term *paper size*, they are not exactly the same.
  - **Page size** is the dimensions of a finished document page.
  - Paper size is the dimensions of the sheet of paper on which the document is printed.
- It is sometimes useful to combine custom margins with custom paper sizes. For example, when you are printing on a small paper size, you may want to use narrower margins.

Business Information Management II | Word | Chapter 8

Try It! Setting Paper Size

1. Start Word, and open **W55Try** from the data files for this lesson.
2. Save the file as **W55Try_xx** in the location where your teacher instructs you to store the files for this lesson.
3. Click VIEW > One Page so you can see the entire page on your screen.
4. On the PAGE LAYOUT tab, in the Page Setup group, click the Size button to display the gallery of built-in paper sizes.
5. In the gallery, click 5x7in. Word changes the paper size to 5" wide by 7" high.
6. Click the Size button again and click More Paper Sizes to display the Paper tab of the Page Setup dialog box.
   ✓ *You can also open the Page Setup dialog box by clicking the dialog box launcher in the Page Setup group on the Ribbon.*
7. Under Paper size, use the increment arrows to set the Width to 3.5".
8. Use the increment arrows to set the Height to 3.5" and click OK.
9. Click PAGE LAYOUT > Margins and click Narrow.
10. Save the changes to **W55Try_xx**, and leave it open to use in the next Try It.

Set a custom paper size

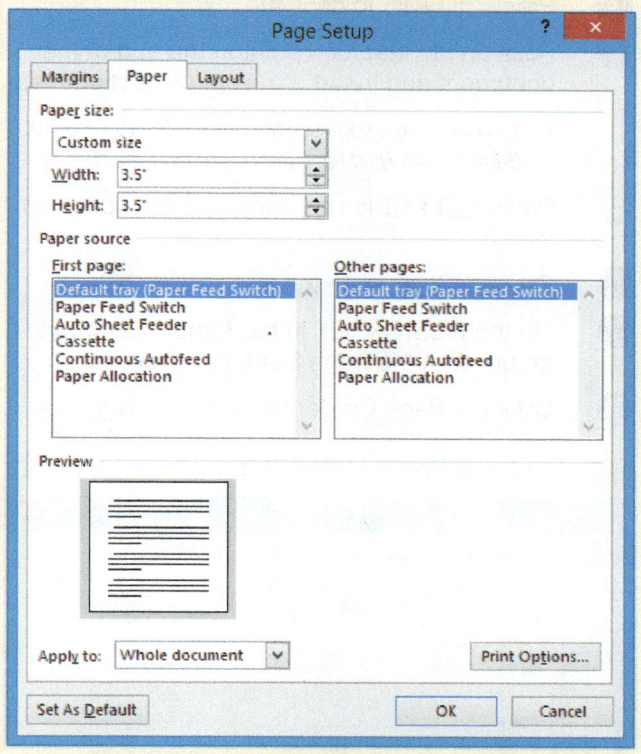

Word 2013, Windows 8, Microsoft Corporation

Creating and Modifying a Page Border

- You can apply a border to pages in a document to enhance visual interest.
- Page border commands are on the Page Border tab of the Borders and Shading dialog box. You can access the dialog box by clicking the Page Borders button on the DESIGN tab.
- In the Preview area of the Page Border tab, you can click the diagram or buttons to apply borders. Likewise, you can click the diagram or buttons to remove borders.
- Using the Apply to drop-down menu, you can apply the borders to all pages of your document, to all pages in only a section of your document, to only the first page of a section, or to all pages of a section except the first page.
- Clicking the Options button on the Page Border tab opens the Border and Shading Options dialog box, where you can adjust margins and other settings to refine the position of the border.

Try It! Creating a Page Border

1. In the **W55Try_xx** file, adjust the zoom so you can see the entire page on your monitor.
2. Press CTRL + A to select all text.
3. Press CTRL + C to copy the text.
4. Position the insertion point at the end of the document and insert a next page section break.
   - ✓ *To insert a next page section break, click PAGE LAYOUT > Breaks. Click Next Page under Section Breaks.*
5. Press CTRL + V to paste the text you copied in step 3.
6. On page 2, change the text *10%* to *25%*.
7. On the DESIGN tab, in the Page Background group, click the Page Borders button.
8. Click the Page Border tab, if necessary.

Use the Preview area to apply a border

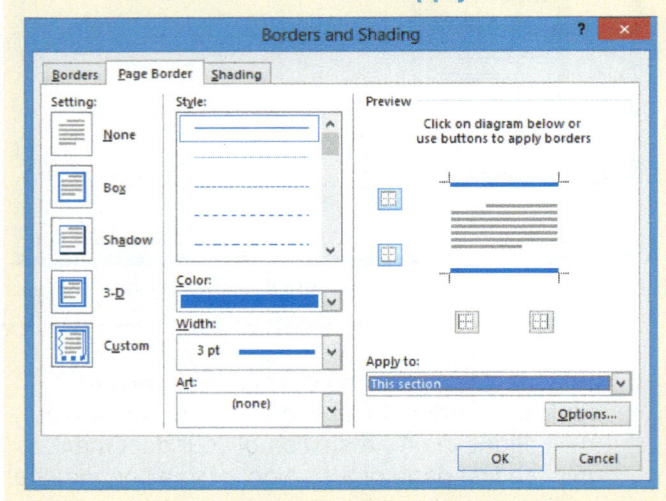

Word 2013, Windows 8, Microsoft Corporation

9. Click the Color drop-down arrow and, under Standard Colors, click Blue.
10. Click the Width drop-down arrow and click 3 pt.
11. In the Preview area, click the top of the diagram to add a border to the top of the page.
12. Click the bottom of the diagram to add a border to the bottom of the page.
13. Click the Apply to drop-down arrow and click This section.
14. Click OK. The borders appear on page 2 only.
15. Save the changes to **W55Try_xx**, and leave it open to use in the next Try It.

Apply a border to a document section

Word 2013, Windows 8, Microsoft Corporation

Business Information Management II | Word | Chapter 8

Try It! Modifying a Page Border

1. In the **W55Try_xx** file, position the insertion point at the beginning of page 2.
2. Click DESIGN > Page Borders.
3. Click the Page Border tab, if necessary.
4. Click the Art drop-down arrow and click the first option, apples.
5. Under Width, use the increment arrows to set the Width to 20 pt.
6. In the Preview area, click the top, left and right borders in the diagram to remove them.
7. Click the Apply to drop-down arrow and click This section.
8. Click the Options button.
9. Under Margin, use the increment arrows to set the Bottom margin to 30 pt.
10. Click OK.
11. Click OK.
12. Save the changes to **W55Try_xx**, and leave it open to use in the next Try It.

Hiding or Displaying White Space

- By default, in Print Layout view, Word displays white space. In this context, the term "white space" refers to the space between the bottom of one page and the top of the next page, as well as the header and footer.
- You can hide white space by double-clicking the top or bottom edge of any page in the document.
  ✓ *Word also hides any page borders applied to the document.*
- When white space is hidden, a gray line marks the location where one page ends and the next begins.
- To display white space, double-click the gray line between pages. If your document has only one page, double-click the top or bottom edge of the page.
- You can also select or clear the Show white space between pages in Print Layout view check box on the Display tab in the Word Options dialog box.

Try It! Hiding or Displaying White Space

1. In the **W55Try_xx** file, click VIEW > Print Layout to change to Print Layout view, if necessary.
2. Scroll down so you can see the bottom of the first page and the top of the second page onscreen at the same time.
3. Position the mouse pointer over the bottom edge of page 1. The pointer changes to resemble arrows pointing up and down.
4. Double-click.
5. Position the mouse pointer on the gray line between the pages. Double-click again.
6. Leave the file open to use in the next Try It.

Display white space between pages

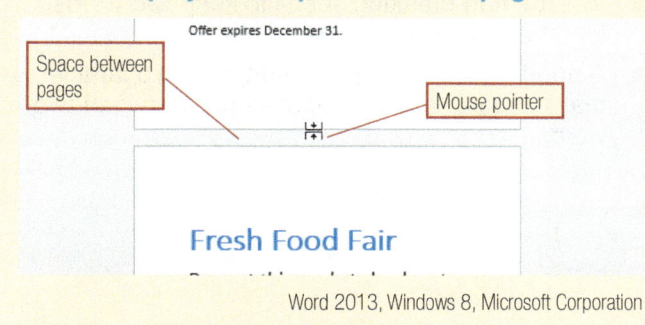

Space between pages — Offer expires December 31. — Mouse pointer

Fresh Food Fair

Word 2013, Windows 8, Microsoft Corporation

Hide white space between pages

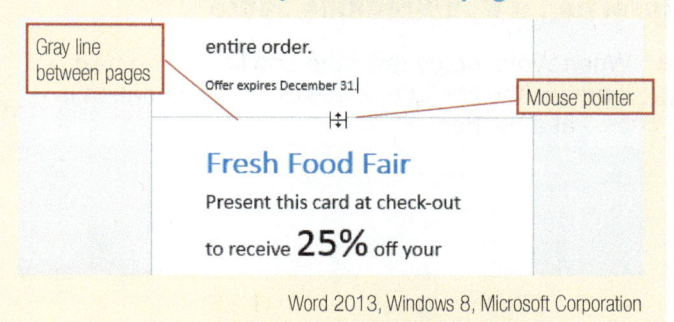

Gray line between pages — entire order. Offer expires December 31. — Mouse pointer

Fresh Food Fair
Present this card at check-out
to receive **25%** off your

Word 2013, Windows 8, Microsoft Corporation

Adjusting Character Spacing

- Use character spacing to improve the readability of the text, as well as to control the amount of text that fits on a line or on a page.
- In Word, the amount of space between characters is determined by the current font set.
- When certain characters that are wider than other characters in a font set are next to each other, they may appear to run together.
- Character spacing options are available on the Advanced tab of the Font dialog box.
- Set the **kerning** to automatically adjust the space between selected characters, when the characters are larger than a particular point size.
- You can also adjust spacing between characters by changing the scale, the spacing, or the position.
  - Set the scale to stretch or compress selected text based on a percentage. For example, set the character spacing scale above 100% to stretch the text, or below 100% to compress the text.
  - Set the spacing to expand or condense the spacing between all selected characters by a specific number of points.
  - Set the position to raise or lower characters relative to the text baseline by a specific number of points.

Try It! Adjusting Character Spacing

1. In the **W55Try_xx** file, select the text *Fresh Food Fair* on page 1.
2. On the HOME tab, click the Font group dialog box launcher.
3. In the Font dialog box, click the Advanced tab.
4. Under Character Spacing, click the Spacing drop-down arrow and click Condensed.
5. Use the Spacing By box increment arrows to change the value to 2 pt and click OK.
   - ✓ To see how the change affects the selected text, Undo the change and then Redo it.
6. On page 1, with the text *Fresh Food Fair* still selected, click the Font group dialog box launcher.
7. On the Advanced tab in the Font dialog box, click to clear the Kerning for fonts check box and click OK.
8. Open the Font dialog box again and click to select the Kerning for fonts check box and click OK.
9. Select the text *10%*, and click the Font group dialog box launcher.
10. On the Advanced tab in the Font dialog box, click the Scale drop-down arrow and click 150%. Click the Position drop-down arrow, click Lowered, and click OK.
11. Select the last line of text on page 1, and click the Font group dialog box launcher.
12. On the Advanced tab in the Font dialog box, click the Spacing drop-down arrow, click Expanded, and use the Spacing By increment arrows to set the value to 2.5 pt. Click OK.
13. Save the changes to **W55Try_xx**, and leave it open to use in the next Try It.

Inserting a Non-Breaking Space

- When Word wraps text from one line to the next, it breaks the line at a space or—if hyphenation is on—at a hyphen.
- Insert a non-breaking space to keep two words together on the same line.
- A non-breaking space is a nonprinting character that looks like a small superscript o between two words.

Business Information Management II | Word | Chapter 8   181

Try It! Inserting a Non-Breaking Space

1. In the **W55Try_xx** file, click HOME > Show/Hide ¶ ¶ to toggle on the display of nonprinting characters, if necessary.

2. On page 1, select the space between the words *your* and *entire*.

3. Press CTRL + SHIFT + SPACE to replace the selected space with a non-breaking space.

   ✓ You can also select a non-breaking space on the Special Characters tab in the Symbol dialog box.

4. Save and close the document, and exit Word.

Insert a non-breaking space

Fresh·Food·Fair¶

Present·this·card·at·check-out·

to·receive· **10%** ·off·

your°entire·order.¶

Offer·expires·December·31.

Word 2013, Windows 8, Microsoft Corporation

Lesson 55—Practice

You work at Liberty Blooms, a flower shop. The owner has asked you to create discount cards that will be placed at the cashier station for customers to take. In this project, you will create a discount card using custom paper size, page border, and character spacing options.

DIRECTIONS

1. Start Word, if necessary, and save a new blank document as **W55Practice_xx** in the location where your teacher instructs you to store the files for this lesson.

2. Apply the **Retrospect** theme and the **Shaded** style set.

3. In the header, type your full name and today's date. Close the header and footer.

4. Position the mouse pointer on the top edge of the page, so it changes to look like this ⇌. Double-click to hide white space.

5. Click **PAGE LAYOUT** > **Size**, and click **More Paper Sizes**.

6. On the **Paper** tab in the Page Setup dialog box, under Paper size, use the **Width** increment arrows to set the paper width to **4"**.

7. Use the **Height** increment arrows to set the paper height to **4.5"**, and click **OK**.

8. In the Page Setup group, click the **Margins** button and click **Narrow**.

9. On the first line of the document, type **Liberty Blooms' Annual Fall Sale**. Format it with the **Title** style and center it horizontally.

10. Press ENTER and type **September 15 through October 10**. Format it with the **Heading 1** style and center it horizontally.

11. Press ENTER, click the **Bullets** button and type the following three items:

    Perennials, including various types of ground cover and shade-loving plants

    Spring Bulbs, such as daffodils, hyacinths, crocuses, lilies of the valley, and tulips

    Shrubbery and more!

12. Press ENTER twice to end bullet list formatting and type **Present this coupon to receive 10% off.**
13. Select the text *Fall* in the title, click the Font group dialog box launcher, and click the **Advanced** tab. Click the **Position** drop-down arrow, click **Lowered**, and click **OK**.
14. Select all bulleted items and click the Font group dialog box launcher. Click the **Spacing** drop-down arrow, click **Expanded**, and click **OK**.
15. If necessary, adjust the Spacing after all bulleted items to **0 pt**.
16. Select the text *10%* and click the Font group dialog box launcher. Click the **Scale** drop-down arrow, click **150%**, and click **OK**.
17. Select the last line of text and click the Font group dialog box launcher. Click the **Spacing** drop-down arrow and click **Condensed**.
18. In the Spacing By box, change the value to **0.5 pt** and click **OK**.
19. Click **HOME > Show/Hide ¶** to toggle on the display of nonprinting characters, if necessary.
20. In the second bulleted item, select the space between the words *the* and *valley*.
21. Press CTRL + SHIFT + SPACE.
22. Position the mouse pointer on the top edge of the page, so it changes to look like this. Double-click to display white space.
23. On the DESIGN tab, in the Page Background group, click the **Page Borders** button.
24. Click the **Page Border** tab, if necessary.
25. Under Style, click the first double line in the list.
26. Click the **Color** drop-down arrow and click **Brown, Accent 3**.
27. Click the **Options** button.
28. Under Margin, change the Top, Bottom, Left, and Right values to **18 pt**. Click **OK**.
29. Click **OK** to close the Borders and Shading dialog box.
30. Check and correct the spelling and grammar in the document.
31. **With your teacher's permission**, print the document. It should look similar to Figure 55-1.

    ✓ *You can cut paper to the selected size, or print on standard letter paper.*

32. Save and close the document, and exit Word.

Figure 55-1

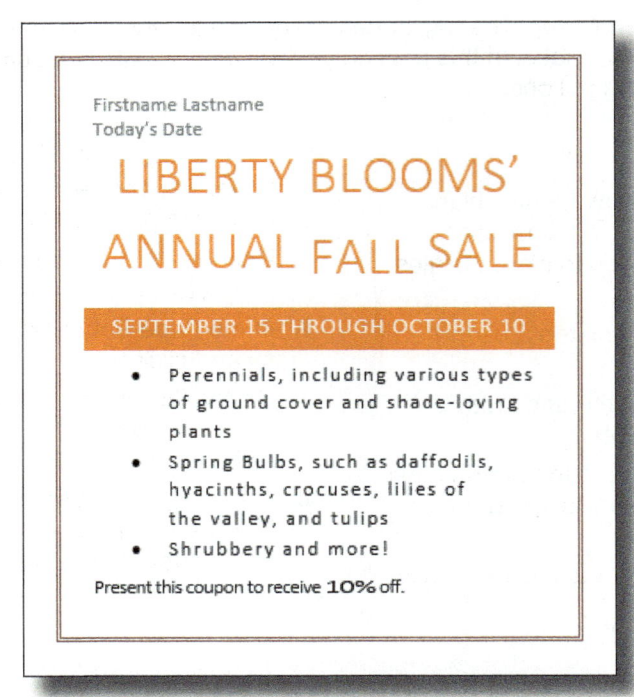

Lesson 55—Apply

The owner of Liberty Blooms wants you to create a special discount card for loyal shoppers. In this project, you will create two designs for the owner to choose from.

DIRECTIONS

1. Start Word, if necessary, and open **W55Apply** from the data files for this lesson.
2. Save the file as **W55Apply_xx** in the location where your teacher instructs you to store the files for this lesson.
3. In the header, type your full name and today's date. Close the header and footer.
4. Hide white space.
5. Apply the **Depth** theme and the **Basic (Elegant)** style set.
6. Set the paper size to **5"** wide by **5"** high.
7. Set the margins to **Narrow**.
8. Expand the spacing of the first paragraph of body text by **2 pt**.
9. Scale the percentages in the three bullet items to **150%**.
10. Condense the spacing of the last paragraph by **0.5 pt**.
11. Raise the position of the word *Flower* in the heading by **5 pt**.
12. Insert a non-breaking space between the words *at* and *Liberty* in the main paragraph.
13. Display white space.
14. Change the width of the page border to **3 pt** and remove the top and bottom borders.
15. Copy all text in the document.
16. Insert a next page section break at the end of the document.
17. Paste the text you copied in step 15.
18. On page 2, center the headings *LIBERTY BLOOMS FLOWER SHOP* and *LOYAL SHOPPER DISCOUNTS*.
19. On page 2, change the page border setting to **Box** and the border color to **Aqua, Accent 1.**
20. Check and correct the spelling and grammar in the document.
21. **With your teacher's permission**, print the document. It should look similar to Figure 55-2.

    ✓ *You can cut paper to the selected size, or print on standard letter paper.*

22. Save and close the document, and exit Word.

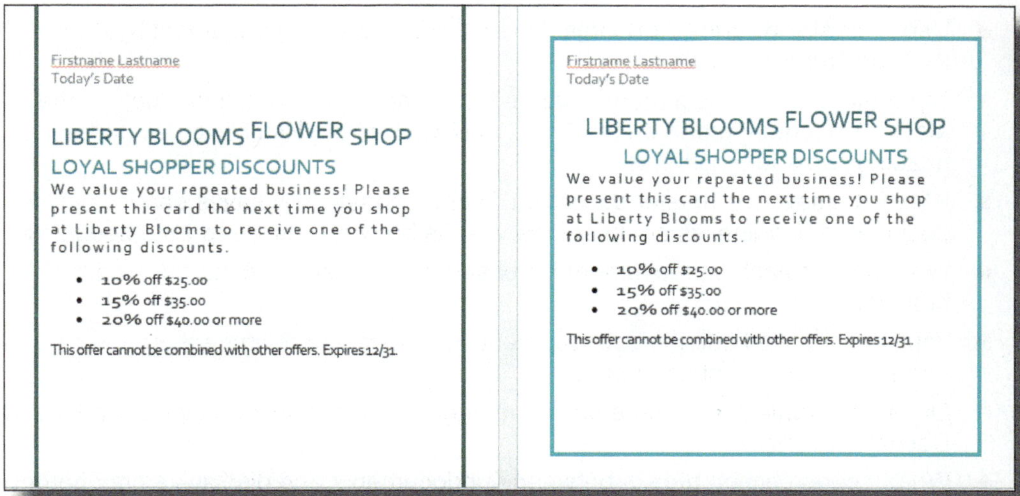

Figure 55-2

Word 2013, Windows 8, Microsoft Corporation

Lesson 56

Working with Master Documents

> ### What You Will Learn
>
> Creating a Master Document
> Managing a Master Document
> Revising a Master Document

WORDS TO KNOW

Master document
A document that contains a set of related documents.

Subdocument
A document contained in a master document.

Software Skills When you need to organize and manage long documents, you can create a master document with subdocuments. For example, use a master document to manage a book that has multiple chapters, or a report that has many sections.

What You Can Do

Creating a Master Document

- Use a **master document** to organize and manage a long document by dividing it into **subdocuments**.
- To create a master document, change to Outline view and use the tools in the Master Document group on the OUTLINING tab of the Ribbon to designate headings as subdocuments.
- When you save the master document, Word automatically saves each designated heading, its subheadings, and its body text as a separate document.
- Word names each subdocument file based on the text in the subdocument heading.
- You can view and edit the subdocuments in the master document, or you can open a subdocument separately.
- Once you create subdocuments, the master document outline appears in Master Document view.
- Word inserts section breaks between subdocuments and displays a gray border around each subdocument.

Lesson 60
Copying, Moving, and Embedding Data and Objects

- Copying and Moving Data from One Office Document to Another
- Embedding Objects
- Editing Embedded Objects
- Pasting Content with Specific Formatting

Lesson 61
Linking Files and Objects

- Linking Files
- Editing a Linked Object
- Updating Links

Lesson 62
Integrating Word and PowerPoint

- Pasting PowerPoint Slides As Graphics
- Embedding a PowerPoint Slide in a Word Document
- Exporting PowerPoint Slides and Notes to a Word Document
- Exporting PowerPoint Text to a Word Document
- Using a Word Outline to Create a PowerPoint Presentation

Lesson 63
Using Merge to Create Letters, Envelopes, Labels, and E-mail

- Reviewing the Mail Merge Process
- Merging Letters Using the Mail Merge Wizard
- Merging Envelopes
- Creating Mailing Labels
- Creating an E-mail Merge
- Filtering Recipients
- Applying Rules to a Merge

Lesson 64
Creating a Directory with Mail Merge

- Creating a Directory Merge
- Adding Formatting to a Field Code
- Sorting Records in the Data Source
- Selecting Specific Records
- Customizing Fields in an Address List

Lesson 65
Working with Macros

- Recording a Macro
- Running a Macro
- Deleting and Re-recording a Macro
- Editing a Macro with VBA
- Assigning a Shortcut Key to an Existing Macro
- Copying a Macro Using the Organizer
- Managing Macro Security

End-of-Chapter Activities

Lesson 60

Copying, Moving, and Embedding Data and Objects

> ### What You Will Learn
> Copying and Moving Data from One Office Document to Another
> Embedding Objects
> Editing Embedded Objects
> Pasting Content with Specific Formatting

WORDS TO KNOW

Acceptable use policy
A set of rules governing how a network or the Internet may be used.

Active window
The window in which you are currently working.

Destination file
The file where the data is pasted.

Embed
To insert an object in a file. The embedded object is not linked to a source file, but it is linked to the source application. You edit the object using the source application, but changes do not affect the source file data.

Source file
The file that contains the data to be copied.

Software Skills You may find it necessary to work with more than one Office application at a time and to share data between them. For example, you might want to create a report detailing your department's decreased costs by combining a Word document with an Excel spreadsheet or a table from Access. You can easily copy and embed all types of data among applications.

What You Can Do

Copying and Moving Data from One Office Document to Another

- You can open multiple program windows at the same time. This is useful for comparing the data in different files, as well as for exchanging data between files.
- Only one window can be active at a time. The **active window** appears on top of other open windows. Its title bar is a different color than the title bars of other open windows, and its taskbar button appears pressed in.
- You can use Windows to switch among open windows to make a different window active. For example, you can press ALT + TAB to cycle between open windows, or click a window's taskbar button.

- To copy or move content between applications, you can either use the Windows Clipboard or drag-and-drop items from the **source file** to the **destination file**.
- Data pasted into a destination file becomes part of the destination file. There is no link to the source file.
- Different types of content are pasted into Word as different object types than the original in some cases. For example, when you paste Excel cells into Word, they are converted to a table. When you paste a PowerPoint slide into Word, it is converted to a graphic.

Try It! Copying and Moving Data from One Office Document to Another

✓ This Try It assumes you know how to locate and select data in an Excel worksheet. If you do not, ask your teacher for more information.

1. Start Word, and open **W60TryA** from the data files for this lesson. Save the file as **W60TryA_xx** in the location where your teacher instructs you to store the files for this lesson.
2. Start Excel, and open **W60TryB**.
3. In Excel, select the cells B12:J18. Press CTRL + C to copy the range to the Clipboard.
4. Switch to Word and select the text *Copy data here*. Do not select the paragraph mark after the period.
5. Press CTRL + V to paste the data from the Clipboard into Word, replacing the selected text.
6. Save the changes to the Word document. Do not save the Excel workbook. Leave both files open to use in the next Try It.

Embedding Objects

- **Embedding** an object places it into a different application, like copying does, but it retains a connection to the source application. This is useful because it enables you to edit the object later in its original application.
- For example, if you copy data from Excel into Word, the data is converted into a Word table. Word "forgets" that the data came from Excel. However, if you embed the same data into Word, the embedded cells remain Excel cells, and you can edit them using Excel's tools and commands.
- Embedding does not retain a link between the data and its source file—only the source application. Therefore, if you make changes to the original source file, they are not reflected in the copy.

✓ Linking, which you will learn about in Lesson 61, does retain a link to the source file, so that the copy is automatically updated.

- To embed rather than simply pasting, copy or cut the object as you would normally, but instead of using the Paste command (CTRL + V), use the Paste Special command in the Clipboard group on the HOME tab.
- In the Paste Special dialog box, select a paste format that includes the word "object" in it, such as Microsoft Excel Worksheet Object. Only then will the object be embedded; otherwise, it will simply be pasted in the chosen format (covered later in this lesson).

Try It! Embedding Objects

1. With **W60TryB** open in Excel, select cells A22:J31.
2. Press CTRL + C to copy the range.
3. In **W60TryA_xx**, select the text *Embed object here*.
4. On the HOME tab, click the down arrow on the Paste button, and click Paste Special. The Paste Special dialog box opens.
5. In the Paste Special dialog box, select Microsoft Excel Worksheet Object and click OK. The range appears in Word, overrunning the document margins.
6. Drag a corner selection handle of the pasted object toward the inside of the worksheet to resize it to fit on the page.
7. If necessary, delete the text *Embed object here*.
8. In Word, save the changes to **W60TryA_xx**. Leave both files open in Word and Excel for the next Try It.

The Paste Special dialog box

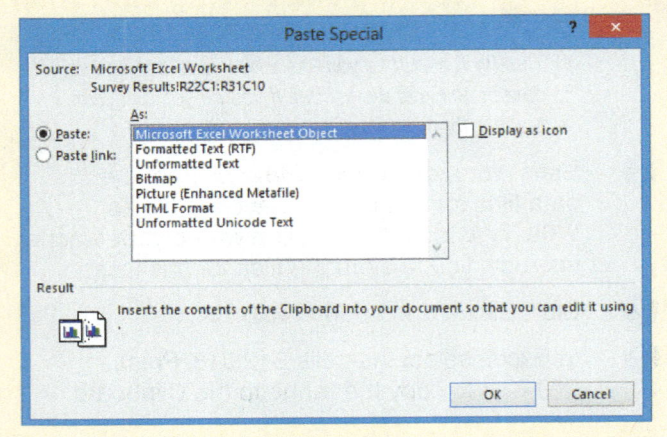

Word 2013, Windows 8, Microsoft Corporation

Editing Embedded Objects

- You can edit and format embedded objects using the source program.
- Double-click an embedded object to open the tools from its source program. Depending on the application, the source program's tools may appear within Word itself, or the object may open in a separate window in the source program.
- Changes you make to the embedded copy do not affect the original file from which the data came.

Try It! Editing Embedded Objects

1. In the **W60TryA_xx** file in Word, double-click the embedded Excel object.
   ✓ *Excel commands become available in Word.*
2. Click in cell D23 and type **60**, changing the value there.
3. Click on the Word document, outside the Excel object. The Word Ribbon reappears.
4. Using Windows, switch to the Excel program, where the original data is still open. Notice that the changes you made to the object in Word did not affect the value in D23 of the original worksheet.
5. Exit Excel. If you are prompted to save changes to **W60TryB**, click No.
6. Save and close **W60TryA_xx**.

(continued)

Business Information Management II | Word | Chapter 9   231

Try It! Editing Embedded Objects (continued)

Edit an embedded Excel Worksheet Object in Word

(Screenshot of Word document with embedded Excel worksheet, labeled with: Word title bar, Excel Ribbon, Worksheet frame, Excel formula bar, Word document window, Word status bar)

Word 2013, Windows 8, Microsoft Corporation

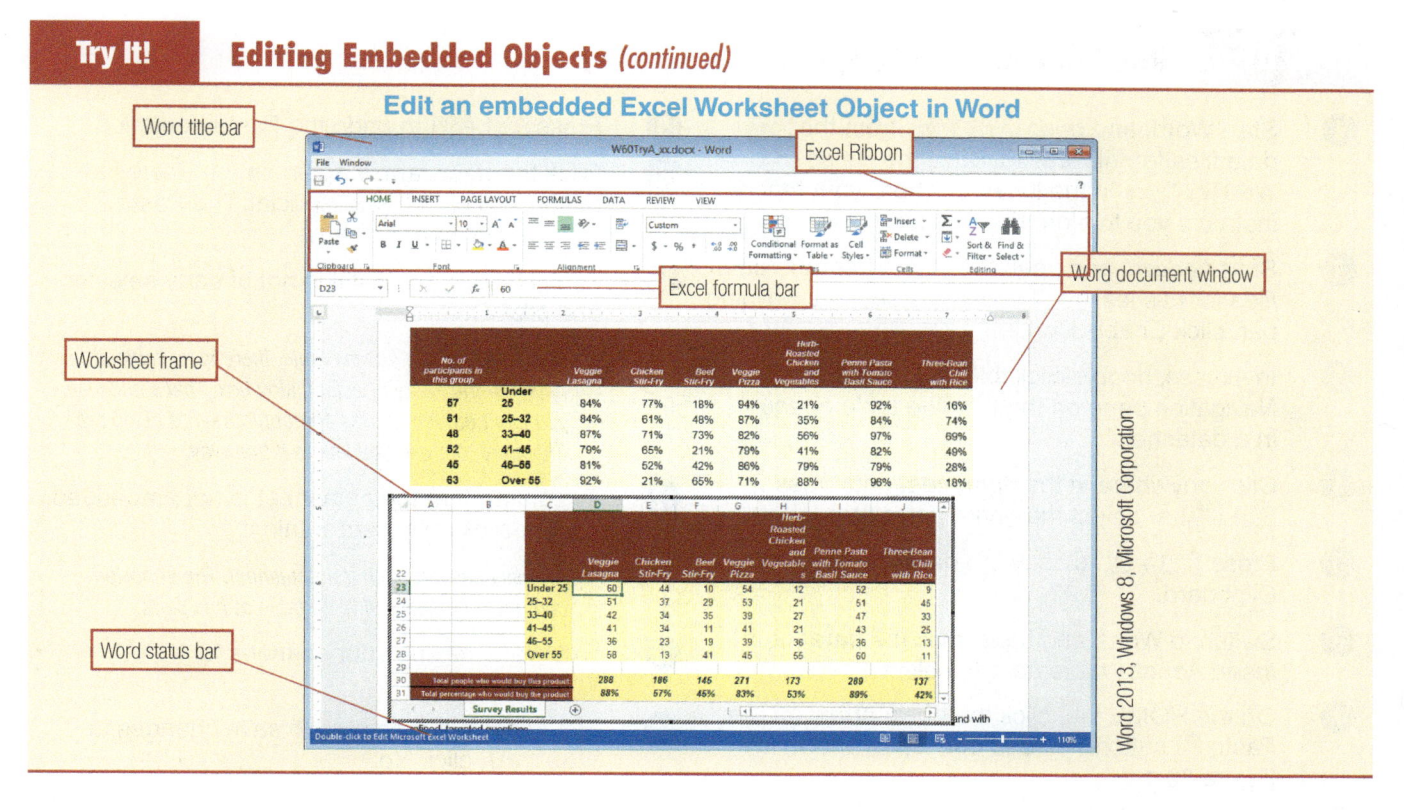

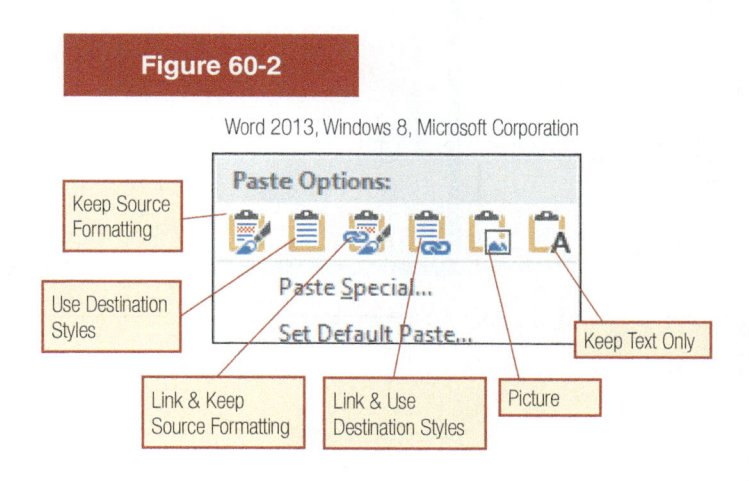

Pasting Content with Specific Formatting

- As you saw in the previous section, Paste Special can be used to embed objects in Word. It can also be used in other ways, such as to insert content in a specific format or insert content with or without its original formatting.
- The Paste button's drop-down list contains a menu that includes the Paste Special command, as you saw in the previous section. It also includes several shortcut buttons that you can use to specify the formatting for the paste operation. Figure 60-1 shows the paste options for an Access table.
- The buttons shown depend on the type of content being pasted. For example, Figure 60-2 shows the options for a range of Excel cells.
- These buttons are shortcuts for some of the commands and options you find in the Paste Special dialog box when you choose Paste Special from the menu (as you did in the previous section when embedding).

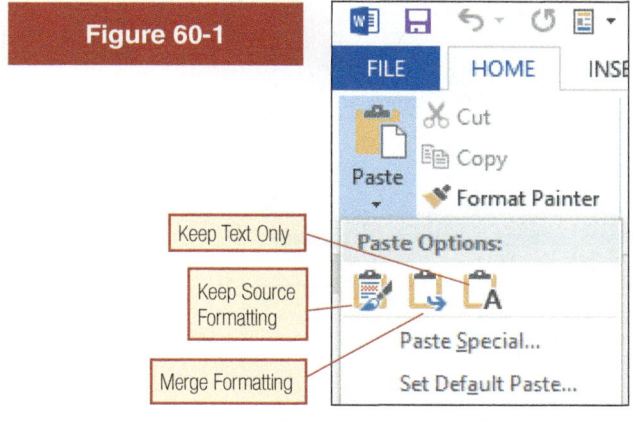

Figure 60-1

(Paste options menu with labels: Keep Text Only, Keep Source Formatting, Merge Formatting)

Word 2013, Windows 8, Microsoft Corporation

Figure 60-2

Word 2013, Windows 8, Microsoft Corporation

(Paste Options panel with labels: Keep Source Formatting, Use Destination Styles, Link & Keep Source Formatting, Link & Use Destination Styles, Picture, Keep Text Only)

Try It!   Pasting Conent with Specific Formatting

1. Start Word, and open **W60TryC** from the data files for this lesson. Save the file as **W60TryC_xx** in the location where your teacher instructs you to store the files for this lesson.

2. Start Access, and open **W60TryD** from the data files for this lesson. If you see a security warning bar, click Enable Content.

3. In Access, double-click tblClients in the Navigation pane on the left. The table opens in a datasheet.

4. Click anywhere in the datasheet and press CTRL + A to select the entire datasheet.

5. Press CTRL + C to copy the datasheet to the Clipboard.

6. Switch to Word, and triple-click the paragraph *Insert Access table here* to select it.

7. On the HOME tab, click the down arrow on the Paste button. A menu opens, as shown in Figure 60-1.

8. Click the Keep Source Formatting button. The table is pasted into the document with default Access formatting retained.

9. Press CTRL + Z to undo the Paste operation.

10. Click the down arrow again on the Paste button and click Paste Special. The Paste Special dialog box opens.

11. Click HTML Format if it is not already selected, and click OK.

   ✓ Notice that for an Access table, there is no "object" option in the Paste Special dialog box. That's because you can't embed Access content into Word using the Clipboard, nor can you link to it that way.

12. To confirm that the datasheet is not embedded, double-click anywhere within it.

   ✓ Access does not open the datasheet. The imported content is in a normal Word table at this point.

13. Exit Word, saving your changes to **W60TryC_xx**.

14. Exit Access. If prompted to save changes to **W60TryD**, click No.

Choose HTML format in which to paste the copied content

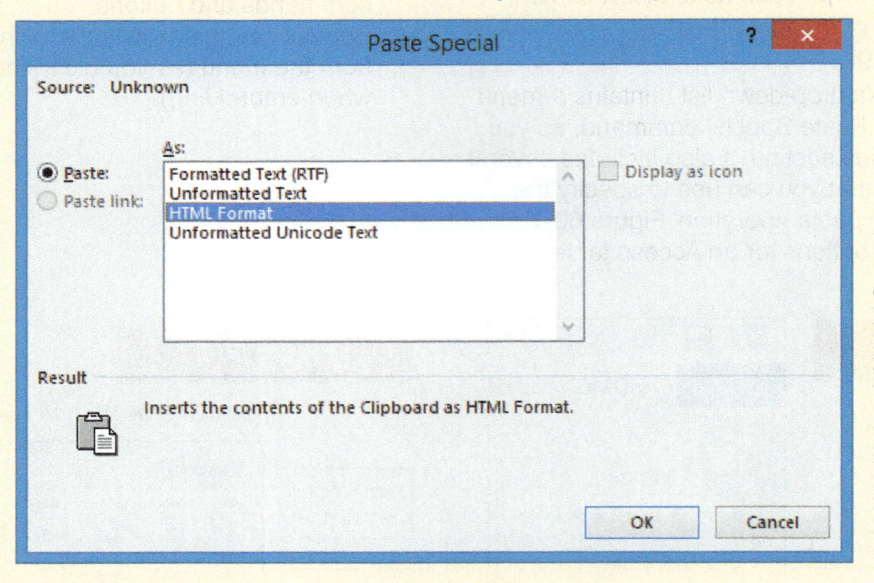

Lesson 60—Practice

You are the business development manager at Fresh Food Fair, a small chain of organic grocery stores. The company's owners are thinking about starting a home delivery service and have asked you to analyze the costs of such a venture. You have collected cost information in an Excel worksheet and have prepared a memo in Word to present your findings. In this project, you will copy some of the data from the worksheet to the memo.

DIRECTIONS

1. Start Word, if necessary, and open **W60PracticeA** from the data files for this lesson. Save the file as **W60PracticeA_xx** in the location where your teacher instructs you to store the files for this lesson.
2. Replace the text **Your Name** with your own name.
3. Replace the text **Today's date** with the current date.
4. Position the insertion point on the blank line at the end of the document.
5. Start Excel, and open the file **W60PracticeB** in Excel.
6. Select cells **A4:B9**.
   - ✓ To select cells, you can drag across them, or you can click in the upper left cell (A4) and hold down SHIFT as you press the arrow keys to extend the selection to B9.
7. Press CTRL + C to copy the selected cells to the Clipboard.
   - ✓ You can use any other copy method if you prefer, such as the HOME > Copy command or right-clicking the selection and choosing Copy.
8. Switch to the Word window.
9. On the **HOME** tab, click the down arrow on the **Paste** button.
10. Click the **Use Destination Styles** button on the menu that appears.
    - ✓ The cells are copied into Word and are formatted to match the Word document's formatting. The document should look similar to Figure 60-3 on the next page.
11. **With your teacher's permission**, print the document.
12. Close Excel without saving changes to the workbook.
13. Save and close the document, and exit Word.

Figure 60-3

Fresh Food Fair
Route 117, Bolton, MA 01740

MEMO

To: Kimberly and Jack Thomson
From: Firstname Lastname
Date: Today's date
Subject: Home Delivery Service

I believe the research bears out the need for a home delivery service. The data indicates we could be profitable within six months. Please review the information and let me know how you want to proceed.

Initial Investment	
Trucks	$100,000.00
Equipment	$55,000.00
Supplies	$52,000.00
Training	$36,500.00
Total	$243,500.00

Lesson 60—Apply

In this project, you will continue to work on the memo for the owners of Fresh Food Fair. You will embed Excel data in the memo. You will also copy a chart from a PowerPoint presentation and paste it into the memo as a picture.

DIRECTIONS

1. Start Word, if necessary, and open **W60ApplyA** from the data files for this lesson. Save the file as **W60ApplyA_xx** in the location where your teacher instructs you to store the files for this lesson.
2. Replace the text **Your Name** with your own name.
3. Replace the text **Today's date** with the current date.
4. Open **W60ApplyB** in Excel, and select cells **E4:F11**.
5. Copy the cells to the Clipboard.
6. Switch to Word and move the insertion point to the end of the document.
7. Press ENTER and type **The estimated monthly expenses are as follows:**. Then press ENTER again to start a new paragraph.
8. Using **Paste Special**, embed the copied cells into the Word document.
    - ✓ *Use the Microsoft Excel Worksheet Object data type in the Paste Special dialog box.*
9. Switch back to Excel, and close it. Do not save changes to **W60ApplyB**.
10. Edit the embedded cells to change the Gas cost to **$3000**.
11. Edit the embedded cells to match the font, font size, and cell borders of the other table earlier in the Word document.
    - ✓ *If you have not already studied Excel formatting, you may not know how to do step 11; ask your teacher for help if needed.*
12. Move the insertion point in Word to the right of the embedded Excel data, and press the spacebar a few times to create extra space there.
13. Open **W60ApplyC** in PowerPoint, and select the chart on slide 7.
14. Copy the chart to the Clipboard.
15. Switch to Word, and paste the chart as a picture at the end of the Word document.
16. Resize the chart so that it fits next to the embedded Excel data, as shown in Figure 60-4 on the next page.
17. **With your teacher's permission**, print the document.
18. Close PowerPoint without saving changes to the presentation.
19. Save your changes in Word, and exit Word.

Figure 60-4

Fresh Food Fair
Route 117, Bolton, MA 01740

MEMO

To: Kimberly and Jack Thomson
From: Firstname Lastname
Date: Today's date
Subject: Home Delivery Service

I believe the research bears out the need for a home delivery service. The data indicates we could be profitable within six months. Please review the information and let me know how you want to proceed.

There are two phases of investment. The initial investment is as follows:

Initial Investment	
Trucks	$100,000.00
Equipment	$55,000.00
Supplies	$52,000.00
Training	$36,500.00
Total	$243,500.00

The estimated monthly expenses are as follows:

Monthly Expenses	
Trucks	
Gas	$3,000.00
Insurance	$550.00
Maintenance	$250.00
Supplies	$18,000.00
Personnel	$73,250.00
Total	$95,050.00

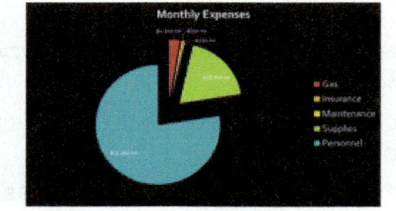

Lesson 61

Linking Files and Objects

➤ What You Will Learn

Linking Files
Editing a Linked Object
Updating Links

Software Skills Link files when you have existing data in one file that you want to use in one or more other files. Whenever the original data is changed, the link ensures that it will be updated in all other files. Linking lets you maintain data in a single file location, yet use it in other files as well.

WORDS TO KNOW

Link
To insert a link to an object in another file, so that when the original is edited, the linked copy also changes.

What You Can Do

Linking Files

- When you want to reference data from another file that might change later, you might want to link to it. A **link** is a pointer to another data file; when you open a document that contains a link, Word retrieves the latest version of the linked data.
- Linked content is different from embedded content. Embedded content retains a memory of the application it came from, but the data itself is stored only within the document in which it is embedded. There is no connection between the embedded data and the original.
- In contrast, linked data maintains information about not only the application it came from, but also the data file it came from. That way when the original changes, the copy changes too, automatically.
- You can link parts of a file by using the Paste Special command with the Paste link option enabled.
- In the Paste Special dialog box, you can also select how you want to format the selected object. The choices depend on the source program.

Try It! Linking Files

1. Start Word, and open **W61TryA** from the data files for this lesson. Save the file as **W61TryA_xx** in the location where your teacher instructs you to store the files for this lesson.
2. Start Excel, and open **W61TryB**. Save the file as **W61TryB_xx** in the location where your teacher instructs you to store the files for this lesson.
3. In Excel, select the cell range A22:J31. Then press CTRL + C to copy.
4. Switch to Word, and triple-click the line *Insert link here* to select it.
5. On the HOME tab, click the down arrow on the Paste button and click Paste Special.
6. In the Paste Special dialog box, click Paste link.
7. Select *Microsoft Excel Worksheet Object*.
8. Click OK.
   ✓ Word inserts the selected cells in the Word document.
9. Resize the object in the Word document so it fits in the document, and add extra paragraph breaks as needed.
10. Exit Excel, saving the changes if prompted. In Word, save the changes to **W61TryA_xx**, and leave it open to use in the next Try It.

Choose Paste link in the Paste Special dialog box

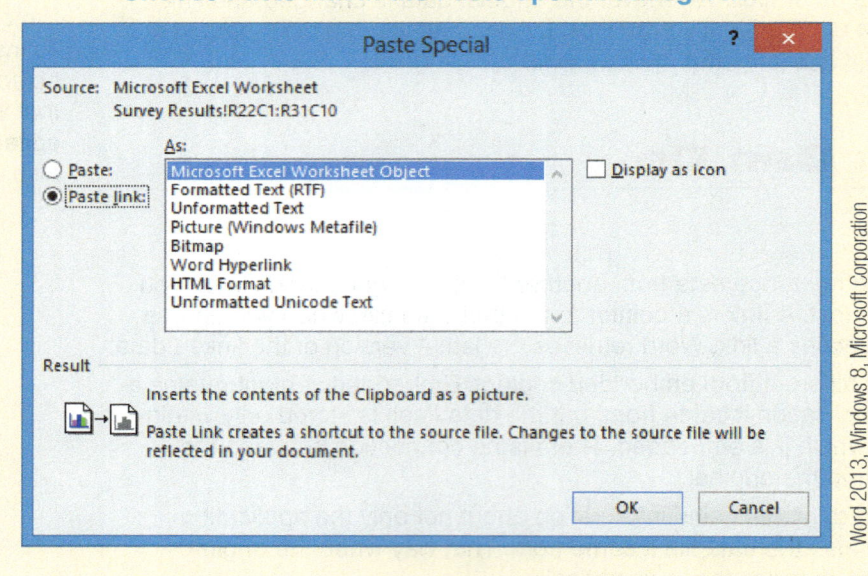

Editing a Linked Object

- You can edit a linked object by opening it via the link in Word, or you can open the source file separately outside of Word. Either way, the same file is being edited. The copy in Word is not a separate copy; it is a pointer to the original.
- When you double-click a linked object in Word, the source program and file open so you can edit the source file directly.
- If you open the source file separately outside of Word, the changes that you make to it are reflected in the linked copy in Word the next time the links are updated.
   ✓ You will learn about link updating in the next section.

Business Information Management II | Word | Chapter 9

Try It! Editing a Linked Object

1. With **W61TryA_xx** open in Word, double-click the linked worksheet object. The original copy opens in Excel.
   ✓ *Unlike with an embedded object, in this case an entirely separate Excel window opens for editing the file; Excel's Ribbon and tools do not appear within Word.*
2. In Excel, change the value in cell J23 to **11**.
3. Exit Excel, saving the changes.
4. In Word, right-click the linked worksheet object. Click Update Link. The change is reflected.
5. Save the changes to **W61TryA_xx**, and leave it open to use in the next Try It.

Updating Links

- By default, links update whenever a file is opened or printed.
- If Word cannot locate the source file (for example, if it has been deleted, renamed, or moved), it will display a warning message telling you that it cannot update the link. You can use the Links dialog box to break the link or to change the location of the source file.
- If there are many links in a file, automatic updating can slow down the process of opening the file. For that reason, you might choose to turn off automatic updating.
- The Links dialog box enables you to manage the links in various ways:
  - You can break a link, leaving the object in the document without a link to the source document.
  - You can change the source file for the link (for example, if the name or location of the source file changed).
  - You can switch between automatic and manual updating.
  - You can lock an individual link to prevent it from updating.

Try It! Switching Between Manual and Automatic Updating

1. With **W61TryA_xx** open in Word, double-click the linked object to reopen it in Excel.
2. In Excel, change the value in cell J23 to **15**, and save.
3. Switch back to Word, and right-click the linked worksheet object. Click Update Link.
4. Click the FILE tab. In the right pane of the Info tab, click Edit Links to Files. The Links dialog box opens.
5. Click Manual update and click OK. Click the Back button to return to the document.
6. Switch back to Excel, and change the value in cell J23 to **7**.
7. Exit Excel, saving the changes.
8. Switch back to Word, and note that the value in cell J23 has not updated. Leave the file open for the next Try It.
   ✓ *You may need to resize the object; it may have reverted to its original inserted dimensions.*

(continued)

Try It! Switching Between Manual and Automatic Updating *(continued)*

Manage links in the Links dialog box

Try It! Manually Updating a Link

1. In the **W61TryA_xx** file, click FILE > Info > Edit Links to Files. The Links dialog box opens.
2. Click Update Now.
3. Click Close to close the dialog box, and click the Back button to return to the document. Note that the value in cell J23 is now updated.

✓ *You may need to resize the object; it may have reverted to its original inserted dimensions.*

4. Save the changes to **W61TryA_xx**, and leave it open to use in the next Try It.

Try It! Breaking a Link

1. In the **W61TryA_xx** file, click FILE > Info > Edit Links to Files.
2. Click Break Link.
3. Click Yes to confirm.
4. Click the Back button to return to the document.

✓ *You may need to resize the object; it may have reverted to its original inserted dimensions.*

5. Double-click the object.

✓ *It no longer opens in Excel; instead picture tools appear on the Ribbon. When you broke the link, you converted the object to a picture.*

6. Save and close the document, and exit Word.

Lesson 61—Practice

As the new training director at Long Shot, Inc., you have been asked to submit the department's expenses for the first quarter to the Director of Human Resources. However, you have only preliminary data available. In this project, you will link the preliminary data stored in an Excel worksheet into a Word memo.

DIRECTIONS

1. Start Word, if necessary, and open **W61PracticeA** from the data files for this lesson. Save the file as **W61PracticeA_xx** in the location where your teacher instructs you to store the files for this lesson.
2. Replace the text **Your Name** with your own name.
3. Replace the text **Today's date** with the current date.
4. Position the insertion point at the end of the document.
5. Open **W61PracticeB** in Excel, and save the file as **W61PracticeB_xx** in the location where your teacher instructs you to store the files for this lesson.
6. In Excel, select **A5:E13**.
7. Press CTRL + C to copy the cells to the Clipboard.
8. Switch to Word.
9. On the **HOME** tab, click the down arrow on the **Paste** button and click **Paste Special**.
10. In the Paste Special dialog box, click **Paste link**.
11. Click **Microsoft Excel Worksheet Object**.
12. Click **OK**. The object is pasted and linked.
13. **With your teacher's permission**, print the document.
14. Save and close the document, and exit Word.
15. Exit Excel, saving your changes if prompted.

Lesson 61—Apply

In this project, you will continue to work on the memo for the Director of Human Resources at Long Shot, Inc. You will change the data to reflect actual expenses, and update the link to update the data in the Word document.

DIRECTIONS

1. Start Word, if necessary, and open **W61ApplyA** from the data files for this lesson. When prompted to update the links, click No.

   ✓ *There is no need to update this link now.*

2. Save the file as **W61ApplyA_xx** in the location where your teacher instructs you to store the files for this lesson.
3. Replace the text **Your Name** with your own name.
4. Replace the text **Today's date** with the current date.
5. Start Excel, and open the workbook **W61ApplyB** from the data files for this lesson. Save the file as **W61ApplyB_xx** in the location where your teacher instructs you to store the files for this lesson.
6. Switch to Word, and change the link in the document to refer to **W61ApplyB_xx**.

   ✓ *Use the Change Source command in the Links dialog box.*

7. Make the following changes to the linked object:
   a. Change the value in cell **C12** to **$350**.
   b. Change the value in cell **C9** to **$2000**.
8. Save the changes in Excel and exit the program.
9. Update the link in the Word document if the changes you made do not immediately appear.

   ✓ *To update the link, you can right-click the object and click Update Link.*

10. **With your teacher's permission**, print the document. It should look similar to Figure 61-1 on the next page.
11. Save and close the document, and exit Word.

Figure 61-1

Long Shot, Inc.

INTERDEPARTMENTAL MEMORANDUM

To: Director of Human Resources
From: Firstname Lastname
Date: Today's date
Re: Training Department Expenses

Per your request, here are the preliminary expense figures for the training department for the first quarter of the year. I will update the figures as soon as I receive the actual amounts.

	Long Shot, Inc.			
	Training Department			
	First Quarter Expenses			
	January	February	March	Total
Salaries	$135,000.00	$135,000.00	$135,000.00	$405,000.00
Overtime	$30,000.00	$32,000.00	$29,000.00	$91,000.00
Entertainment	$1,500.00	$1,750.00	$1,200.00	$4,450.00
Facility rentals	$2,000.00	$2,000.00	$1,500.00	$5,500.00
Books	$500.00	$250.00	$500.00	$1,250.00
Supplies	$250.00	$150.00	$375.00	$775.00
Miscellaneous	$350.00	$350.00	$300.00	$1,000.00
Total	$169,600.00	$171,500.00	$167,875.00	$508,975.00

Lesson 62

Integrating Word and PowerPoint

➤ What You Will Learn

Pasting PowerPoint Slides As Graphics
Embedding a PowerPoint Slide in a Word Document
Exporting PowerPoint Slides and Notes to a Word Document
Exporting PowerPoint Text to a Word Document
Using a Word Outline to Create a PowerPoint Presentation

Software Skills Sharing information between two applications can save you work and provide consistency between documents. If you have a PowerPoint presentation, for example, you can use the presentation information in a Word document. You can embed PowerPoint slides in a Word document as graphics objects, and you can export text and graphics from a PowerPoint presentation into a Word document.

WORDS TO KNOW

Export
To send data from its source file to a different file, usually in a different format.

What You Can Do

Pasting PowerPoint Slides As Graphics

- When you paste slides from PowerPoint into Word, the pasted copies become graphics, like any other graphic you would insert.

Try It!   **Pasting PowerPoint Slides As Graphics**

1. Start Word, and open **W62TryA** from the data files for this lesson. Save the file as **W62TryA_xx** in the location where your teacher instructs you to store the files for this lesson.

2. Start PowerPoint, and open **W62TryB**. Save the file as **W62TryB_xx** in the location where your teacher instructs you to store the files for this lesson.

3. Select slide 4 in the thumbnail pane (on the left) and press `CTRL` + `C` to copy it.

4. Switch to Word, and click to move the insertion point to the bottom of the document.

5. Press `CTRL` + `V` to paste the slide. It is pasted as a graphic.

6. Double-click the slide graphic. Picture formatting tools appear in the Ribbon.

7. Select the slide graphic and press `DEL` to remove it from the document.

8. Leave the document open for the next Try It. Leave the PowerPoint presentation open also.

Embedding a PowerPoint Slide in a Word Document

- You can embed a PowerPoint slide in a Word document. As with other embedding, the slide object remains associated with PowerPoint, so you can double-click to edit it with PowerPoint's own tools at any time.

Try It! Embedding a PowerPoint Slide in a Word Document

1. In **W62TryB_xx** in PowerPoint, select slide 4 and press `CTRL` + `C` to copy it.
2. Switch to Word, where **W62TryA_xx** should already be open, and click to move the insertion point to the bottom of the document.
3. On the HOME tab, click the down arrow on the Paste button and click Paste Special.
4. Click Microsoft PowerPoint Slide Object.
5. Click OK. The slide is embedded.
6. Double-click the embedded object. It opens in PowerPoint within Word.
7. Click away from the embedded object. The Word Ribbon reappears.
8. Close Word, saving your changes. Leave PowerPoint and **W62TryB_xx** open for the next Try It.

Embed the slide as a PowerPoint object

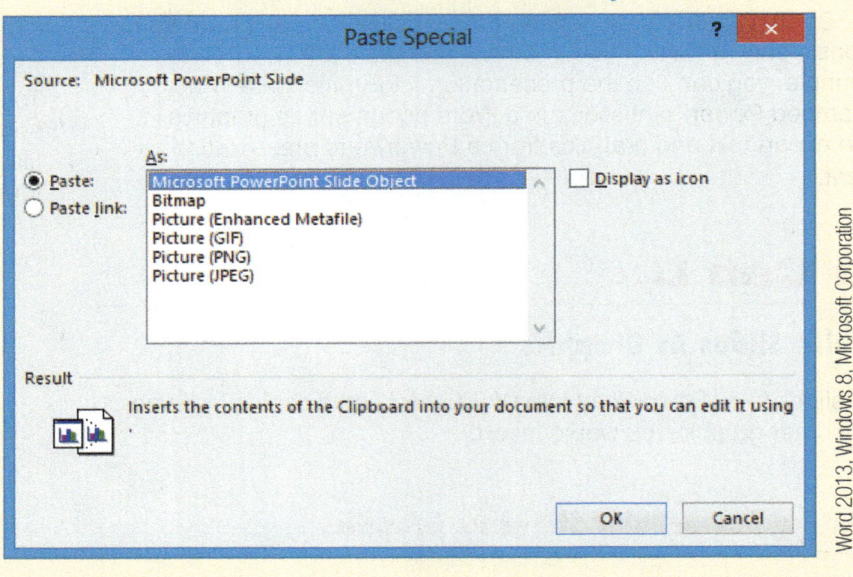

Paste Special dialog box showing Source: Microsoft PowerPoint Slide, with options to Paste as Microsoft PowerPoint Slide Object, Bitmap, Picture (Enhanced Metafile), Picture (GIF), Picture (PNG), Picture (JPEG).

Word 2013, Windows 8, Microsoft Corporation

Exporting PowerPoint Slides and Notes to a Word Document

- For more precise control over the formatting of PowerPoint presentation handouts, you can **export** them to Word. The resulting exported handouts show miniature versions of each slide along with either your speaker notes or blank lines for writing handwritten notes or comments.

- You can optionally link the slides in the Word document to the source presentation, so when you change the source presentation, Word updates the linked slides automatically.

Business Information Management II | Word | Chapter 9   245

Try It! Exporting PowerPoint Slides and Notes to a Word Document

1. In **W62TryB_xx** in PowerPoint, click FILE > Export > Create Handouts > Create Handouts. The Send to Microsoft Word dialog box opens.

2. Click Blank lines next to slides.

   ✓ *Notice the Paste link option at the bottom of the dialog box. This exercise does not use it, but you can choose that option to link to the presentation if desired.*

3. Click OK. Word opens, with the handouts as a new document.

4. Close the Word document without saving it. Leave PowerPoint and **W62TryB_xx** open for the next Try It.

Choose a layout to send to Word

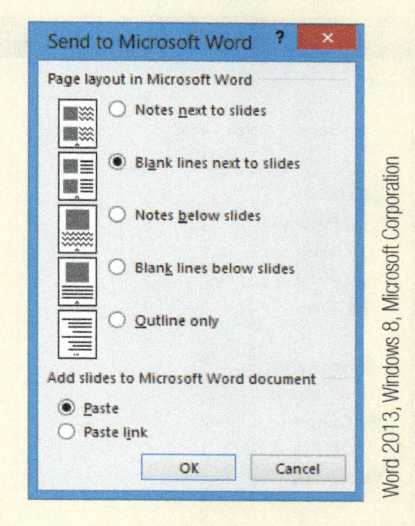

Word 2013, Windows 8, Microsoft Corporation

Exporting PowerPoint Text to a Word Document

- You can export the text from a PowerPoint presentation to Word. In Word, the text appears as an outline, using outline heading levels.

- One way to do this is with the Send to Microsoft Word dialog box, as in the previous section, but choose Outline only instead of one of the other layouts.

- Another way is to save the PowerPoint presentation as an Outline/RTF document. RTF stands for Rich Text Format, a generic word processing format. The following steps show that method.

Try It! Exporting PowerPoint Text to a Word Document

1. In **W62TryB_xx** in PowerPoint, click FILE > Save As.

2. Navigate to the location where your teacher instructs you to store the files for this lesson.

3. In the Save As dialog box, open the Save as type drop-down list and click Outline/RTF.

4. In the File name box, type **W62TryC_xx**.

5. Click Save.

6. Close PowerPoint without saving changes.

7. Open Word, and open **W62TryC_xx**. If a Convert File dialog box opens, click OK to accept the default of RTF and open the document.

   ✓ *This dialog box might not appear, depending on your settings.*

8. Click VIEW > Outline to see the presentation in outline format.

9. Close Word without saving changes.

(continued)

Try It! — Exporting PowerPoint Text to a Word Document *(continued)*

Save in Outline/RTF format

[Screenshot of Save As dialog box in PowerPoint, showing File name: W62TryC_xx.rtf and Save as type: Outline/RTF (*.rtf)]

Using a Word Outline to Create a PowerPoint Presentation

- You can also go the other way between Word and PowerPoint: you can start with a Word outline and convert it to a PowerPoint presentation.
- The first-level headings in the outline form the slide titles, and the subheadings form the slide content.
- Be sure to reset each slide by clicking HOME > Reset. Otherwise, the slides will continue to show Word styles and colors even after a new design has been applied.
- Apply the correct layouts to the slides, for example, the Title and Content layout.

Try It! — Using a Word Outline to Create a PowerPoint Presentation

1. Start PowerPoint, and click Open Other Presentations.
2. Navigate to the location containing the data files for this lesson.
3. In the Open dialog box, change the file type to All Outlines.
4. Select **W62TryD.docx** and click Open to open the outline in PowerPoint as a presentation.
5. Press and hold the [SHIFT] key and click each slide in the thumbnail pane (on the left) to select all four slides. Release the [SHIFT] key.
6. Click HOME > Reset.
7. Click HOME > Layout and select Title and Content.
8. Save your work in PowerPoint as **W62TryD_xx** and exit PowerPoint.

Business Information Management II | Word | Chapter 9

Lesson 62—Practice

You are the business development manager at Fresh Food Fair and have completed a study on the benefits and costs of starting a new home delivery service. You have been asked to present your findings at a company meeting. You already have a PowerPoint presentation about the study. You can use pieces of the presentation to create documents to distribute as a package at the meeting. In this project, you will create a cover page for the package using a slide from the PowerPoint presentation.

DIRECTIONS

1. Start Word, if necessary, and open **W62PracticeA** from the data files for this lesson. Save the file as **W62PracticeA_xx** in the location where your teacher instructs you to store the files for this lesson.
2. Replace the text **Your Name** with your own name.
3. Replace the text **Today's Date** with the current date.
4. Click to move the insertion point to the bottom of the document.
5. Start PowerPoint, and open **W62PracticeB.pptx** from the data files for this lesson.
6. Select slide 1 and press `CTRL` + `C` to copy it to the Clipboard.
7. Switch to Word.
8. On the **HOME** tab, click the down arrow on the **Paste** button, and click **Paste Special**.
9. Click **Paste link**.
10. Click **Microsoft PowerPoint Slide Object**.
11. Click **OK**.
12. Center the pasted slide horizontally, and resize the slide so it fits attractively on the page and is approximately 6" in width.
13. **With your teacher's permission**, print the document.
14. Save and close the document, and exit Word.
15. Close PowerPoint without saving changes.

Lesson 62—Apply

In this project, you will continue to work on the documents that you will distribute at your presentation. You will export the entire presentation to a Word document to use as a handout, leaving blank lines for writing notes. You will also export the text from the presentation as an outline to use as a table of contents for the handout package.

DIRECTIONS

1. Start PowerPoint, and open **W62ApplyA.pptx** from the data files for this lesson.
2. Create handouts in Word that use the **Blank lines below slides** layout. Save that document as **W62ApplyB_xx**.
3. In that document, type your full name and today's date in the Header area.
4. **With your teacher's permission**, print the document.
5. Save and close the document, and exit Word.
6. Switch back to PowerPoint, and create handouts in Word that use the **Outline only** layout. Save that document as **W62ApplyC_xx**.
7. In that document, type your full name and today's date in the Header area.
8. Select the entire document (`CTRL` + `A`). Remove the bullets and change the font size to 12-point.
9. **With your teacher's permission**, print the document.
10. Save and close the document, and exit Word.
11. Close the PowerPoint presentation without saving changes, and exit PowerPoint.

Lesson 63

Using Merge to Create Letters, Envelopes, Labels, and E-mail

➤ What You Will Learn

Reviewing the Mail Merge Process
Merging Letters Using the Mail Merge Wizard
Merging Envelopes
Creating Mailing Labels
Creating an E-mail Merge
Filtering Recipients
Applying Rules to a Merge

Software Skills Use Mail Merge to customize mass mailings such as letters and e-mails. You type the letter or message text you want each recipient to read, and insert merge fields to customize or personalize the message. Create merged envelopes or labels to send letters by mail. Word can automatically use your e-mail program to send merged e-mail messages. Filter the recipient list to quickly select the records you want to use.

WORDS TO KNOW

Criteria
Specific conditions used to match a record or entry in a data source file or list.

Filter
To apply one or more criteria to data and exclude data that does not match the criteria.

MAPI
A Microsoft standard that allows messaging programs to work together.

Merge document
The customized document resulting from a merge.

What You Can Do

Reviewing the Mail Merge Process

- Use Mail Merge to create mass mailings, envelopes, labels, or e-mail messages.
- During the merge, Word generates a series of **merge documents** in which the variable information from the data source replaces the merge fields entered in the main document.
- You may use the commands on the MAILINGS tab of the Ribbon to conduct a merge or use the Mail Merge Wizard.

25. Reduce the width of the left column to fit contents, and then apply the **Grid Table 3 - Accent 1** table style. Turn off formatting for the header row. Your form should look like Illustration 9C.
26. Click **MAILINGS** > **Finish & Merge** > **Edit Individual Documents**.
27. Click **OK**.
28. Save the new document as **WPB09F_xx**.
29. Save and close all Word documents, and exit Word.

Illustration 9C

Firstname Lastname
Today's Date

«First_Name»:

Join the Horticultural Shop Owners' Association on an exciting four-day trip to the Botanical Gardens in Montreal, Canada. Last year, twenty members of the association joined a similar tour. When asked whether they were pleased with the experience, the overwhelming majority answered with a resounding "YES!"

Please fill out the following form and return it to the HSOA to help us in our trip planning.

Your full name	Click here to enter text.
Are you interested in the trip?	Yes ☐ No ☐
Lodging preference	Choose an item.
Food preference	Choose an item.

Chapter 6

(Courtesy Brocreative/Shutterstock)

Managing Large Workbooks

Lesson 49
Customizing the Excel Interface and Converting Text
- Customizing the Quick Access Toolbar
- Customizing the Ribbon
- Customizing Excel Options
- Converting Text to Columns

Lesson 50
Formatting Cells
- Using Advanced Formatting of Dates and Times
- Creating Custom Number Formats
- Clearing Formatting from a Cell

Lesson 51
Hiding and Formatting Workbook Elements
- Hiding Data Temporarily
- Hiding and Printing Worksheet Gridlines
- Hiding Row and Column Headings
- Using Custom Views

Lesson 52
Customizing Styles and Themes
- Customizing a Workbook Theme
- Customizing a Cell Style
- Merging Cell Styles
- Customizing a Table Style

Lesson 53
Customizing Data Entry
- Entering Labels on Multiple Lines
- Entering Fractions and Mixed Numbers
- Using Form Controls

Lesson 54
Formatting and Replacing Data Using Functions
- Formatting Text with Functions
- Replacing Text with Functions

Lesson 55
Working with Subtotals
- Using Go To and Go To Special
- Creating Subtotals
- Creating Nested Subtotals
- Hiding or Displaying Details
- Removing Subtotals
- Manually Outlining and Adding Subtotals

End-of-Chapter Activities

Lesson 49

Customizing the Excel Interface and Converting Text

➤ What You Will Learn

Customizing the Quick Access Toolbar
Customizing the Ribbon
Customizing Excel Options
Converting Text to Columns

Software Skills Like other Office programs, Excel is designed to be customized to your needs. You can customize Excel Options, the Ribbon, and the Quick Access Toolbar to have easy access to the tools and features you use most often.

What You Can Do

Customizing the Quick Access Toolbar

- The Quick Access Toolbar (QAT) appears at the top-left corner of the Excel window. It provides a set of quick shortcuts to the most common functions and features.
- You can choose to show the Quick Access Toolbar below the Ribbon.
- By default the Quick Access Toolbar contains three buttons: Save, Undo, and Redo. You can also customize it by adding shortcuts to most other Excel features.
- To add any button to the Quick Access Toolbar, right-click it and select Add to Quick Access Toolbar.
- To remove a button from the Quick Access Toolbar, right-click it and choose Remove from Quick Access Toolbar.
- You can use the Quick Access Toolbar section of the Excel Options dialog box to add Excel features that don't appear on the tabs of the Ribbon.
- You can also use the Quick Access Toolbar section of the Excel Options dialog box to remove features or to reset any customizations.

Business Information Management II | Excel | Chapter 6

Try It! Customizing the Quick Access Toolbar

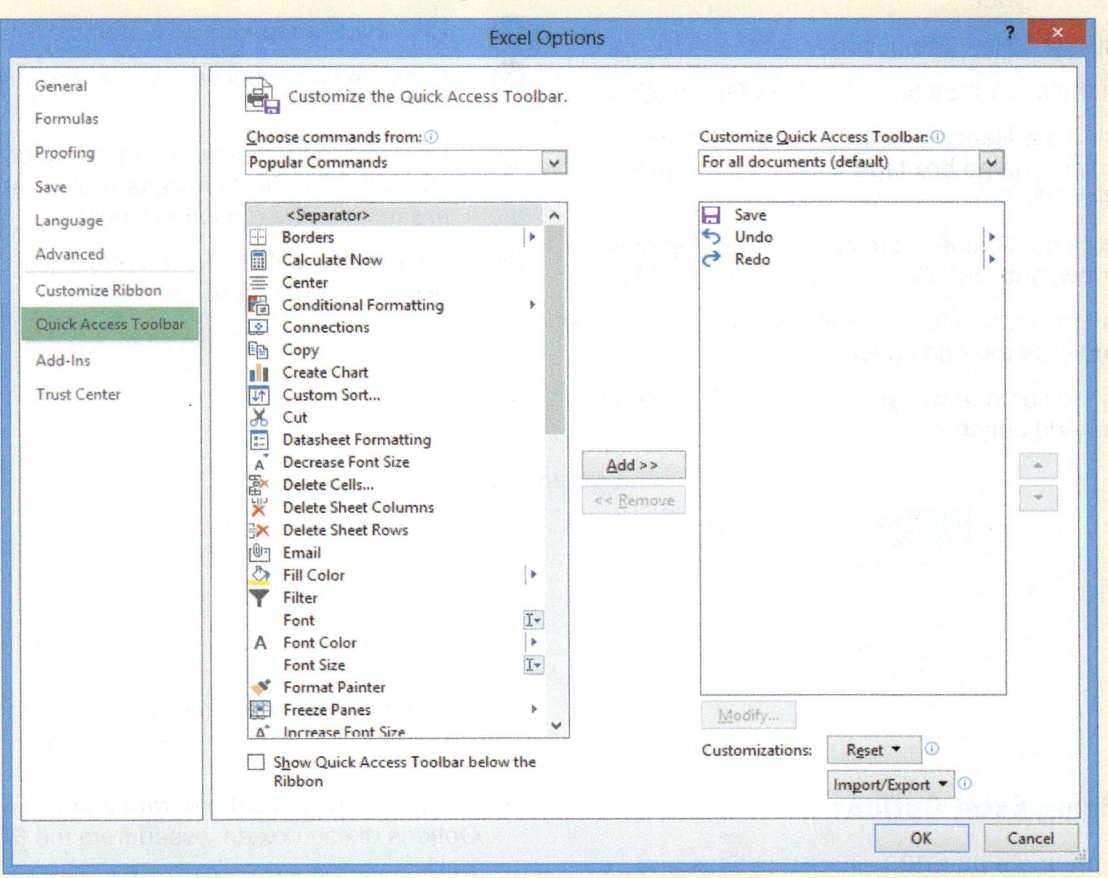

1. Start Excel, and create a new, blank workbook.
2. Click the REVIEW tab, right-click Spelling, and click Add to Quick Access Toolbar.
3. Click Customize Quick Access Toolbar > Sort Ascending.
4. Click FILE > Options > Quick Access Toolbar.
5. Click the Choose commands from drop-down arrow, and click Formulas Tab.
6. In the list of commands, click Average, and click the Add button.
7. In the list below the Customize Quick Access Toolbar box, select Average, and click the Remove button.
8. Click the Reset button > Reset only Quick Access Toolbar.
9. Click Yes in the confirmation dialog box, and click OK. The Quick Access Toolbar is reset.
10. Leave the blank workbook and Excel open for the next Try It.

Customizing the Quick Access Toolbar

Customizing the Ribbon

- In Excel 2013 you can customize the Ribbon by adding commands that you use frequently or removing those commands that you don't use.
- You can create new groups on a Ribbon tab, and you can create a new tab with new groups.
- Commands for customizing the Ribbon are on the Customize Ribbon tab of the Excel Options dialog box.
- You can also use the Customize Ribbon section of the Excel Options dialog box to remove features or to reset any customizations.

Try It! Customizing the Ribbon

1. In Excel, click FILE > Options to open the Excel Options dialog box.
2. Click Customize Ribbon.
3. On the right side of the dialog box, under Main Tabs, click to clear the check mark to the left of Page Layout.
4. Click the New Tab button [New Tab].
5. In the Main Tabs box, click New Group (Custom).
6. Click the Rename button [Rename...], in the Display name box type **Learning Excel**, and click OK.
7. Click the Choose commands from drop-down arrow, and click Commands Not in the Ribbon.
8. In the commands list, scroll down, click Zoom In, and click the Add button [Add >>].
9. In the commands list, click Zoom Out, and click the Add button [Add >>].
10. Click OK to apply the change and close the Excel Options dialog box. Notice that the PAGE LAYOUT tab no longer appears on the Ribbon and that the new tab named New Tab displays.
11. Click New Tab to view the Learning Excel group of commands.
12. Click FILE > Options > Customize Ribbon.
13. Click the Reset button [Reset ▼] > Reset all customizations.
14. Click Yes in the confirmation dialog box, and click OK. The Quick Access Toolbar and Ribbon are reset to the default settings.
15. Leave the blank workbook and Excel open to use in the next Try It.

Modified Ribbon

| FILE | HOME | INSERT | New Tab | FORMULAS | DATA | REVIEW | VIEW |

Zoom In   Zoom Out
Learning Excel

Excel 2013, Windows 8, Microsoft Corporation

Customizing Excel Options

- There are more than 100 different options and settings that you can use to control the way Excel operates.
- Excel options are organized in categories, such as Formulas, Proofing, Save, and Add-Ins.
- You can view and set program options in the Excel Options dialog box accessed from the Backstage view.
- When you set up Microsoft Excel 2013 on your computer, you enter a user name and initials.
- Excel uses this information to identify you as the author of new workbooks that you create and save, and as the editor of existing workbooks that you open, modify, and save.

- In addition, your user name is associated with revisions that you make when you use the Track Changes features, and the initials are associated with comments that you insert.

- You can change the user name and initials using options in the General group in the Excel Options dialog box.

Try It! Customizing Excel Options

1. In Excel, in the blank workbook, click FILE > Options.
2. On the General tab, under Personalize your copy of Microsoft Office, in the User name box, type your full name.
3. In the list on the left side of the dialog box, click Save to display the Save options.
4. Click Proofing to display the Proofing options.
5. Click Advanced, and scroll through the options.
6. Under Display options for this workbook, clear Show sheet tabs.
7. Under Display options for this worksheet, click the Gridline color button.
8. Select Blue (last color on the last row).
9. Click Cancel to close the Excel Options window without saving the changes.
10. Close the blank workbook without saving the changes, and leave Excel open to use in the next Try It.

Excel's advanced display options

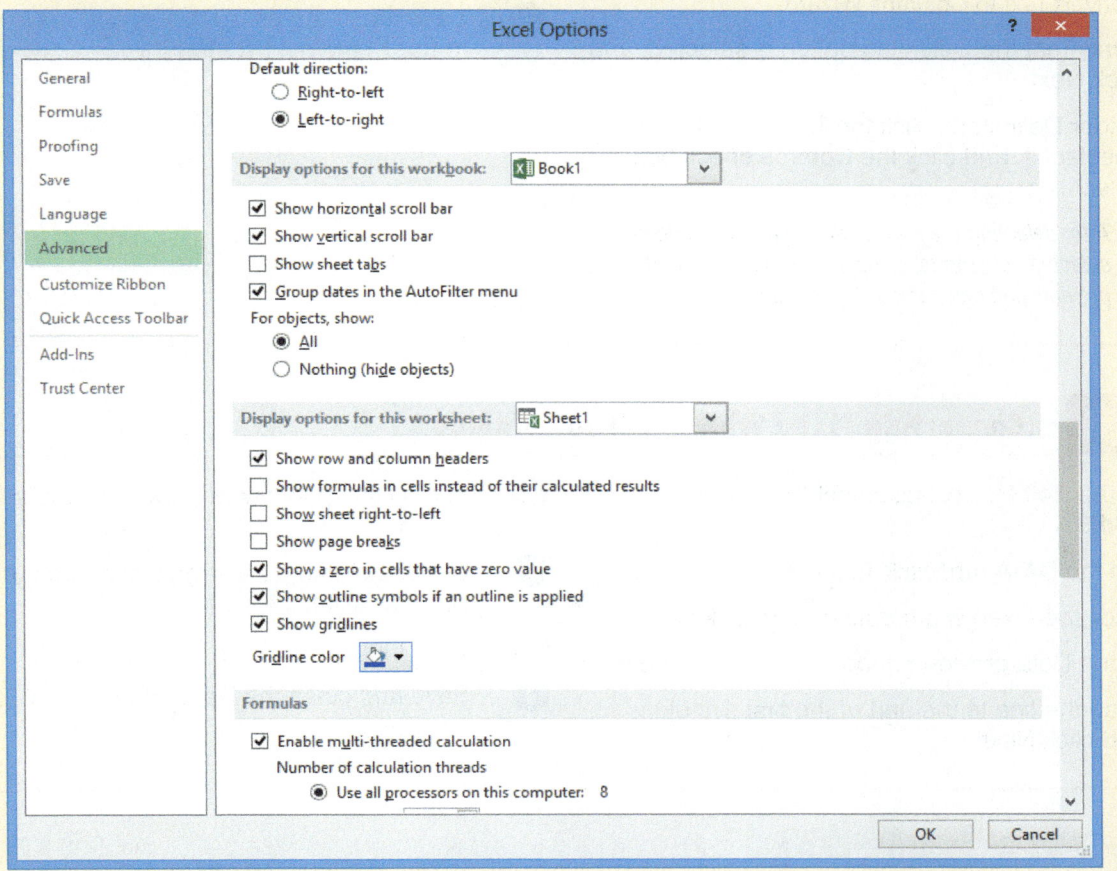

Converting Text to Columns

- When working with large amounts of text data in Excel, pre-planning is often critical.
  - For example, when creating a long list of customers, it's useful to place first names in one column and last names in another so that you can sort on the column with last names and arrange the customer list alphabetically.
- It is useful to separate out the parts of a customer's address into different columns—one each for street address, city, state, and ZIP Code—so the customer list can be sorted by state or ZIP Code.
- You can split the contents of one cell across several cells.
- You can split the contents of a single cell, a range, or an entire column in one step.

Try It! Converting Delimited Text to Columns

1. In Excel, open the open the **E49Try** file from the data files for this lesson.
2. Save the file as **E49ATry_xx** in the location where your teacher instructs you to store the files for this lesson.
3. Select the cell range I6:I57.
4. Click DATA > Text to Columns to display the Convert Text to Columns Wizard.
5. Verify that the Delimited option is selected, and click Next.
6. Under Delimiters, click the Tab check box to deselect it, and click the Comma check box to select it.
   ✓ After selecting the correct delimiter, the fields in the selected cell, range, or column will appear in the Data preview pane, separated by vertical lines.
7. To skip empty columns, click the Treat consecutive delimiters as one check box, and click Next.
8. In the Data preview window, click the last column to select it.
9. Under Column data format, click the Text option.
10. Click Finish.
11. Save the changes to the file, and leave it open to use in the next Try It.

Try It! Converting Fixed Width Text to Columns

1. In the **E49Try_xx** file, select the cell range F6:F57.
2. On the DATA tab, click Text to Columns.
3. Click the Fixed width option, and click Next.
4. In the Data preview window, click 10 on the ruler.
5. Drag the line to the end of the first five digits, and click Next.
6. In the Data preview window, click the second column.
7. Under Column data format, click Do not import column (skip).
8. Click Finish.
9. Save and close the file, and exit Excel.

Business Information Management II | Excel | Chapter 6

Lesson 49—Practice

Your manager at The Little Toy Shoppe wants you to create a newsletter to inform clients of new products and to entice them to return to the store on special sales days. Rob the intern has been keeping track of customer names and addresses in a new worksheet, but the worksheet is not formatted correctly. Unfortunately, Rob doesn't know the first thing about creating a workable database. In this project, you will take Rob's list and convert the data into usable columns.

DIRECTIONS

1. Start Excel, if necessary, and open **E49Practice** from the data files for this lesson.
2. Save the file as **E49Practice_xx** in the location where your teacher instructs you to store the files for this lesson.
3. Add a header to the worksheet that has your name at the left, the date code in the center, and the page number code at the right, and change back to **Normal** view.
4. Select the column headers for columns C and D, right-click the headers, and select **Insert** from the shortcut menu.
5. Select cells **E2** and **E3**, and drag them to cells **C2** and **C3**.
6. In cell **B5**, replace the text by typing **First Name**; type **Last Name** in cell **C5**.
7. Select the cell range **B6:B57**.
8. Click DATA > Text to Columns.
9. Verify that the **Delimited** option is selected, and click **Next**.
10. Under Delimiters, click the Comma check box to deselect it, click the **Space** check box to select it, and click **Next**.
11. Click the first column in the Data preview window, and under Column data format, click the **Text** option.
12. Click the second column in the Data preview window, and under Column data format, click the **Text** option.
13. Click **Finish**.
14. Click **OK** in the confirmation dialog box.
15. Click the **Customize Quick Access Toolbar** button ⇁, and click **Spelling**.
16. Click the **Customize Quick Access Toolbar** button ⇁, and click **Spelling** to remove it.
17. **With your teacher's permission**, print the worksheet. It should look similar to Figure 49-1 on the next page.
18. Save and close the file, and exit Excel.

Figure 49-1

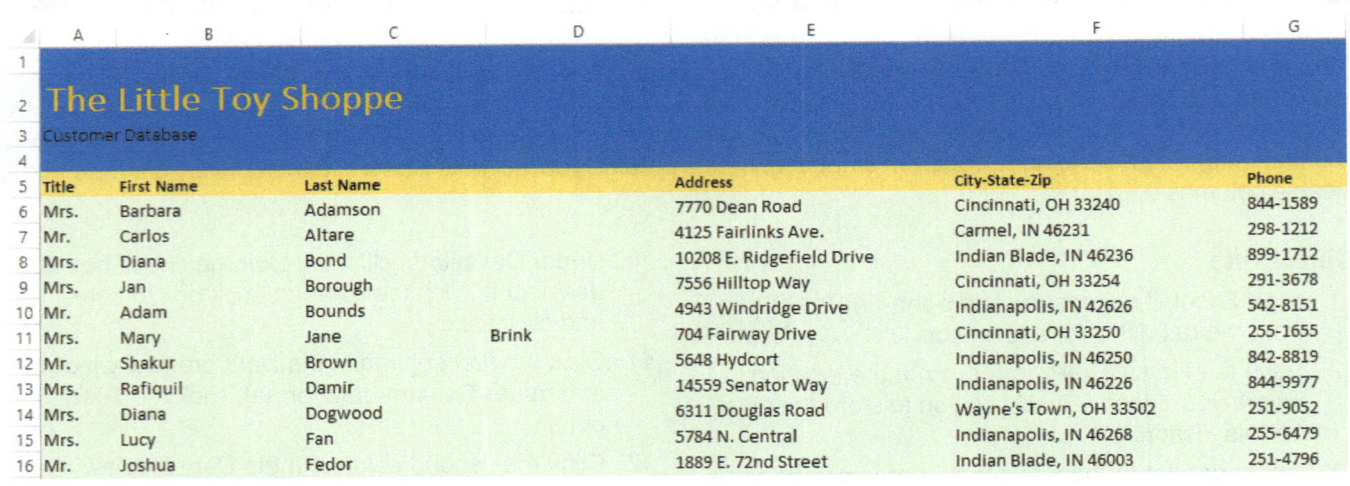

	A	B	C	D	E	F	G
1							
2	The Little Toy Shoppe						
3	Customer Database						
4							
5	Title	First Name	Last Name		Address	City-State-Zip	Phone
6	Mrs.	Barbara	Adamson		7770 Dean Road	Cincinnati, OH 33240	844-1589
7	Mr.	Carlos	Altare		4125 Fairlinks Ave.	Carmel, IN 46231	298-1212
8	Mrs.	Diana	Bond		10208 E. Ridgefield Drive	Indian Blade, IN 46236	899-1712
9	Mrs.	Jan	Borough		7556 Hilltop Way	Cincinnati, OH 33254	291-3678
10	Mr.	Adam	Bounds		4943 Windridge Drive	Indianapolis, IN 42626	542-8151
11	Mrs.	Mary	Jane	Brink	704 Fairway Drive	Cincinnati, OH 33250	255-1655
12	Mr.	Shakur	Brown		5648 Hydcort	Indianapolis, IN 46250	842-8819
13	Mrs.	Rafiquil	Damir		14559 Senator Way	Indianapolis, IN 46226	844-9977
14	Mrs.	Diana	Dogwood		6311 Douglas Road	Wayne's Town, OH 33502	251-9052
15	Mrs.	Lucy	Fan		5784 N. Central	Indianapolis, IN 46268	255-6479
16	Mr.	Joshua	Fedor		1889 E. 72nd Street	Indian Blade, IN 46003	251-4796

Excel 2013, Windows 8, Microsoft Corporation

Lesson 49—Apply

You are creating a newsletter to inform clients of new products and to entice them to return to the store on special sales days. You are working with a worksheet of customer names and addresses created by Rob the intern. However, the worksheet data is not in the most usable format. In this project, you will prepare the data and convert it into usable columns.

DIRECTIONS

1. Start Excel, if necessary, and open **E49Apply** from the data files for this lesson.
2. Save the file as **E49Apply_xx** in the location where your teacher instructs you to store the files for this lesson.
3. Add a header to the worksheet that has your name at the left, the date code in the center, and the page number code at the right, and change back to **Normal** view.
4. Notice that two of the names use all three columns; these names have two-part first names. Fix the names to appear in the correct columns.
    a. Type **Mary Jane** in cell **B11**, and type **Brink** in cell **C11**.
    b. Type **Chu Gi** in cell **B34**, and type **Nguyen** in cell **C34**.
    c. Delete column **D**.
5. Insert two columns between columns E and F.
6. Type **City** in cell **E5**, type **State** in cell **F5**, and type **ZIP Code** in cell **G5**.

7. Split the addresses in column E into two columns:
   a. Select the cell range **E6:E57**.
   b. Click Text to Columns .
   c. Select the **Delimited** option and **Comma** as the delimiter used.
   d. Select **Text** as the format for first column.
8. Split the state and ZIP Codes in column F into two columns:
   a. Select the cell range **F6:F57**.
   b. Click Text to Columns .
   c. Select the **Fixed Width** option.
   d. Add a delimiting line at the beginning of the Zip codes in the Data preview window.
   e. Select **Text** as the format for first column, and **General** for the second column.
9. Adjust the column widths as needed.
10. Customize the Quick Access Toolbar with the features of your choices.
11. Customize the Ribbon with the tabs and commands of your choice.
12. **With your teacher's permission**, print page 1 of the worksheet in landscape orientation. It should look similar to Figure 49-2.
13. Reset the Quick Access Toolbar and the Ribbon to their default settings.
14. Save and close the file, and exit Excel.

Figure 49-2

	A	B	C	D	E	F	G	H
1								
2	The Little Toy Shoppe							
3	Customer Database							
4								
5	Title	First Name	Last Name	Address	City	State	ZIP Code	Phone
6	Mrs.	Barbara	Adamson	7770 Dean Road	Cincinnati	OH	33240	844-1589
7	Mr.	Carlos	Altare	4125 Fairlinks Ave.	Carmel	IN	46231	298-1212
8	Mrs.	Diana	Bond	10208 E. Ridgefield Drive	Indian Blade	IN	46236	899-1712
9	Mrs.	Jan	Borough	7556 Hilltop Way	Cincinnati	OH	33254	291-3678
10	Mr.	Adam	Bounds	4943 Windridge Drive	Indianapolis	IN	42626	542-8151
11	Mrs.	Mary Jane	Brink	704 Fairway Drive	Cincinnati	OH	33250	255-1655
12	Mr.	Shakur	Brown	5648 Hydcort	Indianapolis	IN	46250	842-8819
13	Mrs.	Rafiquil	Damir	14559 Senator Way	Indianapolis	IN	46226	844-9977
14	Mrs.	Diana	Dogwood	6311 Douglas Road	Wayne's Town	OH	33502	251-9052
15	Mrs.	Lucy	Fan	5784 N. Central	Indianapolis	IN	46268	255-6479
16	Mr.	Joshua	Fedor	1889 E. 72nd Street	Indian Blade	IN	46003	251-4796
17	Mrs.	Michele	Floyd	3203 Wander Wood Ct	Indianapolis	IN	46220	291-2510
18	Mrs.	Jennifer	Flynn	9876 Wilshire Ave.	Cincinnati	OH	33240	975-0909
19	Ms.	Katerina	Flynn	4984 Wander Wood Lane	Indianapolis	IN	42626	542-0021
20	Mr.	Eram	Hassan	8123 Maple Ave.	Cincinnati	OH	33250	722-1487
21	Mrs.	Betty	High	7543 Newport Bay Drive	Cincinnati	OH	33250	722-1043
22	Mrs.	Addie	Howard	7960 Susan Drive, S.	Westland	IN	46215	849-3557
23	Mr.	Tyrell	Johnson	11794 Southland Ave.	Wayne's Town	OH	33505	846-9812
24	Mr.	Michael	Jordain	4897 Kessler Ave.	Indianapolis	IN	46220	255-1133
25	Mrs.	Ashley	Kay	8738 Log Run Drive, S.	Carmel	IN	46234	299-6136
26	Mrs.	Rhoda	Kuntz	567 W. 72nd Street	Indian Blade	IN	46003	251-6539
27	Ms.	Verna	Latinz	14903 Senator Way	Indianapolis	IN	46226	844-4333
28	Mr.	Wu	Lee	6467 Riverside Drive	Carmel	IN	46220	257-1253
29	Mr.	Chu	Lee	5821 Wilshire Ave.	Cincinnati	OH	33240	975-0484
30	Mr.	Shamir	Lewis	11684 Bay Colony Drive	Plainsville	IN	46234	297-1894
31	Mrs.	Martha	Luck	4131 Brown Road	Cincinnati	OH	33454	547-7430
32	Mrs.	Maria	Navarro	3847 Shipshore Drive	Indianapolis	IN	46032	873-9664
33	Mr.	Tony	Navarro	7998 Maple Ave.	Westland	IN	46215	849-1515
34	Mr.	Chu Gi	Nguyen	8794 Dean Road	Cincinnati	OH	33240	853-1277

- Total Row: Applies a formatting choice to the final totals row in a table.
- First Header Cell: Applies a formatting choice to the first cell in the header row. This cell often contains no data.
- Last Header Cell: Applies a formatting choice to the final cell in the header row in a table.
- First Total Cell: Applies a formatting choice to the first cell in the total row. This cell often contains the heading "Total".
- Last Total Cell: Applies a formatting choice to the final cell in the total row. This cell often holds an overall total number.
- A new table style only consists of the formatting you apply as you create the table style. It will not automatically use any direct cell formatting you may have applied or use new cell styles you have created.

Try It! Creating a New Table Style

1. In the **E52TryA_xx** file, clear the cell formatting from the cell range A2:H2.
    a. Select the cell range A2:H2.
    b. On the HOME tab, click Clear > Clear Formats.
2. Select the cell range A2:H7, and format it as a table.
    a. On the HOME tab, click Format as Table.
    b. Select Table Style Light 1.
    c. Verify that the data range shown in the Format As Table dialog box reflects the cell range A2:H7.
    ✓ Excel will automatically insert absolute references. Recall that you learned about absolute references in Excel, Lesson 8.
    d. Verify that the My table has headers check box is selected, and click OK.
    e. On the TABLE TOOLS DESIGN tab, select the following options in the Table Style Options group: Header Row, Total Row, Last Column. Deselect any other options.
    ✓ If your custom cell style is applied to cell A8 when you have added the Total row, click in cell A8 and then Clear > Clear Formats to remove the cell style.
3. Click HOME > Format as Table > New Table Style. The New Table Style dialog box displays.
4. In the Name box, type your name.
5. In the Table Element box, click Header Row > Format. The Format Cells dialog box displays.
6. Click the Fill tab, and under Background Color click Black.
7. Click the Font tab, and in the Font style list, click Bold.
8. On the Font tab, click the Color drop-down arrow, click White, Background 1, and click OK.
9. In the Table Element box, click Total Row > Format.
10. On the Font tab, in the Font style list, click Bold.
11. Click the Border tab, in the Style box click the double line option (last option in the second column), and under Presets click Outline.
12. Click the Fill tab, click the brighter blue in the theme colors (fifth option in the first row), and click OK.
13. In the Table Element box, scroll down, click Last Total Cell > Format.
14. Click the Fill tab, on the Standard colors palette click Orange, and click OK.
15. In the Table Element box, scroll up, click Whole Table > Format.
16. Click the Border tab, click the Color drop-down arrow, click Blue-Gray, Text 2, Lighter 40%, under Presets click Inside, and click OK.
17. Click OK to apply the changes and close the New Table Style dialog box.
18. Click inside the table, click TABLE TOOLS DESIGN, and in the Table Styles gallery click your custom table style.
    ✓ Depending on the width of your screen, you may need to click the Quick Styles button to display the table styles.
19. Save and close the file, and exit Excel.

(continued)

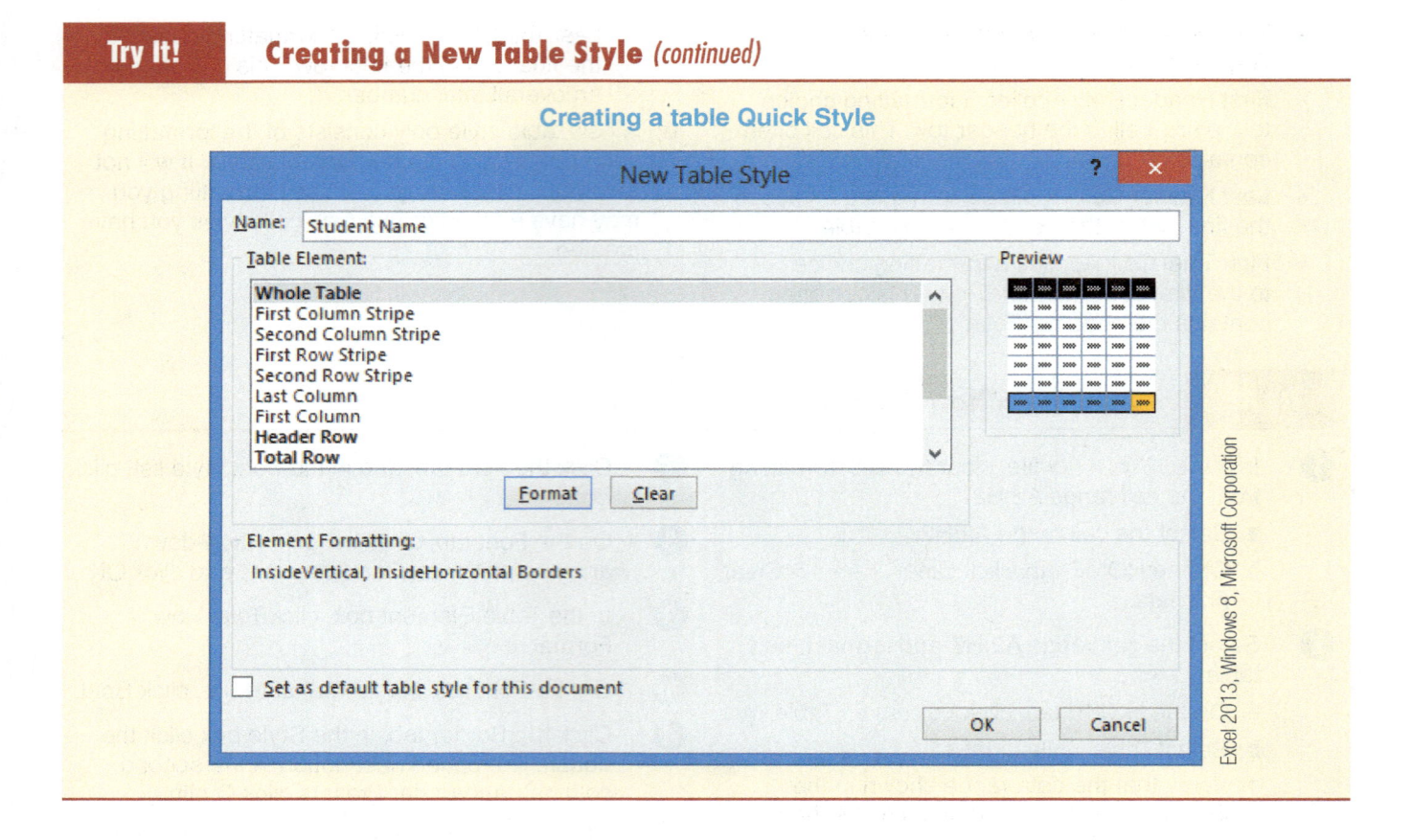

> **Try It!** **Creating a New Table Style** (continued)
>
> Creating a table Quick Style
>
> [Dialog box: New Table Style — Name: Student Name; Table Element list showing Whole Table, First Column Stripe, Second Column Stripe, First Row Stripe, Second Row Stripe, Last Column, First Column, Header Row, Total Row; Format and Clear buttons; Element Formatting: InsideVertical, InsideHorizontal Borders; Set as default table style for this document checkbox; OK and Cancel buttons; Preview pane]
>
> *Excel 2013, Windows 8, Microsoft Corporation*

Lesson 52—Practice

The worksheet you designed to track accessories sold each day at your PhotoTown store has proven very helpful, and the corporate headquarters may adopt it throughout the company. In this project, you will create a custom theme that follows the company publication standards.

DIRECTIONS

1. Start Excel, if necessary, and open **E52Practice** from the data files for this lesson.
2. Save the file as **E52PracticeA_xx** in the location where your teacher instructs you to store the files for this lesson.
3. Add a header that has your name at the left, the date code in the center, and the page number code at the right, and change back to **Normal** view.
4. Click **PAGE LAYOUT** > **Colors** > **Customize Colors**.
5. Click the **Accent 5** button and select **More Colors**.
6. Set Red to **224**, Green to **183**, and Blue to **119** and click **OK**.
7. Click the **Accent 6** button, and click **More Colors**.
8. Change Red to **160**, Green to **113**, and Blue to **255**, and click **OK**.
9. In the Name box, type **PhotoTown**, and click **Save** to save the new color set.
10. Select the cell range **A6:C6**.
11. Click **HOME** > **Fill Color** > **Gold, Accent 4, Lighter 40%**.
12. Click **HOME** > **Font Color** > **Blue, Accent 1, Darker 25%**.

13. Click **PAGE LAYOUT** > **Fonts** A > **Customize Fonts**.
14. Click the Heading font drop-down arrow, and click **Arial Rounded MT Bold**.
15. Click the Body font drop-down arrow, and click **Baskerville Old Face**.
16. In the Name box, type **PhotoTown**, and click **Save** to save the new font set.
17. Select cell range **A6:C6**, press and hold CTRL, and click cell **A2**.
18. Click **HOME** > **Font** > **Arial Rounded MT Bold**.
19. Click **PAGE LAYOUT** > **Themes** > **Save Current Theme**.
20. Save the theme as **E52PracticeB_xx** in the location where your teacher instructs you to store the files for this lesson.
21. **With your teacher's permission**, print the worksheet. It should look similar to Figure 52-1.
22. Save and close the file, and exit Excel.

Figure 52-1

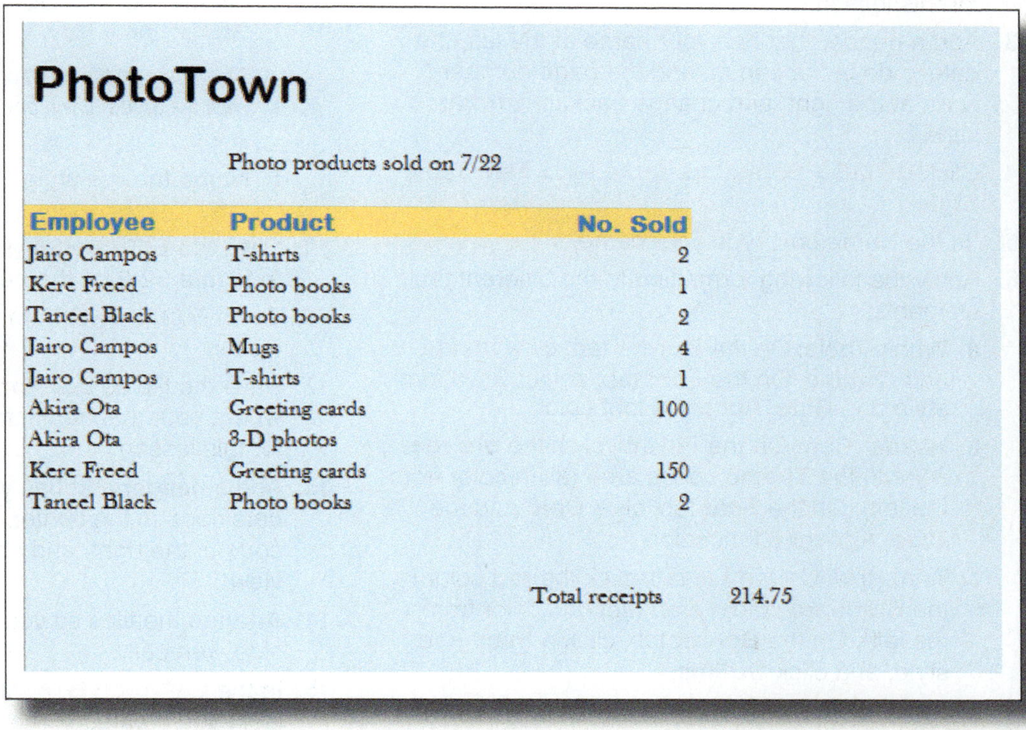

PhotoTown

Photo products sold on 7/22

Employee	Product	No. Sold
Jairo Campos	T-shirts	2
Kere Freed	Photo books	1
Taneel Black	Photo books	2
Jairo Campos	Mugs	4
Jairo Campos	T-shirts	1
Akira Ota	Greeting cards	100
Akira Ota	3-D photos	
Kere Freed	Greeting cards	150
Taneel Black	Photo books	2
	Total receipts	214.75

Excel 2013, Windows 8, Microsoft Corporation

Lesson 52—Apply

PhotoTown corporate headquarters is looking to adopt the worksheet you designed throughout the company. In this project, you will create a custom table style that follows the company publication standards. You will also create a custom cell style and merge the style into another worksheet.

DIRECTIONS

1. Start Excel, if necessary, and open **E52ApplyA** from the data files for this lesson.
2. Save the file as **E52ApplyA_xx** in the location where your teacher instructs you to store the files for this lesson.
3. Add a header that has your name at the left, the date code in the center, and the page number code at the right, and change back to **Normal** view.
4. Click **HOME** > **Format as Table** > **New Table Style**.
5. In the Name box, type your name.
6. Apply the following formatting to the different table elements:
   a. Whole Table: On the **Border** tab, click **Inside** and **Outline**. On the **Font** tab, select **Bold** font style and **Blue, Accent 1** font color.
   b. Header Row: On the **Fill** tab, click the **orange** color in the **Theme** colors area (sixth color from the left). On the **Font** tab, click **Bold** and the **Blue, Accent 5** font color.
   c. Total Row: On the **Fill** tab, click the **red** color in the **Standard** colors area (second color from the left). On the **Border** tab, click a **thick line** style, and click **Outline**.
   d. Second Row Stripe: On the **Fill** tab, click the **light gray** color in the **Theme** colors area (third color from the left).
   e. Last Column: On the **Fill** tab, click the **blue-gray** color in the **Theme** colors area (fourth color from the left). On the **Font** tab, click **Bold**.
7. Select the cell range **A5:E14**, and format this range as a table with your new table style.
8. Click TABLE TOOLS DESIGN, verify that the **Header Row** and **Banded Rows** options are checked, and click to select the **Total Row** and **Last Column** check boxes.
9. Create a new cell style:
   a. Click the cell range **A1:B1**.
   b. Format the cell with a **Black, Text 1** fill color, **White, Background 1** font color, and a **28 pt** font size.
   c. On the TABLE TOOLS DESIGN tab, click **Cell Styles** > **New Cell Style**.
   ✓ *Depending on the width of your screen, you may need to click the Styles dialog box launcher to display the cell styles.*
   d. Name the cell style **PhotoTown Title**, and click **OK**.
10. Save the **E52ApplyA_xx** file. It should look similar to Figure 52-2 on the next page.
11. Open **E52ApplyB** from the data files for this lesson.
12. Save the file as **E52ApplyB_xx** in the location where your teacher instructs you to store the files for this lesson.
13. Add a header that has your name at the left, the date code in the center, and the page number code at the right, and change back to **Normal** view.
14. Arrange the files so you can view them side by side, vertically.
15. In the **E52ApplyB_xx** file, merge the custom cell style you created in the **E52ApplyA_xx** file.
    a. In the **E52ApplyB_xx** file, click **HOME** > **Cell Styles** > **Merge Styles**.
    b. In the **Merge styles from** box, click **E52ApplyA_xx.xlsx** > **OK**.
16. In the **E52ApplyB_xx** file, apply the **PhotoTown Title** cell style to the cell range **A1:B1**.
17. Save the **E52ApplyB_xx** file. It should look similar to Figure 52-3 on the next page.
18. **With your teacher's permission**, print both worksheets.
19. Save and close both files, and exit Excel.

Figure 52-2

PhotoTown

Photo products sold on 7/22

Employee	Product	No. Sold	Cost per Item	Total Sales
Akira Ota	T-shirts	2	10	20
Kere Freed	Photo books	1	6.25	6.25
Taneel Black	Photo books	2	6.25	12.5
Jairo Campos	Mugs	4	4	16
Jairo Campos	T-shirts	1	10	10
Akira Ota	Greeting cards	100	0.55	55
Akira Ota	3-D photos	3	2.25	6.75
Kere Freed	Greeting cards	150	0.55	82.5
Jairo Campos	Photo books	2	6.25	12.5
Total				221.5

Figure 52-3

PhotoTown

Photo products sold on 7/23

Employee	Product	No. Sold	Cost per Item	Total Sales
Akira Ota	T-shirts	5	10	50
Kere Freed	Photo books	6	6.25	37.5
Taneel Black	Photo books	8	6.25	50
Jairo Campos	Mugs	0	4	0
Jairo Campos	T-shirts	2	10	20
Akira Ota	Greeting cards	80	0.55	44
Akira Ota	3-D photos	3	2.25	6.75
Kere Freed	Greeting cards	75	0.55	41.25
Jairo Campos	Photo books	2	6.25	12.5
Total				262

Lesson 53

Customizing Data Entry

➤ What You Will Learn
Entering Labels on Multiple Lines
Entering Fractions and Mixed Numbers
Using Form Controls

WORDS TO KNOW

ActiveX
Reusable software components developed by Microsoft.

Form
A document used to collect and organize information.

Format
To apply attributes to cell data to change the appearance of the worksheet.

Form controls
Tools used to create forms.

Line break
A code inserted into text that forces it to display on two different lines.

Software Skills Excel offers a variety of ways to customize data entry. When entering labels, especially long ones, you may want to display them on more than one line so the column will not need to be as wide. Entering fractions requires a special technique so they display properly. You can create a form by inserting form controls on a worksheet to make data entry even easier.

What You Can Do

Entering Labels on Multiple Lines

- If you have long column labels, you can adjust the column width to fit them.
- This doesn't always look pleasing, however, especially when the column label is much longer than the data in the column.
  - For example, the two columns shown here are much larger than their data:
    Unit Number   Total Annual Sales
    2               $125,365.97
- One of the easiest ways to fix this problem is to enter the column label with **line breaks**.
- Entering line breaks between words in a cell enables you to place several lines of text in the same cell, like this next example:

    Unit   Total
    Number   Annual
                  Sales
    2             $125,365.97
- The height of the row adjusts automatically to accommodate the multiple-line column label.
- You can also use the Wrap Text command in the Alignment group of the HOME tab to wrap multiple lines of text within a cell.

Try It! Entering Labels on Multiple Lines

1. Start Excel, and open **E53Try** from the data files for this lesson.
2. Save the file as **E53Try_xx** in the location where your teacher instructs you to store the files for this lesson.
3. Click cell C11, and type **Cases**.
4. Press ALT + ENTER to insert a line break, and type **Ordered**.
5. In cell D11, type **Price per Case**.
6. In cell E11, type **Product Total Sales**.
7. Click cell D11, and on the HOME tab, click Wrap Text.
8. With cell D11 still selected, on the HOME tab, click Format Painter, and click cell E11.
9. Click cell D11, in the formula bar, place the insertion point after Price, press ALT + ENTER, and press ENTER.
10. Save the changes to the file, and leave it open to use in the next Try It.

Enter a line break within a cell

		Sales Tracker			
	Date:	9/21/2017			
	Customer:	3829992			
	Salesperson:	Alice Harper			
			Cases Ordered	Price per Case	Product Total Sales
	Chew Toys, asst.			$ 18.75	$ -
	Med. Bonie			$ 53.00	$ -
	Leash			$ 190.00	$ -
	Puppy Food			$ 24.50	$ -
				Grand Total	$ -

Entering Fractions and Mixed Numbers

- If you type the value 1/3 into a cell with a General number format, Excel formats it as a date (in this case, January 3).
- To enter a fraction, you must precede it with a zero (0) and a space, which tells Excel that the data is a number. For example, to enter 1/3, type 0 1/3.
- When Excel recognizes the data as a fraction, it applies the Fraction number format to the cell.
- A fraction appears as a decimal value in the Formula bar. The fraction 1/3 appears as 0.333333333333333 in the Formula bar.
- When entering a mixed number (a number and a fraction), simply type it. For example, type 4, a space, and the fraction 1/2 to result in 4 1/2.
- You can **format** existing data to look like fractions using the Format Cells command.

> **Try It!** **Entering Fractions and Mixed Numbers**

1. In the **E53Try_xx** file, click cell C12 and type **0**, press SPACEBAR, type **3/4**, and press ENTER.
2. In cell C13, type **0 1/2**, and press ENTER.
3. In cell C14, type **1 1/8**, and press ENTER.
4. In cell C15 type **5 1/2**, and press ENTER.
5. Save the changes to the file, and leave it open to use in the next Try It.

Entering fractions and mixed numbers

Date:	9/21/2017		
Customer:	3829992		
Salesperson:	Alice Harper		
	Cases Ordered	Price per Case	Product Total Sales
Chew Toys, asst.	3/4	$ 18.75	$ 14.06
Med. Bonie	1/2	$ 53.00	$ 26.50
Leash	1 1/8	$ 190.00	$ 213.75
Puppy Food	5 1/2	$ 24.50	$ 134.75
		Grand Total	$ 389.06

Using Form Controls

- You can insert **form controls** in a worksheet to create a **form** for collecting information that can be stored and analyzed.
- For example, a human resources department might use a form to collect and store employee information.
- Use the commands in the Controls group on the DEVELOPER tab of the Ribbon to insert form controls.
    ✓ Recall that the DEVELOPER tab does not display by default; you must use the Excel Options to make it available.
- Available form controls include the following:
  - Button: Performs an action, such as a running macro.
  - Combo box: Also known as a drop-down list box. You can type an entry or choose one item from the list.
  - Check box: Turns a value on or off. A check box can be selected (turned on), cleared (turned off), or mixed (allow multiple selection).
  - Spin button: Increases or decreases a value, such as a number increment, time, or date. You can also type a value directly into the cell.
  - List box: Displays a list of one or more text items from which a user can choose.
  - Option button: Allows a single choice in a set of mutually exclusive choices. An option button can be selected (turned on), cleared (turned off), or mixed (allow multiple selection). An option button is also referred to as a radio button.
  - Group box: Groups related controls into a rectangle and can include a label.
  - Label: Descriptive text (such as titles, captions, pictures) or brief instructions.
  - Scroll bar: Scrolls through a range of values.
- Some form controls are disabled by default. You can enable them by changing the **ActiveX** Settings in the Trust Center Settings on the Trust Center tab in the Excel Options; however, this may allow potentially dangerous controls to run on your computer.
    ✓ If you need additional controls or more flexibility than form controls allow, you can insert ActiveX controls using the commands in the Controls group on the DEVELOPER tab of the Ribbon.
- Consider the form layout and the order of the form controls when inserting form controls.
- The insertion point moves from control to control based on the order in which controls are inserted in the document, not based on the order in which the controls are arranged.

Business Information Management II | Excel | Chapter 6   325

Try It! Using Form Controls

1. In the **E53Try_xx** file, click cell C9, and on the HOME tab, in the Editing group, click Clear ⬇ Clear ▾ > Clear All.

2. Click FILE > Options > Customize Ribbon.

3. Under Customize the Ribbon, click to select the Developer check box, and click OK. The DEVELOPER tab displays on the Ribbon.

4. Click DEVELOPER.

5. In the Controls group, click Insert, and click the Combo Box form control button.

6. Position the insertion point at the top edge of cell C9.

   ✓ *The insertion pointer changes to a crosshair symbol* +.

7. Click and drag the crosshair insertion pointer across the cell range C9:D9, and release the mouse button.

8. Click the New Sheet button ⊕ to create a new sheet.

9. On Sheet1, click cell A1, type **Alice Harper**, and press ENTER.

10. Click cell A2, type **Greg Bimmel**, and press ENTER.

11. Click cell A3, type **Lucinda Diego**, and press ENTER.

12. Click the Sales Tracker tab, right-click the list box form control, and click Format Control. The Format Control dialog box displays.

13. On the Control tab, click in the Input range text box, click Sheet2, and select the cell range A1:A3.

14. Click OK.

15. Click the combo box drop-down arrow, and click Greg Bimmel.

16. Save and close the file, and exit Excel.

Form controls on the DEVELOPER tab

Pete's Pets
214 North Place Street, Cumberland, OH 43732

Sales Tracker

Date:	9/21/2017				
Customer:	3829992				
Salesperson:	Greg Bimmel ▼				
	Alice Harper				
	Greg Bimmel			Product	
	Lucinda Diego	Ordered	per Case	Total Sales	
Chew Toys, asst.		3/4	$ 18.75	$ 14.06	
Med. Bonie		1/2	$ 53.00	$ 26.50	
Leash		1 1/8	$ 190.00	$ 213.75	
Puppy Food		5 1/2	$ 24.50	$ 134.75	
		Grand Total	$	389.06	

Excel 2013, Windows 8, Microsoft Corporation

Lesson 53—Practice

As assistant manager for a local PhotoTown store, you have been asked to create a weekly payroll tracker. In this project, you will use line breaks and text wrapping to make the worksheet visually appealing and easy to read.

DIRECTIONS

1. Start Excel, if necessary, and open **E53Practice** from the data files for this lesson.
2. Save the file as **E53Practice_xx** in the location where your teacher instructs you to store the files for this lesson.
3. Add a header that has your name at the left, the date code in the center, and the page number code at the right, and change back to **Normal** view.
4. In cell **E6**, type **Hourly**, press ALT + ENTER, type **Rate**, and press ENTER.
5. In cell **D6**, type **Regular Weekly Hours**, and press ENTER.
6. In cell **C6**, type **Full or Part Time**, and press ENTER.
7. Select the cell range **C6:E6**, and on the HOME tab, click **Center**.
8. Select cell **C6** > **Wrap Text**.
9. On the HOME tab, click **Format Painter**, and click cell **D6**.
10. Select cell **C6**, and click in the formula bar. Move the insertion point to just before the **P**, press ALT, and press ENTER.
11. Click cell **G24**, type **Weekly Payroll** and press ENTER.
12. Click cell **G24** > **Align Right**.
13. **With your teacher's permission**, print the worksheet. It should look similar to Figure 53-1.
14. Save and close the file, and exit Excel.

Figure 53-1

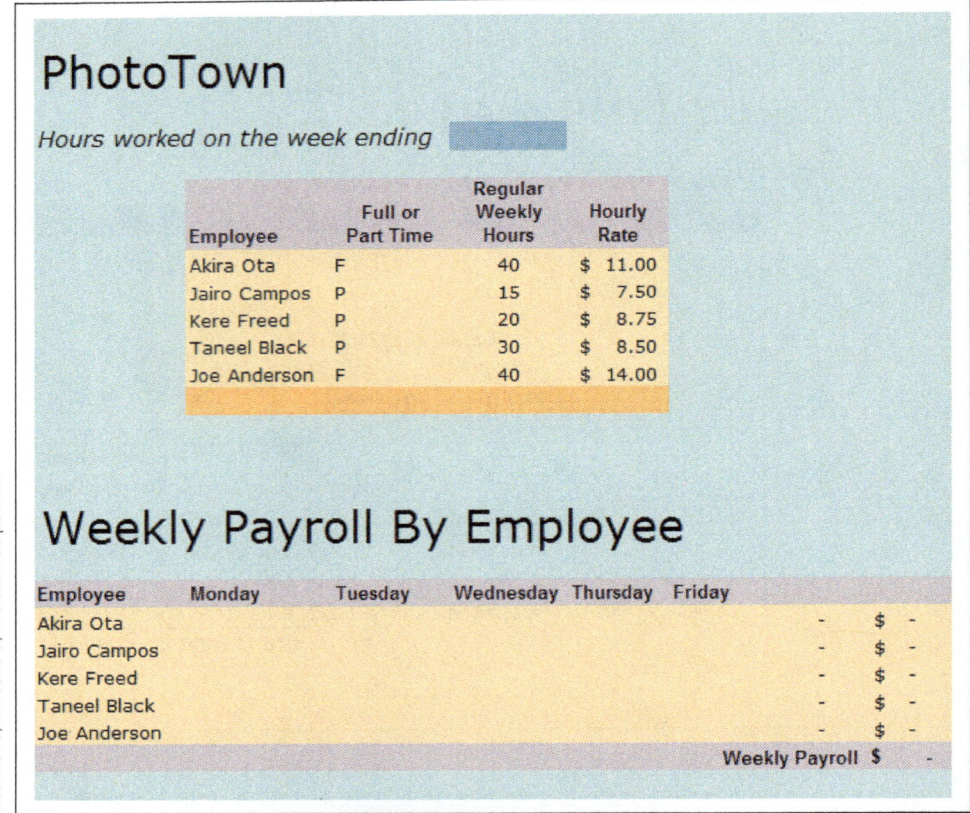

PhotoTown

Hours worked on the week ending

Employee	Full or Part Time	Regular Weekly Hours	Hourly Rate
Akira Ota	F	40	$ 11.00
Jairo Campos	P	15	$ 7.50
Kere Freed	P	20	$ 8.75
Taneel Black	P	30	$ 8.50
Joe Anderson	F	40	$ 14.00

Weekly Payroll By Employee

Employee	Monday	Tuesday	Wednesday	Thursday	Friday		
Akira Ota						-	$ -
Jairo Campos						-	$ -
Kere Freed						-	$ -
Taneel Black						-	$ -
Joe Anderson						-	$ -
					Weekly Payroll	$	-

Excel 2013, Windows 8, Microsoft Corporation

Business Information Management II | Excel | Chapter 6

Lesson 53—Apply

As assistant manager for a local PhotoTown store, you have created a weekly payroll tracker. In this project, you will calculate the total weekly hours worked for each clerk and insert a form control.

DIRECTIONS

1. Start Excel, if necessary, open **E53Apply** from the data files for this lesson.
2. Save the file as **E53Apply_xx** in the location where your teacher instructs you to store the files for this lesson.
3. Add a header that has your name at the left, the date code in the center, and the page number code at the right, and change back to **Normal** view.
4. In cell **G18**, type **Total Hours This Week**, and press ENTER.
5. In cell **H18**, type **Weekly Income**, and press ENTER.
6. Select cells **G18:H18** > **Wrap Text**.
7. Change the column width for column G to **11**, and adjust the row height for row 18.
8. In cell **D4**, enter the fraction **8/15**, and press ENTER. Notice that Excel autmatically interprets the fraction as a date.
9. Enter the following hours for the employees:

Employee	Day	Hours
Kere Freed	Monday	3/4
Taneel Black	Tuesday	4 1/2
Taneel Black	Thursday	5 1/2
Joe Anderson	Thursday	6 1/2

   ✓ When entering the Monday hours, remember to type a zero followed by a space before typing the fraction.

10. Click cell **G4** > DEVELOPER > Insert.
11. Click the Check Box form control button.
12. Position the insertion point at the top edge of cell G4, drag the crosshair insertion pointer across the cell range G4:H4, and release the mouse button
14. Right-click the check box form control > **Edit Text**.
15. Replace the existing text label with **Approved by manager**, right-click the check box form control > **Exit Edit Text**.
16. Click outside of the form control, and click the check box of the form control.
19. **With your teacher's permission**, print the worksheet. It should look similar to Figure 53-2 on the next page.
20. Save and close the file, and exit Excel.

Figure 53-2

PhotoTown

Hours worked on the week ending 15-Aug   ☑ Approved by manager

Employee	Full or Part Time	Regular Weekly Hours	Hourly Rate
Akira Ota	F	40	$ 11.00
Jairo Campos	P	15	$ 7.50
Kere Freed	P	20	$ 8.75
Taneel Black	P	30	$ 8.50
Joe Anderson	F	40	$ 14.00

Weekly Payroll By Employee

Employee	Monday	Tuesday	Wednesday	Thursday	Friday	Total Hours This Week	Weekly Income
Akira Ota	8	8	8	8	8	40	$ 440.00
Jairo Campos	3		3		3	9	$ 67.50
Kere Freed	3/4		5	5		11	$ 94.06
Taneel Black	5	4 1/2	5	5 1/2	5	25	$ 212.50
Joe Anderson	5	5	6	6 1/2	8	31	$ 427.00
					Weekly Payroll	$ 1,241.06

Excel 2013, Windows 8, Microsoft Corporation

Lesson 54

Formatting and Replacing Data Using Functions

➤ What You Will Learn

Formatting Text with Functions
Replacing Text with Functions

Software Skills Using a series of simple text functions, such as PROPER, UPPER, and LOWER, you can quickly change text that has been entered incorrectly. For example, with the UPPER function, you can change the text in a cell to all uppercase. You can use the SUBSTITUTE and REPLACE functions to update existing data (such as department names, cost codes, or dates).

WORDS TO KNOW

Case
The use of capital (uppercase) and small letters (lowercase) in text.

What You Can Do

Formatting Text with Functions

- If you enter your own text into a worksheet, chances are that you entered it with the correct **case**. For example, every sentence probably begins with a capital letter.
- If you're using text from another source, however, it may or may not be properly capitalized. Excel provides some functions that might be able to solve such a problem:
  - PROPER (*text*)—Capitalizes the first letter at the beginning of each word, plus any letters that follow any character that is not a letter, such as a number or a punctuation mark.
  - UPPER (*text*)—Changes all letters to uppercase.
  - LOWER (*text*)—Changes all letters to lowercase.

Try It! Formatting Text Using the PROPER Function

1. Start Excel, and open **E54Try** from the data files for this lesson.
2. Save the file as **E54Try_xx** in the location where your teacher instructs you to store the files for this lesson.
3. Click cell C33.
4. Click FORMULAS > Text.
5. Click PROPER. The Function Arguments dialog box displays.
6. In the Text box, type **C12** (the source data).
7. Click OK.
8. Save the changes to the file, and leave it open to use in the next Try It.

The Text function in the Functions Library

Excel 2013, Windows 8, Microsoft Corporation

Try It! Formatting Text Using the UPPER Function

1. In the **E54Try_xx** file, select cell D28.
2. Click FORMULAS > Text ⓐ.
3. Click UPPER.
4. In the Text box, type **D7** (the source data).
5. Click OK.
6. Save the changes to the file, and leave it open to use in the next Try It.

The Function Arguments dialog box

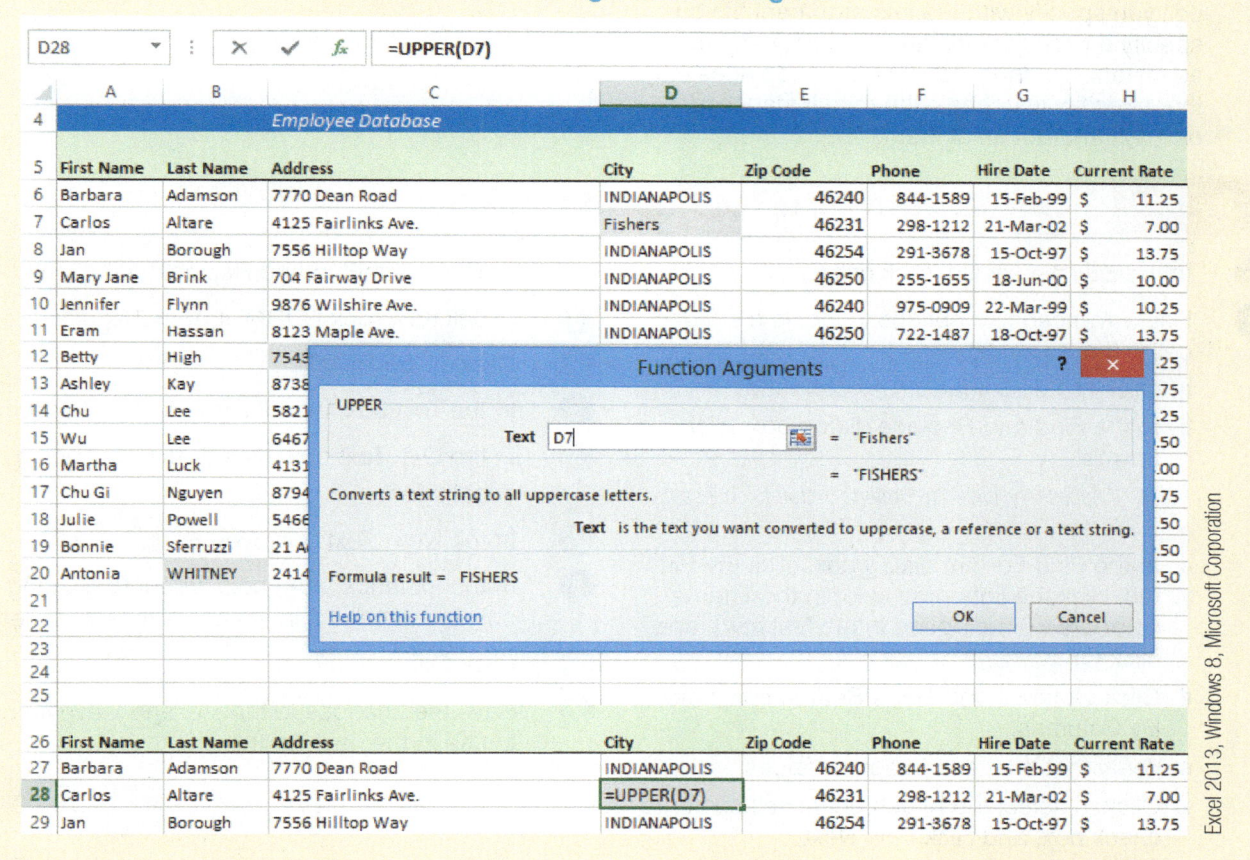

Try It! Formatting Text Using the LOWER Function

1. In the **E54Try_xx** file, select cell B41.
2. Click FORMULAS > Text ⓐ.
3. Click LOWER.
4. In the Text box, type **B20** (the source data).
5. Click OK.
6. Save the changes to the file, and leave it open to use in the next Try It.

Replacing Text with Functions

- Sometimes, all an old worksheet needs in order to be useful again is an update.
- One way in which you can update data (such as department names, cost codes, or dates) is to substitute good text for the outdated text.
  - SUBSTITUTE (*text, old_text, new_text, instance_num*)—Replaces *old_text* with *new_text* in the cell you specify with the text argument. If you specify a particular *instance* of *old_text*, such as instance 3, then SUBSTITUTE replaces only that specific instance—the third instance—of *old_text* and not all of them.
  - REPLACE (*old_text, start_num, num_chars, new_text*)—Replaces *old_text* with *new_text*, beginning at the position (*start_num*) you specify. The argument *num_chars* tells Excel how many characters to replace. This allows you to replace 4 characters with only 2 if you want.

Try It! Changing Text Using the SUBSTITUTE Function

1. In the **E54Try_xx** file, click cell E7.
2. Use advanced find options to locate a shaded cell without any data:
   a. Click HOME > Find & Select > Find.
   b. In the Find and Replace dialog box, click Format.
      ✓ If necessary, click the Options button to access the Format feature.
   c. In the Find Format dialog box, click the Fill tab, click the light gray color in the Theme color area (third option in the first row), and click OK.
   d. Click Options, and in the Search box, select By Columns.
   e. Verify that the Look in box is Values.
   f. Click to select the Match entire cell contents check box, and click Find Next.
   g. Close the Find and Replace dialog box.
3. In cell K27, click FORMULAS > Text.
4. Click SUBSTITUTE.
5. In the Text box, type **K6** (the source data).
6. In the Old_Text box, type **2** (the item being substituted).
7. In the New_Text box, type **6**.
8. In the Instance_num box, type **2** (indicating that only the second 2 in the cell will be changed).
9. Click OK.
10. Save the changes to the file, and leave it open to use in the next Try It.

The Function Arguments dialog box for the SUSTITUTE function

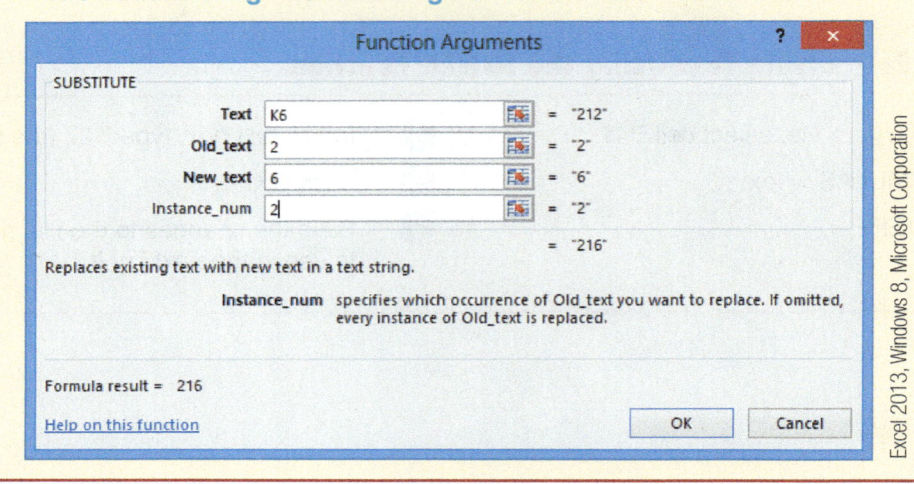

Business Information Management II | Excel | Chapter 6

Try It! Changing Text Using the REPLACE Function

1. In the **E54Try_xx** file, select cell Q27.
2. Click **FORMULAS** > **Text**.
3. Click **REPLACE**.
4. In the Old Text box, type **P27** (the source data).
5. In the Start_num box, type **4** (to indicate that the change should begin at the fourth digit from the left).
6. In the Num_chars box, type **2** (to indicate that 2 digits should be changed).
7. In the New_text box, type **50** (indicating that the Adjusted Rate should end in .50).
8. Click **OK**.
9. Save and close the file, and exit Excel.

Lesson 54—Practice

As the new Human Resources Manager for PhotoTown, you've been getting familiar with various worksheets. You notice that the Payroll worksheet needs to be updated with new department numbers. In this project, you will correct the text using Excel's SUBSTITUTE text function to avoid retyping the data.

DIRECTIONS

1. Start Excel, if necessary, and open **E54Practice** from the data files for this lesson.
2. Save the file as **E54Practice_xx** in the location where your teacher instructs you to store the files for this lesson.
3. Insert a new column between columns E and F:
   a. Click the column header for column **F**.
   b. Right-click, and click **Insert**.
4. Click cell **E7**, click at the beginning of the formula bar, type **Old** and a space, and press ENTER.
5. Click cell **F7**, type **New Department Number**, aand press ENTER.
6. Use the SUBSTITUTE text function to change all of the department numbers beginning with a 6 to begin with a 9 instead:
   a. With cell **F8** selected, click **FORMULAS** > **Text** > **SUBSTITUTE**.
   b. In the Text box, type **E8**.
   c. In the Old_text box, type **6**.
   d. In the New_text box, type **9**.
   e. In the Instance_num box, type **1** and click **OK**.
7. Copy the formula down the cell range **F9:F37**:
   a. In cell F8, click **HOME** > **Copy**.
   b. Select the cell range **F9:F37**.
   c. On the **HOME** tab, click the **Paste** drop-down arrow > **Formulas**.
8. Click **INSERT** > **Header & Footer** > **Header** > **Prepared by UserName Today's Date, Page 1**.
9. In PAGE LAYOUT view, in the header, replace the username with your name.
10. **With your teacher's permission**, print the worksheet. It should look similar to Figure 54-1 on the next page.
11. Save and close the file, and exit Excel.

Figure 54-1

Prepared by Firstname Lastname 12/27/2015   Page 1

PhotoTown Employee Listing
Miller Rd
Unit #2166

Employee ID Number	Title	First Name	Last Name	Old Department Number	New Department Number	Department Name	Rate	Soc Sec No.
63778	Mr.	Carlos	Altare	610412pr	910412pr	processing	$6.30	504-12-3131
71335	Mr.	Taneed	Black	218975am	218975am	asst. manager	$7.00	775-15-1315
31524	Mrs.	Jan	Borough	611748qc	911748qc	quality control	$6.50	727-25-6981
18946	Mr.	Shakur	Brown	482178ca	482178ca	cashier	$7.00	505-43-9587
22415	Mr.	Jairo	Campos	614522in	914522in	inker	$7.20	110-56-2897
20965	Mrs.	Rafiquil	Damir	611748qc	911748qc	quality control	$6.15	102-33-5656
64121	Mrs.	Diana	Dogwood	618796so	918796so	special orders	$6.20	821-55-3262
30388	Mrs.	Lucy	Fan	610412pr	910412pr	processing	$6.55	334-25-6959
44185	Mrs.	Jennifer	Flynn	482178ca	482178ca	cashier	$7.00	221-32-9585
32152	Ms.	Katerina	Flynn	271858kc	271858kc	kiosk control	$7.10	107-45-9111
31885	Ms.	Kere	Freed	610412pr	910412pr	processing	$7.10	222-15-9484
33785	Mr.	Eram	Hassan	271858kc	271858kc	kiosk control	$6.85	203-25-6984
55648	Mr.	Tyrell	Johnson	218975am	218975am	asst. manager	$6.50	468-25-9684
60219	Ms.	Verna	Latinz	611748qc	911748qc	quality control	$6.30	705-85-6352
28645	Mr.	Wu	Lee	618796so	918796so	special orders	$7.00	255-41-9784
67415	Mr.	Shamir	Lewis	610412pr	910412pr	processing	$7.10	112-42-7897
27995	Mrs.	Maria	Navarro	610412pr	910412pr	processing	$6.30	302-42-8465
32151	Mr.	Tony	Navarro	271858kc	271858kc	kiosk control	$6.35	401-78-9855
28499	Mr.	Chu Gi	Nguyen	611748qc	911748qc	quality control	$6.85	823-55-6487
17564	Mr.	Juan	Nuniez	614522in	914522in	inker	$7.00	208-65-4932
14558	Mr.	Akira	Ota	611748qc	911748qc	quality control	$7.25	285-68-9853
31022	Mrs.	Meghan	Ryan	610412pr	910412pr	processing	$7.00	421-85-6452
41885	Mrs.	Kate	Scott	482178ca	482178ca	cashier	$6.85	489-55-4862
25448	Mr.	Jyoti	Shaw	611748qc	911748qc	quality control	$6.50	389-24-6567
23151	Ms.	Jewel	Vidito	611748qc	911748qc	quality control	$6.55	885-63-7158
37785	Mrs.	Corrine	Walters	618796so	918796so	special orders	$6.65	622-34-8891
58945	Mrs.	Antonia	Whitney	271858kc	271858kc	kiosk control	$6.75	312-86-7141
57445	Mr.	Shale	Wilson	482178ca	482178ca	cashier	$7.00	375-86-3425
36684	Mrs.	Shiree	Wilson	482178ca	482178ca	cashier	$7.10	415-65-6658
55412	Mrs.	Su	Yamaguchi	610412pr	910412pr	processing	$6.30	324-75-8021

Excel 2013, Windows 8, Microsoft Corporation

Lesson 54—Apply

You are the new Human Resources Manager for PhotoTown, and you've been working with various worksheets. It's been brought to your attention that the Payroll worksheet has several text-related problems. In this project, you will correct the text using Excel's text functions.

DIRECTIONS

1. Start Excel, if necessary, and open **E54Apply** from the data files for this lesson,
2. Save the file as **E54Apply_xx** in the location where your teacher instructs you to store the files for this lesson.
3. Add a header that has your name at the left, the date code in the center, and the page number code at the right, and change back to **Normal** view.
4. Insert a new column between columns F and G:
   a. Click the column header for column **G**.
   b. Right-click, and click **Insert**.
5. Use the UPPER text function to capitalize the letters at the end of each new department number:
   a. Click cell **G8** > **FORMULAS** > **Text** > **UPPER**.
   b. In the Text box, type **F8**, and click **OK**.
   c. Drag the fill handle down to copy this formula down the cell range **G9:G37**.
6. Copy the text in cell F7 to G7:
   a. Click cell **F7**.
   b. Drag the fill handle to **G7**.
7. Insert a new column between columns H and I:
   a. Click the column header for column **I**.
   b. Right-click, and click **Insert**.
8. Use the PROPER text function to capitalize the department names using title case in column H:
   a. Click cell **I8** > **FORMULAS** > **Text** > **PROPER**.
   b. In the Text box, type **H8**, and click **OK**.
   c. Drag the fill handle down to copy this formula down the cell range **I9:I37**.
9. Copy the text in cell H7 to I7 using the fill handle method in step 6.
10. Hide columns F and H:
    a. Click the **F** column header, press and hold [CTRL], and click the **H** column header.
    b. Right-click, and click **Hide**.
11. **With your teacher's permission**, print the worksheet. It should look similar to Figure 54-2 on the next page.
12. Save and close the file, and exit Excel.

Figure 54-2

Student Name 12/27/2015 1

PhotoTown Employee Listing
Miller Rd
Unit #2166

Employee ID Number	Title	First Name	Last Name	Old Department Number	New Department Number	Department Name	Rate	Soc Sec No.
63778	Mr.	Carlos	Altare	610412pr	910412PR	Processing	$6.30	504-12-3131
71335	Mr.	Taneed	Black	218975am	218975AM	Asst. Manager	$7.00	775-15-1315
31524	Mrs.	Jan	Borough	611748qc	911748QC	Quality Control	$6.50	727-25-6981
18946	Mr.	Shakur	Brown	482178ca	482178CA	Cashier	$7.00	505-43-9587
22415	Mr.	Jairo	Campos	614522in	914522IN	Inker	$7.20	110-56-2897
20965	Mrs.	Rafiquil	Damir	611748qc	911748QC	Quality Control	$6.15	102-33-5656
64121	Mrs.	Diana	Dogwood	618796so	918796SO	Special Orders	$6.20	821-55-3262
30388	Mrs.	Lucy	Fan	610412pr	910412PR	Processing	$6.55	334-25-6959
44185	Mrs.	Jennifer	Flynn	482178ca	482178CA	Cashier	$7.00	221-32-9585
32152	Ms.	Katerina	Flynn	271858kc	271858KC	Kiosk Control	$7.10	107-45-9111
31885	Ms.	Kere	Freed	610412pr	910412PR	Processing	$7.10	222-15-9484
33785	Mr.	Eram	Hassan	271858kc	271858KC	Kiosk Control	$6.85	203-25-6984
55648	Mr.	Tyrell	Johnson	218975am	218975AM	Asst. Manager	$6.50	468-25-9684
60219	Ms.	Verna	Latinz	611748qc	911748QC	Quality Control	$6.30	705-85-6352
28645	Mr.	Wu	Lee	618796so	918796SO	Special Orders	$7.00	255-41-9784
67415	Mr.	Shamir	Lewis	610412pr	910412PR	Processing	$7.10	112-42-7897
27995	Mrs.	Maria	Navarro	610412pr	910412PR	Processing	$6.30	302-42-8465
32151	Mr.	Tony	Navarro	271858kc	271858KC	Kiosk Control	$6.35	401-78-9855
28499	Mr.	Chu Gi	Nguyen	611748qc	911748QC	Quality Control	$6.85	823-55-6487
17564	Mr.	Juan	Nuniez	614522in	914522IN	Inker	$7.00	208-65-4932
14558	Mr.	Akira	Ota	611748qc	911748QC	Quality Control	$7.25	285-68-9853
31022	Mrs.	Meghan	Ryan	610412pr	910412PR	Processing	$7.00	421-85-6452
41885	Mrs.	Kate	Scott	482178ca	482178CA	Cashier	$6.85	489-55-4862
25448	Mr.	Jyoti	Shaw	611748qc	911748QC	Quality Control	$6.50	389-24-6567
23151	Ms.	Jewel	Vidito	611748qc	911748QC	Quality Control	$6.55	885-63-7158
37785	Mrs.	Corrine	Walters	618796so	918796SO	Special Orders	$6.65	622-34-8891
58945	Mrs.	Antonia	Whitney	271858kc	271858KC	Kiosk Control	$6.75	312-86-7141
57445	Mr.	Shale	Wilson	482178ca	482178CA	Cashier	$7.00	375-86-3425
36684	Mrs.	Shiree	Wilson	482178ca	482178CA	Cashier	$7.10	415-65-6658
55412	Mrs.	Su	Yamaguchi	610412pr	910412PR	Processing	$6.30	324-75-8021

Excel 2013, Windows 8, Microsoft Corporation

Lesson 55

Working with Subtotals

➤ What You Will Learn

Using Go To and Go To Special
Creating Subtotals
Creating Nested Subtotals
Hiding or Displaying Details
Removing Subtotals
Manually Outlining and Adding Subtotals

Software Skills You can use the Go To command to instantly jump to any cell in a worksheet. With the Subtotals feature, you can create automatic totals within the records of a database to help you perform more complex analyses. For example, if the database contains sales records for various stores, you can create totals for each store or each salesperson. Use the Subtotals feature to total numeric data instantly without having to insert rows, create formulas, or copy data.

What You Can Do

Using Go To and Go To Special

- Go To is a feature that allows you to tell Excel the exact address of the cell that you want to be the current active cell.
- Using Go To changes the location of the active cell.
- If your goal is not to locate data, but to find particular kinds of cells quickly and select them, then you need a different kind of Find command—Go To Special.
- Using Go To Special, you can locate cells that contain the following:
  - Comments
  - Constants
  - Formulas
  - Row differences, Column differences
  - Precedents, Dependents
  - Blanks
  - Conditional formats
  - Data validation

WORDS TO KNOW

Database function
A specialized type of function for databases/lists. For example, the DSUM function totals the values in a given range, but only for the database records that match criteria you supply.

Function
A preprogrammed calculation. For example, the SUM function totals the values in a specified range.

Business Information Management II | Excel | Chapter 6

End-of-Chapter Activities

➤ Excel Chapter 6—Critical Thinking

Payroll Calculations

You are the corporate payroll clerk at PhotoTown, and you've been calculating payroll checks manually ever since you were hired a month ago. Now that you're familiar with Excel, you want to use the features you have learned to complete this weekly task more easily.

DIRECTIONS

1. Start Excel, if necessary, and open **ECT06** from the data files for this chapter.
2. Save the file as **ECT06_xx** in the location where your teacher instructs you to store the files for this chapter.
3. Type the following column labels on two lines:
    a. In cell **A7**, type **Check Number**.
    b. In cell **B7**, type **Employee ID Number**.
    c. In cell **E7**, type **Hours Worked**.
    d. Adjust the column widths as needed.
4. Separate the **Name** column into **First Name** and **Last Name**:
    a. Insert a column to the right of column D.
    b. Select the cell range **D8:D37**, click **DATA** > **Text to Columns**.
    c. Click the **Delimited** file type option, if necessary.
    d. Click the **Space** Delimiter option, and deselect the **Tab** Delimiter option.
    e. Format both columns as text, and set the Destination to cell $D$8.
    f. In cell **D7**, type **First Name**, and in cell **E7**, type **Last Name**.
5. Enter the hours everyone has worked as mixed fractions, as shown in Illustration A.
6. Use **Go To** to locate the cell that displays the total cost of the payroll this week:
    a. Click **HOME** > **Find & Select** > **Go To**.
    b. Choose **PayrollTotal** from the list, and click **OK** to select cell **L41**.
7. Enter today's date in cell **H3**, and apply the Short Date format.
8. In the cell range **J2:L2**, insert a group box form control.
    a. Click **DEVELOPER** > **Insert** > **Group Box (Form Control)**.
    b. Draw the group box form control over the cell range **J2:L6**.
    c. Edit the text label to be **Featured Employee**.
9. In the group box form control, in the cell **K3**, insert a label form control.
    a. On the **DEVELOPER** tab, click **Insert** > **Label (Form Control)**.
    b. Draw the label box form control over cell **K3**.
    c. Edit the text label to be **Kere Freed**.
10. Format the cells with the coloring shown in Illustration 6A on the next page.
    a. Fill all cells in the worksheet with the **Gold, Accent 4, Lighter 60%** color.
    b. Fill rows 1–6 with the **Gold, Accent 4, Lighter 40%** color.
    c. Select the cell range **A7:L7**, and use the Cell Styles gallery to apply the **Accent 5** style.
11. Create two custom views:
    a. Save the current settings as a custom view called **Full View**.
    b. Hide columns **C-G**, and create a view named **Payroll Checks**.
    c. **With your teacher's permission**, print the worksheet.
12. View the worksheet using the **Full View** custom view.

13. Click **INSERT** > **Header & Footer**, type your name, and change back to **Normal** view.
14. Set the print area for the cell range **A1:L41**, and adjust the page breaks.
15. **With your teacher's permission**, print the worksheet in **Full View** in landscape orientation. It should look similar to Illustration 6A.
16. Save and close the file, and exit Excel.

Illustration 6A

Student Name

PhotoTown
Miller Rd
Unit #2166

Date 4/22/2017

Featured Employee

Kere Freed

Check Number	Employee ID Number	Title	First Name	Last Name	Hours Worked	Rate	Gross Pay	Fed	SS	State	Net Pay
41289	63778	Mr.	Carlos	Altare	12	$6.30	$75.60	$14.36	$5.86	$4.16	$51.22
41290	31524	Mrs.	Jan	Borough	22	$6.50	$143.00	$27.17	$11.08	$7.87	$96.88
41291	18946	Mr.	Shakur	Brown	40	$7.00	$280.00	$53.20	$21.70	$15.40	$189.70
41292	71335	Mr.	Taneed	Black	38 1/2	$7.00	$269.50	$51.21	$20.89	$14.82	$182.59
41293	22415	Mr.	Jairo	Campos	21 3/4	$7.20	$156.60	$29.75	$12.14	$8.61	$106.10
41294	20965	Mrs.	Rafiquil	Damir	10 1/2	$6.15	$64.58	$12.27	$5.00	$3.55	$43.75
41295	64121	Mrs.	Diana	Dogwood	19 3/4	$6.20	$122.45	$23.27	$9.49	$6.73	$82.96
41296	30388	Mrs.	Lucy	Fan	31 1/4	$6.55	$204.69	$38.89	$15.86	$11.26	$138.68
41297	44185	Mrs.	Jennifer	Flynn	30	$7.00	$210.00	$39.90	$16.28	$11.55	$142.28
41298	32152	Ms.	Katerina	Flynn	30	$7.10	$213.00	$40.47	$16.51	$11.72	$144.31
41299	31885	Ms.	Kere	Freed	32 1/2	$7.10	$230.75	$43.84	$17.88	$12.69	$156.33
41300	33785	Mr.	Eram	Hassan	27 1/2	$6.85	$188.38	$35.79	$14.60	$10.36	$127.62
41301	55648	Mr.	Tyrell	Johnson	22	$6.50	$143.00	$27.17	$11.08	$7.87	$96.88
41302	60219	Ms.	Verna	Latinz	12 1/2	$6.30	$78.75	$14.96	$6.10	$4.33	$53.35
41303	28645	Mr.	Wu	Lee	10 3/4	$7.00	$75.25	$14.30	$5.83	$4.14	$50.98
41304	67415	Mr.	Shamir	Lewis	20	$7.10	$142.00	$26.98	$11.01	$7.81	$96.21
41305	27995	Mrs.	Maria	Navarro	20	$6.30	$126.00	$23.94	$9.77	$6.93	$85.37
41306	32151	Mr.	Tony	Navarro	18 3/4	$6.35	$119.06	$22.62	$9.23	$6.55	$80.66
41307	28499	Mr.	Chu	Nguyen	23 1/2	$6.85	$160.98	$30.59	$12.48	$8.85	$109.06
41308	17564	Mr.	Juan	Nuniez	39 1/4	$7.00	$274.75	$52.20	$21.29	$15.11	$186.14
41309	14558	Mr.	Akira	Ota	14 1/2	$7.25	$105.13	$19.97	$8.15	$5.78	$71.22
41310	31022	Mrs.	Meghan	Ryan	31 3/4	$7.00	$222.25	$42.23	$17.22	$12.22	$150.57
41311	41885	Mrs.	Kate	Scott	23	$6.85	$157.55	$29.93	$12.21	$8.67	$106.74
41312	25448	Mr.	Jyoti	Shaw	32 1/4	$6.50	$209.63	$39.83	$16.25	$11.53	$142.02
41313	23151	Ms.	Jewel	Vidito	35	$6.55	$229.25	$43.56	$17.77	$12.61	$155.32
41314	37785	Mrs.	Corrine	Walters	35 1/2	$6.65	$236.08	$44.85	$18.30	$12.98	$159.94
41315	58945	Mrs.	Antonia	Whitney	21 1/4	$6.75	$143.44	$27.25	$11.12	$7.89	$97.18
41316	57445	Mr.	Shale	Wilson	35 3/4	$7.00	$250.25	$47.55	$19.39	$13.76	$169.54
41317	36684	Mrs.	Shiree	Wilson	39	$7.10	$276.90	$52.61	$21.46	$15.23	$187.60
41318	55412	Mrs.	Su	Yamaguchi	27 1/4	$6.30	$171.68	$32.62	$13.30	$9.44	$116.31

Excel 2013, Windows 8, Microsoft Corporation

Excel Chapter 6—Portfolio Builder

Women and Children First

In American History, your class is studying the *Titanic*. Questions have been raised as to whether the rule of the sea, "women and children first," was followed. You and your classmates hope to analyze the data and come up with an analysis of who was most likely to survive.

DIRECTIONS

1. Start Excel, if necessary, and open **EPB06** from the data files for this chapter.
2. Save the file as **EPB06_xx** in the location where your teacher instructs you to store the files for this chapter.
3. Add a header that has your name at the left, the date code in the center, and the page number code at the right, and change back to **Normal** view.
4. The first thing you notice is that the data is not as readable as it might be. Use **Find & Replace** to replace the numbers with the text: **Yes** and **No**:
    a. Select the cell range **C6:C1318**, and on the HOME tab, click **Find & Select** > **Replace**.
    b. Replace **1** with **Yes**, and **0** with **No**.
    c. Close the Find and Replace dialog box.
5. Next, sort the database into two groups—those who survived and those who did not:
    a. Select the cell range **A5:K1318**, and click **DATA** > **Filter**.
    b. On the DATA tab, click **Sort**, and create a custom sort on the values of the following:

Survived?	**Z to A**
Class	**A to Z**
Sex	**Z to A**
Age	**Smallest to largest**

6. Add subtotals that count the survivors (or non-survivors):
    a. Create an initial subtotal based on count of the records based on **Survived?**. Add a page break between groups.
    b. Create a nested subtotal that calculates the average age based on **Class**. Do not add a page break between groups.
    c. Add another nested subtotal that counts the number of survivors (or non-survivors) by sex.
7. Use the outline controls to display only the totals, and adjust the column widths as needed to display data. **With your teacher's permission**, set the print area, and print the worksheet in landscape orientation on one page.
8. Redisplay all data and remove the subtotals.
9. Set up criteria ranges to do some further analysis on the survivors, as shown in Illustration 6B. In order to determine how many children survived, you will need to separate children from the total male and female survivors.
    a. First, create a criteria range that identifies all male survivors who are 18 or younger. Do not apply this criteria range, or any of the others you create.
    b. Next, create a second criteria range that identifies all male survivors.
    c. Repeat steps 9a and 9b to create criteria ranges for females 18 or younger and all females.
    d. Next, create a criteria range that identifies all survivors 18 or younger.

10. Insert the labels shown in Illustration 6B on the next page to identify Total, % of Survivors, % of Total, Male survivors, Female survivors, and Child survivors.

11. You can use the criteria ranges you have already set up as an argument in the **DCOUNT** function to calculate total survivors. To determine the numbers of male and female survivors, subtract males and females who are 18 or younger from the total male and female survivors. Proceed as follows:

    a. In the Total cell for male survivors, type **=DCOUNT($A$5:$K$1318,$A$5**, and select the total male survivor criteria range. Type **)** to end this portion of the formula. To subtract the male children from the total number of male survivors, type a minus sign (-), insert the **DCOUNT** function again, and use the same arguments except use the criteria range for the males **<=18**. If you have set up criteria ranges as shown in Illustration 6B, your formula for male survivors would be:
    =DCOUNT($A$5:$K$1318,$A$5,N7:X8)-DCOUNT($A$5:$K$1318,$A$5,N5:X6).

    b. Repeat this process to identify the adult female survivors.

    c. Use the same function and arguments to count the child survivors. (You do not have to do any subtracting for the child survivors, so **DCOUNT** is used only once in the cell.)

12. Total the number of all survivors in the cell beneath the Child survivors total.

13. Create criteria ranges and formulas similar to those for the survivors to calculate the total non-survivors, as shown in Illustration 6B. Total the non-survivors as you did for the survivors.

14. Now you are ready to perform the final calculations for percentages of survivors and non-survivors:

    a. In the **% of Survivors** cell for male survivors, divide the number of male survivors by the total of all survivors. Format the result as a percent with two decimal places. Copy the formula for the female and child survivors.

    b. Use the same procedure to calculate the percentage of non-survivors for male, female, and child.

    c. To calculate what percent of the total number of passengers were male survivors, divide the total male survivors by the sum of the total survivors and total non-survivors. Format the result as a percent with two decimal places. Copy the formula for female and child survivors.

    d. Use the same procedure to show the percentages of non-survivors for male, female, and child.

15. Adjust the column widths as needed.

16. Set the cell range **N5:X41** as the print area, and adjust the page breaks.

17. **With your teacher's permission**, print the print area.

18. Save and close the file, and exit Excel.

Illustration 6B

	H	I	J	K	L	M	N	O	P	Q	R	S	T	U	V	W	X
4																	
5	Room	Ticket #	Boat	Sex			Order	Class	Survived?	Name	Age	Embarked	Destination	Room	Ticket #	Boat	Sex
6									Yes		<=18						male
7	B-5	24160 L221	4	female			Order	Class	Survived?	Name	Age	Embarked	Destination	Room	Ticket #	Boat	Sex
8	B-18	11136 L L57 19s 7d	2	female					Yes								male
9			9	female			Order	Class	Survived?	Name	Age	Embarked	Destination	Room	Ticket #	Boat	Sex
10			3	female					Yes		<=18						female
11		17608 L262 7s 6d	8	female			Order	Class	Survived?	Name	Age	Embarked	Destination	Room	Ticket #	Boat	Sex
12			4	female					Yes								female
13			6	female													
14		17754 L224 10s 6d	8	female			Order	Class	Survived?	Name	Age	Embarked	Destination	Room	Ticket #	Boat	Sex
15			4	female					Yes		<=18						
16	B-49		7	female							% of Total						
17	C-125	17582 L153 9s 3d	3	female			Male survivors			119	9.06%						
18			5	female			Female survivors			267	59.47%						
19			5	female			Child survivors			63	14.03%						
20			10	female					Total	449	4.80%						
21	D-?	13502 L77	4	female													
22		17608 L262 7s 6d	6	female													
23			5	female													
24																	
25			7	female			Order	Class	Survived?	Name	Age	Embarked	Destination	Room	Ticket #	Boat	Sex
26			5	female					No		<=18						male
27			7	female			Order	Class	Survived?	Name	Age	Embarked	Destination	Room	Ticket #	Boat	Sex
28			10	female					No								male
29			6	female			Order	Class	Survived?	Name	Age	Embarked	Destination	Room	Ticket #	Boat	Sex
30			7	female					No		<=18						female
31			10	female			Order	Class	Survived?	Name	Age	Embarked	Destination	Room	Ticket #	Boat	Sex
32			7	female					No								female
33	C-87		4	female													
34			3	female			Order	Class	Survived?	Name	Age	Embarked	Destination	Room	Ticket #	Boat	Sex
35			6	female					No		<=18						
36			8	female							% of Total						
37			10	female			Male non-survivors			678	51.64%						
38	B-5	24160 L221	2	female			Female non-survivors			142	78.47%						
39	C-7		8	female			Child non-survivors			44	16.44%						
40			5	female					Total	864	10.81%						
41			6	female							5.09%						
42	C-7		8	female							3.35%						

Chapter 7

(Courtesy NAN728/Shutterstock)

Creating Charts, Shapes, and Templates

Lesson 56
Formatting Chart Elements
- Changing Chart Elements
- Setting Data Label Options
- Setting Data Table Options
- Formatting a Data Series

Lesson 57
Formatting the Value Axis
- Creating a Stock Chart
- Modifying the Value Axis
- Formatting Data Markers
- Formatting a Legend
- Adding a Secondary Value Axis to a Chart

Lesson 58
Creating Stacked Area Charts
- Creating a Stacked Area Chart
- Formatting the Chart Floor and Chart Walls
- Displaying Chart Gridlines
- Applying a Chart Layout and Chart Styles

Lesson 59
Working with Sparklines and Trendlines
- Inserting a Line, Column, or Win/Loss Sparkline
- Formatting a Sparkline
- Inserting a Trendline
- Using a Trendline to Predict

Lesson 60
Drawing and Positioning Shapes
- Drawing Shapes
- Resizing, Grouping, Aligning, and Arranging Shapes

Lesson 61
Formatting Shapes
- Formatting Shapes
- Adding Shape Effects

Lesson 62
Enhancing Shapes with Text and Effects
- Adding Text to a Text Box, Callout, or Other Shape
- Adding 3-D Effects
- Rotating Shapes
- Inserting a Screen Capture

Lesson 63
Working with Templates
- Adding a Watermark or Other Graphics
- Formatting the Worksheet Background
- Creating a Workbook Template
- Creating a Chart Template

End-of-Chapter Activities

Lesson 56

Formatting Chart Elements

➤ What You Will Learn

Changing Chart Elements
Setting Data Label Options
Setting Data Table Options
Formatting a Data Series

WORDS TO KNOW

Categories
For most charts, a category is information in a worksheet row. If you select multiple rows of data for a chart, you'll create multiple categories, and these categories will be listed along the x-axis.

Data series
For most charts, a data series is the information in a worksheet column. If you select multiple columns of data for a chart, you'll create multiple data series. Each data series is then represented by its own color bar, line, or column.

Data table
This optional table looks like a small worksheet, and displays the data used to create the chart.

Legend key
Symbol in a legend that identifies the color or pattern of a data series in a chart.

Plot area
The area that holds the data points on a chart.

Software Skills A chart presents complex numerical data in a graphical format. Because a chart tells its story visually, you must make the most of the way your chart looks. There are many ways in which you can enhance a chart; for example, you can add color or pattern to the chart background, and format the value and category axes so that the numbers are easier to understand.

What You Can Do

Changing Chart Elements

- A chart may include some or all of the parts shown in Figure 56-1 on the next page.
- You can format various chart elements such as the data labels, data table, plot area, legend, chart title, axis titles, and the data series.
- As you move your mouse pointer over a chart, the name of the chart element appears in the ScreenTip.
- You can select specific chart elements for formatting from the Current Selection group of the CHART TOOLS LAYOUT tab.
- A chart title describes the purpose of the chart. You can change the font, color, and size of the chart title as with any other text.
- The **plot area** of a chart is the element that holds the data points on a chart. You can change the plot area of the chart by modifying the border color or style, or applying a shadow or pattern to the background. You can also apply 3-D formatting effects to the plot area if a chart has a background.

Business Information Management II | Excel | Chapter 7   355

Figure 56-1

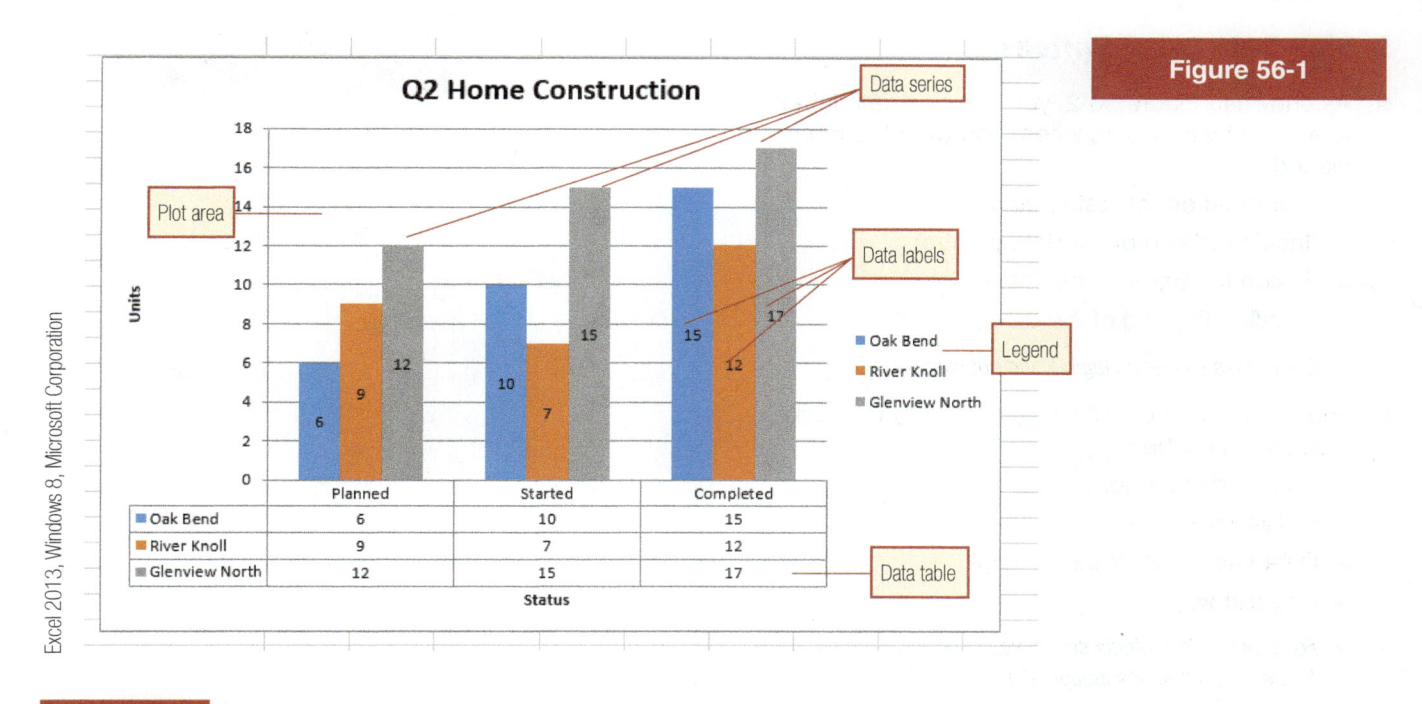

Chart labeled with: Data series, Plot area, Data labels, Legend, Data table. Q2 Home Construction bar chart with Planned, Started, Completed for Oak Bend (6, 10, 15), River Knoll (9, 7, 12), Glenview North (12, 15, 17).

Try It! Changing Chart Elements

1. Start Excel, and open **E56Try** from the data files for this lesson.
2. Save the file as **E56Try_xx** in the location where your teacher instructs you to store the files for this lesson.
3. Click the Country Antiques Q3 Sales Chart tab, if necessary.
4. Click CHART TOOLS DESIGN > Add Chart Element > Chart Title > Above Chart.
5. Type **Third Quarter Sales**, and press ENTER.
6. Move the mouse pointer over the chart, and click when you see the ScreenTip for Plot Area.
7. With the plot area selected, click CHART TOOLS FORMAT, and, in the Current Selection group, click Format Selection to display the Format Plot Area task pane.
8. Click FILL > Gradient fill.
9. Click the Effects button > 3-D FORMAT > Top bevel > Circle.
10. Click Bottom bevel > Circle.
11. In the Lighting group, in the Angle box, type **60**.
12. Close the Format Plot Area task pane.
13. Save the changes to the file, and leave it open to use in the next Try It.

The Format Plot Area task pane

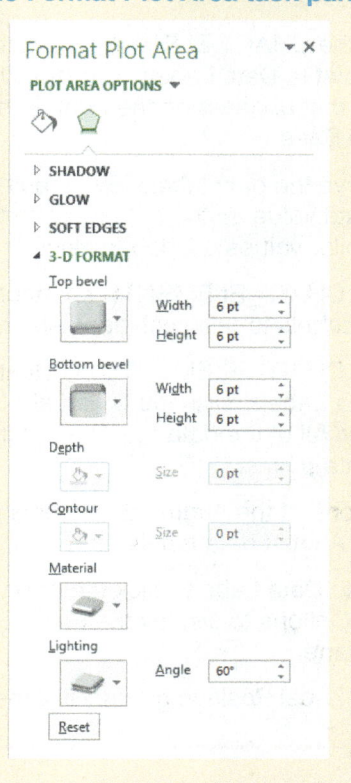

Screenshot of Format Plot Area pane showing PLOT AREA OPTIONS with SHADOW, GLOW, SOFT EDGES, 3-D FORMAT expanded (Top bevel Width 6 pt, Height 6 pt; Bottom bevel Width 6 pt, Height 6 pt; Depth Size 0 pt; Contour Size 0 pt; Material; Lighting Angle 60°; Reset).

Setting Data Label Options

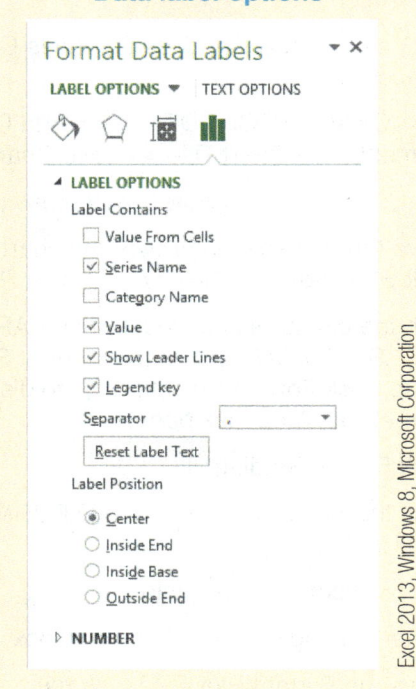

- As shown in Figure 56-2, you can add data labels to a chart by choosing where you want the labels placed:
  - Centered on the data point(s)
  - Inside the end of the data point(s)
  - Inside the base of the data point(s)
  - Outside the end of the data point(s)
  ✓ *Data labels should be legible and not overlap.*

- You can choose exactly what to display in the data label, such as the:
  - Data series name
  - **Category** name
  - Data value and/or percentage
  - **Legend key**
  ✓ *For charts with multiple series, you have to format the data labels for each series independently.*

Figure 56-2

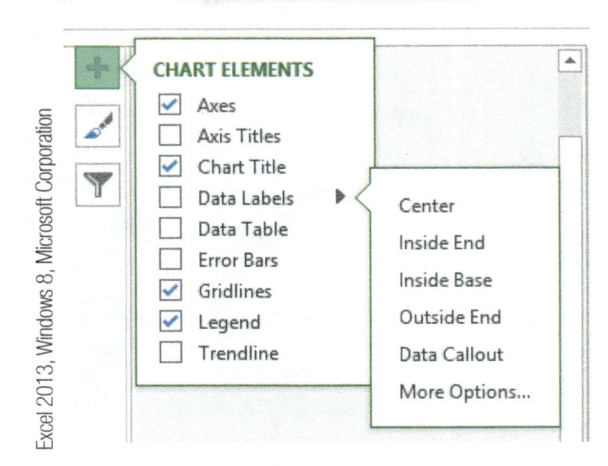

Try It! Setting Data Label Options

1. In the **E56Try_xx** file, select the chart on the Country Antiques Q3 Sales Chart tab, if necessary.

2. Click the CHART ELEMENTS shortcut button ➕, point to Data Labels, click the Data Labels arrow that appears on the right ▶, and click Inside Base.

3. Observe the data labels. By default, Excel uses the data value as the data label. In this instance, the dollar values overlap, making them illegible.

4. In the CHART ELEMENTS shortcut menu, click Data Labels to unselect it and clear the labels.

5. In the CHART ELEMENTS shortcut menu, point to Data Labels, click the Data Labels arrow ▶ > Center. All of the data labels are centered within the data points.

6. Click one of the August data labels to select all of the August data labels.

7. Point to Data Labels, click the arrow ▶, and click More Options to display the Format Data Labels task pane.

8. In the Label Position group, click Inside End.

9. Click one of the September data labels to select all of the September data labels.

Data label options

(continued)

Business Information Management II | Excel | Chapter 7

Try It! Setting Data Label Options (continued)

10. In the Label Contains group, click Series Name.
11. In the Label Contains group, click Legend key.
12. Notice that the gray legend key and the name September appear beside the data value in the data label.
13. Click to unselect Series Name, click to unselect Legend key, click Inside End, and close the Format Data Labels task pane.
14. Save the changes to the file, and leave it open to use in the next Try It.

Setting Data Table Options

- You can add a data table to the bottom of a chart.
- The **data table** looks like a small worksheet, and it lists the data used to create the chart.
- Adding a data table to a chart allows a viewer to easily understand the values plotted on the chart.
- Data tables have only a few basic options beyond normal formatting such as the fill and border colors.
- You can add a border around the cells in the data table—horizontally, vertically, or around the table's outline.
- You can choose whether or not to display the legend keys as part of the table.
- Data table formatting options, such as fill and shadow, are applied to the data inside the cells of the table, not to the table itself.

Try It! Setting Data Table Options

1. In the **E56Try_xx** file, click the chart on the Country Antiques Q3 Sales Chart tab to select it.
2. Click the CHART ELEMENTS shortcut button ➕ > Data Table. A data table appears below the chart with the legend key displayed next to the data series name.
3. Click the CHART ELEMENTS shortcut button ➕, point to Data Table, click the Data Table arrow ▶, and click More Options.
4. In the Format Data Table task pane, click Fill & Line ◇ > FILL > Solid fill.
5. In the FILL group, click Fill Color ▼, and click Orange from the Standard Colors group.
6. In the FILL group, click No fill, and close the Format Data Table task pane.
7. Save the changes to the file, and leave it open to use in the next Try It.

The Format Data Table task pane

Format Data Table
TABLE OPTIONS ▼ | TEXT OPTIONS

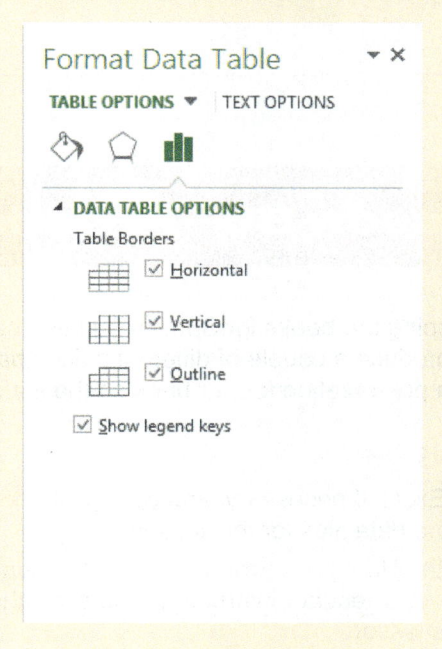

▲ DATA TABLE OPTIONS
Table Borders
☑ Horizontal
☑ Vertical
☑ Outline
☑ Show legend keys

Excel 2013, Windows 8, Microsoft Corporation

Try It! Inserting a Trendline

1. In the **E59TryA_xx** file, select cells D8:G14.
2. Click the INSERT tab > Insert Column Chart > Clustered Column Chart in the 2-D Column group.
3. Drag the chart below the worksheet data.
4. Click the CHART ELEMENTS button + > Trendline.
5. In the Add Trendline dialog box, click September > OK.
6. Click the trendline to select it, right-click, and click Format Trendline.
7. In the Format Trendline task pane, in the TRENDLINE OPTIONS group, click Polynomial.
8. Close the Format Trendline task pane.
9. Save and close the file.
10. Leave Excel open.

Using a Trendline to Predict

- You can use trendlines to chart the trends of a set of data and to project into the future based on the slope of the curve.
- Trendlines can deal with any data over time. Income and expense reports are a good example of this type of data.

Try It! Projecting Income and Expenses with Trendlines

1. Start Excel, and open **E59TryB** from the data files for this lesson.
2. Save the file as **E59TryB_xx** in the location where your teacher instructs you to store the files for this lesson.
3. Select the data range C2:D38.
4. Click INSERT > Insert Line Chart.
5. Under 2-D, click Line. A line chart displays showing the trend.
6. Click the CHART ELEMENTS button +, hover over Trendline, click the Trendline arrow ▶, and click Linear Forecast.
7. In the Add Trendline dialog box, click Income > OK.
8. In the CHART ELEMENTS shortcut menu, hover over Trendline, click the Trendline arrow ▶, and click Linear Forecast.
9. In the Add Trendline dialog box, click Expense > OK.
10. Save and close the file, and exit Excel.

Income and expense trendlines

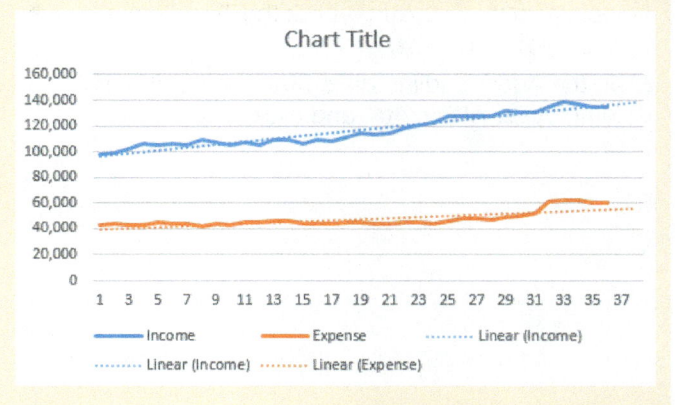

Excel 2013, Windows 8, Microsoft Corporation

Lesson 59—Practice

As the manager of PhotoTown, you are concerned that sales have fallen off lately. You decide to track each individual's gross sales for a week and try to identify a trend. In this project, you will insert a trendline. In addition, you think the employees should be selling more T-shirts than they are, so you decide to track their sales and talk to anyone you feel is underperforming.

DIRECTIONS

1. Start Excel, if necessary, and open **E59Practice** from the data files for this lesson.
2. Save the file as **E59Practice_xx** in the location where your teacher instructs you to store the files for this lesson.
3. Click the **Daily Sales** worksheet tab.
4. Create a scatter chart for employee sales.
   a. Select the cells **A4:G8**.
   b. Click **INSERT** > **Insert Scatter (X, Y) or Bubble Chart**.
   c. In the Scatter group, click **Scatter**.
5. Move the new chart to its own tab.
   a. Click the chart to select it.
   b. On the CHART TOOLS DESIGN tab, in the Location group, click **Move Chart**.
   c. In the New sheet box, type **Employee Sales Chart**, and click **OK**.
6. Click the **Chart Elements** button, hover the pointer over **Trendline**, click the Trendline arrow > **Linear Forecast**.
7. In the Add Trendline dialog box, select the first employee, **Akira Ota**, and click **OK**.
8. Repeat steps 6 and 7 for each of the other three employees.
9. Highlight the data series that is trending upward.
   a. Click the **CHART TOOLS FORMAT** tab, click the **Chart Elements** box Chart Area, **Series "Taneel Black" Trendline 1**.
   b. On the CHART TOOLS FORMAT tab, click the **More** button to display the Shape Styles gallery.
   c. Click **Intense Line – Accent 6** from the gallery.
10. Add a chart title.
    a. On the chart, click the chart title to select it.
    b. Type **PhotoTown Daily Sales by Employee**, and press ENTER.
11. For all worksheets, add a header that has your name at the left, the date code in the center, and the page number code at the right, and change back to **Normal** view.
12. **With your teacher's permission**, print the chart. Your chart should look like Figure 59-2 on the next page.
13. Save and close the file, and exit Excel

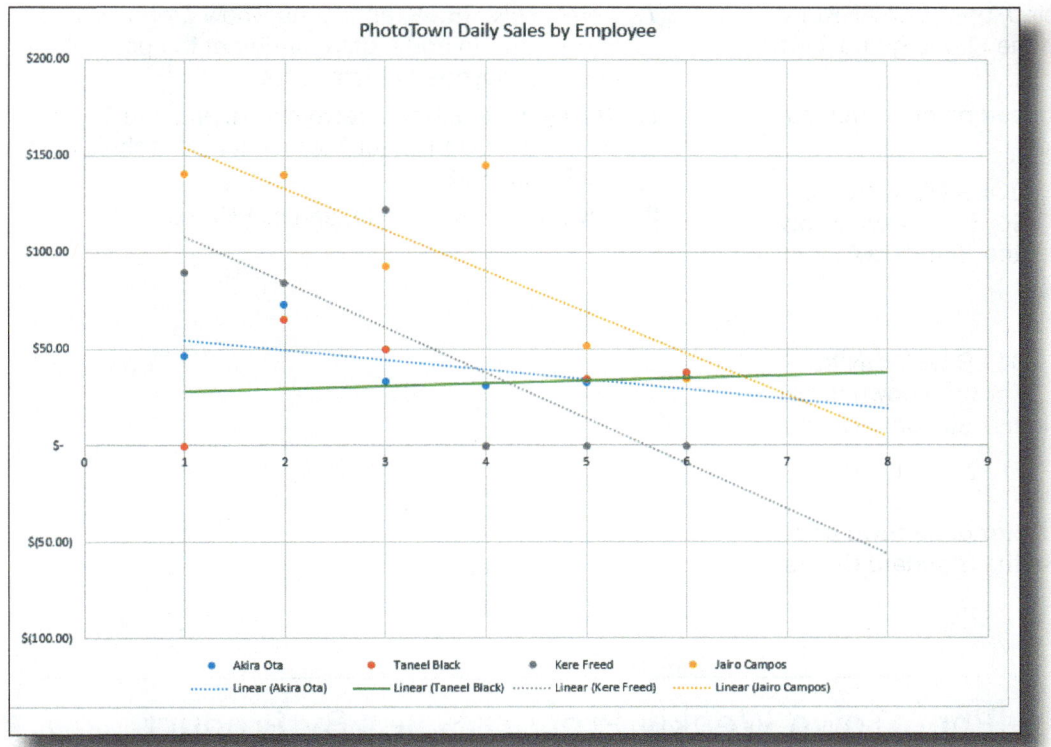

Figure 59-2

PhotoTown Daily Sales by Employee chart with trend lines for Akira Ota, Taneel Black, Kere Freed, and Jairo Campos

Lesson 59—Apply

You are the manager of PhotoTown, and you think the employees should be selling more T-shirts than they are. Because you are concerned that sales have fallen off, you decide to track each individual's gross sales for a week to identify a trend. You need this data so that you can talk to anyone you feel is underperforming. In this project, you will insert a sparkline to track the employees' sales.

DIRECTIONS

1. Start Excel, if necessary, and open **E59Apply** from the data files for this lesson.
2. Save the file as **E59Apply_xx** in the location where your teacher instructs you to store the files for this lesson.
3. Click the **Sales by Product** worksheet tab.
4. Add sparklines to the T-shirt sales.
   a. Click cell **J5** to select it.
   b. Click **INSERT** > **Line** in the Sparklines group.
   c. Select cells **B5:G5** to fill the Data Range box of the Create Sparklines dialog box, and click **OK**.
   d. Drag the AutoFill Handle down to cell **J8**.

5. With the cells still selected, on the SPARKLINE TOOLS DESIGN tab, in the Group group, click **Ungroup**.
6. Format the sparklines based on performance.
   a. Click cell **J5** to select it.
   b. On the SPARKLINE TOOLS DESIGN tab, click the **Sparkline Color** drop-down arrow *Sparkline Color*, and in the Standard Colors palette click **Red**.
   c. Click cell **J6** to select it.
   d. On the SPARKLINE TOOLS DESIGN tab, click the **Sparkline Color** drop-down arrow *Sparkline Color*, and in the Standard Colors palette click **Green**.
   e. Select the cell range **J7:J8**.
   f. Click the **Sparkline Color** drop-down arrow *Sparkline Color*, and in the Standard Colors palette click **Yellow**.
7. Select cells **J5:J8**, and in the Show group click **High Point** to add a data marker at the point of each employee's highest sales.
8. **With your teacher's permission**, print the **Sales by Product** worksheet. Your worksheet should look like Figure 59-3.
9. Save and close the file, and exit Excel.

Figure 59-3

	A	B	C	D	E	F	G	H	I	J
1	PhotoTown Weekly Product Sales By Product									
2										
3	T-shirts									
4	Employee	Monday	Tuesday	Wednesday	Thursday	Friday	Saturday	Price	Receipts	Tracking
5	Akira Ota	2	4	0	1	2	1	$ 10.00	$ 100.00	
6	Taneel Black	0	1	2	0	1	2	$ 10.00	$ 60.00	
7	Kere Freed	4	2	3	0	0	0	$ 10.00	$ 90.00	
8	Jairo Campos	5	10	3	4	2	1	$ 10.00	$ 250.00	
9								Total Receipts	$ 500.00	
11										
12	Photo books									
13	Employee	Monday	Tuesday	Wednesday	Thursday	Friday	Saturday	Price	Receipts	Tracking
14	Akira Ota	1	1	1	1	1	2	$ 6.25	$ 43.75	
15	Taneel Black	0	5	1	0	2	1	$ 6.25	$ 56.25	
16	Kere Freed	1	2	2	0	0	0	$ 6.25	$ 31.25	
17	Jairo Campos	5	1	3	5	2	1	$ 6.25	$ 106.25	
18								Total Receipts	$ 237.50	

Business Information Management II | Excel | Chapter 7

Lesson 60

Drawing and Positioning Shapes

➤ What You Will Learn
Drawing Shapes
Resizing, Grouping, Aligning, and Arranging Shapes

Software Skills After putting all that hard work into designing and entering data for a worksheet, of course you want it to look its best. You already know how to add formatting, color, and borders to a worksheet to enhance its appeal. To make your worksheet stand out from all the rest, you may need to do something "unexpected," such as adding your own art. You can insert predesigned shapes (such as stars or arrows) or combine them to create your own designs.

What You Can Do

Drawing Shapes

- You can use the Shapes button in the Illustration group of the INSERT tab to create many **shapes**.
    - ✓ *Depending on the size of your screen, you may need to click the Illustrations button to access the Shapes button.*
- You can add lines, rectangles, arrows, equation shapes, stars and banners, and callouts as shown in Figure 60-1, on the next page, to highlight important information in your worksheet.
- You can add a text box or a callout—a shape in which you can type your own text.
- A text box or callout, like other shapes, can be placed anywhere on the worksheet.
- The Shapes button presents you with a palette of shapes sorted by category that makes it easy for you to select the shape you want to insert.
- To insert a shape, select the shape, and drag in a cell to create it—no actual drawing skills are needed.
- After inserting a shape, you can format it as needed.

WORDS TO KNOW

Adjustment handle
A yellow diamond-shaped handle that appears with some objects. You can drag this handle to manipulate the shape of the object, such as the width of a wide arrow, or the tip of a callout pointer.

Group
Objects can be grouped together so they can act as a single object. Grouping makes it easier to move or resize a drawing that consists of several objects.

Order
The position of an object with respect to other objects that are layered or in a stack.

Shape
A predesigned object (such as a banner or star) that can be drawn with a single dragging motion.

Sizing handles
Small white circles that appear around the perimeter of the active drawing object. You can resize an object by dragging one of these handles.

Stack
A group of drawing objects layered on top of one another, possibly partially overlapping. Use the Order command to change the position of a selected object within the stack.

- When you insert a shape, the DRAWING TOOLS FORMAT tab displays.
- You can insert more shapes from the Shapes gallery in the Insert Shapes group.

Figure 60-1

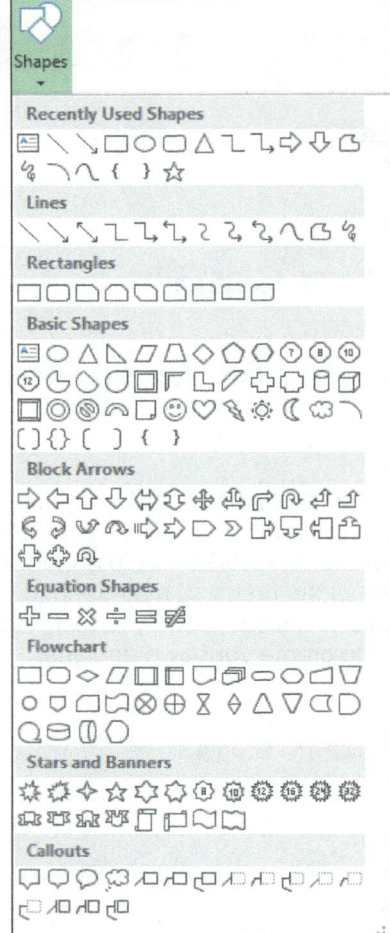

Excel 2013, Windows 8, Microsoft Corporation

Try It! Drawing Shapes

1. Start Excel, and open **E60Try** from the data files for this lesson.
2. Save the file as **E60Try_xx** in the location where your teacher instructs you to store the files for this lesson.
3. Select the P&L sheet, if necessary.
4. Click INSERT > Shapes.
5. In the Rectangles group, click Rounded Rectangle (second item from the left).
6. Click and hold at the upper-left corner of cell F6, drag downward to the lower-right corner of cell J9, and release the pointer.

✓ *All shapes will appear using a default style and color.*

7. On the DRAWING TOOLS FORMAT tab, in the Insert Shapes group, click the More button.
8. In the Rectangles group, click Rectangle.
9. Click and hold at the upper-left corner of cell G14, drag downward to the lower-right corner of cell I16, and release the pointer.
10. Save the changes to the file, and leave it open to use in the next Try It.

Resizing, Grouping, Aligning, and Arranging Shapes

- A shape can also be resized, moved, and copied, like any other object, such as clip art.
  - To resize an object, drag one of the **sizing handles**.
  - To manipulate the shape of an object, drag the **adjustment handle** if one is available with that particular object.
- You can move shapes so that they partially cover other shapes.
  - To move a shape, drag it.
  - To move a shape more precisely, use Snap to Grid. When you drag a shape, it snaps automatically to the closest gridline or half-gridline.
  - The Snap to Shape command is similar, but it snaps a shape to the edge of a nearby shape when you drag the first shape close enough.
- Shapes can be aligned in relation to each other automatically.
  - For example, you might align objects so that their top edges line up.
  - Shapes can be aligned along their left, right, top, or bottom edges.
  - Shapes can also be aligned horizontally through their middles.
- When needed, you can change the **order** of objects that are layered (in a **stack**) so that a particular object appears on top of or behind another object.
- Click an object to select it.
  - Sometimes, selecting one object in a stack is difficult because the objects overlap and even obscure other objects below them in the stack.
  - The Selection task pane makes it easy to select a specific object because all the objects on a worksheet appear in a list. Click an object in the task pane to select it.
  - The Selection task pane also makes it easy to rearrange objects in the stack.
- You can **group** two or more objects together so they act as one object.

Try It!   **Resizing, Grouping, Aligning, and Arranging Shapes**

1. In the **E60Try_xx** file, on the P&L tab, click the rounded rectangle, and drag it into place fitting the area between cells F14 and J17.
2. Select the rectangle and drag it inside the rounded rectangle, as shown in the figure.
3. To draw a third shape, on the DRAWING TOOLS FORMAT tab, in the Insert Shapes group, click the More button.
4. In the Block Arrows group, click Right Arrow, and click anywhere in the worksheet to insert the shape.
5. Move and resize the right arrow shape to fit inside the rounded rectangle, as shown in the figure.
   a. Drag the arrow inside the rounded rectangle.
   b. Drag the center-top sizing handle and the center-bottm sizing handle to stretch the arrow's height to fit just inside the top and bottom border of the rounded rectangle.
6. Click the PAGE LAYOUT tab, and in the Arrange group click Selection Pane to display the Selection task pane.
7. Press and hold CTRL, and click the Right Arrow, Rectangle, and Rounded Rectangle shape names.
8. On the DRAWING TOOLS FORMAT tab, in the Arrange group, click Align > Align Middle.
9. With the shapes still selected, on the DRAWING TOOLS FORMAT tab, in the Arrange group, click Group, and in the drop-down menu click Group.
10. Close the Selection task pane.
11. Save and close the file, and exit Excel.

(continued)

Try It! | **Resizing, Grouping, Aligning, and Arranging Shapes** (continued)

Arranging shapes

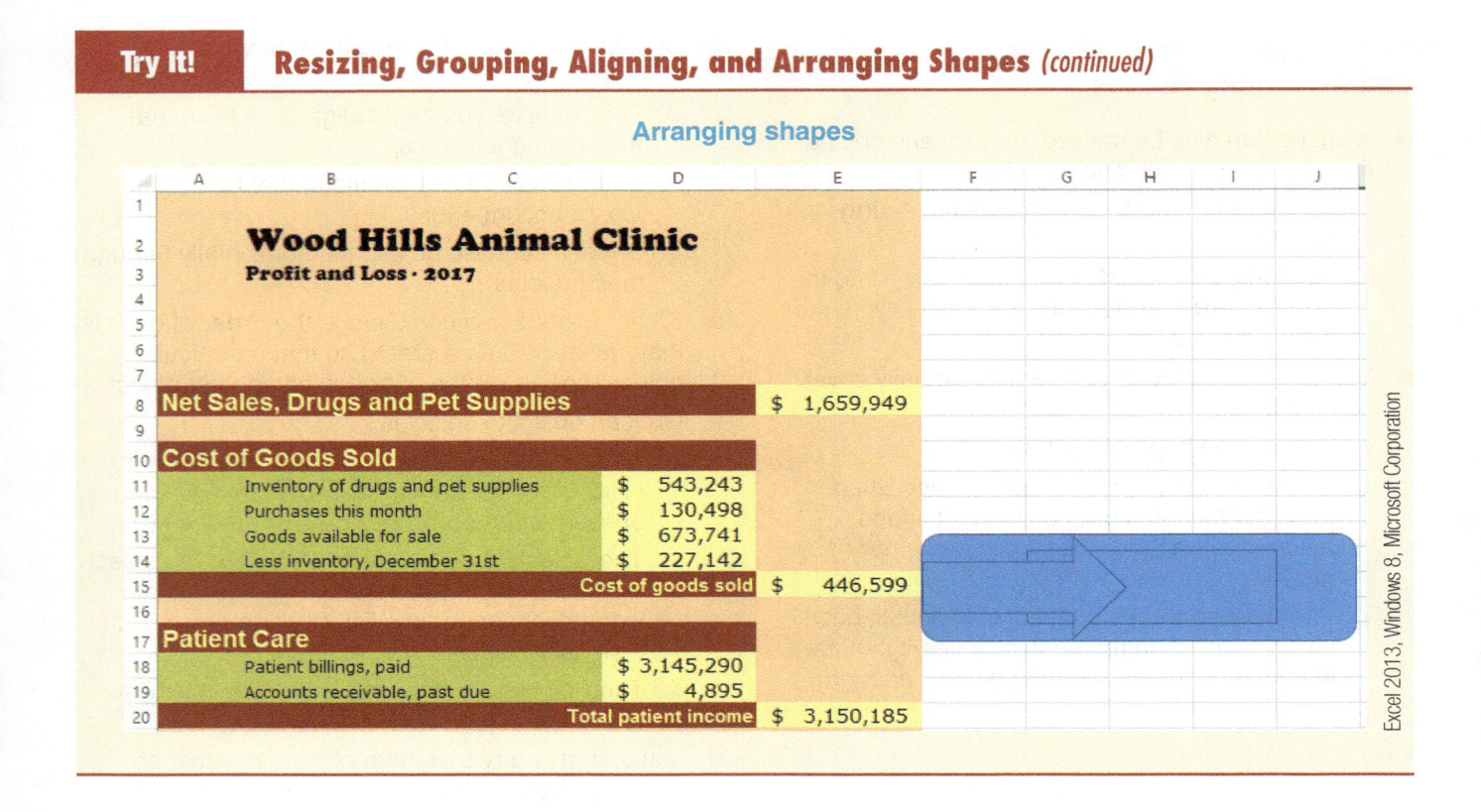

Lesson 60—Practice

You're the accountant at Sydney Crenshaw Realty, and you need to compile a year-to-date spreadsheet showing the total sales and commissions paid. You want to add your company logo. In this project, you will insert, format, arrange, and group shapes to create the company logo.

DIRECTIONS

1. Start Excel, if necessary, and open **E60Practice** from the data files for this lesson.
2. Save the file as **E60Practice_xx** in the location where your teacher instructs you to store the files for this lesson.
3. Add a header that has your name at the left, the date code in the center, and the page number code at the right.
4. Click **PAGE LAYOUT** > **Themes** > **Retrospect**.
5. Click **INSERT** > **Shapes** > **Rectangle** from the Rectangles group.
6. Click and hold at the upper-left corner of cell **B2**, and drag downward and to the right to form a rectangle about the height of the title text.
7. Resize the new rectangle.
   a. On the DRAWING TOOLS FORMAT tab, in the Size group, in the Shape Height box, type **.28**.
   b. On the DRAWING TOOLS FORMAT tab, in the Size group, in the Shape Width box, type **.48**.
8. On the DRAWING TOOLS FORMAT tab, in the Insert Shapes group, click the More button, and in the Basic Shapes group, click **Isosceles Triangle** to add a second shape in cell **B1** about the size of the previously inserted rectangle.

Business Information Management II | Excel | Chapter 7   389

9. Resize the new triangle.
   a. On the DRAWING TOOLS FORMAT tab, in the Size group, in the Shape Height box, type **.22**.
   b. On the DRAWING TOOLS FORMAT tab, in the Size group, in the Shape Width box, type **.48**.
10. Drag the triangle over the top of the rectangle to form the shape of a house.
11. Arrange the house shape.
    a. Press and hold CTRL, click the triangle shape, and click the rectangle shape.
    b. Click **DRAWING TOOLS FORMAT** > **Align** > **Align Center**.
    c. On the DRAWING TOOLS FORMAT tab, click **Group** > **Group**.
    d. Drag the right edge of the "house" even with the right edge of column B.
    e. Align the top edge of the house to just below the column header, as shown in Figure 60-2.
12. Save and close the file, and exit Excel.

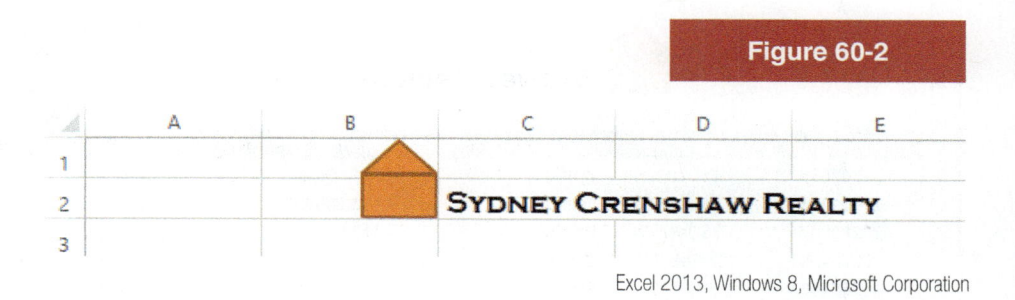

Figure 60-2

Excel 2013, Windows 8, Microsoft Corporation

Lesson 60—Apply

As the accountant at Sydney Crenshaw Realty, you have created a year-to-date spreadsheet showing the total sales and commissions paid. You now want to call attention to some record sales figures. In this project, you will add shapes and format them with color and effects to highlight data in the worksheet.

DIRECTIONS

1. Start Excel, if necessary, and open **E60Apply** from the data files for this lesson.
2. Save the file as **E60Apply_xx** in the location where your teacher instructs you to store the files for this lesson.
3. Add a header that has your name at the left, the date code in the center, and the page number code at the right.
4. Insert a brace that visually groups the data from the month of May:
   a. Click **INSERT** > **Shapes** > **Right Brace** (the last shape in the Basic Shapes group).
   b. Click and hold at the upper-left corner of cell **G21**, and drag downward to the lower-left corner of cell **G23**.
5. Insert an arrow that points to the brace you just inserted:
   a. On the INSERT tab, click **Shapes** > **Left Arrow** (the second arrow in the Block Arrows group).
   b. Click at the upper-left corner of cell **H21**, and drag downward to the lower-right corner of cell **I23**.
6. Align the brace and arrow together.
   a. Drag the arrow closer to the right brace, press and hold CTRL, and select both the left arrow and the right brace.
   b. On the DRAWING TOOLS FORMAT tab, click **Align** > **Align Middle**.
   c. With both shapes still selected, click **Group** > **Group**.

7. Select the **12-Point Star** from the Stars and Banners group.
8. Click at the upper-left corner of the **F1** cell and drag downward to the lower-right corner of the **F3** cell.
9. With the shape still selected, change the shape height to **.76**, and change the shape width to **.93**.
10. **With your teacher's permission**, print the worksheet. Your worksheet should look like Figure 60-3.
11. Save and close the file, and exit Excel.

Figure 60-3

Excel 2013, Windows 8, Microsoft Corporation

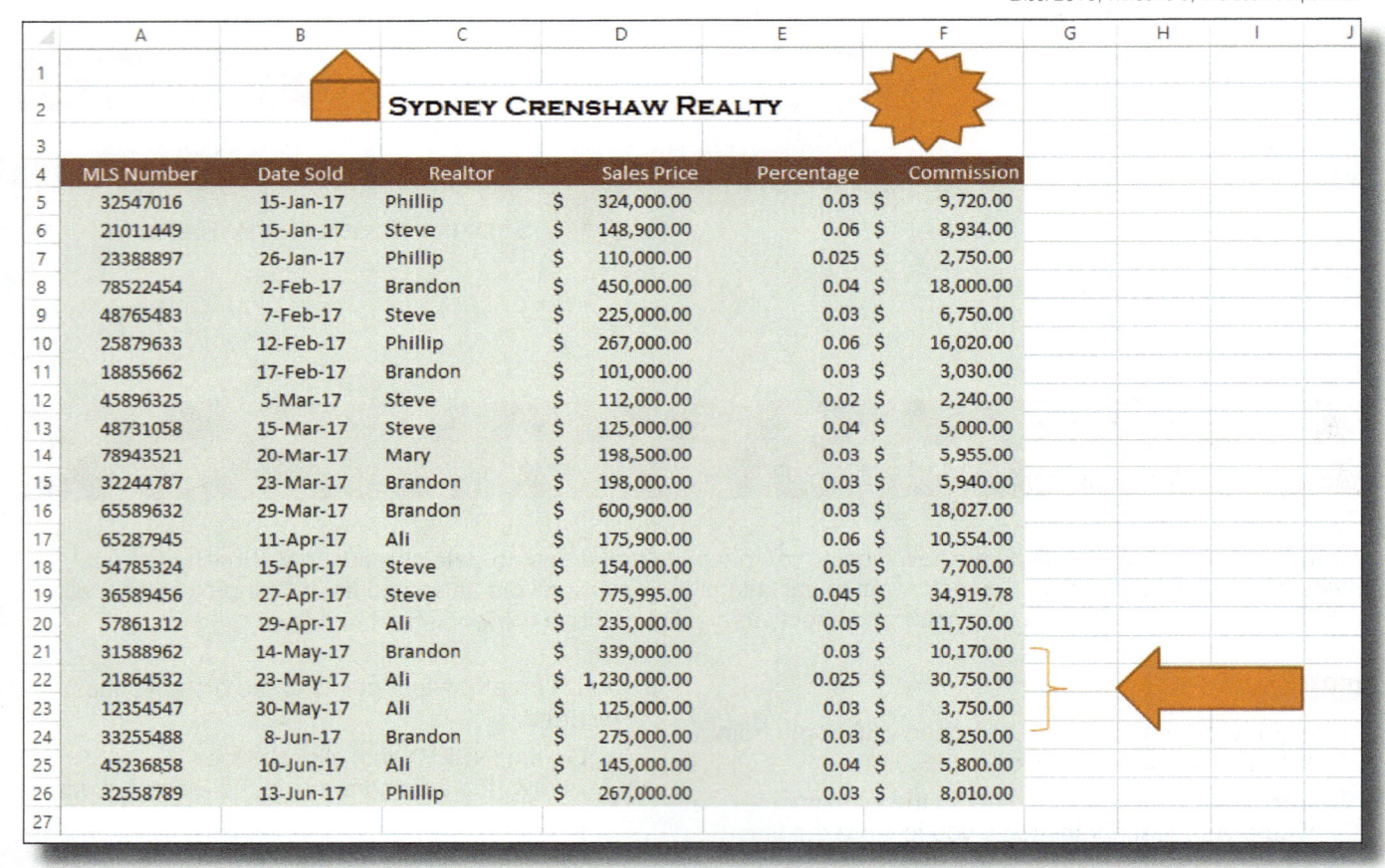

	A	B	C	D	E	F
1						
2			SYDNEY CRENSHAW REALTY			
3						
4	MLS Number	Date Sold	Realtor	Sales Price	Percentage	Commission
5	32547016	15-Jan-17	Phillip	$ 324,000.00	0.03	$ 9,720.00
6	21011449	15-Jan-17	Steve	$ 148,900.00	0.06	$ 8,934.00
7	23388897	26-Jan-17	Phillip	$ 110,000.00	0.025	$ 2,750.00
8	78522454	2-Feb-17	Brandon	$ 450,000.00	0.04	$ 18,000.00
9	48765483	7-Feb-17	Steve	$ 225,000.00	0.03	$ 6,750.00
10	25879633	12-Feb-17	Phillip	$ 267,000.00	0.06	$ 16,020.00
11	18855662	17-Feb-17	Brandon	$ 101,000.00	0.03	$ 3,030.00
12	45896325	5-Mar-17	Steve	$ 112,000.00	0.02	$ 2,240.00
13	48731058	15-Mar-17	Steve	$ 125,000.00	0.04	$ 5,000.00
14	78943521	20-Mar-17	Mary	$ 198,500.00	0.03	$ 5,955.00
15	32244787	23-Mar-17	Brandon	$ 198,000.00	0.03	$ 5,940.00
16	65589632	29-Mar-17	Brandon	$ 600,900.00	0.03	$ 18,027.00
17	65287945	11-Apr-17	Ali	$ 175,900.00	0.06	$ 10,554.00
18	54785324	15-Apr-17	Steve	$ 154,000.00	0.05	$ 7,700.00
19	36589456	27-Apr-17	Steve	$ 775,995.00	0.045	$ 34,919.78
20	57861312	29-Apr-17	Ali	$ 235,000.00	0.05	$ 11,750.00
21	31588962	14-May-17	Brandon	$ 339,000.00	0.03	$ 10,170.00
22	21864532	23-May-17	Ali	$ 1,230,000.00	0.025	$ 30,750.00
23	12354547	30-May-17	Ali	$ 125,000.00	0.03	$ 3,750.00
24	33255488	8-Jun-17	Brandon	$ 275,000.00	0.03	$ 8,250.00
25	45236858	10-Jun-17	Ali	$ 145,000.00	0.04	$ 5,800.00
26	32558789	13-Jun-17	Phillip	$ 267,000.00	0.03	$ 8,010.00
27						

Lesson 61

Formatting Shapes

➤ What You Will Learn
Formatting Shapes
Adding Shape Effects

Software Skills When shapes such as rectangles, block arrows, and banners are added to a worksheet, they originally appear in the default style—a shape with a blue outline filled with the Accent 1 color. You can change both the color and the outline style of any shape. You can also create custom colors. You can also add special effects such as shadows and soft edges.

WORDS TO KNOW

Effects
Special complex-looking formats that can be applied with a single click, such as shadows, reflection, glows, and beveled edges.

What You Can Do

Formatting Shapes

- When a shape is selected, the DRAWING TOOLS FORMAT tab automatically appears on the Ribbon in anticipation of your need to edit it.
- Since all new shapes appear in the default style, you might want to change:
  - Shape Styles: A set of formats that include the outline color and style, edge effects, and fill.
  - Shape Fill: The color, picture, gradient, or texture that fills a shape.
    - ✓ A line shape cannot be filled. A line's color is determined by the Shape Outline settings.
  - Shape Outline: The color, weight, and style of the border that outlines a shape.
    - ✓ You can change the color, weight, and style of a line. You can also add arrows at one or both ends.
  - Shape Effects: Complex formats applied with a single click.
- When changing any color on a shape, either the fill or the outline, you can use the Colors dialog box to create a custom color, and even to add transparency if desired.

Try It! Formatting Shapes

1. Start Excel, and open **E61Try** from the data files for this lesson.
2. Save the file as **E61Try_xx** in the location where your teacher instructs you to store the files for this lesson.
3. Click the P&L worksheet tab > PAGE LAYOUT > Selection Pane.
4. In the Selection task pane, click Rectangle > DRAWING TOOLS FORMAT.
5. In the Shape Styles group, click the Shape Fill drop-down arrow *Shape Fill*, and in the Theme Colors palette click Orange, Accent 2, Lighter 60%.
6. Click the Shape Outline drop-down arrow *Shape Outline*, and in the Standard Colors palette click Dark Red.
7. In the Selection task pane, click Right Arrow.
8. Click the Shape Fill drop-down arrow *Shape Fill* > Gradient > More Gradients.
9. In the FILL group, click Gradient fill.
10. In the Format Shape task pane, click Preset gradients > Bottom Spotlight, Accent 4.
11. In the Type list, click Linear.
12. In the Direction list, click Linear Diagonal - Top Left to Bottom Right (the first option).
13. Click LINE > Outline color > Gold, Accent 4, Darker 25%.
14. In the Selection task pane, click Rounded Rectangle.
15. On the DRAWING TOOLS FORMAT tab, click the Shape Styles More button > Moderate Effect - Orange Accent 2.
16. Close the Selection and Format Shape task panes.
17. Save the changes to the file, and leave it open to use in the next Try It.

The Selection and Format Shape task panes

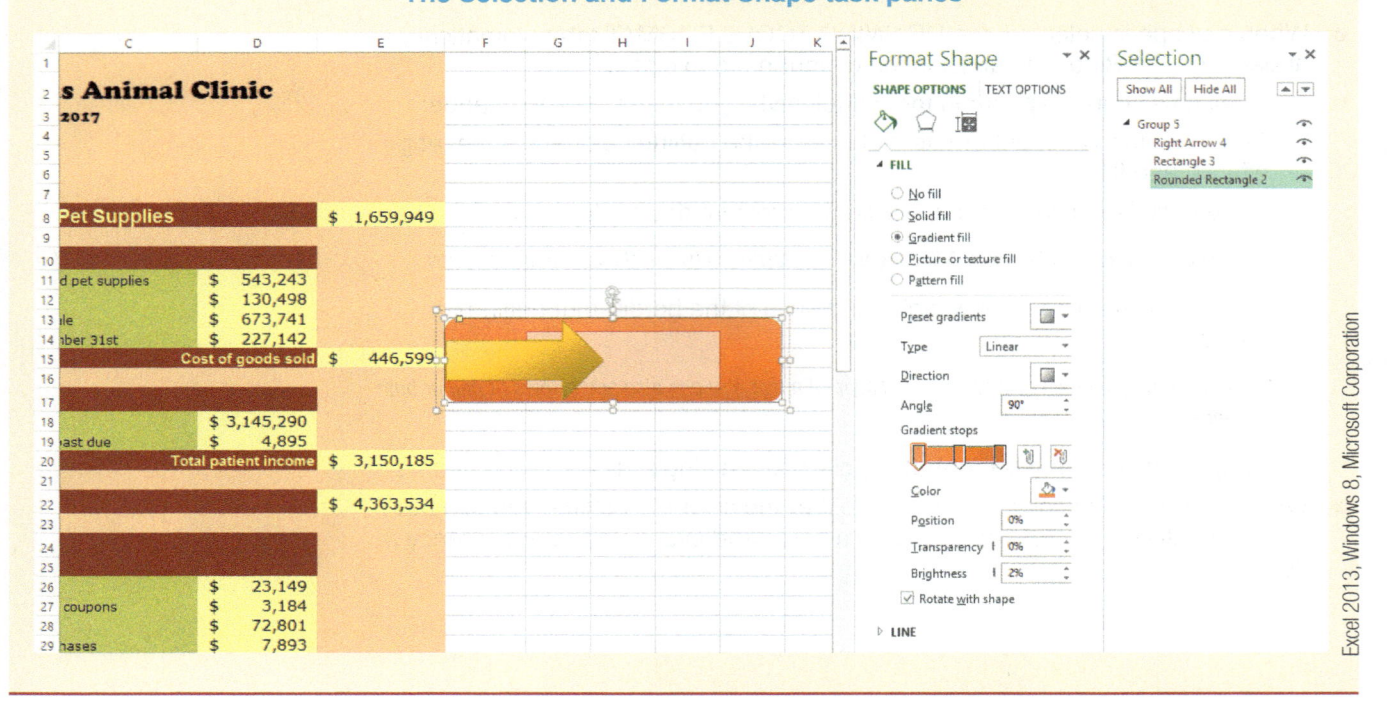

Adding Shape Effects

- Shape **effects** that you can apply to a selected shape include:
  - Shadows
  - Reflections
  - Glows
  - Soft edges
  - Beveled edges
  - 3-D rotations

- Each shape effect style comes with options that allow you to customize the effect to get the look you want.
- The Preset category on the Shape Effects drop-down menu displays a set of common effects, with the options already pre-selected for you.
- Choose one of the Preset effects to change the look of a selected shape.

Try It! Adding Shape Effects

1. In the **E61Try_xx** file, on the P&L tab, click PAGE LAYOUT > Selection Pane.

2. In the Selection task pane, click Rectangle > DRAWING TOOLS FORMAT.

3. In the Shape Styles group, click Shape Effects > Glow > Gold, 8 pt glow, Accent color 4.

4. In the Selection task pane, click Rounded Rectangle and click the DRAWING TOOLS FORMAT tab, if necessary.

5. On the DRAWING TOOLS FORMAT tab, in the Shape Styles group, click Shape Effects > Reflection > Tight Reflection, 4 pt offset.

6. Close the Selection task pane.

7. Save and close the file, and exit Excel.

Lesson 61—Practice

As the accountant for Sydney Crenshaw Realty, you've already created a spreadsheet to track year-to-date sales and commissions with some basic shapes. Now you'd like to format the shapes with some color and dimension.

DIRECTIONS

1. Start Excel, if necessary, and open **E61Practice** from the data files for this lesson.
2. Save the file as **E61Practice_xx** in the location where your teacher instructs you to store the files for this lesson.
3. Add a header that has your name at the left, the date code in the center, and the page number code at the right
4. Click **PAGE LAYOUT** > **Selection Pane**.
5. In the Selection task pane, click **Isosceles Triangle**.
6. Click **DRAWING TOOLS FORMAT**, and click the Shape Styles **More** button to open the gallery.
7. Click **Moderate Effect - Orange, Accent 2**.
8. In the Selection task pane, click **Rectangle**.
9. On the DRAWING TOOLS FORMAT tab, click the Shape Styles **More** button to open the gallery.
10. Click **Moderate Effect - Brown, Accent 3**.
11. On the DRAWING TOOLS FORMAT tab, in the Shape Styles group, click **Shape Effects** > **Reflection**.
12. In the Reflection Variations group, click **Tight Reflection, touching**.
13. Close the Selection task pane.
14. **With your teacher's permission**, print the worksheet. Your worksheet should look like Figure 61-1.
15. Save and close the file, and exit Excel.

Figure 61-1

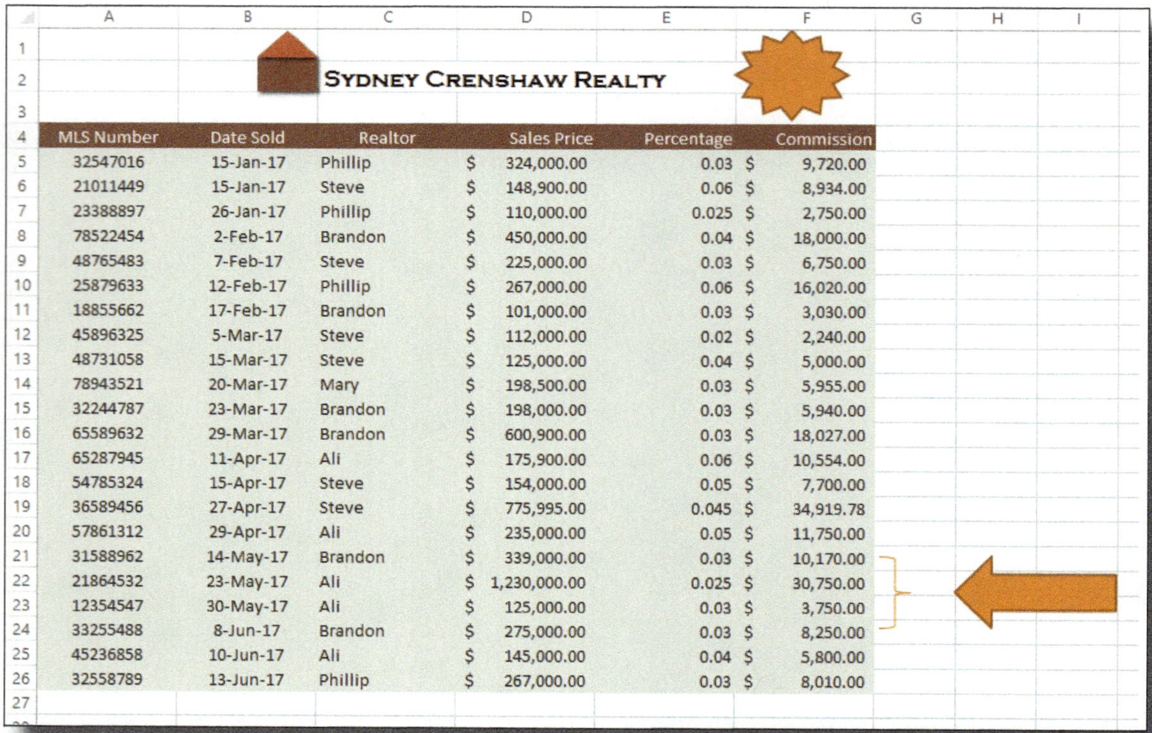

SYDNEY CRENSHAW REALTY

MLS Number	Date Sold	Realtor	Sales Price	Percentage	Commission
32547016	15-Jan-17	Phillip	$ 324,000.00	0.03	$ 9,720.00
21011449	15-Jan-17	Steve	$ 148,900.00	0.06	$ 8,934.00
23388897	26-Jan-17	Phillip	$ 110,000.00	0.025	$ 2,750.00
78522454	2-Feb-17	Brandon	$ 450,000.00	0.04	$ 18,000.00
48765483	7-Feb-17	Steve	$ 225,000.00	0.03	$ 6,750.00
25879633	12-Feb-17	Phillip	$ 267,000.00	0.06	$ 16,020.00
18855662	17-Feb-17	Brandon	$ 101,000.00	0.03	$ 3,030.00
45896325	5-Mar-17	Steve	$ 112,000.00	0.02	$ 2,240.00
48731058	15-Mar-17	Steve	$ 125,000.00	0.04	$ 5,000.00
78943521	20-Mar-17	Mary	$ 198,500.00	0.03	$ 5,955.00
32244787	23-Mar-17	Brandon	$ 198,000.00	0.03	$ 5,940.00
65589632	29-Mar-17	Brandon	$ 600,900.00	0.03	$ 18,027.00
65287945	11-Apr-17	Ali	$ 175,900.00	0.06	$ 10,554.00
54785324	15-Apr-17	Steve	$ 154,000.00	0.05	$ 7,700.00
36589456	27-Apr-17	Steve	$ 775,995.00	0.045	$ 34,919.78
57861312	29-Apr-17	Ali	$ 235,000.00	0.05	$ 11,750.00
31588962	14-May-17	Brandon	$ 339,000.00	0.03	$ 10,170.00
21864532	23-May-17	Ali	$ 1,230,000.00	0.025	$ 30,750.00
12354547	30-May-17	Ali	$ 125,000.00	0.03	$ 3,750.00
33255488	8-Jun-17	Brandon	$ 275,000.00	0.03	$ 8,250.00
45236858	10-Jun-17	Ali	$ 145,000.00	0.04	$ 5,800.00
32558789	13-Jun-17	Phillip	$ 267,000.00	0.03	$ 8,010.00

Lesson 61—Apply

You are working with a spreadsheet of year-to-date sales and commissions for Sydney Crenshaw Realty. You've been enhacing the spreadsheet with basic shapes and formatting. Now you want to format the shapes with color and effects to draw attention to certain data.

DIRECTIONS

1. Start Excel, if necessary, and open **E61Apply** from the data files for this lesson.
2. Save the file as **E61Apply_xx** in the location where your teacher instructs you to store the files for this lesson.
3. Add a header that has your name at the left, the date code in the center, and the page number code at the right
4. Click **PAGE LAYOUT** > **Selection Pane**.
5. In the Selection task pane, click the Group that includes the Left Arrow and the Right Brace.
6. On the DRAWING TOOLS FORMAT tab, click the Shape Styles **More** button to open the gallery, and click **Intense Effect - Orange, Accent 2**.
7. In the Selection pane, select the Right Brace.
8. On the DRAWING TOOLS FORMAT tab, click the Shape Styles **More** button to open the gallery, and click **Subtle Line - Accent 3**.
9. In the Selection task pane, click the **12-Point Star**.
10. On the DRAWING TOOLS FORMAT tab, click the Shape Styles **More** button to open the gallery, and click **Moderate Effect - Tan, Accent 5**.
11. With the shape still selected, click **Shape Effects** > **Shadow** > **Offset Diagonal Top Left** (the third item in the third row of the Outer group).
12. Close the Selection task pane.
13. **With your teacher's permission**, print the worksheet. Your worksheet should look like Figure 61-2.
14. Save and close the file, and exit Excel.

Figure 61-2

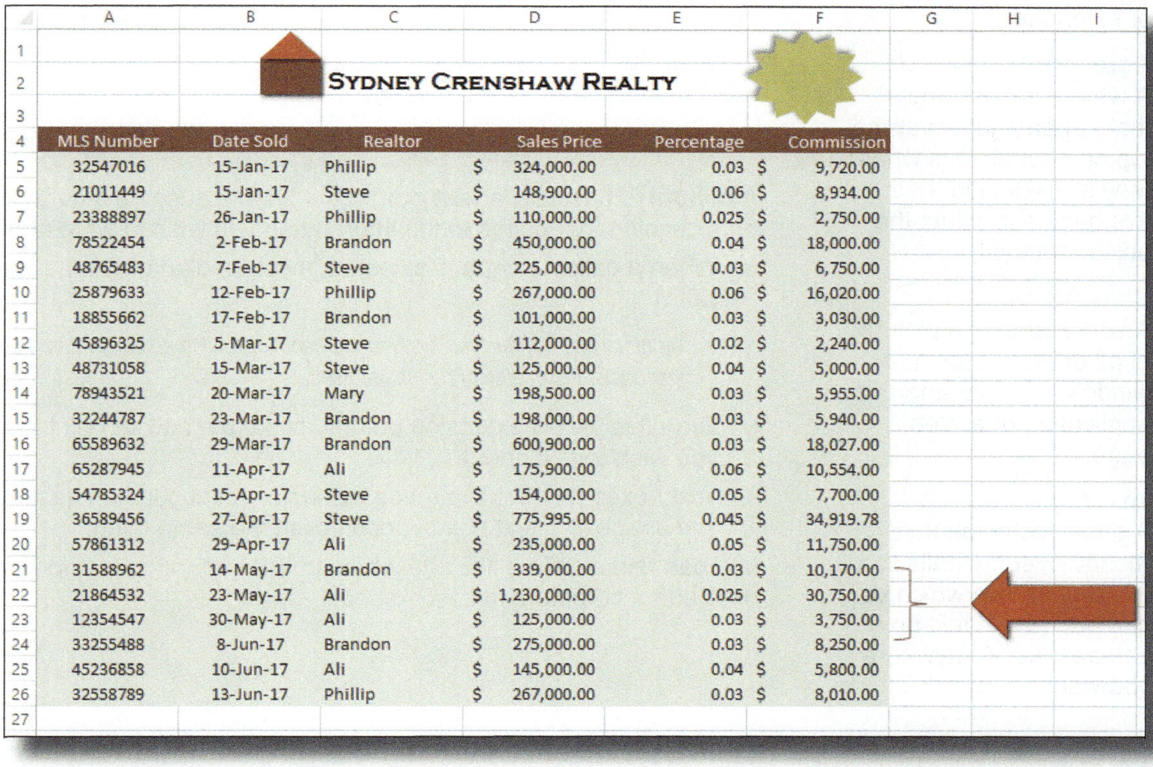

	A	B	C	D	E	F
1						
2			SYDNEY CRENSHAW REALTY			
3						
4	MLS Number	Date Sold	Realtor	Sales Price	Percentage	Commission
5	32547016	15-Jan-17	Phillip	$ 324,000.00	0.03	$ 9,720.00
6	21011449	15-Jan-17	Steve	$ 148,900.00	0.06	$ 8,934.00
7	23388897	26-Jan-17	Phillip	$ 110,000.00	0.025	$ 2,750.00
8	78522454	2-Feb-17	Brandon	$ 450,000.00	0.04	$ 18,000.00
9	48765483	7-Feb-17	Steve	$ 225,000.00	0.03	$ 6,750.00
10	25879633	12-Feb-17	Phillip	$ 267,000.00	0.06	$ 16,020.00
11	18855662	17-Feb-17	Brandon	$ 101,000.00	0.03	$ 3,030.00
12	45896325	5-Mar-17	Steve	$ 112,000.00	0.02	$ 2,240.00
13	48731058	15-Mar-17	Steve	$ 125,000.00	0.04	$ 5,000.00
14	78943521	20-Mar-17	Mary	$ 198,500.00	0.03	$ 5,955.00
15	32244787	23-Mar-17	Brandon	$ 198,000.00	0.03	$ 5,940.00
16	65589632	29-Mar-17	Brandon	$ 600,900.00	0.03	$ 18,027.00
17	65287945	11-Apr-17	Ali	$ 175,900.00	0.06	$ 10,554.00
18	54785324	15-Apr-17	Steve	$ 154,000.00	0.05	$ 7,700.00
19	36589456	27-Apr-17	Steve	$ 775,995.00	0.045	$ 34,919.78
20	57861312	29-Apr-17	Ali	$ 235,000.00	0.05	$ 11,750.00
21	31588962	14-May-17	Brandon	$ 339,000.00	0.03	$ 10,170.00
22	21864532	23-May-17	Ali	$ 1,230,000.00	0.025	$ 30,750.00
23	12354547	30-May-17	Ali	$ 125,000.00	0.03	$ 3,750.00
24	33255488	8-Jun-17	Brandon	$ 275,000.00	0.03	$ 8,250.00
25	45236858	10-Jun-17	Ali	$ 145,000.00	0.04	$ 5,800.00
26	32558789	13-Jun-17	Phillip	$ 267,000.00	0.03	$ 8,010.00
27						

Lesson 62

Enhancing Shapes with Text and Effects

➤ What You Will Learn

Adding Text to a Text Box, Callout, or Other Shape
Adding 3-D Effects
Rotating Shapes
Inserting a Screen Capture

WORDS TO KNOW

Callout
Text that's placed in a special AutoShape balloon. A callout, like a text box, "floats" over the cells in a worksheet—so you can position a callout wherever you like.

Extension point
The yellow diamond handle that indicates the position where a callout can be resized or extended.

Rotation handle
A white rotation symbol that appears just over the top of most objects when they are selected. Use this handle to rotate the object manually.

Screenshot
A screenshot is a picture of all or part of an open window, such as another application or a Web page.

Text box
A small rectangle that "floats" over the cells in a worksheet, into which you can add text. A text box can be placed anywhere you want.

Software Skills If you need to place text in some spot within the worksheet that doesn't correspond to a specific cell, you can "float" the text over the cells by creating a text box or by adding a callout. A text box or callout can be placed anywhere in the worksheet, regardless of the cell gridlines. You can add text to any shape. Add 3-D effects or rotation to shapes to really make them stand out. You can use the screen capture feature to take a picture of any open application or Web page.

What You Can Do

Adding Text to a Text Box, Callout, or Other Shape

- A **callout** is basically a **text box** with a shape, such as a cartoon balloon, with an extension that points to the information you wish to write about.
  - When a callout shape is selected, a yellow diamond indicates the **extension point**.
    - ✓ On other shapes, this yellow diamond handle is called an adjustment handle, because it lets you adjust the outline of the shape itself.
  - Drag this yellow extension point to make the callout point precisely to the data you wish to talk about.
  - Text boxes do not have these extensions, but you can easily add an arrow or line shape to a text box to accomplish the same thing.
- You can use a callout like a text box, to draw attention to important information, or to add a comment to a worksheet.

- You can add text to any shape.
  - ✓ If the shape already contains text, the text you type will be added to the end of the existing text. You can replace text by first selecting it, and then typing new text.

- The border of a selected shape changes to indicate whether you're editing the object itself (solid border) or the text in the object (dashed border).
  - To move, resize, copy, or delete the object, the border must be solid.
  - To edit or add text in a text box or shape, the border must be dashed.

Try It! Adding Text to a Text Box, Callout, or Other Shape

1. Start Excel, and open **E62TryA** from the data files for this lesson.
2. Save the file as **E62TryA_xx** in the location where your teacher instructs you to store the files for this lesson.
3. Click the P&L worksheet tab > PAGE LAYOUT > Selection Pane.
4. In the Selection task pane, click Rectangle, and type **This cost is down because of better inventory management.**
5. Select the text in the shape, and click HOME.
6. Click Font Color, and in the Standard Colors palette click Dark Red.
7. With the text still selected, click te Decrease Font four times to change the font size to 8 points.
8. In the Alignment group, click Center.
9. With the rectangle still selected, right-click the rectangle, and in the shortcut menu click Format Text Effects.
10. In the Format Shape task pane, under TEXT OPTIONS, click Textbox. In the Left Margin box type **.5**, and in the Top margin box type **.1**.
11. Create a callout:
    a. Click INSERT > Shapes and choose Rectangular Callout from the Callouts group.
    b. Draw a callout in the area of F34:I36.
    c. Type **Next year's purchases should be much lower than this.**
    d. Select the text you typed in step 11c, click HOME, and click Decrease Font three times to change the font size to 9.
    e. In the Alignment group, click Center, and close the Format Shape task pane.
    f. Click the border of the callout shape.
       ✓ Clicking the border allows you to change the format of the whole text box, not just the text.
    g. Click DRAWING TOOLS FORMAT, click the Shape Styles More button, and click Intense Effect - Orange, Accent 2.
12. Click and hold the yellow extension point, and drag it until the callout tip points to cell D38.
13. Close the Selection and Format Shapes task panes.
14. Save the changes to the file, and leave it open to use in the next Try It.

Formatting the text options of a shape

Adding 3-D Effects

- When you add 3-D effects to an object, that object appears to have depth.
- You can add 3-D effects to any object, even grouped objects.
- To select a 3-D rotation style, use the Shape Effects button in the Shape Styles group on the DRAWING TOOLS FORMAT tab.
  - If you choose 3-D Rotation Options, the Format Shape task pane displays where you can customize the settings.
  - You can set the exact degree of rotation and other options such as whether you want the text in the shape (if any) to be rotated with the shape.
  - Objects are rotated along three axes—X (horizontal), Y (vertical), and Z (depth dimension).
- In the Format Shape task pane, shown in Figure 62-1, you can adjust the format of a 3-D shape, by selecting the depth, surface texture, and other options.
  - You can adjust the style of the edge of your 3-D shape. You can also change the color and contour of this third dimension.
  - Use the Material feature to select a surface texture—such as the apparent material used.
  - You can change how the surface is lit (both the color of the light and the angle at which it shines on the 3-D object).

Figure 62-1

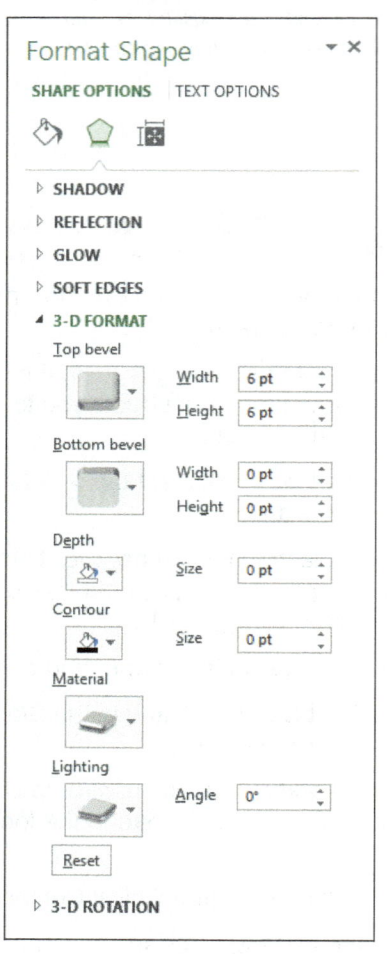

Try It! Adding 3-D Effects

1. In the **E62TryA_xx** file, click the P&L tab, if necessary.
2. Click the callout shape to select it.
3. On the DRAWING TOOLS FORMAT, click Shape Effects, click Bevel, and in the Bevel group click Circle.
4. On the DRAWING TOOLS FORMAT, click Shape Effects, click 3-D Rotation, and in the Oblique group click Oblique Top Right.
5. Save the changes to the file, and leave it open to use in the next Try It.

Saving a Workbook That Contains Macros

- The default file extension for Excel 2013 is .xlsx. This file format cannot contain macros, by design, to avoid potential malware threats associated with macros.

- A workbook must be saved in **.xlsm** format in order to enable it to store macros.
  - ✓ When you save a file in .xlsm format, it does not overwrite the original file in .xlsx format.

Try It! Saving a Workbook That Contains Macros

1. Open **E64TryA** from the data files for this lesson.
2. Click FILE > Save As.
3. Navigate to the location where your teacher instructs you to store the files for this lesson.
4. In the Save As dialog box, click the Save as type drop-down list > Excel Macro-Enabled Workbook.
5. In the File name box, change the file name to **E64TryA_xx**.
6. Click Save.
7. Leave the **E64TryA_xx** file open to use in the next Try It.

Recording a Macro

- The Macro Recorder records every action you take, and stores them in a macro that you can later play back to reproduce the steps.
  - ✓ Recording a macro requires planning and some practice. It is not uncommon to have to record a macro several times because errors were made in the recording process. If you make a mistake, delete the macro and record a new one.

- By default, Excel records the actual addresses of the cells you affect when recording. For example, if the active cell happens to be cell D2 when you begin recording a macro that makes the active cell bold, the macro will always make cell D2 bold, regardless of the position of the active cell when you run that macro. This is called **absolute recording**, and it is the default behavior.

- If you go with the default setting of absolute recording, the macro begins recording your actions based on the cell that is active. When you create the macro, select the desired cell before you click Record.

- The alternative is **relative recording**, which performs the recorded action on whatever cell or range is selected before running the macro.

- On the DEVELOPER tab, click Use Relative References or Use Absolute References to switch between absolute and relative recording.

- You can name a macro to make it easier to reference; however, you cannot use spaces in a macro name.

Try It! Recording a Macro

1. In the **E64TryA_xx** file, click cell B2, and click the DEVELOPER tab.
2. Click Record Macro.

   OR

   Click the Record Macro button on the status bar.
3. In the Record Macro dialog box, in the Macro name text box, type **TopSales**.
   - ✓ The macro name cannot have spaces.
4. In the Shortcut key text box, type **t**.
   - ✓ This will be your shortcut key used to run the macro. If you choose a shortcut key that Excel already has assigned to another action, the macro will override the other action in this workbook.

(continued)

Try It! Recording a Macro (continued)

5. In the Description text box, type **Date, sales by Z-A order, top seller**.

Define the macro before recording it

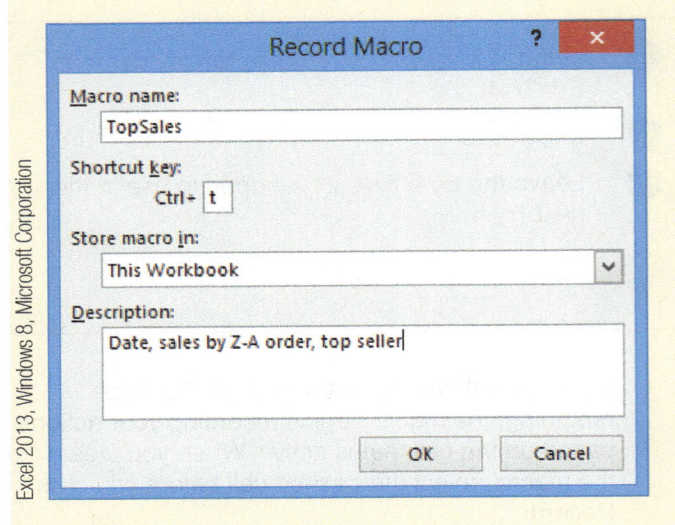

Record Macro dialog box:
- Macro name: TopSales
- Shortcut key: Ctrl+ t
- Store macro in: This Workbook
- Description: Date, sales by Z-A order, top seller
- OK / Cancel

6. Click OK. The recording begins.

7. Without re-clicking in cell B2, but with the cell still selected, type **=NOW()**, and press ENTER.

✓ This will place the current date and time in this cell each time the file is opened. Notice that this cell has a date format applied to it so that only the date displays.

8. Select cells A5:B9.

9. Click DATA > Sort.

10. In the Sort dialog box, open the Sort by drop-down list and click Column B.

11. Click OK.

12. Click cell B3, type **=**, click cell A9, and press ENTER.

✓ This will place the top sales person's name in cell B3 when the macro is run.

13. Click DEVELOPER > Stop Recording.

OR

Click the Stop Record Macro button on the status bar.

14. Save the changes to the file, and leave it open to use in the next Try It.

Running a Macro

- To run a macro, you can use the Macros command on the DEVELOPER tab to open a Macro dialog box from which you can select the macro you want.
- You can also use the shortcut key combination you defined when you created the macro.
- You can also assign a macro to the Quick Access Toolbar or the Ribbon, and then run it from its button.

Try It! Running a Macro

1. In the **E64TryA_xx** file, select the cell range A5:B9, and click DATA > Sort A to Z to re-sort the list by name, so you can test the macro.

2. Click cell B2 and press CTRL + T. The macro runs.

3. Click cell E2 and press CTRL + T again. The macro runs again.

✓ This time the macro places =NOW() in cell E2. It does that because you did not click B2 after beginning the macro recording but before typing =NOW(). You recorded a relative reference macro that begins running at the active cell. We'll fix that later in the lesson, when you learn about editing a macro in VBA. Notice that the references to A5:B9 still work, though, because they are absolute references by default.

(continued)

Business Information Management II | Excel | Chapter 8

Try It! Running a Macro (continued)

4. Widen column E so that the content of cell E2 is visible.
5. Select cell E2, and press DEL.
6. Click cell B5, and type **5000**.
7. Click cell B2.
8. Click DEVELOPER > Macros to display the Macro dialog box.

✓ *The Macro dialog box provides an alternate way of running a macro. You must use this method for macros for which there is no shortcut key combination or button.*

9. Click the TopSales macro, and click Run to run the macro again.
10. Save the changes to the file, and leave it open to use in the next Try It.

Try It! Adding a Macro to the Quick Access Toolbar

1. In the **E64TryA_xx** file, click FILE > Options.
2. Click Quick Access Toolbar.
3. Open the Choose commands from drop-down list, and click Macros.
4. Click TopSales.
5. Click Add.
6. Click OK. A button for the macro now appears on the Quick Access Toolbar.
7. Click cell B7, and type **100**.
8. Click cell B2.
9. On the Quick Access Toolbar, click the TopSales macro button. The macro re-runs and re-sorts the list with the new value.
10. Save the changes to the file, and leave it open to use in the next Try It.

Editing a Macro

- If you make a mistake during recording, you can delete the macro, or you can edit the macro in **Visual Basic for Applications (VBA)**.
- Editing the macro requires a basic understanding of VBA, which you may not have yet. However, many of the commands are simple to figure out by their names, so that you can identify unwanted parts of the macro to delete or correct typos.

Try It! Editing a Macro

1. In the **E64TryA_xx** file, click DEVELOPER > Macros to open the Macro dialog box.
2. Click TopSales, and click Edit. Visual Basic for Applications opens, showing the macro code.
3. Click to place the insertion point at the beginning of the text: **ActiveCell.FormulaR1C1 = "=NOW()"**.
4. Type **Range("B2").Select**, and press ENTER.

   ✓ *Adding this line of code selects cell B2 as the first action in the macro.*

5. Click FILE > Close and Return to Microsoft Excel.
6. Save the changes to the file, and leave it open to use in the next Try It.

Try It! Deleting a Macro

1. In the **E64TryA_xx** file, click DEVELOPER > Macros to open the Macro dialog box.
2. Click TopSales, and click Delete.
3. Click Yes to confirm.
4. Right-click the macro button you placed on the Quick Access Toolbar earlier, and click Remove from Quick Access Toolbar.
5. Close the workbook without saving your changes to it so that macro is still in the saved copy.
6. Leave Excel open to use in the next Try It.

Copying Macros Between Workbooks

- Macro code is stored in a **module** within the file.
- You can access VBA modules in the Microsoft Visual Basic for Applications window from the Visual Basic button on the DEVELOPER tab.
- You can open a module like a file and edit its content.
- Each time you create a new macro in the worksheet, Excel adds it to the Modules folder of the Visual Basic project with the name Module1, Module2, etc.
- You can copy a module to another macro-enabled Excel workbook to make the macros in the module available for use in that workbook.
    - ✓ When you copy a macro from one workbook to another, Excel does not copy its shortcut key. You will need to reassign the shortcut key by editing the macro.
- You can edit or delete individual macros in a workbook by using the Organizer.

Try It! Copying Macros Between Workbooks

1. In Excel, open **E64TryA_xx** from the location where your teacher instructs you to store the files for this lesson.
2. In the SECURITY WARNING bar, click Enable Content to enable the macro.
3. Create a new, blank workbook.
4. Click FILE > Save As.
5. Navigate to the location where your teacher instructs you to store the files for this lesson.
6. In the Save As dialog box, in the File name box, type **E64TryB_xx**.
7. Click the Save as type drop-down list > Excel Macro-Enabled Workbook.
8. Click Save.
9. In the **E64TryB _xx** file, click DEVELOPER > Visual Basic.
10. In the Microsoft Visual Basic for Applications window, on the Standard shortcut menu, click Project Explorer. Notice that Module1 of the E64TryA_xx.xlsm file is highlighted in the Project - VBAProject pane.

(continued)

Business Information Management II | Excel | Chapter 8 | 427

Try It! Copying Macros Between Workbooks (continued)

11. Click and hold Module1, and drag it on top of the VBAProject(E64TryB_xx.xlsm) project. The macro is copied in a Modules folder.
12. Under VBAProject(E64TryB_xx.xlsm), click the plus sign next to the Modules folder to open it and view the macro.
13. Close the Microsoft Visual Basic for Applications window.
14. Save and close the **E64TryA_xx** and **E64TryB_xx** files, and exit Excel.

Copying a macros module to another workbook

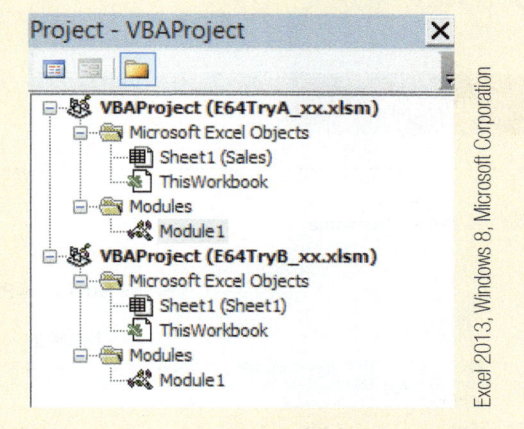

Lesson 64—Practice

The Membership Chairperson for the Small Business Professional Organization is tracking attendance for the organization's quarterly meeting. She has asked you to create a worksheet to show the RSVP replies and to track who said they would come to the meeting but did not show up. In this project, you will create a macro that shows the members who said they would attend, but who did not actually attend the meeting.

DIRECTIONS

1. Start Excel, if necessary, and open **E64Practice** from the data files for this lesson.
2. Click **FILE** > **Save As**.
3. Navigate to the location where your teacher instructs you to store the files for this lesson.
4. In the File name box, type **E64Practice_xx**.
5. Click the **Save as type** drop-down list > **Excel Macro-Enabled Workbook**.
6. Click **Save**.
7. Add a header with your full name on the left, and today's date on the right. Return to **Normal** view.
8. Select the range **A2:G62**.
9. Click **INSERT** > **Table**.
10. In the Create Table dialog box, verify that the cell range is **A2:G62**, verify that the **My table has headers** check box is selected, and click **OK**.
11. Click cell **A2** to make this the active cell.
12. Click **DEVELOPER** > **Record Macro** to display the Record Macro dialog box.
13. In the Macro Name text box, type **MeetingAttendance**. Do not put a space in the macro name.
14. In the Shortcut key box, type **t**.
    ✓ *If you receive a message telling you a macro is already assigned to that key, choose another key.*
15. In the Description box, type **People who said they would attend, but did not**.
16. In the Store macro in box, verify that This Workbook is selected, and click **OK**.
17. Click the down arrow on cell **E2**, click to clear the **No** check box, and click **OK**.
    ✓ *This shows all the people who said they would attend the meeting.*
18. Click the down arrow on cell **F2**, click to clear the **Yes** check box, and click **OK**.
    ✓ *This shows who said they would attend, but did not attend the meeting.*

19. Click **DEVELOPER** > **Stop Recording**.
20. Click **DATA** > **Clear** to remove the filters.
21. Click **A2**.
22. Press CTRL + T to run the macro.
23. **With your teacher's permission,** print the worksheet. Your worksheet should look like the one shown in Figure 64-1.
24. Save and close the file, and exit Excel.

Figure 64-1

Firstname Lastname					1/5/2016

Small Business Professional Organization

Spring Networking Meeting

Last Name	First Name	RSVP Received	Reminder	RSVP Response	Attended
Chang	Joshua	yes		Yes	No
Copp	Seth	No	Yes	Yes	No
Devereaux	Domique	yes		Yes	No
Huang	Griffin	No	Yes	Yes	No
Klein	Nathaniel	yes		Yes	No
Nishiba	Arielle	No	Yes	Yes	No
Reisman	Sophia	yes		Yes	No

Lesson 64—Apply

You are a member of the Small Business Professional Organization. The Membership Chairperson has asked you to create a chart comparing the revenue from the sales of products and services over a period of six months. Since the Membership Chairperson has asked you to do this in the past, you want to record a macro to create the chart.

DIRECTIONS

1. Start Excel, if necessary, and open **E64ApplyA** from the data files for this lesson. Notice that this file is already in a macro-enabled file format.
2. Save the file as **E64ApplyA_xx** in the location where your teacher instructs you to store the files for this lesson.
3. For all worksheets, add a header that has your name at the left, the date code in the center, and the page number code at the right, and change back to **Normal** view.
4. Prepare to record a macro that creates a chart comparing the revenue from the sales of products and services over a period of six months:

    Macro name: **Sales**

    Shortcut key: **Ctrl+s**

    Store macro in: **This Workbook**

    Description: **Sales and services revenue chart**

    ✓ If you receive a message saying a macro is already assigned to the shortcut key, choose another key.

5. Perform the following actions as the macro recorder records them:
   a. On the Sales tab, select the cell range **A2:C8**.
   b. Click **INSERT** > **Insert Column Chart** > **3-D Clustered Column** (the first option in the 3-D Column group).
   c. Click **CHART TOOLS DESIGN**, and in the Chart Styles group click **Style 4**.
6. End the recording.
7. Delete the chart from the workbook, and run the macro to re-create the chart.
8. Edit the macro in the VBA Editor to change the style applied to the chart to **Style 3**:
   a. Click **DEVELOPER** > **Macros**.
   b. In the Macros dialog box, click the **Macros in** drop-down arrow, and click **This Workbook**.
   c. Click **Edit**.
   d. In the E64Apply_xx.xlsm - Module1 (Code) window, change the ActiveChart.Chartstyle to **288**.
   e. Save the macro project.
   f. Close the VBA window.
9. Delete the chart from the workbook, and run the macro to re-create the chart.
10. Reposition the chart so that the upper-left corner of the chart is at the upper-left corner of cell C10.
11. **With your teacher's permission,** print the **Sales** worksheet. Your chart should look like the one shown in Figure 64-2.
12. Copy the macro to a blank workbook:
    a. Create a new, blank workbook.
    b. Save the file as a Macro-Enabled Workbook named **E64ApplyB_xx** in the location where your teacher instructs you to store the files for this lesson.
    c. In the **E64ApplyB_xx** file, click **DEVELOPER** > **Visual Basic**.
    d. In the Microsoft Visual Basic for Applications window, on the Standard shortcut menu, click **Project Explorer** to view the Project - VBAProject pane, if necessary.
    e. Under VBAProject(E64ApplyA_xx.xlsm), click the plus sign next to the Modules folder to open it and view the Module1 macro.
    f. Click and hold **Module1**, and drag it on top of the VBAProject(E64ApplyB_xx.xlsm) project.
    g. Under VBAProject(E64ApplyB _xx.xlsm), click the plus sign next to the Modules folder to open it and view the macro.
13. Close the Microsoft Visual Basic for Applications window.
14. Save and close the **E64ApplyA_xx** and **E64ApplyB_xx** files, and exit Excel.

Figure 64-2

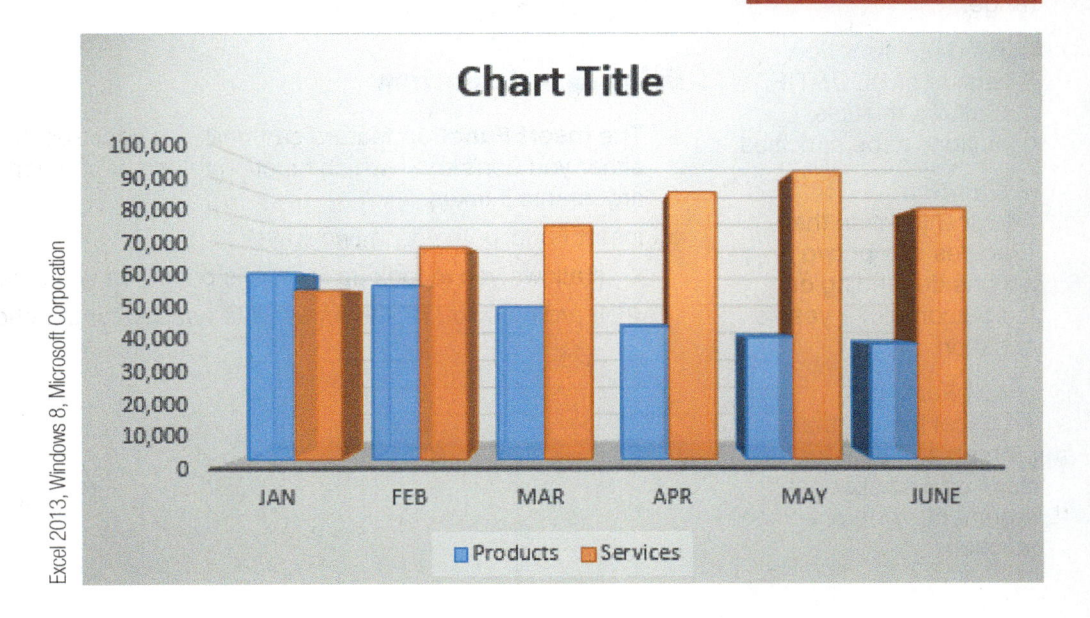

Lesson 65

Using Functions

> **What You Will Learn**
>
> Using Insert Function
> Creating an IF Function
> Creating SUMIF, COUNTIF, and AVERAGEIF Functions
> Creating SUMIFS, COUNTIFS, and AVERAGEIFS Functions
> Using the TODAY Function and the NOW Function
> Using the TRANSPOSE Function

WORDS TO KNOW

Array
An orderly arrangement of numbers.

AVERAGEIF function
A function that averages the values in a range that meet a certain condition.

AVERAGEIFS function
A version of AVERAGEIF that allows multiple conditions to be specified.

COUNTIF function
A function that uses a criteria to count the number of items in a range.

COUNTIFS function
A version of COUNTIF that allows multiple conditions to be specified.

IF function
A logical function that executes one of two actions depending on the outcome of a yes/no question.

Insert Function
An Excel feature that prompts the user for the required and optional arguments for a specified function.

Software Skills Excel includes logical functions that enable you to set up conditions where a calculation is performed only if the conditions are met, such as IF, SUMIF, COUNTIF, and AVERAGEIF. Such functions are somewhat more complex to set up than other functions, so you may prefer to construct them using Insert Function, a built-in utility in Excel that prompts you for the necessary arguments. You can use functions to automate the insertion of data in your worksheet, such as using the TODAY and NOW functions to add today's date. You can also use functions to reposition data, such as using the TRANSPOSE function to switch the position of row and column data.

What You Can Do

Using Insert Function

- The **Insert Function** feature can help you construct functions in cases where either you don't know which function to use or you don't remember what arguments it takes.
- Insert Function helps in two ways:
  - It allows you to look up functions based on what they do.
  - It prompts you for the arguments needed for the chosen function.

Business Information Management II | Excel | Chapter 8   431

Try It!   Inserting a Function

1. Start Excel, and open **E65Try** from the data files for this lesson.

2. Save the file as **E65Try_xx** in the location where your teacher has instructed you to save your work.

3. On the IF worksheet tab, click cell A13, and type **Total**.

4. Click cell B13, and click the Insert Function *fx* button on the formula bar to open the Insert Function dialog box.

The Insert Function button

Insert Function button

Excel 2013, Windows 8, Microsoft Corporation

5. In the Search for a Function box, type **add**, and click Go.

   ✓ We already know that we want the SUM function in this case; step 5 is just for practice.

6. In the list of functions that appears, click SUM, and read the description of it at the bottom of the dialog box.

7. Click OK to open the Function Arguments dialog box with text boxes for each of the arguments.

   ✓ The SUM function has only one required argument. Labels for required arguments are bold.

8. Confirm that the Number1 argument displays B5:B12.

   ✓ If Excel guesses at the range incorrectly, you can manually correct it, or you can select the range yourself. You can click the Collapse Dialog Box button to the right of the argument to get the dialog box out of the way, select the desired range, and then click the Expand Dialog Box button or press Enter to bring the dialog box back to full view.

9. Click OK to display the formula result in the cell.

10. Save the changes to the file, and leave it open to use in the next Try It.

Arguments for the SUM function

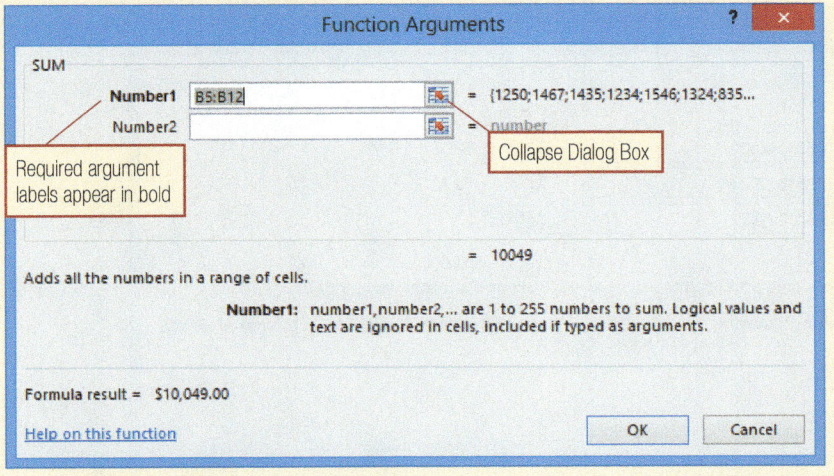

Function Arguments

SUM
Number1 B5:B12   = {1250;1467;1435;1234;1546;1324;835...
Number2   = number

Required argument labels appear in bold

Collapse Dialog Box

= 10049

Adds all the numbers in a range of cells.

Number1: number1,number2,... are 1 to 255 numbers to sum. Logical values and text are ignored in cells, included if typed as arguments.

Formula result = $10,049.00

Help on this function   OK   Cancel

Excel 2013, Windows 8, Microsoft Corporation

Logical function
A function that evaluates a yes/no condition and then takes an action based on the result.

NOW function
A function that displays the current date and time on a worksheet or calculates a value based on the current date and time.

SUMIF function
A function that sums the values in a range that meet a certain condition.

SUMIFS function
A version of SUMIF that allows multiple conditions to be specified.

TODAY function
A function that obtains the current date from the computer.

TRANSPOSE function
A function that copies data located in a row into a column or copies data located in a column into a row.

Creating an IF Function

- **Logical functions** enable you to set up yes/no questions, and then perform one action or another based on the answer
- **IF** is the simplest of the logical functions. It has three arguments:
  - The logical condition
  - What to do if it is true
  - What to do if it is false
- For example, suppose that if cell A1 contains 100, you want cell B1 to show "Perfect Score"; otherwise, B1 should show "Thanks for Playing." To achieve this, you would place the following function in B1:

  =IF(A1=100,"Perfect Score","Thanks for Playing")

- Enclose text strings in quotation marks, and use commas to separate the arguments.
- You can use Insert Function to enter the arguments instead of typing them manually.
- Like most other functions, you can use the IF function in conjunction with other functions, such as AND or OR.
- For example, suppose you want to find out who sold item number 15634 for $150 in a range of sales data where column A contains the name of the salesperson, column B contains the item number, and column C contains the cost of the item. To achieve this, you would use the following function:

  =IF(AND(C1=150)B1=15634,A1)

Try It! Creating an IF Function

1. In the **E65Try_xx** file, on the IF worksheet tab, click cell C5.
2. Click Insert Function.
3. Click the Or select a category list > Logical.
4. In the Select a function list, click IF.
5. Click OK to open the Function Arguments dialog box.
6. In the Logical test box, type **B5>=1000**.
7. In the Value_if_true box, type **B5*0.05**.
8. In the Value_if_false box, type **B5*0.02**.
9. Click OK to place the function in cell C5.
10. Copy the function from cell C5 to the range C6:C12.
    ✓ Use any copy method you like. You can drag the fill handle, or use the Copy and Paste commands.
11. Save the changes to the file, and leave it open to use in the next Try It.

Arguments for the IF function

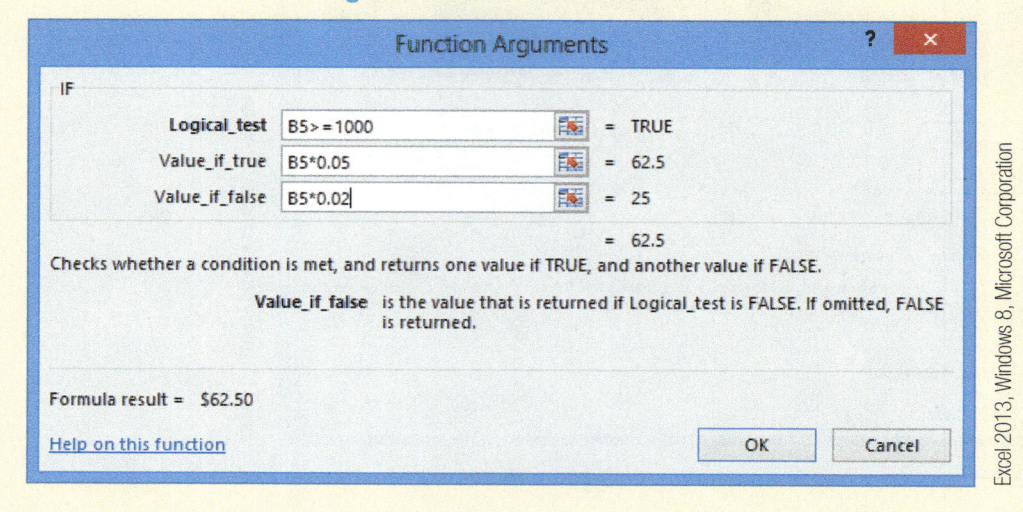

Creating SUMIF, COUNTIF, and AVERAGEIF Functions

- The **SUMIF**, **COUNTIF**, and **AVERAGEIF** functions combine the IF function with either SUM, COUNT, or AVERAGE. The SUM, COUNT, or AVERAGE operation is performed upon cells within the specified range that meet a certain logical condition.
- The syntax is:

  =SUMIF(range,criteria,sum_range)

- In some cases the range to evaluate (*range*) and the range to calculate (*sum_range*) are the same. In that case, you can omit the *sum_range* argument.
- To specify that a criterion not be a certain value, precede the value with <>. For example, to exclude records where the value is 500, you would use <>500 as the criterion.
- COUNTIF and AVERAGEIF work the same way as SUMIF, with the same types of arguments.

Try It! Creating a SUMIF Function

1. In the **E65Try_xx** file, click the SUMIF worksheet tab.
2. Click cell B15 > Insert Function.
3. Type **SUMIF**, and click Go.
4. Click SUMIF in the list of functions, if necessary, and click OK.
5. In the Range box, type **D4:D13**.
6. In the Criteria box, type **Yes**.

   ✓ *Quotation marks around the criteria are required, even if the criteria are numeric. Insert Function automatically puts quotation marks around the criteria for you.*

7. In the Sum Range box, type **C4:C13**.
8. Click OK. The result ($802.00) appears in cell B15.
9. Save the changes to the file, and leave it open to use in the next Try It.

Enter the arguments for the SUMIF function

Creating SUMIFS, COUNTIFS, and AVERAGEIFS Functions

- The **SUMIFS**, **COUNTIFS**, and **AVERAGEIFS** functions are the same as SUMIF, COUNTIF, and AVERAGEIF except that they allow multiple criteria.
- For the function to be evaluated as true, all the criteria must be met.

Try It! Creating an AVERAGEIFS Function

1. In the **E65Try_xx** file, on the SUMIF worksheet tab, click cell A16, and type **Avg Due for Dog Items**.
2. Click cell B16 > Insert Function.
3. Type **AVERAGEIFS**, and click Go > OK.
4. In the Average_range box, type **C4:C13**.
5. In the Criteria_range1 box, type **D4:D13**.
6. In the Criteria1 box, type **No**.
7. In the Criteria_range2 box, type **E4:E13**.
8. In the Criteria2 box, type **Dog**.
9. Click OK. The function appears in the cell.
10. Save the changes to the file, and leave it open for the next Try It.

Arguments for the AVERAGEIFS function

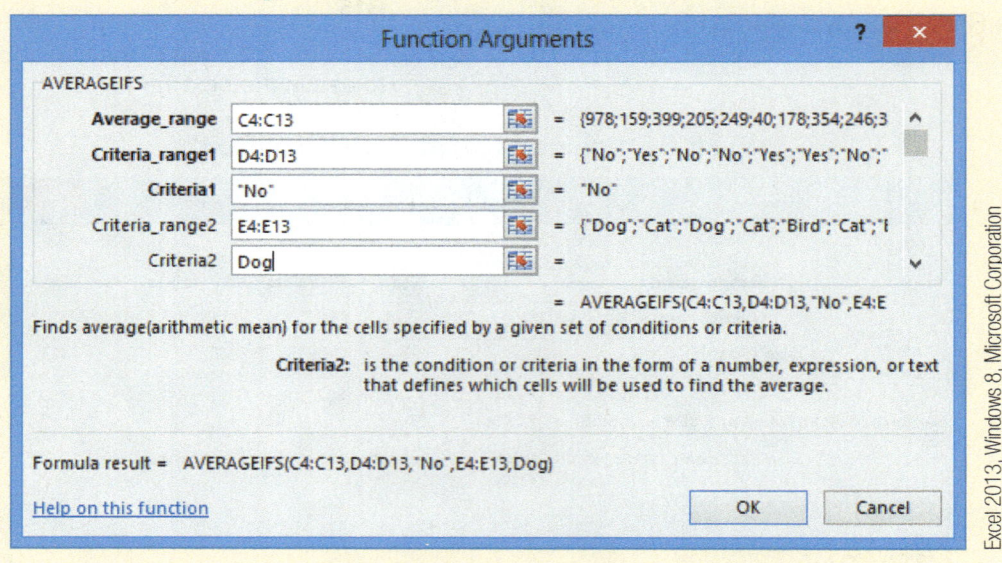

Using the TODAY Function and the NOW Function

- You can use the **TODAY function** to add today's date to a worksheet cell.
- Excel stores dates as sequential serial numbers so that they can be used in calculations using January 1, 1900 as serial number 1. For example, January 1, 2015 is serial number 42005 because it is 42,005 days after January 1, 1900.
- The TODAY function obtains the serial number of the date from your computer, and formats it as a date.
- The syntax for the TODAY function is: **=TODAY ()**
- The **NOW function** displays the current date and time on a worksheet. It can also be used to calculate a value based on the current date and time. Each time the worksheet is opened, the value is updated.
- The syntax for the NOW function is: **=NOW ()**

Try It! Using the TODAY Function and the NOW Function

1. In the **E65Try_xx** file, on the SUMIF worksheet, click cell C1.
2. Type **=TODAY()**.
3. Press ENTER to display the formula result in the cell.
4. Click cell D1, and type **=NOW()**.
5. Press ENTER to display the formula result in the cell. (Adjust the column width as necessary.)
6. Save the changes to the file, and leave it open to use in the next Try It.

The TODAY function

| C1 | : | × | ✓ | fx | =TODAY() |

	A	B	C
1	Sales and Payments		5/17/2013
2			

Excel 2013, Windows 8, Microsoft Corporation

Using the TRANSPOSE Function

- The **TRANSPOSE function** is one of Excel's Lookup & Reference functions.
- You can use the TRANSPOSE function to switch the position of rows and columns.
  ✓ TRANSPOSE does not work with data in a table. First convert the table to text, and then TRANSPOSE.
- The TRANSPOSE function requires an **array** argument.
- The syntax for the TRANSPOSE function is:
  { = TRANSPOSE (Array)}
  ✓ The curly braces—{ }— around the function indicate that the function is an array function.
- Use the first row of the array as the first column of the new array, the second row of the array as the second column of the new array, and so on.
- You must enter the TRANSPOSE function as an array formula in a range that has the same number of rows and columns, respectively, as the source range has columns and rows.
  - For example, to transpose a cell range of two columns and five rows, you must indicate a cell range of five rows and two columns in the worksheet.
  - You can transpose a cell range to a range of blank cells, as long as there are enough blank cells to contain the data that will be transposed.
- You must indicate the array or range of cells on a worksheet that you want to transpose before using the Insert Function button.

Try It! Using the TRANSPOSE Function

1. In the **E65Try_xx** file, on the SUMIF worksheet, select the cell range H3:R7.
2. Click FORMULAS > Lookup & Reference > TRANSPOSE to display the Function Arguments dialog box.
3. In the Array box, type **A3:E13**.
   OR
   Click the collapse dialog button, select the **A3:E13** cell range, and click the expand dialog button.
4. Press CTRL, SHIFT, and ENTER at the same time to insert the TRANSPOSE array formula into the cell range H3:R7.
   ✓ If you click OK instead of using the Control, Shift, and Enter key combination, the formula will return an error value.
5. Adjust the column widths.
6. Save and close the file, and exit Excel.

Lesson 65—Practice

Your boss at Wood Hills Animal Clinic has asked you to modify the monthly sales report and create an analysis of sales based on several factors such as animal type (cat versus dog, for example) and purpose (ear infection versus flea control, for example). In this project, you will insert functions to aid in the analysis of the data.

DIRECTIONS

1. Start Excel, if necessary, and open **E65Practice** from the data files for this lesson.
2. Save the file as **E65Practice_xx** in the location where your teacher instructs you to store the files for this lesson.
3. Add a header that has your name at the left, the date code in the center, and the page number code at the right, and change back to **Normal** view.
4. Click cell D99, and type the formula **=SUM(K8:K94)** to compute the total sales revenues.
5. Use Insert Function to create a formula in cell D100 to sum the sales from dog products:
   a. Click cell **D100**.
   b. On the formula bar, click **Insert Function** *fx* to open the Insert Function dialog box.
   c. In the Search for a function box, type **SUMIF** > **Go** > **OK**.
   d. In the Function Arguments dialog box, for the Range argument, type **C8:C94**.
   e. In the Criteria argument, type **"Dog"**.
      ✓ Typing the quotation marks is optional; if you do not type them, Excel will add them for you automatically.
   f. In the Sum_range argument, type **K8:K94**.
   g. Click **OK**.
6. Use the process in step 5 to sum the sales of cat products in cell D101.
   ✓ The function to be placed in cell D101 is identical to the one in cell D100 except it uses Cat rather than Dog in the criteria argument.
7. Use Insert Function to create a formula in cell D103 to sum the sales from flea products:
   a. Click cell **D103**.
   b. On the formula bar, click **Insert Function** *fx*.
   c. Click **SUMIF** > **OK**.
   d. In the Function Arguments dialog box, for the Range argument, type **B8:B94**.
   e. In the Criteria argument, type **"Flea"**.
   f. In the Sum_range argument, type **K8:K94**.
   g. Click **OK**.
8. Use the process in step 7 to insert SUMIF functions in cells **D104** and **D105**. For cell D104, use **"Flea and Tick"** as the critieria argument. For cell D105, use **"Heartworm"** as the criteria argument.
9. Complete the functions for cells **D108:D114** using the same methods as in steps 5–8 except use **AVERAGE** and **AVERAGEIF** functions.
   ✓ Notice that cell D108 is the average sales and D112 is the average sales of flea products.
10. In cell **D106**, type **=D99-SUM(D103:D105)**.
11. In cell **D115**, enter an **AVERAGEIFS** function that averages the values that are not Flea, Flea and Tick, or Heartworm:
    a. Click cell **D115**.
    b. On the formula bar, click **Insert Function** *fx*.
    c. Type **AVERAGEIFS** > **Go** > **OK**.
    d. In the Average_range argument, type **K8:K94**.
    e. In the Criteria_range1 argument, type **B8:B94**.
    f. In the Criteria1 argument, type **"<>Flea"**.
       ✓ Make sure you put the <> inside the quotation marks.
    g. In the Criteria_range2 argument, type **B8:B94**.
    h. In the Criteria2 argument, type **"<>Flea and Tick"**.
    i. In the Criteria_range3 argument, type **B8:B94**.
    j. In the Criteria3 argument, type **"<>Heartworm"**.
    k. Click **OK**.
12. Use a function to insert today's date in cell E98:
    a. Click cell **E98**.
    b. Type **=TODAY()**.
    c. Press ENTER.

Business Information Management II | Excel | Chapter 8   437

13. **With your teacher's permission**, print the cell range **A98:E117**. Your worksheet should look like the one shown in Figure 65-1.

14. Save and close the file, and exit Excel.

Figure 65-1

Sales Analysis		5/27/2013
	Total Sales	$263,465.96
	Sales of dog only products	$157,691.75
	Sales of cat only products	$24,091.11
	Sales of flea products	$18,630.10
	Sales of flea and tick products	$1,748.85
	Sales of heartworm products	$70,944.70
	Other sales	$172,142.31
	Average Sales	$3,028.34
	Average sales of dog only products	$3,583.90
	Average sales of cat only products	$1,853.16
	Average sales of flea products	$1,693.65
	Average sales of flea and tick products	$874.43
	Average sales of heartworm products	$7,094.47
	Average of other sales	$2,689.72

Excel 2013, Windows 8, Microsoft Corporation

Lesson 65—Apply

You work in the sales department of Pete's Pets. Your manager has asked you to create an analysis of the store's sales based on several factors such as animal type and salesperson. Your manager also wants you to find out who sold a particular item. In this project, you will insert functions and transpose data to aid in the analysis of the sales report.

DIRECTIONS

1. Start Excel, if necessary, and open **E65Apply** from the data files for this lesson.
2. Save the file as **E65Apply_xx** in the location where your teacher instructs you to store the files for this lesson.
3. Add a header that has your name at the left, the date code in the center, and the page number code at the right, and change back to **Normal** view.
4. In cell **D54**, use the **COUNTIF** function to compute the number of **Cats** sold.
5. In cell **D55**, use the **COUNTIF** function to compute the number of **Fish** sold.
6. In cell **D62**, use the **SUMIF** function to compute the total sales for **Alice Harper**.
7. In cell **D63**, use the **SUMIF** function to compute the total sales for **Bob Cook**.
8. In cell **E62**, use the **AVERAGEIF** function to compute the average sale for **Alice Harper**.
9. In cell **E63**, use the **AVERAGEIF** function to compute the average sale for **Bob Cook**.

10. In cell **D66**, use **SUMIFS** to compute the total fish sales for **Alice Harper**.
11. In cell **D67**, use **SUMIFS** to compute the total fish sales for **Bob Cook**.
12. In cell **E66**, use **SUMIFS** to compute the total accessory sales for **Alice Harper**.
13. In cell **E67**, use **SUMIFS** to compute the total accessory sales for **Bob Cook**.
14. In cell **D70**, use **AVERAGEIFS** to calculate the average fish sale for **Alice Harper**.
15. In cell **D71**, use **AVERAGEIFS** to calculate the average fish sale for **Bob Cook**.
16. In cell **E70**, use **AVERAGEIFS** to calculate the average accessory sale for **Alice Harper**.
17. In cell **E71**, use **AVERAGEIFS** to calculate the average accessory sale for **Bob Cook**.
18. In cell **E52**, use the **TODAY** function to insert today's date.
19. In cells **H61:J63**, use the **TRANSPOSE** function to transpose the rows and columns of the cell range C61:E63.
20. In cell **J65**, use the **VLOOKUP** function to find out who sold item 51478.

    ✓ You learned about LOOKUP functions in Excel Lesson 35.

    a. Click cell **H65**.
    b. Type **Who sold item 51478?**
    c. Click cell **J65**.
    d. In the Lookup_value argument, type **51478**.
    e. In the Table_array argument, type **B10:G49**.
    f. In the Col_index_num argument, type **4**.
    g. Click **OK**.

21. In cell **J67**, use the **HLOOKUP** function to find out what item was sold for $27.65.

    a. Click cell **H67**.
    b. Type **What item # sold for $27.65?**
    c. Click cell **J67**.
    d. In the Lookup_value argument, type **"Item #"**.
    e. In the Table_array argument, type **B9:G49**.
    f. In the Row_index_num argument, type **20**.

    ✓ Notice that the row index number is the row number in the table, not the worksheet.

    g. In the Range_lookup argument, type **FALSE**.

    ✓ Use FALSE to find the exact match.

    h. Click **OK**.

21. Apply **Accounting Format** with two decimal places to all the functions you created.
22. Adjust the column widths as needed.
23. **With your teacher's permission**, print cells **B52:K71**. Your worksheet should look like the one shown in Figure 65-2.
24. Save and close the file, and exit Excel.

Figure 65-2

Sales Recap					6/25/2013
Dogs sold			3		
Cats sold			2		
Fish sold			9		
Pet sales		$	1,696.37		
Feed sales		$	200.71		
Accessories		$	464.16		
Salesperson	Total Sales			Average Sales	
Alice Harper		$	1,059.37	$	48.15
Bob Cook		$	1,301.87	$	72.33
				Total Accessories	
Salesperson	Total Fish Sales			Sales	
Alice Harper		$	135.15	$	297.96
Bob Cook		$	17.22	$	166.20
				Average Accessories	
Salesperson	Average Fish Sales			Sales	
Alice Harper		$	22.53	$	27.09
Bob Cook		$	5.74	$	18.47

Salesperson	Alice Harper	Bob Cook
Total Sales	$ 1,059.37	$ 1,301.87
Average Sales	$ 48.15	$ 72.33
Who sold item 51478?		Alice Harper
What item # sold for $27.65?		48681

Business Information Management II | Excel | Chapter 8

Lesson 66

Working with Absolute References and Using Financial Functions

➤ What You Will Learn

Using Absolute, Relative, and Mixed References
Enabling Iterative Calculations
Using Financial Functions

Software Skills Usually when you create a function, the cell references are relative. When you copy the function to another cell, the cell references change in relation to the new location. Sometimes, though, you may not want the cell reference to change. In cases like that, you need an absolute reference. Excel enables you to create relative, absolute, or mixed references as needed. Absolute references come in handy when you are creating functions that calculate interest rates, payments, loan periods, and other financial information.

What You Can Do

Using Absolute, Relative, and Mixed References

- When you create a formula and then copy or move the formula, a **relative reference** changes to reflect the new position.
- For example, in Figure 66-1 on the next page, cell D3 contains the formula =B3+C3. If you copy that formula to cell D4, it will automatically change to =B4+C4. It increments the row number by one because the copy is being placed one row below the original.
- Cell references are relative by default in Excel; you do not need to do anything special to create a relative cell reference.
- An **absolute reference** to a cell locks the cell's reference when the formula is moved or copied. Absolute references are created by placing a dollar sign ($) before both the row and the column of the cell reference, like this: $B$3.

WORDS TO KNOW

Absolute reference
A cell reference that remains fixed when copied to another cell.

Circular reference
When a formula in Excel refers to the cell that contains the formula, either directly or indirectly.

FV
The Future Value function. Calculates the future value of an investment when given the rate, the number of periods, and the payment amount.

Iterative calculation
A repeated calculation

Mixed reference
A cell reference in which the row is absolute and the column is relative, or vice-versa.

NPER
The Number of Periods function. Calculates the number of payments on a loan when given the rate, payment amount, and present value.

PMT
The Payment function. Calculates a payment when given the rate, number of periods, and present value.

PV
The Present Value function. Calculates the present value of an investment when given rate, number of periods, and payment amount.

Relative reference
A cell reference that changes when copied to another cell. The default setting.

Figure 66-1

- For example, in Figure 66-2, in cell C5, the following formula appears: =B5+$B$1. If you copy that formula to cell C6, the reference to B5 will change because it is relative, but the reference to B1 will not because it is absolute. The resulting formula in cell C6 will be =B6+$B$1.

Figure 66-2

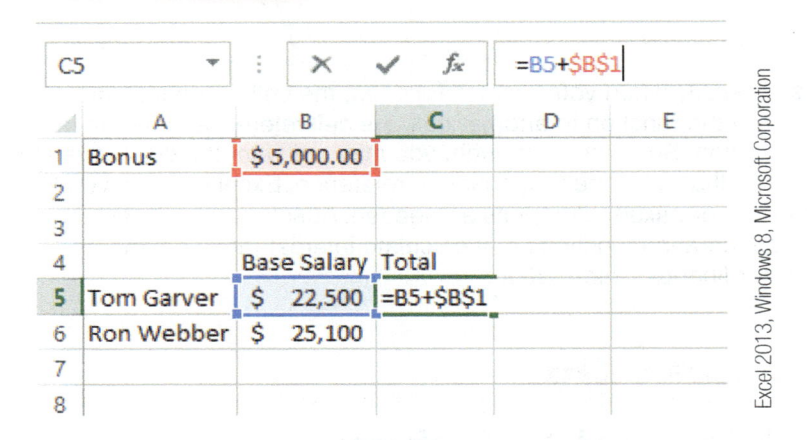

- A **mixed reference** is one in which only one dimension is absolute. For example, $B1 locks the column but not the row, and B$1 locks the row but not the column.
- To create absolute or mixed references, you can manually type the dollar signs into the formulas in the appropriate places.
- You can also toggle a cell reference among all the possible combinations of absolute, relative, and mixed by pressing F4 when the insertion point is within the cell reference.

Business Information Management II | Excel | Chapter 8   441

Try It! Using Absolute References

1. Start Excel, and open **E66Try** from the data files for this lesson.

2. Save the file as **E66Try_xx** in the location where your teacher instructs you to store the files for this lesson.

3. On the Taxes worksheet, click cell H3, type **=G3*$A$18**, and press ENTER.

4. Click cell H3, and press CTRL + C to copy the formula to the Clipboard.

5. Select the cell range H4:H15, and press CTRL + V to paste the formula into those cells.

6. Browse the contents of several of the pasted cells to confirm that the reference to A18 remained absolute.

7. Save the changes to the file, and leave it open to use in the next Try It.

The reference to the Total is relative; the reference to the Tax rate is absolute

	A	B	C	D	E	F	G	H
1				Sally's Shoes				
2		Clarks	Easy Spirit	Converse	Bali	Sketchers	Total	Total Taxes
3	January	$865.00	$657.00	$357.00	$456.00	$321.00	$2,656.00	$232.40
4	February	$561.00	$358.00	$159.00	$789.00	$654.00	$2,521.00	$220.59
5	March	$891.00	$159.00	$456.00	$321.00	$789.00	$2,616.00	$228.90
6	April	$236.00	$753.00	$789.00	$159.00	$159.00	$2,096.00	$183.40
7	May	$458.00	$159.00	$321.00	$357.00	$357.00	$1,652.00	$144.55
8	June	$695.00	$456.00	$582.00	$159.00	$456.00	$2,348.00	$205.45
9	July	$498.00	$987.00	$471.00	$753.00	$258.00	$2,967.00	$259.61
10	August	$285.00	$123.00	$693.00	$852.00	$123.00	$2,076.00	$181.65
11	September	$795.00	$951.00	$214.00	$741.00	$852.00	$3,553.00	$310.89
12	October	$125.00	$357.00	$236.00	$369.00	$456.00	$1,543.00	$135.01
13	November	$952.00	$458.00	$785.00	$196.00	$951.00	$3,342.00	$292.43
14	December	$159.00	$852.00	$985.00	$852.00	$528.00	$3,376.00	$295.40
15	Total	$6,520.00	$6,270.00	$6,048.00	$6,004.00	$5,904.00	$30,746.00	$2,690.28

H15 fx =G15*$A$18

Excel 2013, Windows 8, Microsoft Corporation

Try It! Using Mixed References

1. In the **E66Try_xx** file, click the Area worksheet tab.

2. In cell C5, type **=$B5*C$4**, and press ENTER.

3. Click cell C5, and drag the fill handle down to fill the cell range C6:C9 with the formula.

4. Click in any filled cell, and look at the formula bar. Notice that the relative references changed, and that the absolute references remained the same.

5. Copy the formula from cell C5 into the remainder of the range (through cell F9).

6. Save the changes to the file, and leave it open to use in the next Try It.

Figure 69-2

	A	B	C	D	E
1					
2					
3					
4					
5		**Old Southern Fu**			
6		*Biweekly Earnings Review*			
7		42736			
8					
9	Commission Rate	0.06			
10	Bonus on sales over $40K	200			
11					
12	Salesperson	Sales	Comm.	Bonus	Total Earnings
13	Carl Jackson	44202	=B13*$B$9	=IF(B13>40000,$B$10,0)	=SUM(B13:D13)
14	Ni Li Yung	41524	=B14*$B$9	=IF(B14>40000,$B$10,0)	=SUM(B14:D14)
15	Tom Wilson	43574	=B15*$B$9	=IF(B15>40000,$B$10,0)	=SUM(B15:D15)
16	Jill Palmer	39612	=B16*$B$9	=IF(B16>40000,$B$10,0)	=SUM(B16:D16)
17	Rita Nuez	39061	=B17*$B$9	=IF(B17>40000,$B$10,0)	=SUM(B17:D17)
18	Maureen Baker	38893	=B18*$B$9	=IF(B18>40000,$B$10,0)	=SUM(B18:D18)
19	Kim Cheng	31120	=B19*$B$9	=IF(B19>40000,$B$10,0)	=SUM(B19:D19)
20	Lloyd Hamilton	41922	=B20*$B$9	=IF(B20>40000,$B$10,0)	=SUM(B20:D20)
21	Ed Fulton	45609	=B21*$B$9	=IF(B21>40000,$B$10,0)	=SUM(B21:D21)
22	Maria Alvarez	30952	=B22*$B$9	=IF(B22>40000,$B$10,0)	=SUM(B22:D22)
23	Katie Wilson	31472	=B23*$B$9	=IF(B23>40000,$B$10,0)	=SUM(B23:D23)
24	Tim Brown	44783	=B24*$B$9	=IF(B24>40000,$B$10,0)	=SUM(B24:D24)
25					

Excel 2013, Windows 8, Microsoft Corporation

End-of-Chapter Activities

▶ Excel Chapter 8—Critical Thinking

Analyzing a Business Opportunity

You are interested in purchasing a business, and you want to analyze the financial numbers of the business from the past two years to see if it is a profitable, growing company. You will analyze the raw data that the current owner has provided to make sure the business would be a good investment.

If you do purchase the business, you will need to get a small business loan. You are considering two different loans, each with different terms. You will use what you know about financial functions to determine which loan is a better deal.

DIRECTIONS

1. Start Excel, if necessary, and open **ECT08** from the data files for this chapter.
2. Save the file as **ECT08_xx** in the location where your teacher instructs you to store the files for this chapter.
3. On the **Expenses** worksheet, in cell **G5**, create a **SUMIF** function that sums the values from **D5:D124** where "Facility Rental" appears in column C.
4. Enter the appropriate **SUMIF** functions in columns **G** and **I** that summarize the data in the ways described by the labels in columns **F** and **H**. Illustration 8A shows the totals that should appear in the cells when the functions are correctly created.
   - ✓ If you apply absolute references to all the cells in the function in G5, it makes it easier to copy and paste the function into other cells and then modify the copies to meet the new criteria. For example, you can copy the function into G6 and change Facility Rental to Loan Payment.
5. On the **Summary** tab, examine the **SUMIFS** functions in cells **C5** and **D5**.
   - ✓ Notice that in both functions, the date Jan-13 is being referenced as a general number: 40179. To determine the numeric equivalent of a date, temporarily set the cell's number format to General.
6. Using C5 and D5 as examples, complete the rest of the functions for the cell range **C6:D28**.
   - ✓ Because the cell references are absolute, you can copy and paste the functions from cells C5 and D5 into the remaining cells, and then edit each copy.
   - ✓ You may want to set all the dates in column A temporarily to General format to make it easier to see what numbers to use for the dates. Don't forget to set them back to the custom Date format of MMM-YY when you are finished.
   - ✓ Another shortcut: after completing column C's functions, copy them to column D, and use Find and Replace to replace all instances of "Fixed" with "Variable."
7. Copy the formula from cell **E5** to the cell range **E6:E28**.
8. Create a line chart from the values in column **E**, using the dates in column **A** as labels. Display the legend.
9. Add an exponential trend line to the chart.
10. Place the chart on its own sheet in the workbook. Name the sheet **Net Profit**.
    - ✓ To place the chart on its own sheet, right-click the chart border and click Move Chart.
11. On the **Loans** sheet, use the **PMT** function to calculate the monthly payments on two different loans, both for **$2 million**:

    Loan 1: **6% APR for 60 months**

    Loan 2: **5% APR for 48 months**
12. On the **Loans** worksheet, in cell **B10**, create a formula that evaluates whether the amount in cell **B9** is less than the smallest value in column **E** of the **Summary** worksheet (hint: use the =MIN function). If it is less, display **OK**. If it is not less, display **No**. Copy the formula to cell **C10**, changing any cell references as needed.

13. Create a scenario for the current values on the **Loans** sheet, with cell **B4** as the changing cell. Name the scenario **2 Million Loan**.

14. Create another scenario in which the loan amount is **$2,500,000**. Name it **2.5 Million Loan**. Show the **2.5 Million Loan** scenario, then show the **2 Million Loan** scenario.

15. For all worksheets, add a header that has your name at the left, the date code in the center, and the page number code at the right, and change back to **Normal** view.

16. **With your teacher's permission**, print the **Loans** worksheet and the **Net Profit** chart.

17. Save and close the file, and exit Excel.

Illustration 8A

2-Year Total of Expenses		2-Year Total Expenses by Type	
Facility Rental	$19,200	Fixed	$48,000
Loan Payment	$28,800	Variable	$6,268,911
Materials	$5,567,857		
Payroll	$694,826	**2013 Expenses by Type**	
Utilities	$6,228	Fixed	$24,000
		Variable	$2,642,102
2013 Expenses			
Facility Rental	$9,600	**2014 Expenses by Type**	
Loan Payment	$14,400	Fixed	$24,000
Materials	$2,344,531	Variable	$3,626,809
Payroll	$294,522		
Utilities	$3,049		
2014 Expenses			
Facility Rental	$9,600		
Loan Payment	$14,400		
Materials	$3,223,326		
Payroll	$400,304		
Utilities	$3,179		

Excel Chapter 8 — Portfolio Builder

Projecting Business Scenarios

The purchase of the business seems to be a good decision. However, the net profit per month seems to fluctuate quite a bit, making it difficult to predict how much money you can safely borrow to purchase the business. You can be more confident by calculating a moving average of the monthly profits, and by setting up several scenarios with varying degrees of optimism, ranging from worst case to best case.

DIRECTIONS

1. Start Excel, if necessary, and open **EPB08** from the data files for this chapter.
2. Save the file as **EPB08_xx** in the location where your teacher instructs you to store the files for this chapter.
3. On the **Summary** worksheet, in the **F** column, create a 5-interval moving average of the values in the **E** column, and chart the output.
   ✓ Enable the Analysis Toolpak Add-On, if necessary.
4. Move the chart to its own sheet. Name the sheet **Profit Moving Average**.
5. On the **Summary** sheet, in the cell range **B29:B40**, use the **GROWTH** function to predict the future monthly gross revenues for 2015. Use the cell ranges for 2014 only in the **GROWTH** function arguments.
6. Copy the formula from cell **E28** to the cell range **E29:E40**.
7. In cell **C29**, enter **$1,500**. Copy that value to the cell range **C30:C40**.
8. In cell **D29**, enter **$370,000**. Copy that value to the cell range **D30:D40**.
9. Use **Format Painter** to copy the formatting from cell **B29** to the cell range **C29:E40**.
10. Type **$1,500** in cell **I29**. Enter **$200,000** in cell **I30**.
11. In cell **C29**, enter a formula that provides an absolute reference to **I29**.
12. In cell **D29**, enter a formula that provides an absolute reference to **I30**.
13. Copy the formulas from the cell range **C29:D29** to the cell range **C30:D40**.
14. Create a scenario called **Best Case** that allows **I29** and **I30** to change, and uses the current values of those cells.
15. Create another scenario called **Most Likely** that sets cell **I29** to **$1750** and cell **I30** to **$300,000**.
16. Create another scenario called **Worst Case** that sets cell **I29** to **$2000** and cell **I30** to **$400,000**.
17. Show the **Most Likely** scenario.
18. For all worksheets, add a header that has your name at the left, the date code in the center, and the page number code at the right, and change back to **Normal** view.
19. **With your instructor's permission**, print the range **A29:E40** on the **Summary** worksheet, and print the **Profit Moving Average** chart.
20. Save and close the file, and exit Excel.

Chapter 9

(Courtesy Goodluz/Shutterstock)

Importing and Analyzing Database Data

Lesson 70
Importing Data into Excel
- Importing Data from an Access Database
- Importing Data from a Web Page
- Importing Data from a Text File
- Importing Data from an XML File

Lesson 71
Working with Excel Tables
- Converting Ranges to Tables
- Showing a Totals Row in a Table
- Viewing Two Tables Side-by-Side
- Applying Icon Sets

Lesson 72
Using Advanced Filters, Slicers, and Database Functions
- Using Advanced Filters
- Working with Slicers
- Using Database Functions

Lesson 73
Using Flash Fill and Data Consolidation
- Working with Flash Fill
- Consolidating Data
- Working with Consolidated Data

Lesson 74
Linking Workbooks
- Linking Workbooks
- Modifying a Linked Workbook

Lesson 75
Using PivotTables
- Working with PivotTables
- Working with PivotTable Fields
- Sorting PivotTable Fields
- Formatting a PivotTable

Lesson 76
Using PivotCharts
- Creating a PivotChart from a PivotTable
- Creating a PivotChart from an External Data Source
- Working with PivotChart Fields
- Formatting a PivotChart

Lesson 77
Using PowerPivot and Power View
- Using PowerPivot to Manage Data
- Creating a Power View Report
- Working with Power View Fields
- Formatting a Power View Report

End-of-Chapter Activities

473

Lesson 70

Importing Data into Excel

> ### ➤ What You Will Learn
> Importing Data from an Access Database
> Importing Data from a Web Page
> Importing Data from a Text File
> Importing Data from an XML File

WORDS TO KNOW

Database
An organized collection of data. Database data is commonly organized by rows (records) and columns (fields).

Datasheet
In Access, a spreadsheet-like view of a table.

Delimited
Separated. A delimited text file, for example, uses consistent characters such as a tab or comma to separate data into columns.

Software Skills You may want to use Excel to manipulate data that originates in other programs. Excel can import data from many sources, including Access, text files, Web pages, and XML files.

What You Can Do

Importing Data from an Access Database

- You can import the data from an Access **database** table into Excel and then use the features of Excel to format the data, add calculations, create charts, and so on, to help you analyze the data in a meaningful way.
- Access databases store data in **tables**.
- A table is most commonly viewed in a **datasheet**, which is very much like an Excel worksheet. Each row in a datasheet represents a **record**, and each column represents a **field**. See Figure 70-1.
- Once you import data from Access, you cannot use the undo command to undo the import. If you don't like the results, close the file without saving the changes.

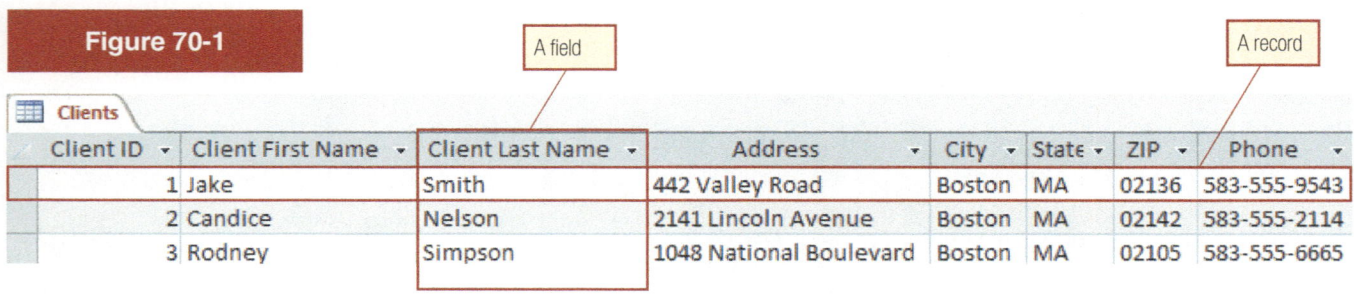

Figure 70-1

Client ID	Client First Name	Client Last Name	Address	City	State	ZIP	Phone
1	Jake	Smith	442 Valley Road	Boston	MA	02136	583-555-9543
2	Candice	Nelson	2141 Lincoln Avenue	Boston	MA	02142	583-555-2114
3	Rodney	Simpson	1048 National Boulevard	Boston	MA	02105	583-555-6665

A field (Client Last Name column) — A record (row 1: Jake Smith)

Excel 2013, Windows 8, Microsoft Corporation

Business Information Management II | Excel | Chapter 9   475

Try It!   Importing Data from an Access Database

1. Start Excel, and open **E70TryA.xlsx** from the data files for this lesson.

2. Save the file as **E70TryA_xx** in the location where your teacher instructs you to store the files for this lesson.
   - ✓ The file has no data in it; however, notice that the tabs are named Access, Web, Text, and XML.

3. Click cell A2. This is the location where you want to import the data.

4. Click DATA > Get External Data > From Access. The Select Data Source dialog box opens.
   - ✓ If the Excel window is wide enough, From Access appears as its own button, and you do not have to click Get External Data to see it.

5. Navigate to the data files for this lesson, and click **E70TryB.accdb**.

The Import Data dialog box

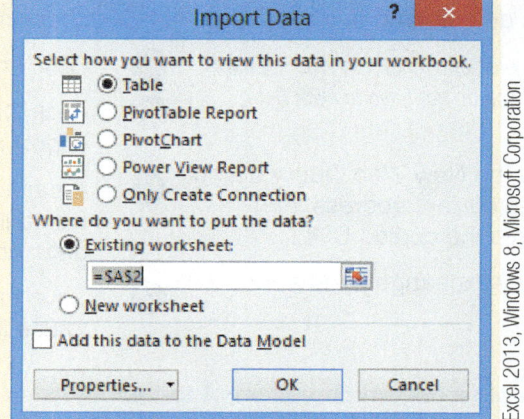

6. Click Open to display the Import Data dialog box.

7. Click OK to accept the default settings in the dialog box and =$A$2 as the start of the import range. Excel imports the data and formats it as a table.

8. Save the changes to the file, and leave it open to use in the next Try It.

Delimiter character
In a delimited text file, the character that is used to separate columns. Tabs and commas are the most common.

Field
A single column in a database.

Markup language
A set of codes inserted into a text file to indicate the formatting and purpose of each block of text. HTML and XML are both markup languages.

Record
A single row in a database.

Table
In Access, a container for database records.

XML
Stands for EXtensible Markup Language. It is a markup language similar to HTML, but designed for use with databases rather than Web sites. XML is widely used for a variety of data storage and retrieval applications.

Importing Data from a Web Page

- In Excel 2013, you can download data from Web pages with a few clicks. This process works best when the data being imported is already in a tabular format.

Try It!   Importing Data from a Web Page

1. In the **E70TryA_xx** file, click the Web worksheet tab.

2. Click cell A2. This is the location where you want to import the data.

3. Open a Web browser, and navigate to **http://www.global-view.com/forex-trading-tools/chartpts.html**.
   - ✓ If the URL provided is no longer available, explore other pages that include currency exchange tables that could be imported into Excel.

4. On the main page, under Printer-Friendly Tables, click the USD hyperlink.
   - ✓ USD stands for U.S. Dollars.

5. In the Address bar in the Web browser, select the URL of the page, and press CTRL + C to copy it.

6. Close the browser window.

(continued)

Try It! Importing Data from a Web Page *(continued)*

7. Switch to Excel, and click DATA > Get External Data > From Web. A New Web Query dialog box opens, with your default Web page showing.

   ✓ If the Excel window is wide enough, From Web appears as its own button, and you do not have to click Get External Data to see it.

8. In the Address bar of the New Web Query dialog box, click to select the current address, and press CTRL + V to paste the copied URL.

9. Click Go. The currency exchange page appears in the dialog box.

10. Click the yellow arrow to the left of the table's upper-left corner. The arrow turns to a green check mark and the table is selected.

11. Click Import. The Import Data dialog box opens.

12. Click OK to accept =$A$2 as the start of the import range. The data is imported.

13. Clean up the worksheet and format as you would like. For example, format cell A2 as a date, and adjust the column widths.

14. Save the changes to the file, and leave it open to use in the next Try It.

Selecting the table from which you want to import in the New Web Query dialog box

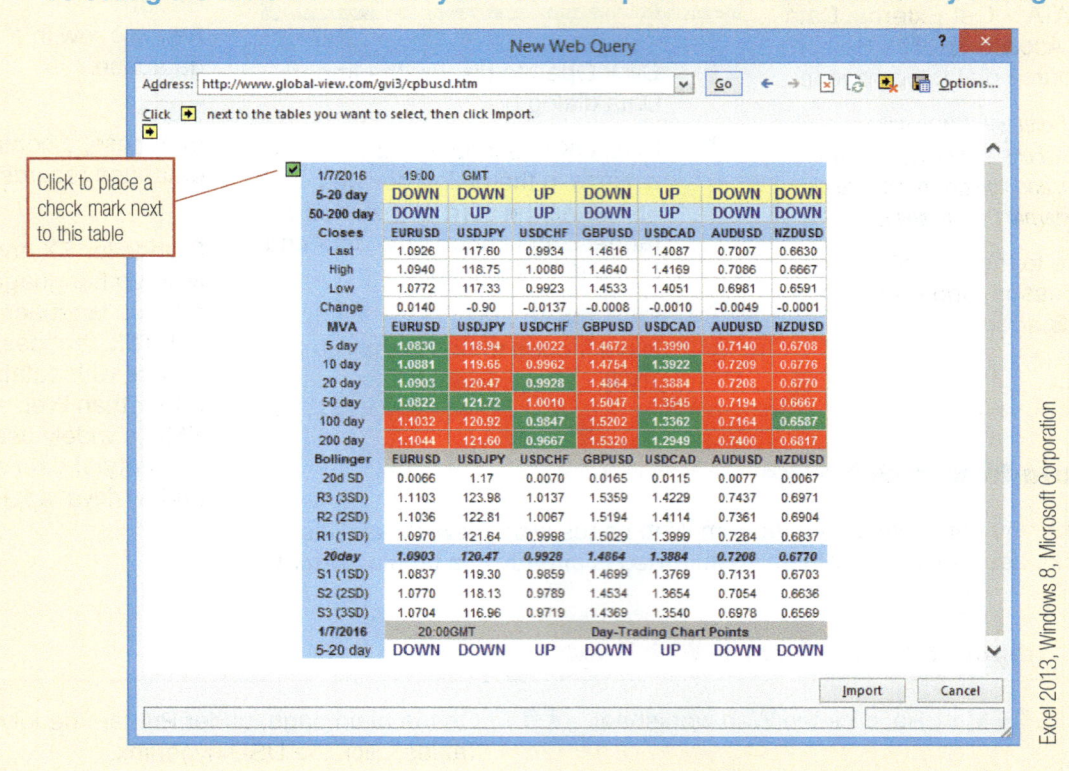

Importing Data from a Text File

- Plain text files can store **delimited** data by using a consistent **delimiter character**. For example, columns may be separated by either tabs or commas; rows are typically separated by paragraph breaks.

- Delimited text files typically have a .txt or .csv extension. CSV stands for comma-separated values.

Try It! Importing Data from a Text File

1. In the **E70TryA_xx** file, click the Text worksheet tab.
2. Click cell A2. This is the location where you want to import the data.
3. Click DATA > Get External Data > From Text. The Import Text File dialog box opens.
4. Navigate to and select **E70TryC.txt** file, and click Import. The Text Import Wizard runs.
5. Click Next to accept Delimited as the file type.
6. Click Next to accept Tab as the delimiter character.
7. On the Step 3 of 3 screen, click the second column heading (the dates), and click the Date option button.
8. Click Finish to complete the import. The Import Data dialog box opens.
9. Click OK to accept the entry range of =$A$2. The data is imported.
10. Save the changes to the file, and leave it open to use in the next Try It.

Importing Data from an XML File

- **XML** is a relative of HTML. Like HTML, it uses bracketed codes to indicate the formatting and function of each piece of data that the file contains. This is called a **markup language**.
- There may be times when data is in an XML file and you would like to analyze the data using the power of Excel. XML pages are typically viewed via a browser.
- There are two ways to import an XML file. You can use From Other Sources on the DATA tab, or you can click the DEVELOPER tab, and in the XML group, click Import.

Try It! Importing Data from an XML File

1. In the **E70TryA_xx** file, click the XML worksheet tab.
2. Click cell A2. This is the location where you want to import the data.
3. Select DATA > Get External Data > From Other Sources.
4. Click From XML Data Import to open the Select Data Source dialog box.
5. Navigate to the data files for this lesson, and click **E70TryD.xml**.
6. Click Open.
7. In the confirmation box, click OK to confirm that Excel will create a schema for the data being imported.
8. In the Import Data dialog box, click OK to accept the location of $A$2. The data is imported.
9. Save and close the file, and exit Excel.

Lesson 70—Practice

A real estate broker at World Services Real Estate is working for a family from Europe interested in purchasing a second residence in the United States. As the broker's assistant, you have been asked to provide a worksheet with information about the consumer price index in the United States. In this project, you will import data from the Web on exchange rates that will help the real estate agent provide information for the family.

DIRECTIONS

1. Start Excel, if necessary, and open **E70Practice** from the data files for this lesson.
2. Save the file as **E70Practice_xx** in the location where your teacher instructs you to store the files for this lesson.
3. Add a header that has your name at the left, the date code in the center, and the page number code at the right, and change back to **Normal** view.
4. Open a browser, and go to **http://www.bls.gov/news.release/cpi.t01.htm**, the Consumer Price Index Web page. Select the URL, and press CTRL + C to copy it to the Clipboard.
   - ✓ If the URL provided is no longer available, explore other pages at www.bls.gov to find data that could be important to a real estate agent, and that can be imported into Excel.
5. Identify a table that contains consumer price index data.
6. Switch to Excel, and click **DATA** > **Get External Data** > **From Web**.
7. In the Address box of the New Web Query dialog box, press CTRL + V to paste the address copied in step 4. Alternatively, you can type **http://www.bls.gov/news.release/cpi.t01.htm** (or the address of another page you found on that site that contains appropriate data). Click **Go**.
8. If a Script Error dialog box appears, click **Yes** to continue running scripts on the page.
9. (Optional) Drag the border of the New Web Query dialog box to enlarge the window so you can see more of the page.
10. Click the yellow arrow to the left of the main table to select it. It changes to a green check mark.
11. Click **Import**. If a Script Error dialog box appears, click **Yes** to continue running scripts on the page
12. in the Import Data dialog box, in the Existing worksheet box, type **=$A$2**. The data appears in the worksheet.
13. Clean up and format the data where the data did not import perfectly. Refer to the Web page to see how it was formatted.
14. Save and close the file, and exit Excel.

Lesson 70—Apply

A real estate broker at World Services Real Estate was asked to prepare real estate data for a family from Europe interested in purchasing a second residence in the United States. In this project, you will create one workbook with several worksheets of data from various sources to help this client make a decision as to where to buy. You will also provide them with information about the consumer price index in the United States.

DIRECTIONS

1. Start Excel, if necessary, and open **E70ApplyA** from the data files for this lesson.
2. Save the file as **E70ApplyA_xx** in the location where your teacher instructs you to store the files for this lesson.
3. Add a header on all worksheets that has your name at the left, the date code in the center, and the page number code at the right, and change back to **Normal** view.
4. On the **Real Estate** worksheet, import the data as a table from the Access database file **E70ApplyB.accdb**, starting in cell A3.
   ✓ *That database contains only one table, so you are not prompted to choose which table the data is coming from.*
5. Format the list prices with the **Accounting** format, with no decimal places. Adjust the list price column width.
6. Sort the data by the highest list price to the lowest list price. Look at the common characteristics of the houses at the top of the list.
7. Copy the entire table to the Bedrooms tab, and sort the data based on the number of bedrooms, from most to fewest. Adjust the column widths, as necessary.
8. **With your teacher's permission,** print only the first page of the **Bedrooms** worksheet.
9. Save and close the file, and exit Excel.

Lesson 71

Working with Excel Tables

> ## ➤ What You Will Learn
>
> **Converting Ranges to Tables**
> **Showing a Totals Row in a Table**
> **Viewing Two Tables Side-by-Side**
> **Applying Icon Sets**

WORDS TO KNOW

Banded columns
Alternating colors in columns in a table.

Banded rows
Alternating colors in rows in a table.

Filter
To reduce the number of records displayed on the screen by applying one or more criteria.

Icon Sets
Icons that are placed in a cell based on the value of the cell.

Table
In Excel, a range of cells in a datasheet that have been grouped together into a single unit for formatting and data analysis.

Software Skills You can create a table in Excel to sort, filter, and analyze data. A worksheet can have multiple tables, and placing tables side by side is a good way to compare data quickly. Putting the two tables on one worksheet, rather than on separate worksheets, lets the user filter and compare data on a single sheet. Icons can be placed in cells to visually represent criteria of the data in the cell. For example, colored dots can represent a high value, medium value, or low value.

What You Can Do

Converting Ranges to Tables

- Worksheet ranges can be turned into **tables** for easy analysis. A table can easily be sorted and **filtered** via the drop-down lists associated with each column heading.
- A table also offers visually pleasing formatting with **banded rows** or **banded columns**. The alternating lighter and darker colors make it easy to follow data across a row, or down a column, increasing the accuracy of your work. See Figure 71-1 on the next page.
- Banding is added by default when you create a table out of a data range that does not have previously existing fill applied to it. The worksheets in the Try It exercises in this lesson already have background fill, so you will not see banding applied when you create the tables.
- To add or remove banding, use the Banded Rows command on the TABLE TOOLS DESIGN tab.
- Multiple ranges in a worksheet can be converted into separate tables.

   ✓ When inserting two tables on the same worksheet, there must be at least one row or one column between the data ranges in order for Excel to know that the data will be treated as two tables.

Business Information Management II | Excel | Chapter 9

Figure 71-1

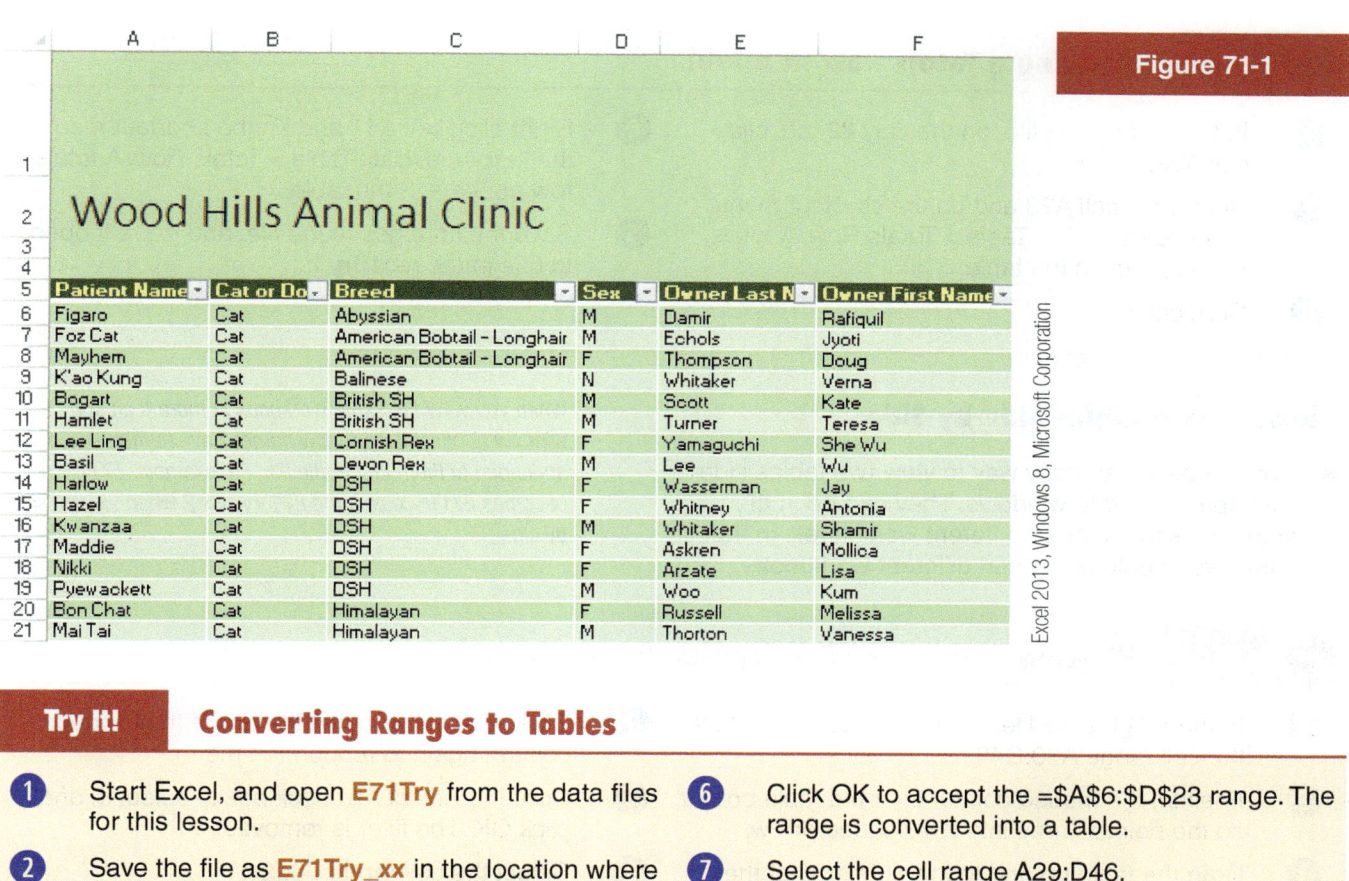

	A	B	C	D	E	F
1						
2	Wood Hills Animal Clinic					
3						
4						
5	Patient Name	Cat or Dog	Breed	Sex	Owner Last N	Owner First Name
6	Figaro	Cat	Abyssian	M	Damir	Rafiquil
7	Foz Cat	Cat	American Bobtail - Longhair	M	Echols	Jyoti
8	Mayhem	Cat	American Bobtail - Longhair	F	Thompson	Doug
9	K'ao Kung	Cat	Balinese	N	Whitaker	Verna
10	Bogart	Cat	British SH	M	Scott	Kate
11	Hamlet	Cat	British SH	M	Turner	Teresa
12	Lee Ling	Cat	Cornish Rex	F	Yamaguchi	She Wu
13	Basil	Cat	Devon Rex	M	Lee	Wu
14	Harlow	Cat	DSH	F	Wasserman	Jay
15	Hazel	Cat	DSH	F	Whitney	Antonia
16	Kwanzaa	Cat	DSH	M	Whitaker	Shamir
17	Maddie	Cat	DSH	F	Askren	Mollica
18	Nikki	Cat	DSH	F	Arzate	Lisa
19	Pyewackett	Cat	DSH	M	Woo	Kum
20	Bon Chat	Cat	Himalayan	F	Russell	Melissa
21	Mai Tai	Cat	Himalayan	M	Thorton	Vanessa

Excel 2013, Windows 8, Microsoft Corporation

Try It! Converting Ranges to Tables

1. Start Excel, and open **E71Try** from the data files for this lesson.
2. Save the file as **E71Try_xx** in the location where your teacher instructs you to store the files for this lesson.
3. Click the July 22 worksheet tab to select it, if necessary.
4. Select the cell range A6:D23.
5. Click INSERT > Table.
6. Click OK to accept the =$A$6:$D$23 range. The range is converted into a table.
7. Select the cell range A29:D46.
8. Click INSERT > Table.
9. Click OK to accept the =$A$29:$D$46 range.
10. Save the changes to the file, and leave it open to use in the next Try It.

Showing a Totals Row in a Table

- Using a Totals row provides a way of summarizing data in the table without having to create formulas or functions for each column. It is one of the many benefits of analyzing data in tabular form in Excel.

Try It! Showing a Totals Row in a Table

1. In the **E71Try_xx** file, on the July 22 tab, click cell A23.
2. Right-click cell A23 and on the shortcut menu that appears, click Table > Totals Row. A totals row appears in the table.
3. Click cell A47.
4. Right-click cell A47 and on the shortcut menu that appears, click Table > Totals Row. A totals row appears in the table.
5. Save the changes to the file, and leave it open to use in the next Try It.

Viewing Two Tables Side-by-Side

- Excel provides an easy way to view two tables side-by-side in separate windows. They can be in the same worksheet, or on different worksheets in the same workbook, or even in different workbooks.

✓ When you view the same workbook in more than one window at once, the window names have numbers appended to them in the title bar. For example, E71Try.xlsx becomes E71Try.xlsx:1 and E71Try.xlsx:2 when viewed side by side.

Try It! Viewing Two Tables Side-by-Side by Moving a Table

1. In the **E71Try_xx** file, on the July 22 tab, select the cell range A30:D48.
2. Position the mouse pointer over the table border, so the pointer turns into a 4-headed arrow.
3. Drag the table up and to the right so that the upper-left corner is in cell F6, and release the mouse button.
4. Adjust the column widths as needed.
5. In the table on the left, click the drop-drop-down arrow at the top of the Product column.
6. Click the Select All check box to deselect it, click the Greeting Cards check box, and click OK.
   ✓ Notice that the left table is sorted on greeting cards, and the right table displays the data that happens to be in the same rows.
7. Click the filter arrow at the top of the Product column again to reopen the menu.
8. Click the Select All check box to select it, and click OK. The filter is removed.
9. Select the cell range F6:I24.
10. Using the same process as in steps 2–3, move the selected table back to its original position, in cells A30:D48.
11. Use the Format Painter to format the fill color of the cell range F24:I24 to match the rest of the filled cells.
12. Save the changes to the file, and leave it open to use in the next Try It.

Side-by-side tables, filtered, in one worksheet

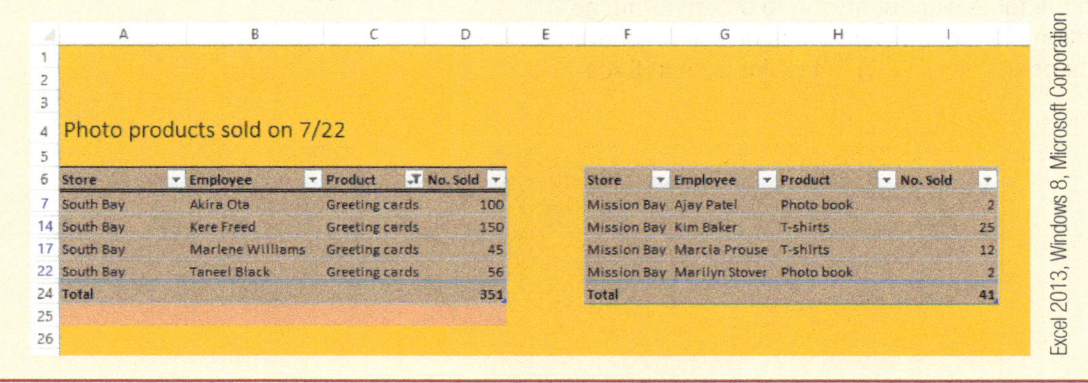

End-of-Chapter Activities

➤ Excel Chapter 9—Critical Thinking

Chamber of Commerce Presentation

At the Center City Chamber of Commerce, you have been asked to gather, analyze, and present some information at a business meeting with guests who may be interested in relocating their businesses to Center City. You will present information to them about local real estate, schools, and existing businesses that will help them make up their minds. You will convey meaningful information in a concise and attractive format, using the skills you learned in this chapter.

DIRECTIONS

1. Start Excel, if necessary, and create a new blank workbook. Save the workbook as **ECT09A_xx** in the location where your teacher instructs you to store the files for this chapter.
2. Insert two new worksheets, and rename the worksheet tabs to match the categories of data you will be presenting: **Real Estate**, **Schools**, and **Local Businesses**.
3. Copy the real estate data from **ECT09B** workbook into the **ECT09A_xx** workbook on the **Real Estate** worksheet.
   - ✓ One way to perform step 3 is to copy the entire worksheet. This method has the advantage of retaining all the content and formatting. Right-click the tab of the sheet to be copied and click Move or Copy. In the Move or Copy dialog box, select your new workbook as the Move To value, and click the Create a Copy check box to select it. Then delete the Real Estate tab you created in step 2, and rename the imported worksheet's tab Real Estate.
4. Create a new worksheet named **Real Estate Summary**. Place it immediately after the **Real Estate** worksheet.
5. On the **Real Estate Summary** worksheet, for each area, create a PivotTable of the areas and their communities, and provide an average price of the homes for sale in each community. Use any method you like. Format the prices with the **Accounting** format.
6. On the **Real Estate Summary** worksheet, create a PivotChart showing the average list price of the homes for sale in each community. Format the PivotChart with **Style 6**. Resize the chart so that all data is legible.
7. On the **Real Estate** worksheet, filter the data to exclude homes with fewer than two bedrooms, and add icon sets to the bedrooms and bathrooms. Determine the most appropriate icon set to use to visually indicate the number of bedrooms and bathrooms in the homes.
8. On the **Schools** worksheet, import the school district SAT score data from the **ECT09C** XML file. Allow Excel to create a schema based on the XML source data. In the imported school data, delete the **avgsqft** and **avgsaleprice** columns. Format the school data by renaming the headings. Sort the data alphabetically by school district name.
9. On the **Schools** worksheet, show the high schools with the highest SAT scores in a separate table below the original table.
   - ✓ One way is to copy the table and use a slicer to filter the highest score.
10. Save the **ECT09A_xx** file, and leave it open for later use.
11. Open the **ECT09D** file from the data files for this project, and save it as **ECT09D_xx** in the location where your teacher instructs you to store the files for this project.
12. Complete the **Sales Summary** worksheet by consolidating the data from each of the month worksheets. Create a link to the source data. Move the label from cell J6 into cell **J7**.
13. On the **Sales Summary** worksheet, convert the cell range **A7:I17** to a table, and then add a **Totals** row to it. Use the drop-down arrow in the Totals row label to show averages for each area, and change the row's label to **Average**.
    - ✓ Hint: Every cell has to have a numeric value for the function to calculate properly.

14. On the **Sales Summary** worksheet, format the cell range **B8:J18** with the **Accounting** format. Make the font usage consistent by using Format Painter to copy the font settings from cell **B8** to the cell range **H8:J17**. Adjust the column widths as needed.
15. Save and close the **ECT09D_xx** file.
16. In the **ECT09A_xx** workbook, on the **Local Businesses** worksheet, import the data from the **Sales Summary** worksheet in the **ECT09D_xx** workbook.
17. For all worksheets, add a header that has your name at the left, the date code in the center, and the page number code at the right, and change back to **Normal** view.
18. **With your teacher's permission,** print the **ECT09A_xx** workbook.
19. Save and close the file, and exit Excel.

▶ Excel Chapter 9—Portfolio Builder

Basketball Team Data

To promote attendance at professional team sports competitions in the state, the Indiana Visitors Bureau has asked you to collect data about the most recent season's win/loss records of the professional basketball teams based in Indiana. You will collect statistics on the Indiana Pacers (men's basketball) and the Indiana Fever (women's basketball) and present it in an attractively formatted Excel workbook.

DIRECTIONS

1. Start Excel, if necessary, and create a new blank workbook. Save the workbook as **EPB09_xx** in the location where your teacher instructs you to store the files for this chapter.
2. Insert two new worksheets, and rename the worksheet tabs as follows: **Summary**, **Pacers**, and **Fever**.
3. Search the Web to collect data about each team's wins and losses for the last full season played, and place it on that team's worksheet in the workbook. For each game played, include at least the date, the opponent, and the final score, with each team's score in a separate column.
    - ✓ If both scores are in a single column, use the Text to Columns feature on the DATA tab to split the scores into separate columns.
4. On each worksheet, if there is already a column that indicates whether it was a win or a loss, delete that column. Then create (or re-create) the Win/Loss column to use an IF function that determines whether the score of the Pacers/Fever was higher than the score of the opponent. If the Pacers'/Fever's score was higher, "**WIN**" should appear in the Win/Loss column. If not, "**LOSS**" should appear there.
5. Convert each team's statistics list into a table.
6. Format the two worksheets attractively and as consistently as possible, given that you may have collected different statistics on each team.
7. On the **Summary** worksheet, summarize the data from the other sheets, providing as many meaningful statistics as you can extrapolate from the data you gathered.

8. On the **Summary** worksheet, use Conditional Formatting to set the team's name in **green** font if it had more wins than losses, or in **red** font if it had more losses than wins.

9. In each of the tables, add a **point difference** column, and calculate its value as the team's final score in the game minus the opponent's final score. The number in this column will be **positive** if the team won, and **negative** if they lost.

10. On the **Summary** worksheet, include **Average Point Difference** as one of the statistics you provide.

11. On each of the team worksheets, create a **Moving Average of Point Difference** column, and calculate a **6-interval moving average** for the point difference. Create a chart for each team, and place the chart on the **Summary** sheet, next to each team's other statistics. Label, size, and format each chart so it is easily understandable.

    ✓ Illustration 9A shows one possible Summary worksheet design.

12. For all worksheets, add a header that has your name at the left, the date code in the center, and the page number code at the right, and change back to **Normal** view.

13. **With your teacher's permission,** print the **Summary** worksheet.

14. Save and close the file, and exit Excel.

Illustration 9A

	A	B
2	**Pacers**	
4	First game:	28-Oct
5	Last game:	14-Apr
6	Total Games:	82
7	Wins:	32
8	Losses:	50
9	# Home Games	41
10	# Away Games	41
11	Average Point Difference	-3
13	**Fever**	
15	First game:	15-May
16	Last game:	22-Aug
17	Total Games:	34
18	Wins:	21
19	Losses:	13
20	# Home Games	17
21	# Away Games	17
22	Average Point Difference	4

Charts: Pacers Moving Average Point Difference; Fever Moving Average Point Difference (Actual and Forecast series).

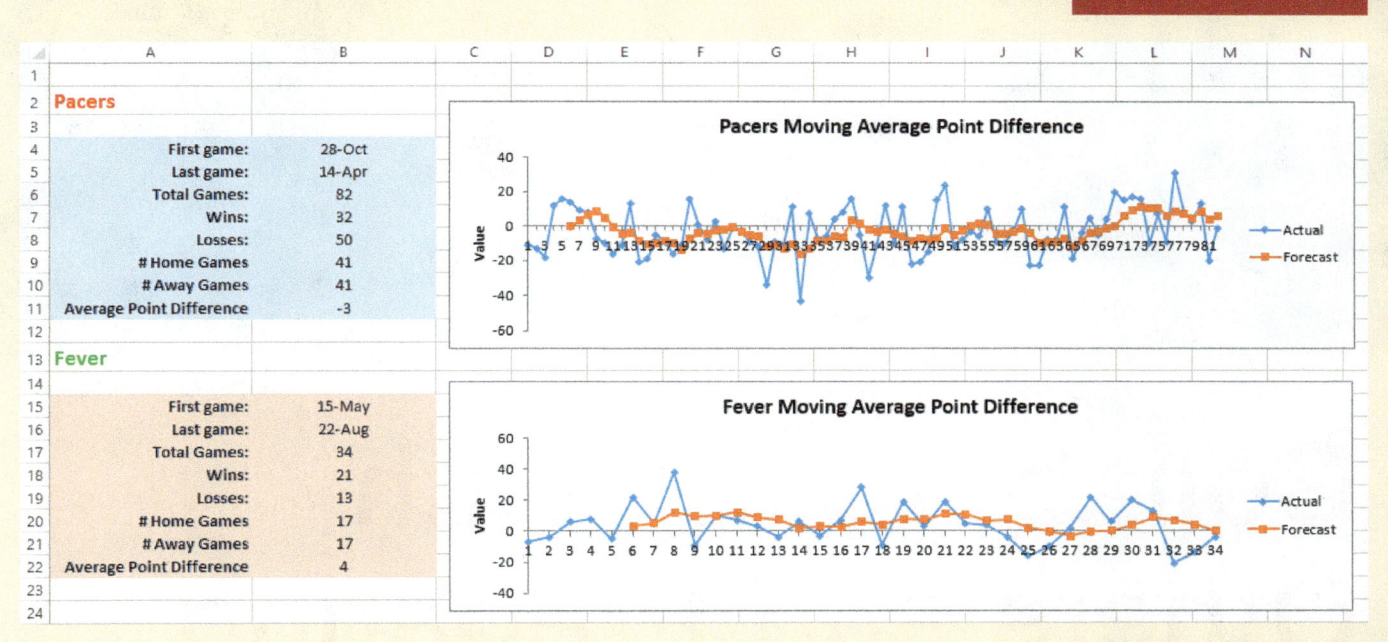

Excel 2013, Windows 8, Microsoft Corporation

Chapter 10

(Courtesy YanLev/Shutterstock)

Collaborating with Others and Preparing a Final Workbook for Distribution

Lesson 78
Tracking Changes
- Creating and Modifying a Shared Workbook
- Tracking Changes in a Shared Workbook
- Managing Comments in a Shared Workbook
- Merging Changes
- Removing Workbook Sharing

Lesson 79
Ensuring Data Integrity
- Turning Off AutoComplete
- Controlling Data Entry with Data Validation
- Circling Invalid Data
- Copying Validation Rules
- Removing Duplicate Data
- Controlling Recalculation

Lesson 80
Protecting Data
- Locking and Unlocking Cells in a Worksheet
- Protecting a Range
- Protecting a Worksheet
- Protecting a Workbook

Lesson 81
Securing a Workbook
- Using Document Inspector
- Encrypting a Workbook
- Identifying Workbooks Using Keywords

Lesson 82
Finalizing a Workbook
- Adding a Digital Signature
- Checking for Accessibility Issues
- Marking a Workbook As Final
- Managing Versions

Lesson 83
Sharing a Workbook
- Setting Precise Margins for Printing
- Uploading a Workbook to Windows OneDrive

End-of-Chapter Activities

Lesson 78

Tracking Changes

➤ What You Will Learn

Creating and Modifying a Shared Workbook
Tracking Changes in a Shared Workbook
Managing Comments in a Shared Workbook
Merging Changes
Removing Workbook Sharing

Software Skills When you are working on a large worksheet or a major project, you may need to work with other members of your team to complete all the parts of the worksheet that need to be completed. Collaborating successfully in Excel 2013 means that you need to be able to create and edit your own sections, add comments to the worksheet, see what changes others are making, merge many changes into one worksheet, and turn off sharing when you no longer need it.

What You Can Do

Creating and Modifying a Shared Workbook

- Sharing a workbook enables you to allow other authors to make changes in the file.
- You can turn a regular workbook into a **shared workbook** by using the Share Workbook command in the Changes group on the REVIEW tab.
- You can restrict the editing of the workbook by removing users from the Share Workbook dialog box.
- On the Advanced tab of the Share Workbook dialog box, you can set sharing options to specify how long changes are kept, when the changes in the file are updated, and how any conflicting changes will be resolved.
- You can tell Excel whether you want to update the file automatically as people work on it or update the file when it is saved.
- You can choose whether you want to see everyone's changes in the file or see only other users' changes.
- If your worksheet contains a table, you will be prompted to convert the table to a range before sharing the file.

WORDS TO KNOW

Change history
A listing of all changes made in a workbook. You can view the change history in the workbook or on its own worksheet.

Comment
A note attached to a worksheet cell for reference.

Track Changes
A process that keeps track of all changes made to a workbook each time you save it.

Shared workbook
An Excel workbook that you are using collaboratively with other users. When you turn on track changes, the workbook becomes a shared workbook automatically.

- You can save a shared workbook to a network location or your Windows Live SkyDrive account so that others can work with the file.

- You can tell Excel whether you want to be prompted to decide about changes that are in conflict or whether you want the saved changes to be the ones that are preserved in the file.

Try It! Sharing a Workbook

1. Start Excel, and open **E78TryA** from the data files for this lesson.
2. Save the file as **E78TryA_xx** in the location where your teacher instructs you to store the files for this lesson.
3. Click REVIEW > Share Workbook.
4. Click the Allow changes by more than one user at the same time check box.
5. Click OK.
6. If prompted, click OK to save the workbook.
7. Save the changes to the file, and leave it open to use in the next Try It.

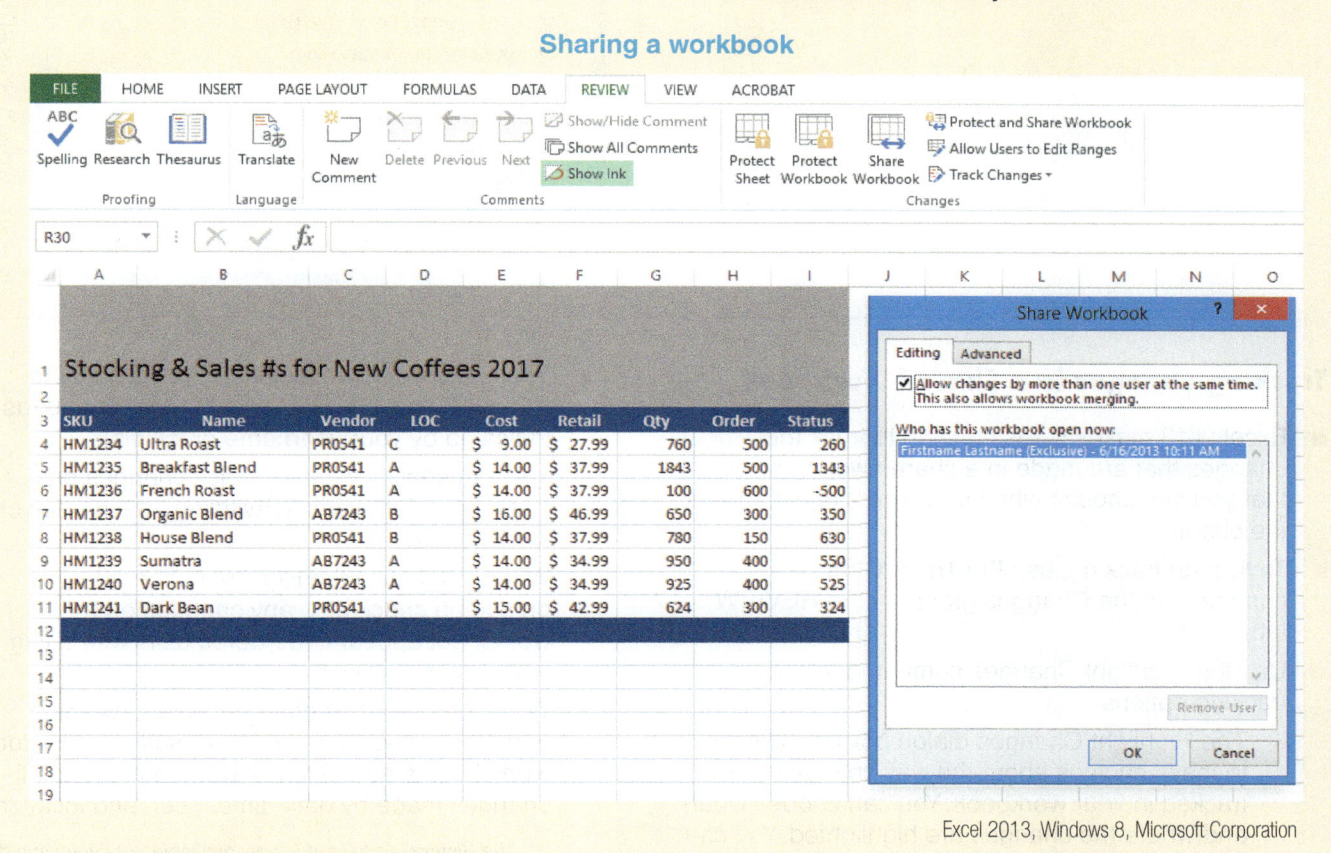

Sharing a workbook

Excel 2013, Windows 8, Microsoft Corporation

Try It! Setting Sharing Options

1. In the **E78TryA_xx** file, click REVIEW > Share Workbook.
2. In the Share Workbook dialog box, click the Advanced tab.
3. Review the Advanced share settings.
4. Under Update changes, click Automatically every.
5. Click OK.
6. Save the changes to the file, and leave it open to use in the next Try It.

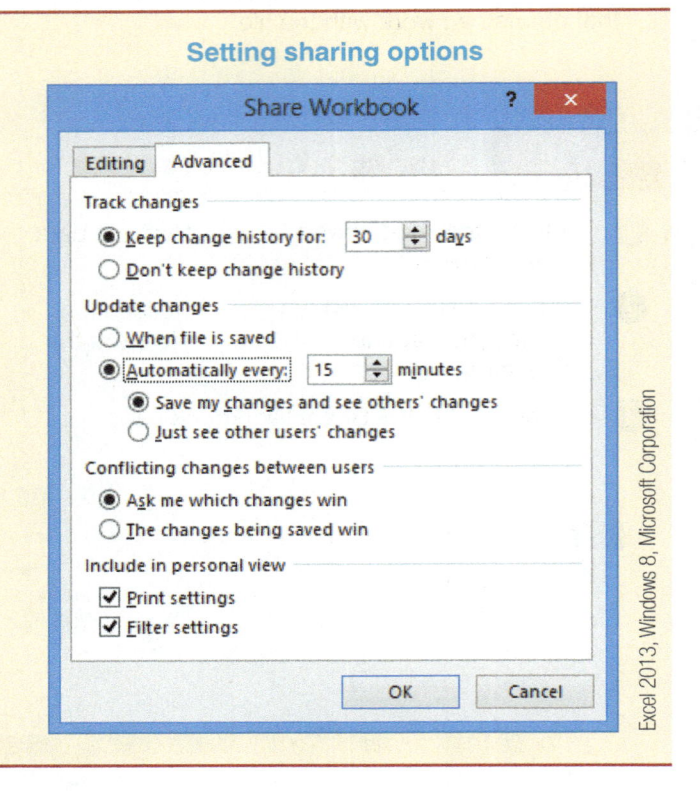

Setting sharing options

Tracking Changes in a Shared Workbook

- Excel 2013 makes it easy for you to track the changes that are made in a shared workbook so that you can choose whether to keep, reject, or edit the changes.
- To turn on tracking, use the **Track Changes** command in the Changes group on the REVIEW tab.
- Use the Highlight Changes command to set the tracking options.
    - The Highlight Changes dialog box enables you to make choices about the way changes are tracked in your workbook. You can choose when and where the changes are highlighted. You can also decide whether you want the changes to be highlighted on the sheet or listed on a new worksheet.
    - You can specify when changes are saved in the Highlight Changes dialog box: Since I last saved, All, Not yet reviewed, or Since date.
    - You can choose whose changes you want to review: Everyone, Everyone but Me, or you (as indicated by your username or initials).
    - You can specify where to track changes on a worksheet, for example, within a specific cell or a cell range.
    - When you select the Highlight changes on screen check box, any changes on the worksheet appear in bordered cells with a flag in the upper-left corner.
    - When you click List changes on a new sheet and All is selected in the When setting, a History worksheet is added to the workbook listing all changes made by date, time, user, and location.
        ✓ *The History worksheet is only available until you save the workbook.*
- When you are ready to accept or reject changes, you can choose to do so based on when changes were made, who made the changes, and where the changes are located.

Business Information Management II | Excel | Chapter 10

Try It! Turning on Tracking

1. In the **E78TryA_xx** file, click REVIEW > Track Changes.
2. Click Highlight Changes.
3. Click the Track changes while editing check box, if necessary.
4. Click the When check box > When drop-down arrow > All.
5. Click the Who check box > Who drop-down arrow > Everyone, if necessary.
6. Click the Highlight changes on screen check box, if necessary.
7. Click OK, and click OK to confirm that no changes were found.
8. Click cell G4, and change the value to **820**. Notice the flag in the upper-left corner of the cell.
9. Click cell H4, and change the value to **550**.
10. Save the changes to the file, and leave it open to use in the next Try It.

Try It! Displaying Change History

1. In the **E78TryA_xx** file, click cell G9, and change the value to **925**.
2. Click cell H9, and change the value to **450**.
3. Save the workbook.
4. On the REVIEW tab, click Track Changes > Highlight Changes.
5. Click List changes on a new sheet.
6. Click OK.
7. Review the History worksheet.
8. Save the changes to the file, and leave it open to use in the next Try It.

The change history

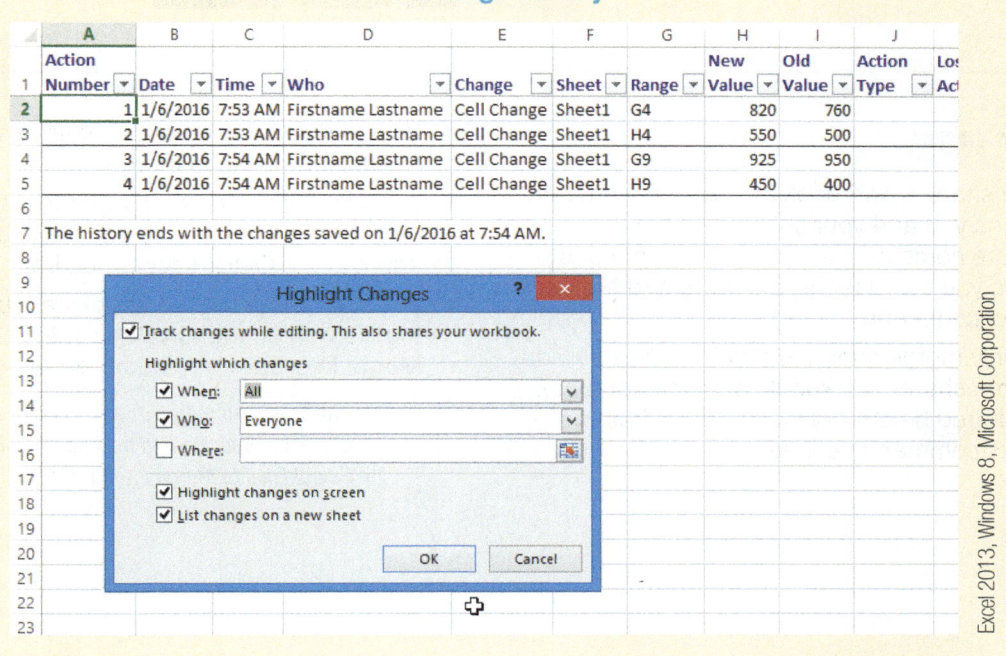

Action Number	Date	Time	Who	Change	Sheet	Range	New Value	Old Value	Action Type
1	1/6/2016	7:53 AM	Firstname Lastname	Cell Change	Sheet1	G4	820	760	
2	1/6/2016	7:53 AM	Firstname Lastname	Cell Change	Sheet1	H4	550	500	
3	1/6/2016	7:54 AM	Firstname Lastname	Cell Change	Sheet1	G9	925	950	
4	1/6/2016	7:54 AM	Firstname Lastname	Cell Change	Sheet1	H9	450	400	

The history ends with the changes saved on 1/6/2016 at 7:54 AM.

Excel 2013, Windows 8, Microsoft Corporation

Managing Comments in a Shared Workbook

- Using **comments** in a shared workbook is the same as doing so in an unshared workbook.
- Use the commands in the Comments group on the REVIEW tab of the Ribbon.
- A red triangle appears in the upper-right corner of any cell with an attached comment.
- You can edit the contents of a comment that has been previously inserted.
- Use the Previous and Next commands to navigate among the comments.
- You can choose to show or hide a single comment, or you can show all comments.
- You can delete a single comment, or you can delete all comments in a worksheet.

Try It! Creating and Editing Comments

1. In the **E78TryA_xx** file, click cell I6.
2. On the REVIEW tab, click New Comment.
3. In the comment box, type **Order more immediately**.
4. Click cell A1.
5. On the REVIEW tab, in the Comments group, click Next to display the comment.
6. On the REVIEW tab, in the Comments group, click Edit Comment.
7. In the comment, replace the text *Order more immediately* with the text **This has been ordered**.
8. Click outside of the comment.
9. On the REVIEW tab, in the Comments group, click Show All Comments.
10. Save the changes to the file, and leave it open to use in the next Try It.

Editing a comment

Qty	Order	Status
820	550	270
1843	500	1343
100	600	-500
650	300	350
780	150	630
925	450	475
925	400	525
624	300	324

Firstname Lastname: This has been ordered

Excel 2013, Windows 8, Microsoft Corporation

Merging Changes

- When you share a workbook and want to compare the changes you and your colleagues have made before combining those changes into one worksheet, you can use the Compare and Merge Workbooks command.
- You can only merge changes that have been made on the same shared workbook, and the workbook must be shared before the Compare and Merge Workbooks command becomes available.
- You can manage workbook versions by selecting which workbooks to merge.
- By default, the Compare and Merge Workbooks command isn't available on the Ribbon; you need to add it to the Quick Access Toolbar.
- You can merge the workbook data by selecting the file with changed values in the Select Files to Merge Into Current Workbook dialog box.
    - ✓ You can open and merge multiple copies of the same workbook by pressing and holding Ctrl while clicking files in the Select Files to Merge Into Current Workbook dialog box.

Try It! Adding the Compare and Merge Workbooks Command to the QAT

1. In the **E78TryA_xx** file, click FILE > Options > Quick Access Toolbar in the left pane.
2. In the Choose commands from list, click All Commands.
3. Scroll down the list, and click Compare and Merge Workbooks > Add.
4. Click OK.
5. Save and close the file. Leave Excel open to use in the next Try It.

Try It! Merging Workbook Data

1. Open the **E78TryB** file from the data files for this lesson.
2. Save the file as **E78TryB_xx** in the location where your teacher instructs you to store the files for this lesson.
3. Click REVIEW > Share Workbook.
4. Click the Allow changes by more than one user at the same time check box.
5. Click OK > OK.
6. Save the file as **E78TryC_xx** in the location where your teacher instructs you to store the files for this lesson.
7. In cell G7, change the value to **400**.
8. Save and close the **E78TryC_xx** file.
9. Open the **E78TryB_xx** file again.
10. On the Quick Access Toolbar, click Compare and Merge Workbooks.
11. In the Select Files to Merge Into Current Workbook dialog box, browse to the location where your teacher instructs you to store the files for this lesson to, and click **E78TryC_xx**.
12. Click OK. The new file data is merged with the current file, and the value you changed is flagged on the worksheet.
13. Save the changes to the **E78TryB_xx** file, and leave it open to use in the next Try It.

Removing Workbook Sharing

- When you are ready to stop sharing the workbook, you can turn the sharing workbook feature off by using the Share Workbook command in the Changes group on the REVIEW tab.
- You can remove other users by clicking the names of colleagues in the Who Has This Workbook Open Now list of the Share Workbook dialog box and clicking Remove User.
- Click to remove the check mark in the Allow changes by more than one user at the same time check box.

✓ *You need to remove workbook protection before sharing or unsharing a workbook. Click Unprotect Shared Workbook in the Changes group of the REVIEW tab to remove protection.*

Lesson 81—Practice

You are working on a workbook for two clients. You will inspect the workbook for issues, apply passwords, and add keywords to the workbook properties.

DIRECTIONS

1. Start Excel, if necessary, and open **E81Practice** from the data files for this lesson.
2. Save the file as **E81Practice_xx** in the location where your teacher instructs you to store the files for this lesson.
3. Click **FILE**.
4. In the Backstage view, on the Info tab, click **Check for Issues** > **Inspect Document**.
5. In the Document Inspector, click **Inspect**.
6. Review the results, and click **Close** to close the Document Inspector.
7. In the Backstage view, on the Info tab, click **Protect Workbook** > **Encrypt with Password**.
8. In the Encrypt Document dialog box, in the Password box, type **pass123#**, and click **OK**.
9. In the Confirm Password dialog box, in the Reenter password box, type **pass123#**, and click **OK**.
10. In the Backstage view, on the Info tab, click **Properties** > **Show Document Panel**.
11. In the Document Properties panel, in the Keywords box, type **inventory, reorders**.
12. Close the Document Properties panel.
13. Save the file.
14. Click **FILE**. The Info tab of the Backstage view should look like the one shown in Figure 81-1.
15. Click the Back button to exit the Backstage view.
16. Save and close the file, and exit Excel.

Figure 81-1

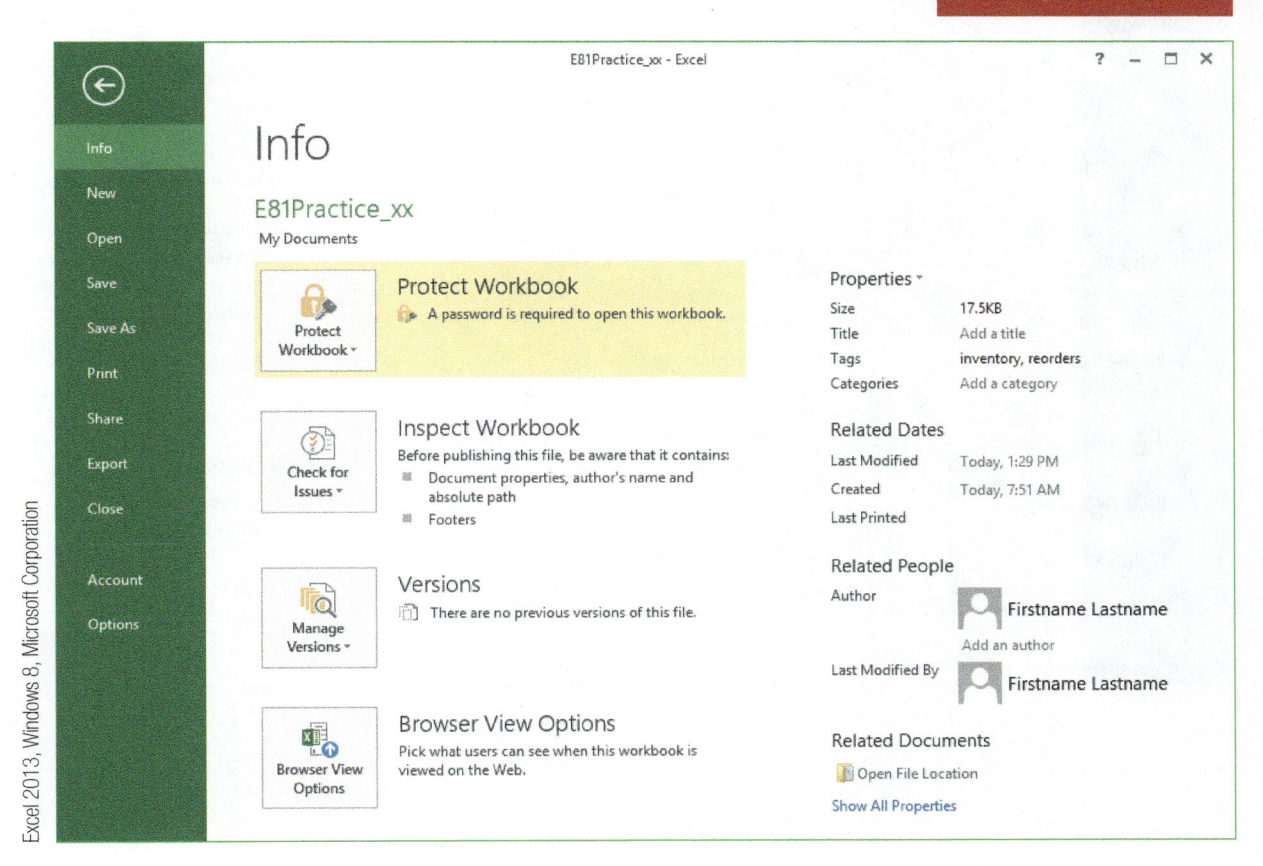

Lesson 81—Apply

You are working on worksheets for two clients. You will inspect the worksheets for issues, apply passwords, and protect the worksheets. You will also add keywords to the properties.

DIRECTIONS

1. Start Excel, if necessary, and open **E81Apply** from the data files for this lesson.
2. Save the file as **E81Apply_xx** in the location where your teacher instructs you to store the files for this lesson.
3. Run the Document Inspector, and remove any found information.
4. Add the password **marketing456&** to the workbook.
5. Add the keywords **marketing, yearly budget** to the workbook, and close the Document Properties panel. Your workbook should look like the one shown in Figure 81-2.
6. Save and close the file, and exit Excel.

Figure 81-2

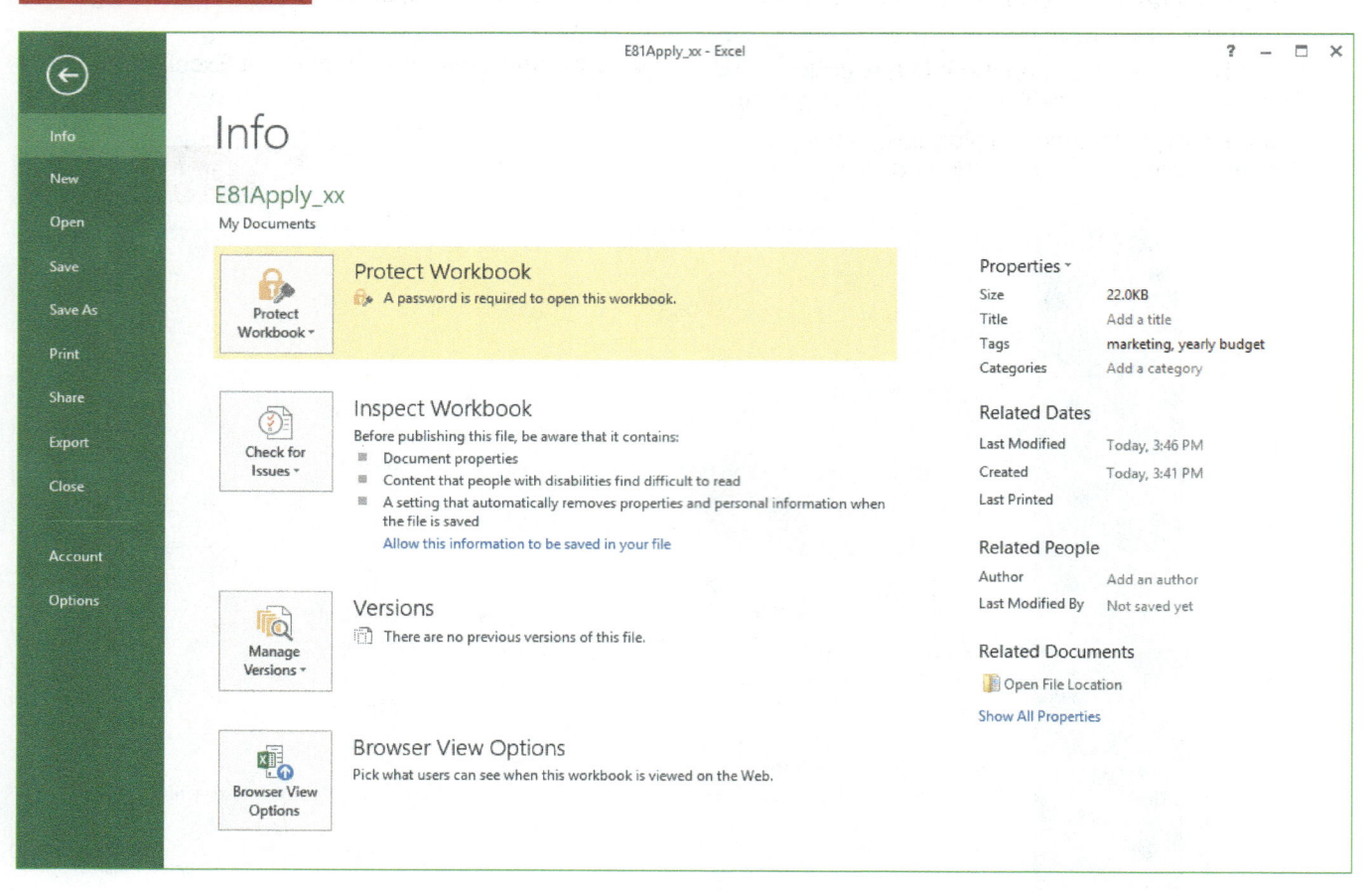

Excel 2013, Windows 8, Microsoft Corporation

Lesson 82

Finalizing a Workbook

➤ What You Will Learn

Adding a Digital Signature
Checking for Accessibility Issues
Marking a Workbook As Final
Managing Versions

Software Skills Especially when you're working with sensitive financial data, you need some way of letting others know a workbook they review is authentically from you. You can digitally sign the workbook to let your colleagues know that they are working with an approved version of the file. Excel 2013 offers features to make workbooks easier for users with disabilities to use. You can check the accessibility of your workbook and correct a workbook for possible issues. When you are finished with your workbook, you can mark it as final to show that no further changes should be made to the file. Use Excel's Manage Versions feature to search for an auto-saved version of a file you have not yet manually saved.

What You Can Do

Adding a Digital Signature

- You can apply a **digital signature** to a worksheet or a workbook to indicate that the information is authentically from you.
- To sign the worksheet or workbook with a digital signature, you need a digital ID. You can obtain a digital ID from a Microsoft Partner.
  - ✓ *Follow your instructor's instruction on how—or whether—to use digital signatures with Microsoft Excel.*
- You can add a digital signature line to a worksheet by using the Signature Line command in the Text group on the INSERT tab.
- To sign a digital signature line, right-click the digital signature line and click Sign.
- You can assign a digital signature to a workbook by clicking FILE, and using the Protect Workbook command on the Info tab in the Backstage view.
- When you add a digital signature, you can enter a purpose or instructions to the signer.
- A digital signature remains valid as long as the workbook is not changed.
- If you change the workbook at a later time, you will need to sign the file again to make the signature valid.

WORDS TO KNOW

Accessibility
The ability to make documents easier for people with disabilities to use.

Accessibility Checker
A feature in Excel that checks for and displays issues in a document that might be challenging for a user with a disability.

Alternative text (alt text)
Text that appears when you move the mouse pointer over a picture or object.

Digital Signature
An electronic signature that is stored with the workbook to let others know the file is authentic or meets a standard that is important to the group.

Try It! Adding a Digital Signature Line to a Worksheet

1. Start Excel, and open **E82Try** from the data files for this lesson.
2. Save the file as **E82Try_xx** in the location where your teacher instructs you to store the files for this lesson.
3. Click cell F16.
4. Click INSERT > Signature Line.
5. In the Signature Setup dialog box, click in the Suggested signer box, and type your name.
6. Click OK. A digital signature line appears.
7. Save the changes to the file, and leave it open to use in the next Try It.

The Signature Setup dialog box

Try It! Adding a Digital Signature

1. In the **E82Try_xx** file, click FILE.
2. In the Backstage view, on the Info tab, click Protect Workbook > Add a Digital Signature.
   - ✓ Follow your instructor's instruction on how—or whether—to use digital signatures with Microsoft Excel.
3. If so instructed, in the Get a Digital ID dialog box, click No.
4. In the worksheet, right-click the digital signature line, and click Sign.
5. If so instructed, in the Get a Digital ID dialog box, click No.
6. Save the changes to the file, and leave it open to use in the next Try It.

Checking for Accessibility Issues

- You can use **accessibility** features in Excel 2013 to make workbooks more accessible to users with disabilities.
- Use the **Accessibility Checker** to check and correct a workbook for possible issues that might make it hard for a user with a disability to read or interpret the content.
- Access the Accessibility Checker from the Check for Issues button on the Info tab on the FILE tab in the Backstage view.
- **Alternative text**, or **alt text**, is an accessibility feature that helps people who use screen readers to understand the content of a picture in a workbook.
   - ✓ Alt text may not work with touch-screen or mobile devices.

- When making a workbook accessible, you should include alt text for objects such as pictures, embedded objects, charts, and tables.
- When you use a screen reader to view a workbook, or save it to a file format such as HTML, alt text appears in most browsers when the picture doesn't display.
   - ✓ You may have to adjust the computer's browser settings to display alt text.
- You can add alt text from the Size & Properties button on the Format Picture task pane.

Business Information Management II | Excel | Chapter 10

Try It! Using the Accessibility Checker

1 In the **E82Try_xx** file, click FILE.

2 In the Backstage view, on the Info tab, click Check for Issues > Check Accessibility. Notice the Missing Alt Text error.

3 Save the changes to the file, and leave it open to use in the next Try It.

The Accessibility Checker task pane

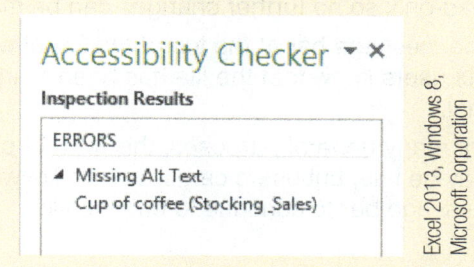

Accessibility Checker
Inspection Results
ERRORS
▲ Missing Alt Text
  Cup of coffee (Stocking_Sales)

Excel 2013, Windows 8, Microsoft Corporation

Try It! Adding Alternative Text (Alt Text)

1 In the **E82Try_xx** file, right-click the picture of the cup of coffee, and click Size & Properties to display the Size & Properties group of the Format Picture task pane.

2 Click ALT TEXT.

3 Click in the Title box, and type **Cup of coffee**.

4 Click in the Description box, and type **A picture of the best coffee from Grounds for Thought**. The Accessibility Checker Inspection Results now finds no accessibility issues.

5 Close the Format Picture and Accessibility Checker task panes.

6 Save the changes to the file, and leave it open to use in the next Try It.

The ALT TEXT group of the Format Picture task pane

Format Picture

▲ SIZE
Height   0.75"
Width   1.2"
Rotation 0°
Scale Height 101%
Scale Width   100%
☑ Lock aspect ratio
☑ Relative to original picture size
Original size
  Height: 0.74" Width: 1.2"
  Reset

▷ PROPERTIES
▷ TEXT BOX
▲ ALT TEXT
Title
[Cup of coffee]
Description
[A picture of the best coffee from Grounds for Thought]

Accessibility Checker
Inspection Results
✓ No accessibility issues found. People with disabilities should not have difficulty reading this workbook.

Additional Information
Select and fix each issue listed above to make this document accessible for people with disabilities.

Read more about making documents accessible

Excel 2013, Windows 8, Microsoft Corporation

Marking a Workbook As Final

- When you mark your workbook as final, colleagues who view the workbook see that it is marked as read-only so no further changes can be made.
- The message bar at the top of the Excel window lets users know that the file has been marked as final.
- For many general purposes, this level of protection may be fine, but users can click Edit Anyway in the message bar to continue to edit the file.
- Users can save the workbook under another name and edit the file as desired.
- If you need stronger security for the workbook, add a password or restrict editing privileges before sharing the file.
- When a file is marked as final, the Marked As Final icon appears in the status bar.
- When you add a digital signature to a file, the file is automatically marked as final.
- Before you can mark a file as final, you must turn off workbook sharing.

Try It! Marking a Workbook As Final

1. In the **E82Try_xx** file, click FILE > Protect Workbook.
2. Click Mark as Final.
3. Click OK.
4. In the information message box, click OK.
5. Close the file, and exit Excel.

Managing Versions

- Excel automatically saves your workbooks to a temporary folder while you are working on them.
- If you forget to save your changes, or if Excel crashes, you can restore the file using AutoRecover.
- If you don't see the file in the AutoRecover list, or if you're looking for an auto-saved version of a file that has no previously saved versions, you can use the Manage Versions feature to search for the file.
- Access the Manage Versions command from the Info tab of the FILE tab.
- You can recover unsaved workbooks from the default location of the UnsavedFiles folder.
- You can also use the Manage Versions command to delete all unsaved workbooks.

Lesson 82—Practice

You work for the Grounds for Thought Coffee Company, and you need to enhance the company's expense report form. This form will allow employees to get reimbursed by the company. You want to add two digital signature lines to the worksheet, one for the employee and one for the manager. You also want to check for any accessibility issues and correct them.

DIRECTIONS

1. Start Excel, if necessary, and open **E82Practice** from the data files for this lesson.
2. Save the file as **E82Practice_xx** in the location where your teacher instructs you to store the files for this lesson.
3. Add a header that has your name at the left, the date code in the center, and the page number code at the right, and change back to **Normal** view.

4. Add a digital signature for an employee signature in cell C20:
   a. Click cell **C20**.
   b. Click **INSERT** > **Signature Line**.
   c. In the Signature Setup dialog box, click in the **Suggested signer** box, and type **Employee Signature**.
   d. Click **OK**.
5. Add a digital signature for a manager in cell F20 using the process in step 4.
6. Check the workbook for accessibility issues:
   a. Click **FILE**.
   b. In the Backstage view, on the Info tab, click **Check for Issues** > **Check Accessibility**.
7. Ignore the Merged Cells errors, and correct the missing alt text error:
   a. Right-click the picture of the cup of coffee, and click **Size & Properties**.
   b. Click **ALT TEXT**.
   c. Click in the **Title** box, and type **Cup of coffee**.
   d. Click in the **Description** box, and type **A picture of a cup of French Roast coffee**.
8. Close the Format Picture and Accessibility Checker task panes.
9. Change the page layout orientation to **Landscape**.
10. **With your teacher's permission,** print the worksheet. Your workbook should look like the one shown in Figure 82-1.
11. Save and close the file, and exit Excel.

Figure 82-1

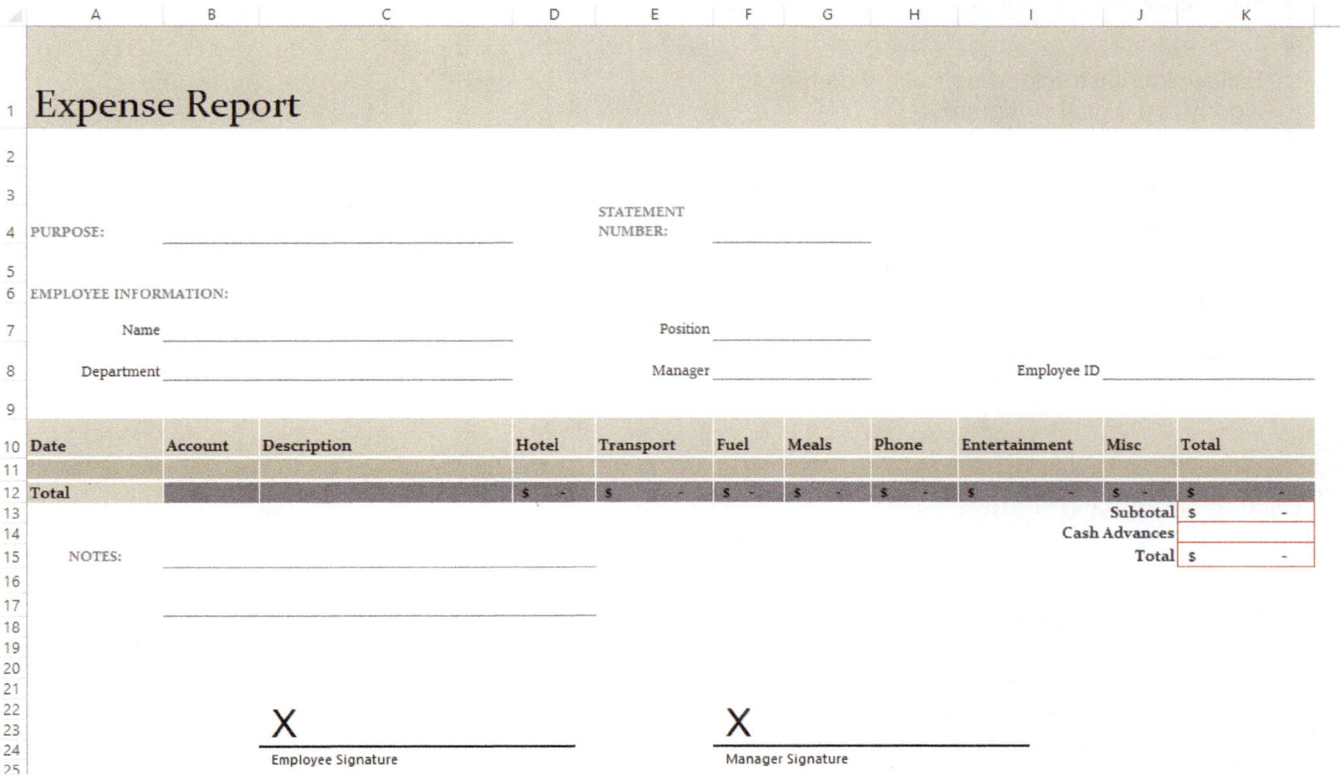

Excel 2013, Windows 8, Microsoft Corporation

Lesson 82—Apply

You have just traveled to a coffee convention for the Grounds for Thought Coffee Company. You now need to complete an expense report to get reimbursed by the company for your travel expenses. You want to complete the worksheet, check for and correct any accessibility issues, and mark the workbook as final before submitting it to your manager.

DIRECTIONS

1. Start Excel, if necessary, and open **E82Apply** from the data files for this lesson.
2. Save the file as **E82Apply_xx** in the location where your teacher instructs you to store the files for this lesson.
3. In cell **C7**, type your name.
4. In cell **A11**, type today's date.
5. Add a digital signature to the Employee Signature line.
    a. Right-click the **Employee Signature line**.
    b. Click **Sign**.
    c. Follow your instructor's instruction on how to sign with a digital signature.
6. Check the workbook for accessibility issues. Ignore the Merged Cells errors.
7. Mark the workbook as final:
    a. Click **FILE** > **Protect Workbook**.
    b. Click **Mark as Final**.
    c. Click **OK**.
    d. In the information message box, click **OK**.
8. Close any open task panes.
9. Close the file, and exit Excel.

Lesson 83

Sharing a Workbook

➤ What You Will Learn

Setting Precise Margins for Printing
Uploading a Workbook to Windows OneDrive

Software Skills After you finish working with workbook content and adding a digital signature, you may be ready to share your file with others. Excel 2013 makes it easy to send a worksheet to colleagues. You can make some last-minute choices about the margins for printing the worksheet information and, if you like, you can post the workbook on Windows OneDrive so that you can access and modify it using Excel 2013 Online.

What You Can Do

Setting Precise Margins for Printing

- Excel 2013 offers a number of ways to control what you want to print.
- You can set a print area by highlighting the range you want to print and clicking Print Area in the PAGE LAYOUT tab. Use the Set Print Area command to let the program know you want to print the highlighted range.
- You can enter precise measurements for the margins by setting print options:
  - Click FILE to display the Backstage view, and click Print. Click the Margins arrow toward the bottom of the center column, and click Custom Margins.
  - Enter the values you want to set for each of the page areas: header, right margin, footer, bottom margin, left margin, and top margin.
  - If you want to center the content horizontally or vertically (or both), click the check boxes in the Center on page area of the Page Setup dialog box.

WORDS TO KNOW

Windows OneDrive
A free Microsoft offering that enables you to post and share documents in a Web-based library. You can also use Windows OneDrive with Excel Online to co-author workbooks.

Excel Online
The online version of Excel 2013 that you can access through Windows OneDrive or Windows SharePoint.

Try It! Setting Precise Margins for Printing

1. Start Excel, and open **E83Try** from the data files for this lesson.
2. Save the file as **E83Try_xx** in the location where your teacher instructs you to store the files for this lesson.
3. Click FILE > Print.
4. Click Normal Margins > Custom Margins.
5. In the Page Setup dialog box, set the Top margin to 1.0, the Bottom margin to 1.25, and the Left and Right margins to 1.2.
6. Under Center on page, click to select the Horizontally check box.
7. Click OK.
8. Save the changes to the file, and leave it open to use in the next Try It.

Setting precise margins

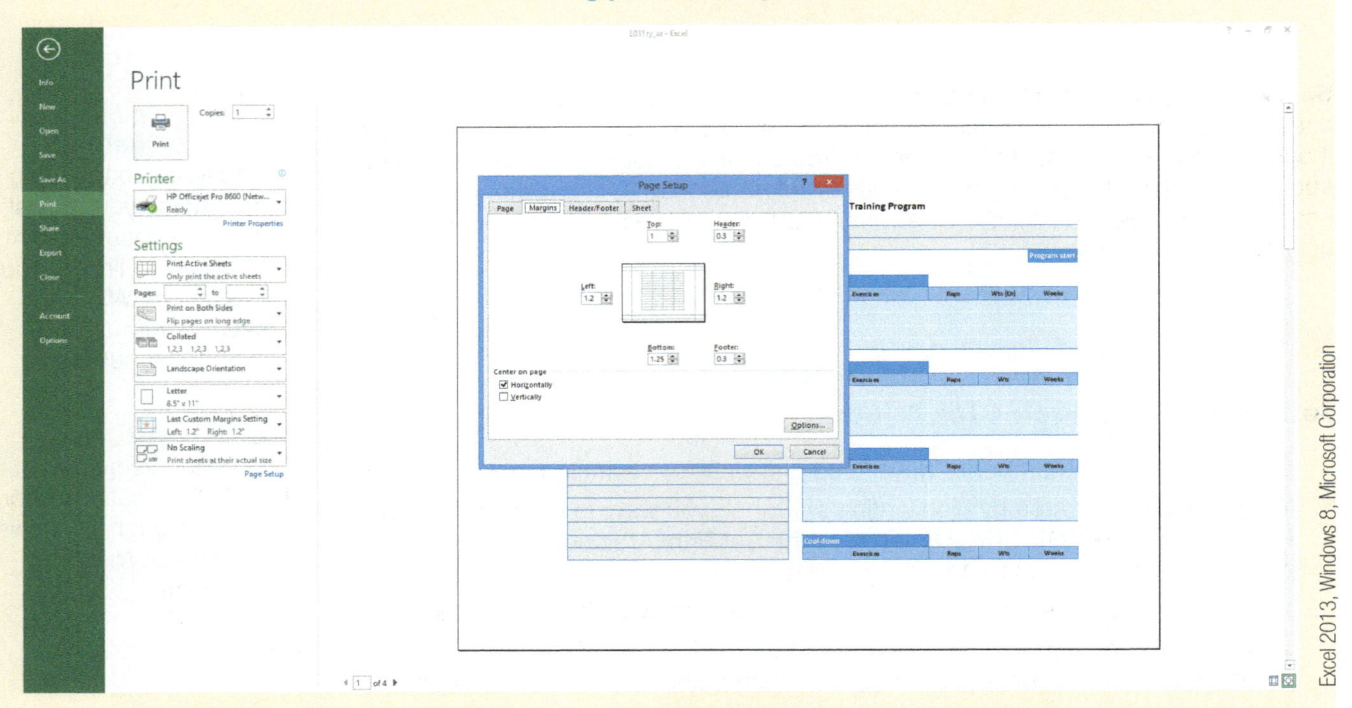

Uploading a Workbook to Windows OneDrive

- Excel 2013 offers you the ability to save a workbook to your **Windows OneDrive** account so that you can work on it from any point you have Web access.
- If you don't have a Windows OneDrive account, Excel 2013 will prompt you to create one when you choose Save To Cloud on the Share tab in the Backstage view.
- After you save the workbook file to your Windows OneDrive account, you can access the file using **Excel Online**.
- Once you have Web access, you can log in to your OneDrive account.
- You can use Excel Online to open, review, and edit your workbook online.
- When you open a workbook in Excel Online, the workbook opens in the Edit in Browser view and automatically displays the Ribbon with the tools you need to review, edit, and save the file.
- You can choose to open the workbook in Excel instead of working in it in Excel Online.
- Your changes to a file in Excel Online are automatically saved.

Business Information Management II | Excel | Chapter 10   583

Try It!   Uploading a Workbook to Windows OneDrive

1. In the **E83Try_xx** file, click FILE > Save As.
2. Click OneDrive - Personal ☁.
3. If you don't have a Windows account, click Sign up now.

   ✓ *Your instructor will let you know if you should sign up for an account.*

   OR

   If you already have an account, click Sign In, enter your Windows e-mail address and password, and click Sign in.

4. Click the folder in which you want to save the file.

   ✓ *Your instructor will let you know which account and folder to use to store the file.*

5. In the Save As dialog box, in the File name box, type **E83Try_online_xx**.
6. Click Save.
7. Close the workbook, and close Excel.

Try It!   Working in Excel Online

1. Open your Web browser, and go to **https://onedrive.live.com**.
2. Log in with your Windows ID.
3. Click the folder in which you saved the workbook file.
4. Click the workbook to display it in the Microsoft Excel Online window. Excel Online automatically displays the Ribbon with the tools you need to review, edit, and save the file.
5. In Excel Online, on the Info & Schedule worksheet tab, click cell E4 and type **Jonas Smith**.
6. Click cell E5, and type your name.
7. In Excel Online, click the OPEN IN EXCEL tab.
8. Click Yes to confirm that you want to open the file. Close the information box that lets you know the workbook is opening in Excel. The workbook opens in Excel.
9. Click cell J6, and type today's date.
10. Save the Excel file, and close Excel.
11. In the browser window, click **E83Try_online_xx**, and view the changes.
12. Review the workbook in the browser.
13. Close the workbook in Excel Online.
14. Close the browser to sign out of OneDrive.

(continued)

> **Try It!** **Working in the Excel Web App** *(continued)*

Working in Excel Online

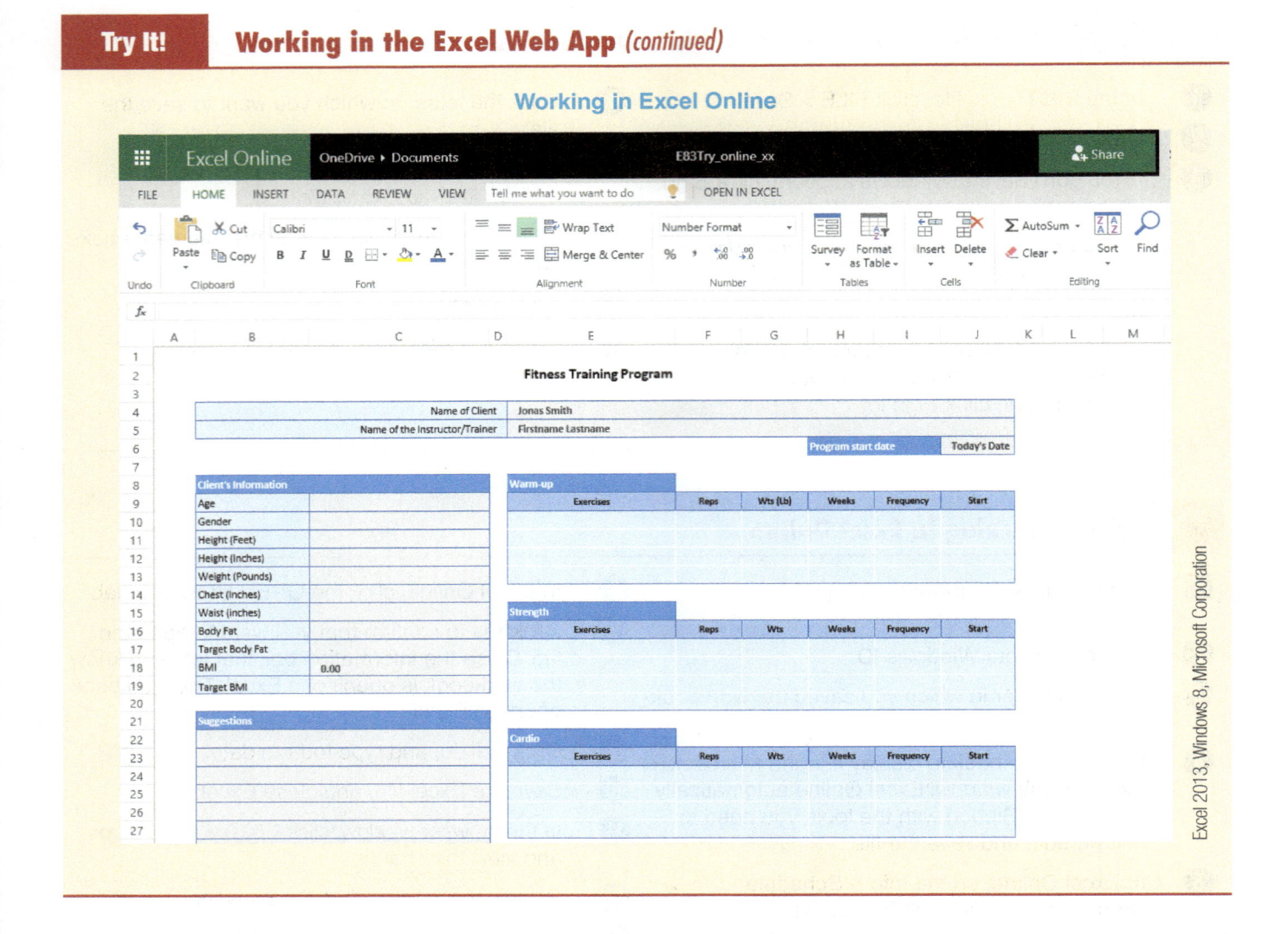

Lesson 83—Practice

You and two of your colleagues are collaborating on a research project that requires you to gather field data from a variety of sites around the United States. During the course of your research, you will need to be able to share your workbook with each other online. You want to change the margins of the data tables so that you can print your results to be included in the final research workbook.

DIRECTIONS

1. Start Excel, if necessary, and open **E83Practice** from the data files for this lesson.
2. Save the file as **E83Practice_xx** in the location where your teacher instructs you to store the files for this lesson.
3. Click **FILE** > **Print**.
4. Click **Normal Margins** > **Custom Margins**.
5. In the Page Setup dialog box, set the **Top** margin to **0.5**, the **Bottom** margin to **0.5**, and the **Left** and **Right** margins to **1.0**.
6. Click **OK**.

7. Click **No Scaling** > **Fit Sheet on One Page**.
8. Click Save.
9. Save the file to the OneDrive:
   ✓ *Your instructor will let you know if you should sign up for an account.*
   a. Click **FILE** > **Save As**.
   b. Click **OneDrive - Personal** ☁, and click the folder in which you want to save the file.
      ✓ *Your instructor will let you know which account and folder to use to store the file.*
   c. In the Save As dialog box, in the File name box, type **E83Practice_online_xx**.
   d. Click **Save**.
10. Close the workbook in Excel.
11. Open your Web browser, and go to **https://onedrive.live.com**.
12. Log in if necessary.
13. Click the folder where you saved the workbook, and click the **E83Practice_online_xx** workbook to display it in Excel Online.
14. Edit the file in your browser by changing the dates in the Survey 1 column to the current date. Your file should look like the one shown in Figure 83-1.
15. Close the workbook in Excel Online.
16. Close the browser to sign out of OneDrive.

Figure 83-1

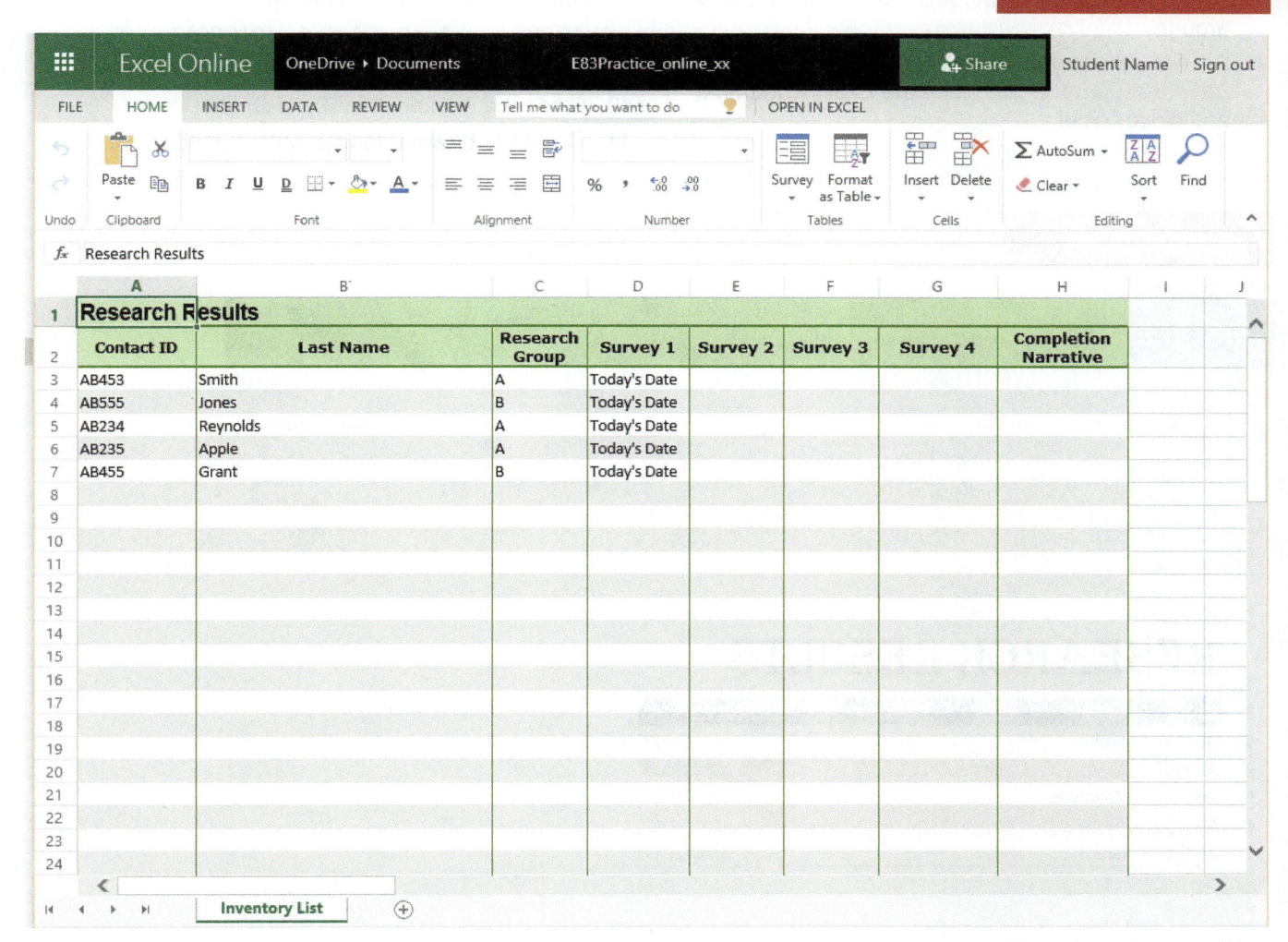

	A	B	C	D	E	F	G	H
1	Research Results							
2	Contact ID	Last Name	Research Group	Survey 1	Survey 2	Survey 3	Survey 4	Completion Narrative
3	AB453	Smith	A	Today's Date				
4	AB555	Jones	B	Today's Date				
5	AB234	Reynolds	A	Today's Date				
6	AB235	Apple	A	Today's Date				
7	AB455	Grant	B	Today's Date				

Excel 2013, Windows 8, Microsoft Corporation

Business Information Management II | Access | Chapter 4

Try It! Formatting a Table

1. Start Access, and open **A28Try** from the data files for this lesson.
2. Save the file as **A28Try_xx** in the location where your teacher instructs you to store the files for this lesson. Click Enable Content if the information bar appears.
3. Double-click the Employees table to open it in Datasheet view.
4. On the HOME tab, click the Font drop-down list, and click Century Schoolbook (or any other font if you do not have that one).
5. Open the Font Size drop-down list and click 10.
6. Click the arrow on the Font Color button and click a dark red square.
7. Click in the ID column and click the Center button.
8. Click the Gridlines button and, on its menu, click None.
9. Click the arrow on the Fill Color button and click a yellow square.
10. Click the arrow on the Alternate Row Color button and click an orange square.
11. Right-click the table's tab and click Close. Click No when prompted to save changes.
12. Leave the database open to use in the next Try It.

Checking Spelling

- Access includes a Spell Check feature. It is not as robust as the Spell Check feature included in Word, but it uses the same dictionaries (including any custom dictionaries you have created). See Figure 28-1.
- When a word is found that is not in the dictionary, a list of suggestions appears. Click the word that represents the correct spelling. Or, if none of the suggestions are right, make a correction directly in the Not In Dictionary text box.
- After selecting or typing the correct spelling, you can click Change to change only the found instance of a word or Change All to change all instances of that word in the table with the same misspelling.
- If the word is actually spelled correctly, you can click Ignore to ignore only this instance, Ignore All to ignore all instances in this table, or Add to add the word to the custom dictionary stored on your PC.

Figure 28-1

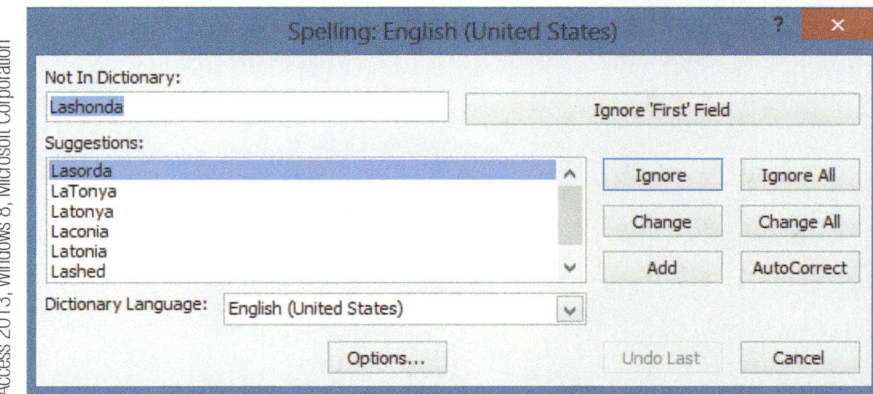

Try It! Checking Spelling

1. In **A28Try_xx**, in the Navigation pane, double-click the Duties table to open it in Datasheet view.
2. Click HOME > Spelling. The Spelling dialog box opens.
   - ✓ *The first misspelled word found is identified in the Not In Dictionary box. On the Suggestions list, Wash is already selected.*
3. Click Change. The next misspelling appears.
4. Click Change. The word is corrected and a message appears that the spelling check is complete.
5. Click OK.
6. Leave the database open to use in the next Try It.

Try It! Adding a Word to the Dictionary

1. In **A28Try_xx**, double-click the Employees table to open it in Datasheet view.
2. Click HOME > Spelling.
   - ✓ *A proper name appears as misspelled, but it is actually correct.*
3. Click Add. A message appears that the spell check is complete.
4. Click OK.
5. Close the database, and exit Access.

Lesson 28—Practice

In this project, you will fix spelling errors and change the alignment of the ID field in the Ace Learning database.

DIRECTIONS

1. Start Access, if necessary, and open **A28Practice** from the data files for this lesson.
2. Save the file as **A28Practice_xx** in the location where your teacher instructs you to store the files for this lesson.
   ✓ If a security warning bar appears, click Enable Content.
3. In the Navigation pane, double-click **tblClasses** to open it in Datasheet view.
4. Click **HOME** > **Spelling**.
5. Click **Change** to change the first misspelled word.
6. Click **Change** to change the second misspelled word.
7. Click **Change** to change the third misspelled word.
8. Click **OK**.
9. Click in the **ID** column.
10. Click the **Align Left** button.
11. Right-click the table's tab and click **Close**. Click **Yes** when prompted to save changes.
12. Close the database, and exit Access. If instructed, submit it to your teacher for grading.

Lesson 28—Apply

The Ace Learning database has been in use for several weeks now, and the staff has been complaining that the datasheet is hard to read and that there are some spelling errors in the data. You will fix these problems.

DIRECTIONS

1. Start Access, if necessary, and open **A28Apply** from the data files for this lesson.
2. Save the file as **A28Apply_xx** in the location where your teacher instructs you to store the files for this lesson.
   ✓ If a security warning bar appears, click Enable Content.
3. Open **tblInstructors** and run a spell check. Ignore all possible spelling errors that are found in the Address field. Correct any other errors found.
4. Open **tblStudents** and run a spell check. Ignore all possible spelling errors that are found in the FirstName, LastName, and Address fields. Correct any other spelling errors found.
5. In **tblStudents**, change the alternate row color to **light green**.
6. In **tblStudents**, change the font to **12-point Times New Roman**.
7. In **tblStudents**, widen all the columns as needed so that the content fits (except the Notes field, which can stay truncated).
   ✓ To widen a column, position the mouse pointer at the right edge of the column header and double-click.
8. Set the **Gridlines** setting to **Horizontal**.
9. Close the table, saving the changes.
10. Close the database, and exit Access. If instructed, submit it to your teacher for grading.

Lesson 29

Creating Macros

> ### ➤ What You Will Learn
>
> **Creating and Running a Standalone Macro**
> **Creating an Embedded Macro**
> **Printing Macro Details**

WORDS TO KNOW

Embedded macro
A macro that is stored in a database object, such as a table, query, form, or report.

Macro
A sequence of steps that are automatically performed when a specific trigger is activated.

Standalone macro
A macro that exists as a separate object in the database from any other table, query, form, or report.

User Interface (UI) macro
An embedded macro.

Software Skills Macros enable you to automate groups of steps so that they can be executed in a single action, such as pressing a key combination or clicking a button. Writing a simple macro requires no programming experience; the interface for creating a macro is point-and-click. More sophisticated macros can also be written in Visual Basic.

What You Can Do

Creating and Running a Standalone Macro

- A **standalone macro** is a macro that is saved as a separate object. You can run the macro from the Navigation pane, activate it with a shortcut key combination you assign, or start it with a button that you add to the Quick Access Toolbar.
- **Macros** are created in Macro Design view. You select commands from a series of drop-down lists, so no typing of programming code is required.
- You can run macros by double-clicking them in the Navigation pane or by using the DATABASE TOOLS > Run Macro command. You can also run a macro from Design view, which is useful for testing the macro as you are constructing it.
- If you aren't sure which command to add to the macro, you can browse for an action by category using the Action Catalog, a task pane that appears on the right side of Macro Design view.
- The Action Catalog also includes some Program Flow options that add special sections to the macro (Comment, Group, If, and Submacro).

Business Information Management II | Access | Chapter 4

Try It! Starting a New Macro

1. Start Access, and open **A29Try** from the data files for this lesson.
2. Save the file as **A29Try_xx** in the location where your teacher instructs you to store the files for this lesson. Click Enable Content if the information bar appears.
3. Click CREATE > Macro. A new Macro object opens, ready for you to enter commands.
4. Open the Add New Action drop-down list, and click OpenTable. Additional drop-down list boxes appear that are specific to that command.
5. Open the Table Name drop-down list and click Assignments.
6. Open the second Add New Action drop-down list, and click OpenTable. A second set of drop-down list boxes appears for the new command.
7. Open the Table Name drop-down list and click Employees.
8. Click the Save button on the Quick Access Toolbar.
9. In the Save As dialog box, type **Open Assignments and Employees** and click OK.
10. Leave the macro open to use in the next Try It.

A command added to the macro

OpenTable	
Table Name	Assignments
View	Datasheet
Data Mode	Edit

+ Add New Action

Access 2013, Windows 8, Microsoft Corporation

Try It! Running a Macro (Macro Open)

1. In the **A29Try_xx** database, with the macro open, click MACRO TOOLS DESIGN > Run. Both of the tables referenced in the macro open.
2. Right-click any open object's tab and click Close All.
3. Leave the database open to use in the next Try It.

Try It! Running a Macro (Macro Not Open)

1. In the **A29Try_xx** database, from the Navigation pane, double-click Open Assignments and Employees.
2. Right-click any open object's tab and click Close All.
3. Leave the database open to use in the next Try It.

Try It! Selecting Commands from the Action Catalog

1. In **A29Try_xx**, click CREATE > Macro. In the Action Catalog, double-click Comment in the Program Flow section.

2. In the comment box that appears, type **This macro closes the current database without exiting Access.**

3. In the Actions section of the Action Catalog pane, click the arrow next to System Commands.

4. Double-click CloseDatabase. The command is added to the macro.

5. Click the Save button on the Quick Access Toolbar. In the Save As dialog box, type **Close Database**. Click OK.

6. Click MACRO TOOLS DESIGN > Run. The macro runs, and the database closes.

7. Reopen the **A29Try_xx** database.

Add a command from the Action Catalog

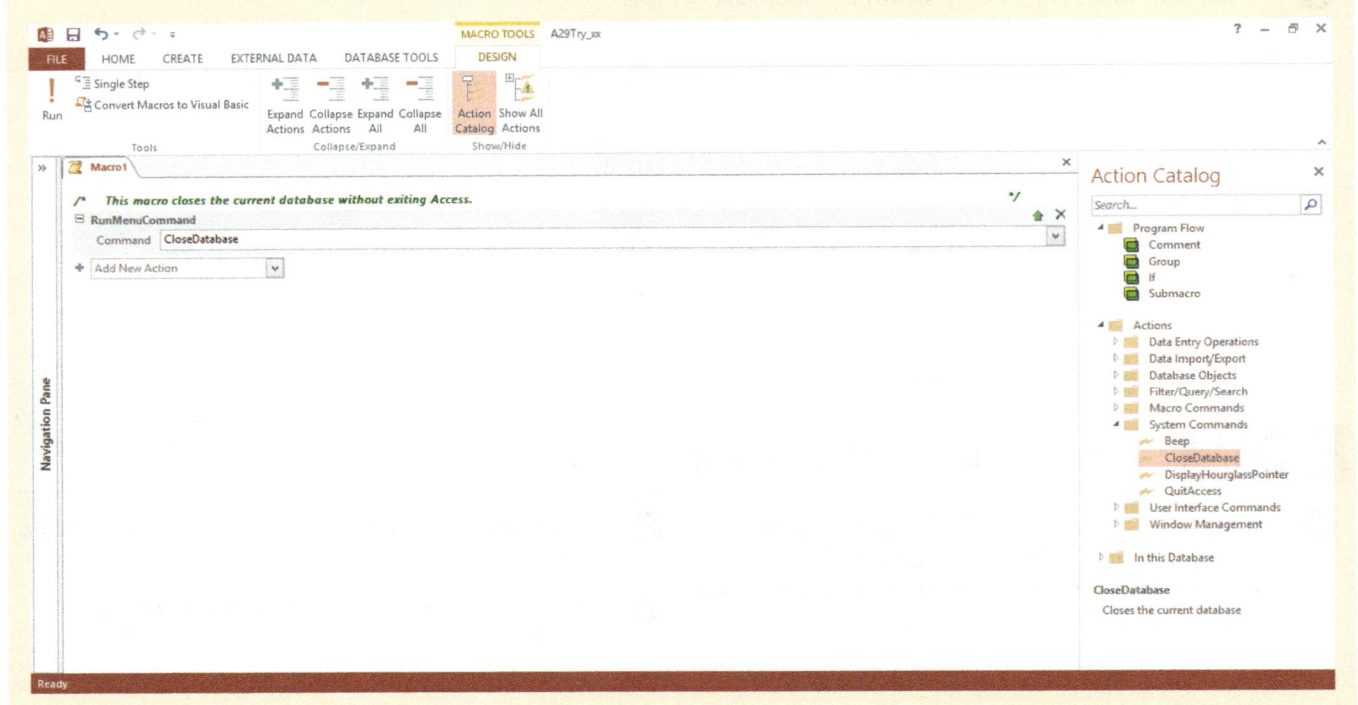

Access 2013, Windows 8, Microsoft Corporation

Creating an Embedded Macro

- An **embedded macro**, also called a **User Interface (UI) macro**, is one that is associated with a particular control. For example, a macro can be assigned to a command button, so that when you click the button a series of actions execute.

- When you create command buttons, you are actually creating embedded macros for the buttons through the Command Button Wizard. You can edit these macros to add or change the actions assigned.

- When you are embedding a macro in a form you need to be sure and select the entire form from the Selection Type drop-down in the Property Sheet.

- You can also embed macros in any database object. For example, you can specify that a certain action occurs when an object opens or closes.

Try It! Editing an Embedded Macro

1. In **A29Try_xx**, in the Navigation pane, right-click Main Form and click Layout View.

2. Click the Assignments Form button, and click FORM LAYOUT TOOLS DESIGN > Property Sheet.

3. In the Property Sheet, click the Event tab.

4. In the On Click property, click the Build button. The macro design interface opens. It is the same interface as with a standalone macro.

5. Open the Add New Action drop-down list and click CloseWindow.

6. Open the Object Type drop-down list and click Form.

7. Open the Object Name drop-down list and click Main Form.

8. Click MACRO TOOLS DESIGN > Close. Click Yes when prompted to save changes.

9. Click the Save button on the Quick Access Toolbar to save the changes to Main Form.

10. Click FORM LAYOUT TOOLS DESIGN > View to switch to Form view.

11. Click the Assignments Form button. The Assignments Form opens and the Main Form closes.

12. Right-click the Assignments Form tab and click Close.

13. Leave the database open to use in the next Try It.

Add another action to the embedded macro

```
OpenForm
    Form Name    Assignments Form
         View    Form
    Filter Name
Where Condition
     Data Mode
   Window Mode   Normal
☐ CloseWindow
    Object Type   Form
    Object Name   Main Form
          Save    Prompt
+ Add New Action
```

Access 2013, Windows 8, Microsoft Corporation

Try It! Creating an Embedded Macro

1. In **A29Try_xx** in the Navigation pane, right-click Assignments Form and click Layout View.
2. If the Property Sheet is not already open, click FORM LAYOUT TOOLS DESIGN > Property Sheet.
3. At the top of the Property Sheet, open the Selection Type drop-down list and click Form.
4. In the Property Sheet, click the Event tab.
5. Click in the On Close property box.
6. Click the Build button.
7. Click Macro Builder and click OK.
8. Open the Add New Action drop-down list and click OpenForm.
9. Open the Form Name drop-down list and click Main Form.
10. Click MACRO TOOLS DESIGN > Close. Click Yes when prompted to save changes.
11. Click Save on the Quick Access Toolbar to save the changes to the Assignments Form.
12. Right-click the form's tab and click Close. The Main Form opens.
13. Right-click the Main Form tab and click Close.
14. Leave the database open to use in the next Try It.

Printing Macro Details

- To keep track of the macros in your database, you may wish to document each macro in printed form.
- When you print a macro, a variety of information about it also prints in addition to the macro commands.

Try It! Printing Macro Details

1. In **A29Try_xx**, in the Navigation pane, right-click the Open Assignments and Employees macro and click Design View.
2. Click FILE > Print > Print Preview. The Print Macro Definition dialog box opens.
3. Click OK to accept all the additional information to print.
    ✓ *The report appears in Print Preview.*
4. Click Close Print Preview.
5. Close the database, and exit Access.

Business Information Management II | Access | Chapter 4

Lesson 29—Practice

You continue to work with the Ace Learning database. In this project, you will create a macro to open the frmClasses form when the frmMenu form closes, and a macro to open the frmMenu form when the frmClasses form closes.

DIRECTIONS

1. Start Access, if necessary, and open **A29Practice** from the data files for this lesson.
2. Save the file as **A29Practice_xx** in the location where your teacher instructs you to store the files for this lesson.
   - ✓ If a security warning bar appears, click Enable Content.
   - ✓ Enabling all content is especially important when working with macros, as macros are one of the content types that are otherwise blocked.
3. Right-click **frmClasses** and click **Layout View**.
4. Click **FORM LAYOUT TOOLS DESIGN** > **Property Sheet**.
5. Open the **Selection Type** drop-down list in the **Property Sheet** pane and click **Form**.
6. Click in the **On Open** property box.
7. Click the **Build button**.
8. Click **Macro Builder** and click **OK**.
9. Open the **Add New Action** drop-down list and click **CloseWindow**.
10. Open the **Object Type** drop-down list and click **Form**.
11. Open the **Object Name** drop-down list and click **frmMenu**.
12. Click **MACRO TOOLS DESIGN** > **Close**. Click **Yes** when prompted to save changes.
13. Click in the **On Close** property box.
14. Click the **Build** button.
15. Click **Macro Builder** and click **OK**.
16. Open the **Add New Action** drop-down list and click **OpenForm**.
17. Open the **Form Name** drop-down list and click **frmMenu**.
18. Click **MACRO TOOLS DESIGN** > **Close**. Click **Yes** when prompted to save changes.
19. Right-click the **frmClasses** tab and click **Close**. Click **Yes** when prompted to save changes.
20. On the **frmMenu** form in Form view, click the **Classes** button. The **frmClasses** form opens, and the **frmMenu** form closes.
21. Right-click the **frmClasses** tab and click **Close**. The **frmClasses** form closes, and the **frmMenu** form opens.
22. Close the database, and exit Access. If instructed, submit it to your teacher for grading.

Lesson 29—Apply

You will create macros to help users navigate the Ace Learning database in a more efficient manner.

DIRECTIONS

1. Start Access, if necessary, and open **A29Apply** from the data files for this lesson.
2. Save the file as **A29Apply_xx** in the location where your teacher instructs you to store the files for this lesson.
   - ✓ *If a security warning bar appears, click Enable Content.*
3. Open **frmVolunteers** in Layout view and set its **On Open** property so that **frmMenu** closes when **frmVolunteers** opens.
4. Set the **On Close** property so that **frmMenu** opens when **frmVolunteers** closes.
5. Save and close **frmVolunteers**. The **frmMenu** form opens automatically.
6. Test each of the buttons on **frmMenu** to confirm that each button opens a form and closes **frmMenu**, and that closing each of the opened forms causes **frmMenu** to reappear.
7. Create a new macro that opens all the tables in the database. Name it **mcrOpenAll**.
8. Run **mcrOpenAll** to test it, and then close all tabs.
   - ✓ *Right-click any tab and click Close All.*
9. Open the **frmClasses** form in Layout view and select the **Notes** text box.
10. Open the **Property Sheet** for the Notes text box and click in the **On Got Focus** property.
11. Open the **Macro Builder**, and create a **MessageBox** action with the following properties:
    Message: **Please enter notes about classes whenever possible**
    Beep: **No**
    Type: **Information**
    Title: **Notes Requested**
12. Save and close the macro.
13. Test the new macro by viewing the **frmClasses** form in Form view and clicking the **Notes** field for a record.
14. Close the database, and exit Access. If instructed, submit it to your teacher for grading.

End-of-Chapter Activities

➤ Access Chapter 4—Critical Thinking

Creating a Multi-table Database

Bugs Be Gone, a pest control company, is not satisfied with their current database. They have a lot of data that they want to organize in a way that will improve their business operations. You have been hired to design a new database that will help them solve problems such as inconsistent customer and client records and scheduling concerns. The initial meeting with the general manager resulted in the notes shown in Illustration 4A.

Your job is to develop a working, multi-table database that accomplishes the key goals identified in the notes.

DIRECTIONS

1. Referring to the notes in Illustration 4A on the next page, make a list (on paper or in a word processing program) of the tables you will create, the fields in each table, the primary key field for each table, and how the tables will be related.
   ✓ *Make sure that your tables are normalized to 3NF.*

2. Start Access, if necessary, and create a new blank database called **ACT04_xx**.

3. Create the needed tables. Use Rich Text for the Notes fields in each table.
   ✓ *When creating fields that will have relationships to the primary key values in other tables, make sure you use the right data type. For example, if the Badge Number field in Employees is Number, make sure that the Employee field in the Schedule table is also set to Number. Otherwise you won't be able to create the relationships.*

4. Create the needed relationships between the tables, and enforce referential integrity where it is helpful to do so.

5. Arrange and size the field lists in the Relationships window so that they are all fully visible and the relationship lines are clear.

6. **With your teacher's permission**, print a Relationships report showing the relationship window.

7. Create reports that deliver the information described in the *Most important information retrieval goals* in Illustration 4A on the next page.

8. Enter one record in each table, for example purposes. (Make up the data.) Check your spelling in each table to make sure you have not made any typos.

9. Close the database, and exit Access. If instructed, submit it to your teacher for grading.

Illustration 4A

Notes from Meeting

Data to include, at a minimum:
- About the customers: contact information (mailing address, phone number, e-mail), notes
- About the services we offer: name, description, cost, time interval between treatments, notes
- About the employees: Badge number, name, job title, hire date, notes
- The service schedule: date, time, customer, service being performed, employee performing the service, whether or not the service has been performed yet, notes

Most important information retrieval goals:
- A list of services that have been scheduled but not yet performed, sorted by date
- A list of services scheduled for a particular day, grouped by employee

Access 2013, Windows 8, Microsoft Corporation

▶ Access Chapter 4—Portfolio Builder

Improving a Database

Marketing Concepts, Inc. has started a database in Access, but they would like you to help them improve its functionality. You will help them by creating forms, adjusting properties, and creating a macro.

DIRECTIONS

1. Start Access, if necessary, and open **APB04** from the data files for this chapter.
2. Save the file as **APB04_xx** in the location where your teacher instructs you to store the files for this chapter.
   - ✓ *If a security warning bar appears, click Enable Content.*
3. Open the **Staff** table in Datasheet view, and change its font to **10-point Arial**. Do the same for the **Clients** and **Promotions** tables.
4. Create a form for each of the tables by doing the following:
   a. Click the table name in the Navigation pane.
   b. Click **CREATE** > **Form**.
   c. Save the form with the same name as the table name, but with frm at the beginning. For example, the form for **Clients** would be **frmClients**.
5. Open the **Clients** table in Layout view.
6. Change the Index of the **ZIP** field to **Yes (Duplicates OK)**.
7. Create a standalone macro that opens all three tables.
8. Save the macro as **Open All Tables**.
9. Close all open tabs.
10. Close the database, and exit Access. If instructed, submit it to your teacher for grading.

Chapter 5

Developing Advanced Queries

(Courtesy Konstantin Chagin/Shutterstock)

Lesson 31
Creating Customized Crosstab Queries
- Using the Crosstab Query Wizard
- Creating a Crosstab Query in Design View

Lesson 32
Creating Queries That Find Unmatched or Duplicate Records
- Using the Find Unmatched Query Wizard
- Using the Find Duplicates Query Wizard

Lesson 33
Creating Queries That Prompt for Input
- Understanding Parameter Queries
- Creating Criteria-Based Prompts
- Showing All Records If No Parameter Is Entered
- Creating a Field Prompt

Lesson 34
Creating Action Queries
- Understanding Action Queries
- Creating an Update Query
- Creating a Delete Query

Lesson 35
Working with Advanced Query Options
- Changing the Join Type in an Ad-Hoc Query
- Changing Field Properties in Query Design View
- Showing Top Values

End-of-Chapter Activities

625

Lesson 31

Creating Crosstab Queries

> ## What You Will Learn
> Using the Crosstab Query Wizard
> Creating a Crosstab Query in Design View

Software Skills Crosstab queries are a rather "special purpose" item. Instead of presenting just summary data, or just detail data, they allow you to combine summary and detail in specific ways to deliver information you need. In this way, they are somewhat like PivotTables.

WORDS TO KNOW

Column heading
The field that provides labels for the columns in a Crosstab query.

Crosstab query
A query that summarizes one field by two or more other category fields. The category fields display in row and column headings. At the intersection of each row and column is a summary (sum, average, count) of the value.

Row heading
One or more fields that label each row of a Crosstab query.

Value
The field that provides the data to summarize for the intersection of each column and row of a Crosstab query.

What You Can Do

Using the Crosstab Query Wizard

- A **Crosstab query** summarizes data in a very specific way that allows you to customize it to answer a specific need.
- For example, in Figure 31-1 on the next page, each product is listed along with its price per unit, and a sum of the quantity of that product ordered appears, first totaled (Total Of Quantity), and then broken out by salesperson's last name.
  ✓ If the fields that you want to summarize are in more than one table, you must create a query that joins those tables before you use the Crosstab Query Wizard and then base the Crosstab query on that query.
- The Crosstab Query Wizard leads you through the steps to create a Crosstab query.
- The Wizard first asks for a table or query on which to base the new query. Then it asks you to choose which field will be the source for **row headings** in the left column of the query. All like **values** from the row heading field are grouped together, and each unique value in the row heading field becomes a heading for each row of the query. You can choose up to three fields for row headings.
- The Wizard then asks you to choose which field will be the source for **column headings** along the top of the query. All like values from the column heading field are grouped together and each unique value in the column heading field becomes a heading for the data columns of the query. You can choose only one field for a column heading.
  ✓ If you choose a field that is a Date data type for a row or column heading, you will be asked how you want to group the dates on the next step of the wizard. You can choose Year, Month, or another date category.

Figure 31-1

Access 2013, Windows 8, Microsoft Corporation

ProductName	PricePerUnit	Total Of Qua	Bastilla	Jackson	Sanchez	Serino	Wakasuki	Wendtworth
4" zinc tealight wicks	$3.45	2					2	
6" zinc votive wicks	$3.45	21	10			10	1	
Container wax, 10lb	$13.80	6		1	3			2
Mold sealant	$2.30	1					1	
Pillar mold 9"x3"	$28.75	1		1				
Stearic acid	$6.90	4			2			2
Tealight candle	$1.20	24					24	
Votive mold, square	$5.75	6			6			
Votive/pillar wax, 10lb	$13.80	3	1	2				
Vybar 103	$5.75	2						2

- The next step of the Wizard enables you to choose which field you are going to summarize. Generally, this field is a number that you can sum. Sometimes this field is a text or other type of field that you may want to count. You choose both the field and the function you want to perform on it.

- Table 31-1 summarizes the functions you can use. The available functions change depending on whether the value data field is a number or other data type. In this step of the wizard, you can also choose if you want a total for each row. (This will total all column values for each row.)

Table 31-1 Functions in the Crosstab Query Wizard

Function	Description
Avg	Sum the numeric values and divide by the number of values.
Count	Count the number of records.
First	Show the field value for the first record.
Last	Show the field value for the last record.
Max	Show the highest value (if a number), the last alphabetic value (if a text string), or the latest date (if a date).
Min	Show the lowest value (if a number), the first alphabetic value (if a text string), or the earliest date (if a date).
StDev	Calculate the standard deviation, which is used to see how close all values are to the average.
Sum	Sum numeric values.
Var	Calculate the variance of the number, which is another way to see how close values are to the average.

Try It! Using the Crosstab Query Wizard

1. Start Access, and open **A31Try** from the data files for this lesson.
2. Save the file as **A31Try_xx** in the location where your teacher instructs you to store the files for this lesson. Click Enable Content if the information bar appears.
3. Click CREATE > Query Wizard. The New Query dialog box opens.
4. Click Crosstab Query Wizard and click OK.
5. In the Crosstab Query Wizard dialog box, click the Queries option button.
6. Click qryOrderInfo on the list of queries.
7. Click Next.

Select the qryOrderInfo query as the basis for the Crosstab query

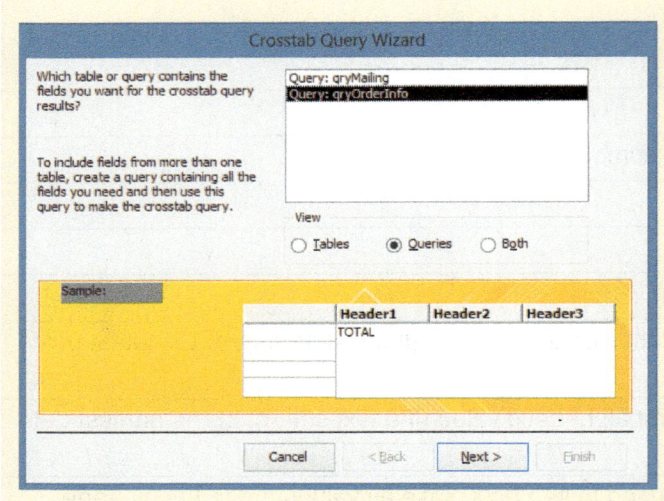

Access 2013, Windows 8, Microsoft Corporation

8. Click ProductName and click Add >.
9. Click PricePerUnit and click Add >.
10. Click Next.

Choose ProductName and PricePerUnit as the rows

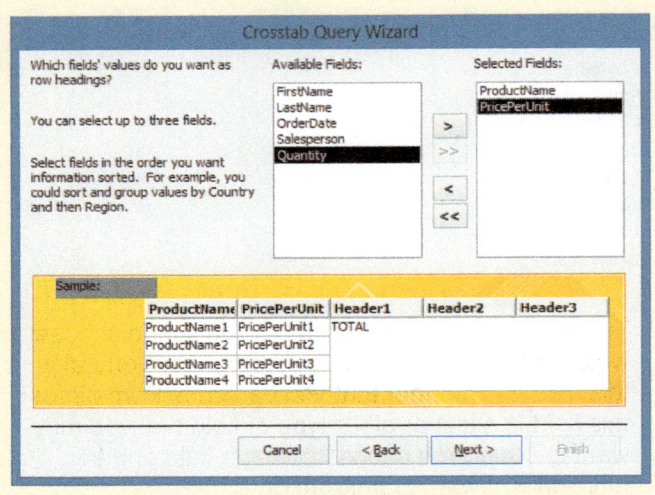

Access 2013, Windows 8, Microsoft Corporation

11. Click LastName to select it for a column heading and click Next.
12. On the Fields list, click Quantity.
13. On the Functions list, click Sum.

Choose to sum the Quantity field

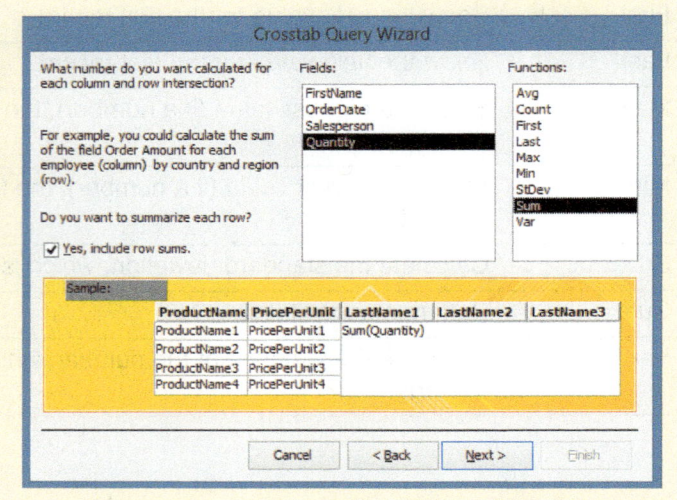

Access 2013, Windows 8, Microsoft Corporation

14. Click Next.
15. Leave the default name and click Finish. The query results appear. Leave the database open for the next Try It.

Creating a Crosstab Query in Design View

- In a Crosstab query, a Crosstab row appears in the query design grid. Figure 31-2 shows the query design grid for the query you created in the last Try It. You can switch to Datasheet view or click the Run button to see the results of the Crosstab query.
- The choices in the Crosstab row are Row Heading, Column Heading, and Value. You must have at least one of each.

  ✓ *You can make any query into a Crosstab query by clicking the Crosstab button on the QUERY TOOLS DESIGN tab.*

- You can have more than one Row Heading field, but not more than one Column Heading or Value field.
- The Total row for the Row Heading and Column Heading fields shows Group By.
- If you choose to display row totals, the Crosstab row also shows Row Heading, but the Total row shows the Sum (or other) function.
- The Total row for the Value field shows the function you want to apply, such as Sum.
- If you want to include only certain records, choose Where in the Total row and type the filtering criteria in the Criteria row.

Figure 31-2

Field:	ProductName	PricePerUnit	LastName	Quantity	Total Of Quantity: Qu
Table:	qryOrderInfo	qryOrderInfo	qryOrderInfo	qryOrderInfo	qryOrderInfo
Total:	Group By	Group By	Group By	Sum	Sum
Crosstab:	Row Heading	Row Heading	Column Heading	Value	Row Heading
Sort:					
Criteria:					
or:					

Access 2013, Windows 8, Microsoft Corporation

Try It! Creating a Crosstab Query in Design View

1. In the **A31Try_xx** file, click CREATE > Query Design.
2. In the Show Table dialog box, click the tblCustomers table. Hold down the CTRL key and click the tblOrderDetails, tblOrders, and tblProducts tables, too.
3. Click Add to add the tables to the query grid. Then click Close to close the Show Table dialog box.

   ✓ *You can drag the query field lists to arrange them so they are more readable if desired.*

4. Double-click the LastName field in tblCustomers to add it to the query grid.
5. Double-click the ProductName field in tblProducts.
6. Double-click the Quantity field in tblOrderDetails.

   ✓ *You needed to add the tblOrders table to the query in step 2 to get the linkage between the other tables; however, none of its fields are used directly in this query.*

7. Click QUERY TOOLS DESIGN > Crosstab.
8. A Crosstab row appears in the grid.
9. In the LastName column, open the Crosstab drop-down list and click Column Heading.
10. In the ProductName column, open the Crosstab drop-down list and click Row Heading.
11. In the Quantity column, open the Crosstab drop-down list and click Value.
12. In the Quantity column, open the Total drop-down list and click Sum.

(continued)

Try It! Creating a Crosstab Query in Design View *(continued)*

13 Click QUERY TOOLS DESIGN > Run ! to see the results.

14 Right-click the Query1 tab and click Close. When prompted to save changes, click Yes.

15 In the Save As dialog box, type **Products Crosstab** and click OK.

16 Close the database, and exit Access.

Create a Crosstab query from scratch in Query Design view

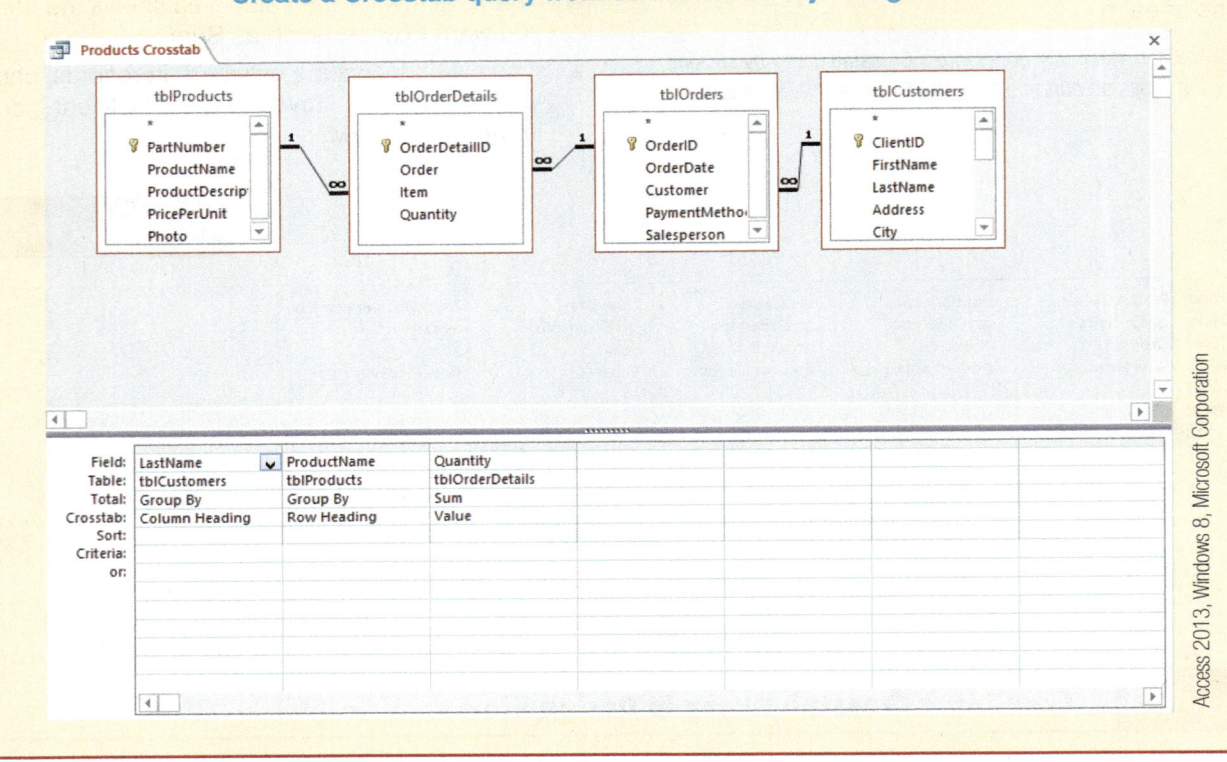

Field:	LastName	ProductName	Quantity
Table:	tblCustomers	tblProducts	tblOrderDetails
Total:	Group By	Group By	Sum
Crosstab:	Column Heading	Row Heading	Value
Sort:			
Criteria:			
or:			

Lesson 31—Practice

You are helping a company called Bookseller Source that offers large quantities of textbooks to bookstores at 50 percent off retail prices. They have already set up the database for this business, and they have three days' worth of sales data entered. Now the owners would like to look at the data for these first few days to evaluate what items are selling well and which salespeople are performing the best. You will use Crosstab queries to produce this data.

DIRECTIONS

1. Start Access, if necessary, and open **A31Practice** from the data files for this lesson.
2. Save the file as **A31Practice_xx** in the location where your teacher instructs you to store the files for this lesson.
   - ✓ *If a security warning bar appears, click Enable Content.*
3. Click **CREATE** > **Query Wizard**.
4. Click **Crosstab Query Wizard** and click **OK**.
5. Click the **Queries** option button.
6. Click **Next**.
7. Click the **Salesperson** field, and click the **Add** button to move it to the Selected Fields list. Then click **Next**.
8. Click the **OrderDate** field and click **Next**.
9. Click **Date** and click **Next**.
10. In the **Fields** column, click **Total**.
11. In the Functions column, click **Sum**. Make sure the **Yes, include row sums** check box is marked.
12. Click **Next**.
13. Replace the default name with **qrySalesValuePerDay-Crosstab**, and click **Finish**.
14. In the query results, double-click the dividers between each set of column headers, expanding the column widths as needed to fit the contents, as shown in Figure 31-3.
15. **With your teacher's permission**, print the query results.
16. Save and close the database, and exit Access. If instructed, submit this database to your teacher for grading.

Figure 31-3

Salesperson	Total Of Total	1/15/2014	1/16/2014	1/17/2014
Christine Cutler	$12,338.00	$7,498.50		$4,839.50
Julie Burrow	$80,291.38	$61,109.00	$14,184.38	$4,998.00
Marjorie Hopper	$108,652.00	$74,420.00	$29,607.50	$4,624.50
Melissa Louks	$53,493.00	$21,495.50		$31,997.50

qrySalesValuePerDay-Crosstab

Access 2013, Windows 8, Microsoft Corporation

Lesson 31—Apply

In this project, you will take the Bookseller Source queries and create Crosstab queries to help them navigate their database more efficiently.

DIRECTIONS

1. Start Access, if necessary, and open **A31Apply** from the data files for this lesson.
2. Save the file as **A31Apply_xx** in the location where your teacher instructs you to store the files for this lesson.
   - ✓ If a security warning bar appears, click Enable Content.
3. Open the **qrySalesValuePerDay-Crosstab** query in Design view.
4. Change the column name of the Total Of Total column to **Total All Days**.
   - ✓ To do this, edit the text in the Field row to read Total All Days:Total.
5. Run the query. Then save and close it.
6. Make a copy of the query, and name the copy **qrySalesQuantityPerDay-Crosstab**.
   - ✓ To do this from the Navigation pane, select the query, press CTRL + C, and then press CTRL + V. You will be prompted for the new name.
7. Open the **qrySalesQuantityPerDay-Crosstab** query in Design view, and edit the query so that it shows the total number of books sold, rather than the value of the books sold, per salesperson per day.
   - ✓ To do this, change the references to the Total field to the Quantity field in the last two columns of the query grid.
8. Save and run the query. It should look like Figure 31-4.
9. Start a new Crosstab query in Design view that is based on **qryOrdersWithDetails**,
10. Enter the appropriate fields and settings to produce the results shown in Figure 31-5.
    - The order dates are the row headings.
    - The salespeople are the column headings.
    - The average price of the books sold (Our Price field) is the value.
11. Run the query, and widen the columns as needed so that no text is truncated.
12. Save the new query as **qryAvgPricePerDay-Crosstab**.
13. **With your teacher's permission**, print the results for all three queries.
14. Close the database, and exit Access. If instructed, submit this database to your teacher for grading.

Figure 31-4

Salesperson	Total All Days	1/15/2014	1/16/2014	1/17/2014
Christine Cutler	600	300		300
Julie Burrow	2675	1600	675	400
Marjorie Hopper	2875	2050	675	150
Melissa Louks	2000	1000		1000

Access 2013, Windows 8, Microsoft Corporation

Figure 31-5

qryAvgPricePerDay-Crosstab

Order Date	Christine Cutler	Julie Burrow	Marjorie Hopper	Melissa Louks
1/15/2014	$27.50	$36.71	$32.92	$20.00
1/16/2014		$18.50	$31.93	
1/17/2014	$17.10	$12.50	$35.00	$32.00

Access 2013, Windows 8, Microsoft Corporation

Lesson 32

Creating Queries That Find Unmatched or Duplicate Records

➤ What You Will Learn

Using the Find Unmatched Query Wizard
Using the Find Duplicates Query Wizard

Software Skills   The Find Unmatched Query Wizard and the Find Duplicates Query Wizard are two special-purpose query types for specific tasks. They do just what their names suggest. The Find Unmatched Query Wizard compares two tables and reports records from one that do not have a corresponding entry in the other. The Find Duplicates query lists records that have the same value for one or more specified fields.

WORDS TO KNOW

Duplicate
Two or more records that contain the same data in a field that ought to be unique for each record.

Unmatched
Records that should have a corresponding reference in another table but do not.

What You Can Do

Using the Find Unmatched Query Wizard

- The Find Unmatched Query Wizard leads you through the steps needed to create a query that will show records that do not match up with corresponding values in another table.
- Suppose, for example, that you have separate tables for Orders and OrderDetails. Every record in OrderDetails should refer to a valid order number in the Orders table. If there are detail records that do not, they are **unmatched**.
  - ✓ *This type of error would not occur if you were enforcing referential integrity in the relationship between the two tables. This illustrates the importance of referential integrity.*
- The results appear in a datasheet, just like a select query. You can print it to use as a reference when fixing the problems.
- You can also use this type of query in cases where there aren't any errors, but you just want information. For example, in the following steps, you'll use it to find payment methods that no customers have used.

Try It! Using the Find Unmatched Query Wizard

1. Start Access, and open **A32Try** from the data files for this lesson.

2. Save the file as **A32Try_xx** in the location where your teacher instructs you to store the files for this lesson. Click Enable Content if the information bar appears.

3. Click CREATE > Query Wizard.

4. Select Find Unmatched Query Wizard and click OK.

5. Click Table: tblPaymentMethods and click Next.

Select the table from which to display unmatched records

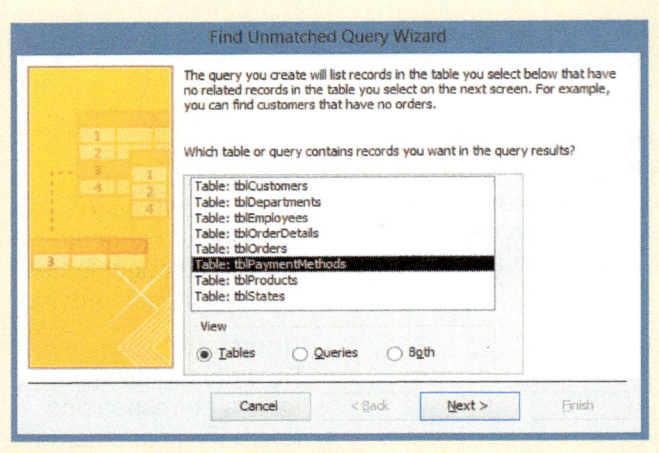

Access 2013, Windows 8, Microsoft Corporation

6. Click Table: tblOrders and click Next.

7. The field matching should already be set correctly, as shown in the next figure. Click Next to accept it.

Access guesses the field matching correctly in this case

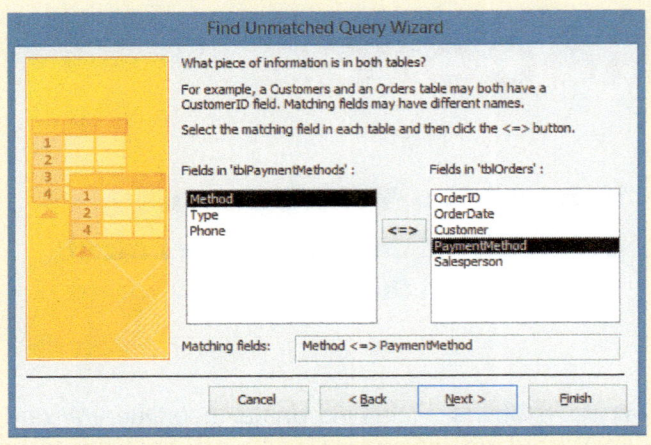

Access 2013, Windows 8, Microsoft Corporation

8. Click the All Fields button >> to select all the fields to include in the query results. Then click Next.

9. Replace the default query name with **qryUnusedPaymentMethods**.

10. Click Finish. Access finds four unmatched records.

11. Right-click the query's tab, and click Close.

12. Leave the database open to use in the next Try It.

Using the Find Duplicates Query Wizard

- The Find Duplicates Query Wizard is like a super "search" that helps flush out duplication in your data.

- For example, suppose you want a single record in your Customers table for each business, but you have ended up with some businesses entered multiple times with different contact people in each record. You could find the **duplicates** with the Find Duplicates Query Wizard.

✓ This error would not occur if you set up the business name field to not allow duplicates. Setting its Indexed property to Yes (No Duplicates) would prevent the problem from happening in the future.

- In the following Try It, you will find products that have the same name in a product table. You can then examine the duplicate products to make sure they are indeed different products and, if they are not, you can delete or combine the duplicates.

Lesson 40

Working with Subforms and Subreports

➤ What You Will Learn

Understanding Subforms and Subreports
Creating a Form and Subform with the Form Wizard
Creating a Subform with the Subform Wizard
Creating a Subreport with Drag-and-Drop
Editing a Subform or Subreport

Software Skills When you have one set of records that is related to another, it is much easier to input new records when you can see the main record and the records that are related to it. For example, if you have an order record that could be related to one or more order detail items, the top half of the form might show the order information in general and the bottom half might show the items within the order.

WORDS TO KNOW

Main form
A form that contains a subform or several subforms.

Subform
A form that is enclosed inside another form.

Subreport
Similar to a subform. A report can have a subreport that is the child side of a parent-to-child relationship.

What You Can Do

Understanding Subforms and Subreports

- **Subforms** and **subreports** allow you to see values related to a main record.
- You can go ten levels deep with a subform within a subform within the **main form**. However, one subform level deep is probably plenty in most circumstances; otherwise your forms get too complicated.
- A subform can be displayed in any view (Form view, Datasheet view, and so on). However, most subforms are displayed in Datasheet view by default because it is the most efficient view for packing a lot of information into a small space, and subforms are usually limited in the amount of space they occupy.

    ✓ There must be a relationship between the table or query that comprises the main form and the one that comprises the subform. You must create that relationship before creating the form.

- In a form with a subform, there are two sets of record-navigation controls. The subform has its own set, as does the main form. Figure 40-1 shows a main form and subform.
    - ✓ Once created, a subform also exists outside of the main form, as a separate form in the object list for your database. You can open and use it as a separate form whenever you like. It is customary to include "subform" in the names you assign to subforms so that you will remember what they were created for.

- To create a subform, you can do any of the following:
    - Use the Form Wizard to create both the main form and the subform at the same time.
    - Create the main form and then use the Subform wizard to build the subform.
    - Drag-and-drop another form onto an existing form in Design view to place it there as a subform.
- A subreport is much like a subform, except there isn't a wizard for creating subreports; you must set them up manually.

Figure 40-1

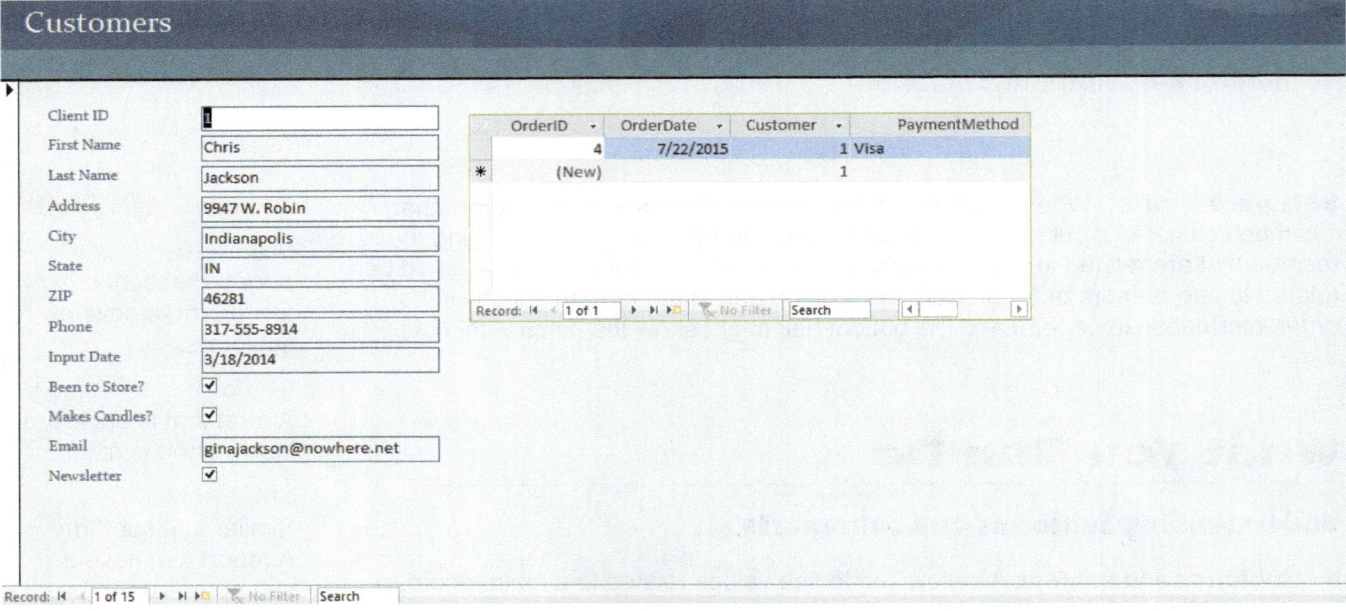

Access 2013, Windows 8, Microsoft Corporation

Creating a Form and Subform with the Form Wizard

- If you create the form and subform at the same time using the Wizard, Access does all the work for you.

- When you select fields from more than one table or query, the Wizard automatically offers to set up the subform.

Try It! Creating a Form and Subform with the Form Wizard

1. Start Access, and open **A40Try** from the data files for this lesson.
2. Save the file as **A40Try_xx** in the location where your teacher instructs you to store the files for this lesson. Click Enable Content if the information bar appears.
3. Click CREATE > Form Wizard. The Form Wizard opens.
4. Open the Tables/Queries drop-down list and click Table: tblOrders.
5. Click the >> button to add all the fields to the form.
6. Open the Tables/Queries drop-down list and click Table: tblOrderDetails.
7. Click the >> button to add all the fields to the form. Then, click Next.
8. When prompted for how you want to view your data, click Next to accept the default of by tblOrders.
   - ✓ The Linked forms option places a button on the main form instead of displaying the subform there. Users can click the button to open the subform separately.
9. Click Next to accept the default of Datasheet for the subform layout. In the Form text box, replace the default name with **frmOrderForm**.
10. In the Subform text box, replace the default name with **frmOrderDetailsSubform**.
11. Click Finish. The new form and subform appear.
12. Right-click the form tab and click Close. You are not prompted to save changes because the Wizard saved the forms.
13. Leave the database open for the next Try It.

Specify that the main form will be tblOrders

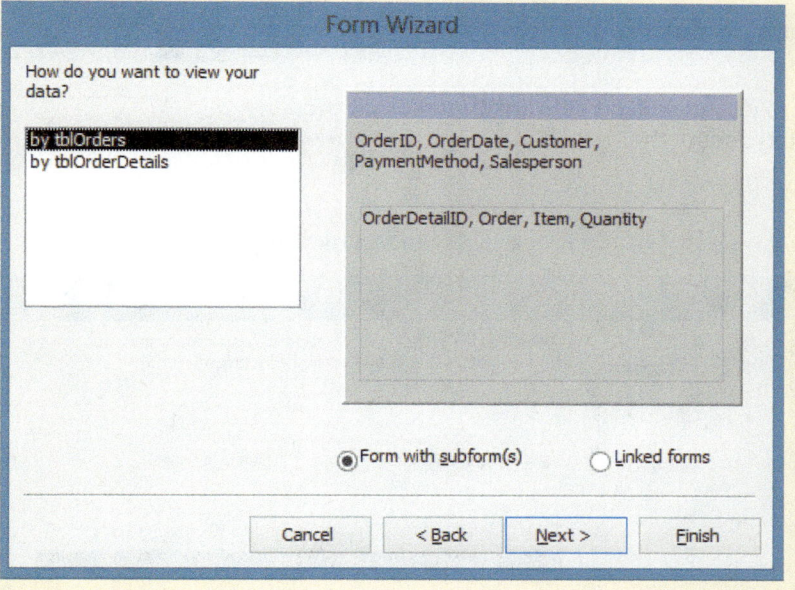

Try It! Creating a Subform with the Subform Wizard

1. In the **A40Try_xx** file, right-click frmCustomers and click Design View.

2. Drag the right border of the form to the 9.0" mark on the horizontal ruler, expanding the form width.

3. On the FORM DESIGN TOOLS DESIGN tab, click the More button for the Controls group.

4. Make sure Use Control Wizards is selected. If it's not, click it to select it, and then repeat step 3.

5. In the Controls group, select the Subform/Subreport icon.

6. Click on the blank area of the form, at approximately the 4" mark on the horizontal ruler and aligned vertically with the top of the ClientID text box. The Subform Wizard opens.

7. Click Next to accept the default of Use existing Tables and Queries.

8. Open the Tables/Queries drop-down list, and click Table: tblOrders.

9. Click the >> button to select all the fields. Then, click Next.

10. When prompted to define which fields link the forms, click Next to accept the default.

11. Replace the default name with **frmOrdersSubform** and click Finish. The subform appears on the form.

12. Click the subform's label to select it, and press DEL to delete the label.

    ✓ Do not worry that the subform appears in Single Item form view rather than Datasheet view. It will appear correctly in Layout and Form views.

13. Right-click the form's tab and click Form View to view your work. Click Next Record ▶ a few times to move through the records in the main form and confirm that the records shown in the subform change.

14. Right-click the form's tab and click Close. Click Yes when prompted to save changes.

15. Leave the database open for the next Try It.

Click the Subform/Subreport button

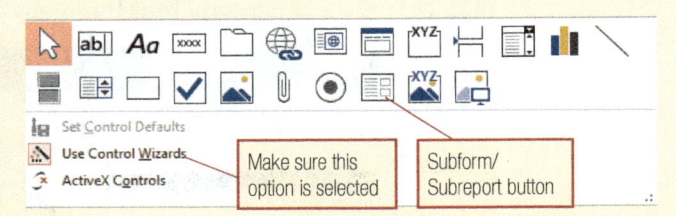

Access 2013, Windows 8, Microsoft Corporation

Define which fields link the forms

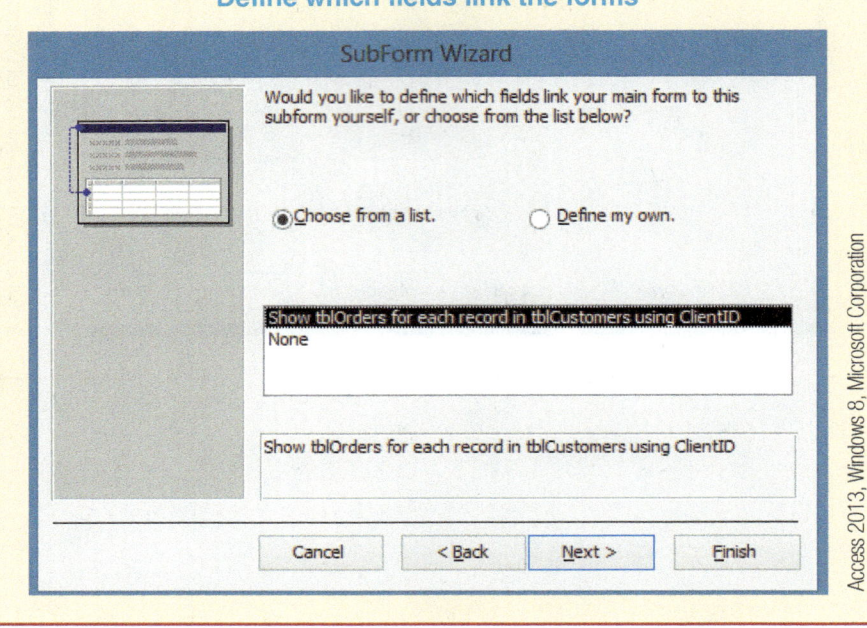

Access 2013, Windows 8, Microsoft Corporation

Creating a Subreport with Drag-and-Drop

- The easiest way to create a subform on a form, or a subreport on a report, is if you have already created both of them separately. You can then drag the subform or subreport onto the main one in Design view from the Navigation pane.

- You can also drag a table directly onto a form or report in Design view, and a wizard will ask you to verify the relationship.

Try It! Creating a Subreport with Drag-and-Drop

1. In the **A40Try_xx** file, in the Navigation pane, right-click rptMailerMain and click Design View.

2. From the Navigation pane, drag rptMailerSub to the report layout grid, below the existing fields.

3. Click the subreport's label (rptMailerSub) on the report design grid and press DEL.

4. Click the Save button on the Quick Access Toolbar.

5. Right-click the report's tab, and click Report View to check your work.

6. Right-click the report's tab and click Close. Click Yes, if prompted to save.

7. Leave the report open to use in the next Try It.

Drag the subreport onto the main report directly from the Navigation pane

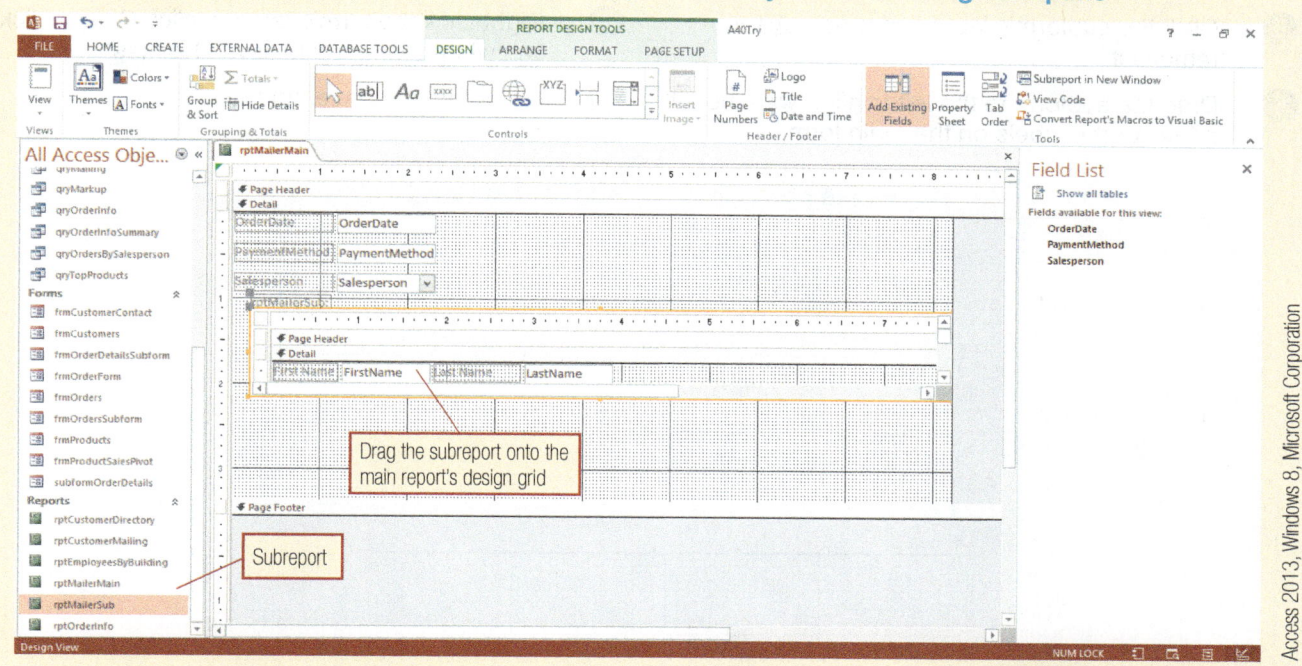

Editing a Subform or Subreport

- You can change the size of the subform or subreport like any other object by selecting it and then dragging its borders.
- When you save the form, both the main form and the subform are saved (or the main report and subreport).
- When using a preexisting form or report as your subform or subreport, there may be fields that you do not want to include on the subform. You can hide them from Layout view by right-clicking the unwanted field and choosing Hide Fields.

Try It! Editing a Subform

1. In the **A40Try_xx** file, right-click the rptMailerMain report and click Design View.
2. Drag the right border of the subreport to the left until it does not overlap the page margin line.
3. Right-click the report's tab and click Close. Click Yes when prompted to save changes.
4. In the Navigation pane, right-click frmOrderForm and click Design View.
5. Click the subform's label and press DEL to remove it.
6. Drag the subform to the left to align with the left edges of the labels on the main form.
7. Drag the right edge of the subform to the left to align with the right edge of the Salesperson field in the main form.
8. On the subform, click the OrderDetailID text box and DEL.
9. Right-click the main form's tab and click Form View.
   ✓ Note that OrderDetailID does not appear in the subform.
10. Right-click the form's tab and click Close. Click Yes when prompted to save changes.
11. Close the database, and exit Access.

Adjust the position of the subform in Design view

Lesson 40—Practice

In this project, you will add a subform to a form and modify it to make the Textbook Exchange's database look more professional.

DIRECTIONS

1. Start Access, if necessary, and open **A40Practice** from the data files for this lesson.
2. Save the file as **A40Practice_xx** in the location where your teacher instructs you to store the files for this lesson.
   ✓ *If a security warning bar appears, click Enable Content.*
3. In the Navigation pane, right-click **frmMembers** and click Design View.
4. Drag **frmForSale** from the Navigation pane to the empty area at the bottom of the **frmMembers** form, making it a subform.
5. Right-click the main form's tab, and click **Form View**.
6. Notice that this does not look very good because of the large form header on the frmForSale form. It is clear that a new subform should be created, rather than trying to use an existing form as a subform.
7. Right-click the main form's tab, and click **Design View**.
8. Select the subform, and press DEL to remove it.
9. Click **FORM DESIGN TOOLS DESIGN > More** to open the palette of controls you can insert.
10. Click **Subform/Subreport**.
11. Click on the main form, below the Phone label. The Subform Wizard opens.
12. Click **Next** to accept the default (Use existing Tables and Queries).
13. Open the **Tables/Queries** drop-down list and click **Table: tblForSale**.
14. Click the **ListingDate** field and click > to add it to the form. Do the same for **Book, Condition**, and **Asking Price**. Then, click **Next**.
15. Click **Next** to accept the default field associations.
16. Replace the default name with **frmForSaleSubform** and click **Finish**.
17. Click the **frmForSaleSubform** label on the form and press DEL.
18. Switch to Layout view and resize the subform and its columns so that all data is visible. See Figure 40-2.
19. Right-click the form's tab and click **Form View**.
20. Right-click the form's tab and click **Close**. When prompted to save changes, click **Yes**.
21. Close the database, and exit Access. If instructed, submit this database to your teacher for grading.

Figure 40-2

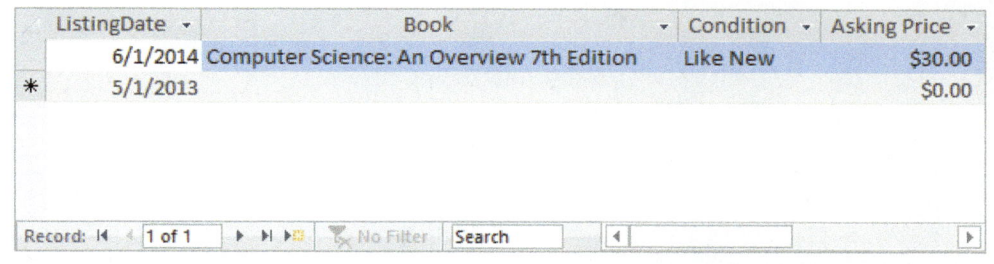

ListingDate	Book	Condition	Asking Price
6/1/2014	Computer Science: An Overview 7th Edition	Like New	$30.00
* 5/1/2013			$0.00

Access 2013, Windows 8, Microsoft Corporation

Lesson 40—Apply

Working for the Textbook Exchange, you will set up a form with a subform that helps salespeople see at a glance the details of each book being offered for sale.

DIRECTIONS

1. Start Access, if necessary, and open **A40Apply** from the data files for this lesson.
2. Save the file as **A40Apply_xx** in the location where your teacher instructs you to store the files for this lesson.
    - ✓ If a security warning bar appears, click Enable Content.
3. Open **frmBookInformation** in Design view and add a subform to it showing which members are selling each book. Name the subform **frmSaleSubform**.
    - ✓ Use any method and settings you wish, but make sure that for each book, the user viewing the form will be able to see who is selling a copy (the member number) and what is the condition and asking price of each book. Check your work in Layout view and make adjustments to the subform's columns and overall width as needed.
4. Save and close all forms.
5. Use the Form Wizard to create a new form/subform combo called **frmBooks2**. The main form should use all the fields from **tblBooks** and the subform should show all fields from **tblForSale** and should open in a linked form. The subform should be named **frmSaleSubform2**.
6. Try out the button for the linked form in Form view. It doesn't work because the form title is covering it.
7. In Design view, move the form's title (in the Form Header) to the right so it does not overlap the button.
8. Switch to Form view, and try the button again. This time it works. The subform opens in a separate tab.
9. Close the subform. Return to Design view and make the following changes:
    a. Change the text on the button to **Copies for Sale**.
    b. Change the form title label to **Books**.
10. Close the form, saving changes.
11. Display **frmSaleSubform2** in Layout view, and delete the form title.
12. Resize columns as needed so all text fits. Go to **frmBooks2**, as well, and resize columns as needed.
13. Save your changes, and close the form.
14. Open **frmBooks2** in Form view again, and test the button.
    - ✓ The subform opens showing only the records that are associated with the record that was showing in the main form.
15. Close the database, and exit Access. If instructed, submit this database to your teacher for grading.

Lesson 41

Working with Charts

➤ What You Will Learn

Inserting a Chart in a Report
Editing a Chart
Changing the Chart Type
Changing Chart Options

Software Skills Although Access is not known for the kind of powerful charting capabilities Excel has, you can still produce attractive and useful charts using Access data.

What You Can Do

Inserting a Chart in a Report

- To create a chart in Access, you can place a Microsoft Graph chart on a report or form.
- **Microsoft Graph** charts use a somewhat awkward user interface from earlier versions of Microsoft Office, but can be placed on any report or form.
- To create a chart report, first create a blank report using the Blank Report button on the CREATE tab. Then, in Design view, use the Chart button on the Design tab to start a new chart.
- The Chart Wizard runs, prompting you to select the table or query from which you want to pull data.

    ✓ After selecting the chart options, the Chart Wizard has a layout section where you can decide how the chart should be formatted. You can also change how the information is to be summarized and preview the chart in this section. Do not be alarmed that the chart does not show the data from your selected data source in Design view. This is one of the quirks of Microsoft Graph. It does not show the actual chart data in Design view. Switch to Layout view or Report view to see your data.

WORDS TO KNOW

Legend
A color-coded key that tells what each color in a chart represents.

Microsoft Graph
A charting tool that creates embedded charts in applications such as Access.

Try It! Inserting a Chart in a Report

1. Start Access, and open **A41Try** from the data files for this lesson.
2. Save the file as **A41Try_xx** in the location where your teacher instructs you to store the files for this lesson. Click Enable Content if the information bar appears.
3. Click CREATE > Blank Report. A blank report appears in Layout view.
4. Right-click the report's tab, and click Design View.
   ✓ Some controls can be inserted from Layout view, but a chart is not one of them.
5. On the REPORT DESIGN TOOLS DESIGN tab, in the Controls group, click the More button to display a palette of available tools.
6. Click the Chart button, and click on the report in the Detail section. The Chart Wizard opens.
7. Click Table: tblOrderDetails and click Next.
8. Click Customers and click > to select it.
9. Click Quantity and click > to select it. Then, click Next.
10. Click Pie Chart (the first chart type in the bottom row of the dialog box) and click Next.
11. Double-click SumOfQuantity. The Summarize dialog box opens.
12. Click None and OK.
13. Click Preview Chart. Click Close.
    ✓ The chart will look strange at this point, but we will fix that later.
14. Click Next.
15. Replace the default name with **chtOrderDetails** and click Finish. The chart appears on the report layout. The actual data does not appear at this point.
16. Right-click the report's tab, and click Report View to see the actual chart.
17. Click the Save button on the Quick Access Toolbar.
18. In the Save As dialog box, type **rptOrderChart** and click OK.
19. Leave the report open to use in the next Try It.

Editing a Chart

- If the chart is the wrong size, you can drag the chart object's border to resize it. You can do this in either Design or Layout view.
- To edit the chart's content, you must return to Design view and double-click the chart. This opens Microsoft Graph. Notice that Microsoft Graph uses a traditional menu and toolbar. See Figure 41-1 on the next page.
- When you are working in Microsoft Graph, the chart displays dummy data, except for the chart title. You can format the labels, **legends**, axes, and so on, and those formatting settings will be passed on to the actual chart that is generated when you are in Layout or Report view.
- The small floating spreadsheet is called the datasheet. You can close it by clicking the View Datasheet button on the toolbar. It does not contain the actual data for the chart; it is only for the sample chart.
  ✓ The Standard and Formatting toolbars in Microsoft Graph appear on a single line, which means both are truncated. You can access hidden buttons on a toolbar by clicking the More button at the right end, or you can click More and then click Show Buttons on Two Rows to separate them so all buttons are visible.

Figure 41-1

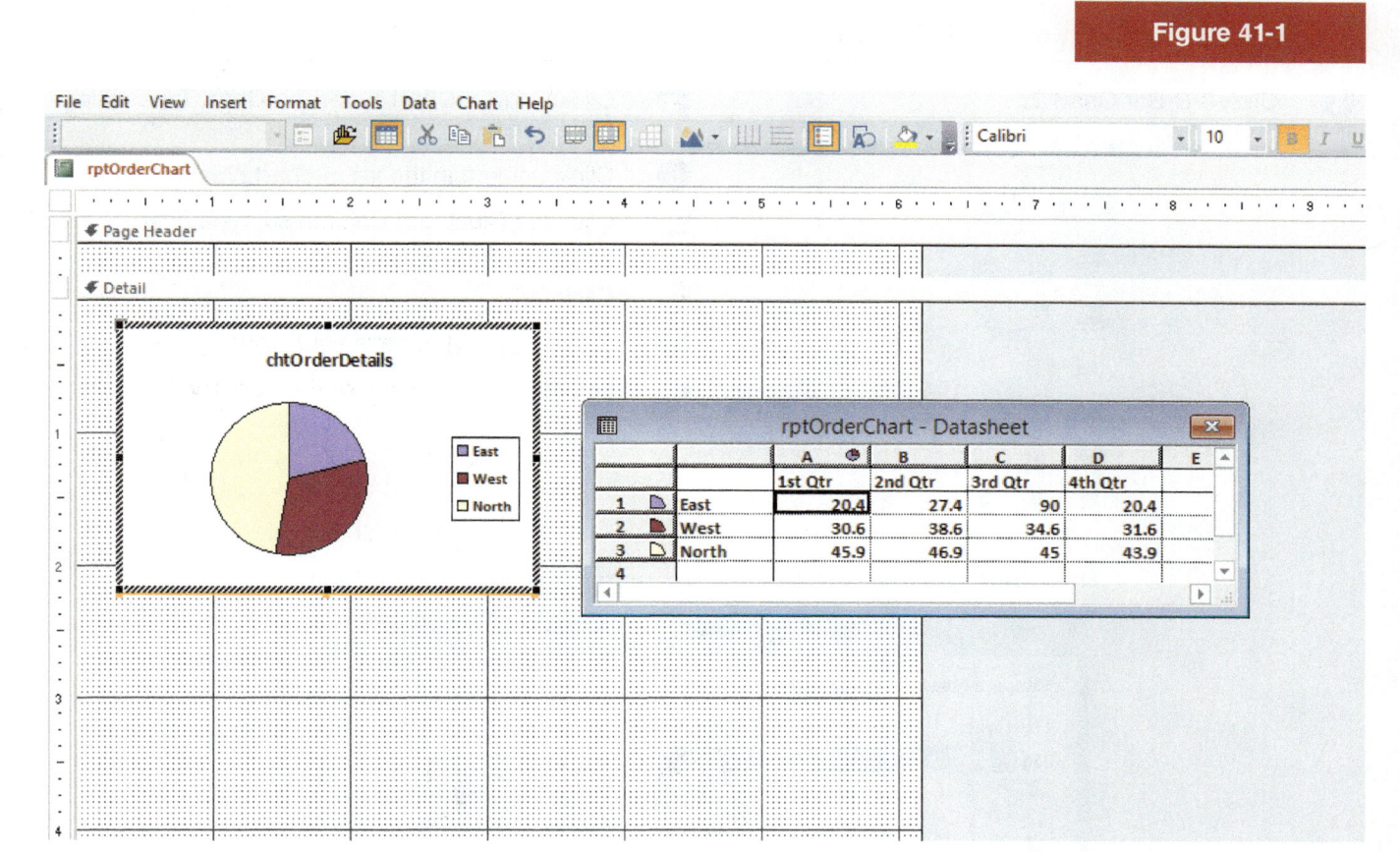

Access 2013, Windows 8, Microsoft Corporation

Changing the Chart Type

- You can change the chart's type without having to recreate it entirely.
- To change the chart's type, open it in Microsoft Graph and then click the drop-down arrow next to the Chart Type button. From the palette of types, click the one you want.

✓ If you have a chart that uses three fields, such as a bar chart, and you switch to a chart that uses only two fields, such as a pie chart, only the first series will show (that is, the first color of the bar from the legend).

- For additional chart types, open the Chart menu and click Chart Type. From the Chart Type dialog box, you can select a type and subtype. There is also a Custom Types tab that has some interesting preset formatting types on it.

Try It!   Editing a Chart

1. In the **A41Try_xx** file, right-click the rptOrderChart tab and click Design View.

2. Double-click the chart to open Microsoft Graph.

3. Click the drop-down arrow on the Chart Type button to open a palette of chart types.

(continued)

Try It! Editing a Chart (continued)

4 Click 3-D Bar Chart.

Select a different chart type

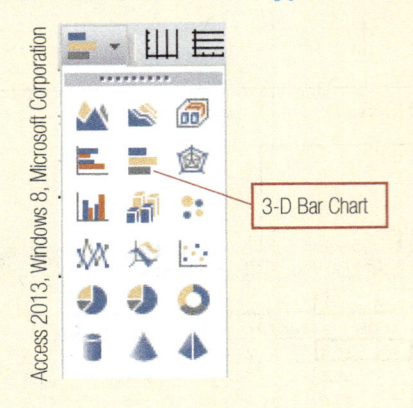

3-D Bar Chart

5 Click Chart > Chart Type. The Chart Type dialog box opens.

6 Click Column in the list of chart types.

7 Click the Clustered Column subtype (first sample in the top row).

8 Click OK.

9 Press CTRL + S to save your work.

10 Leave the chart open for the next Try It.

The Chart Type dialog box contains more chart subtype options

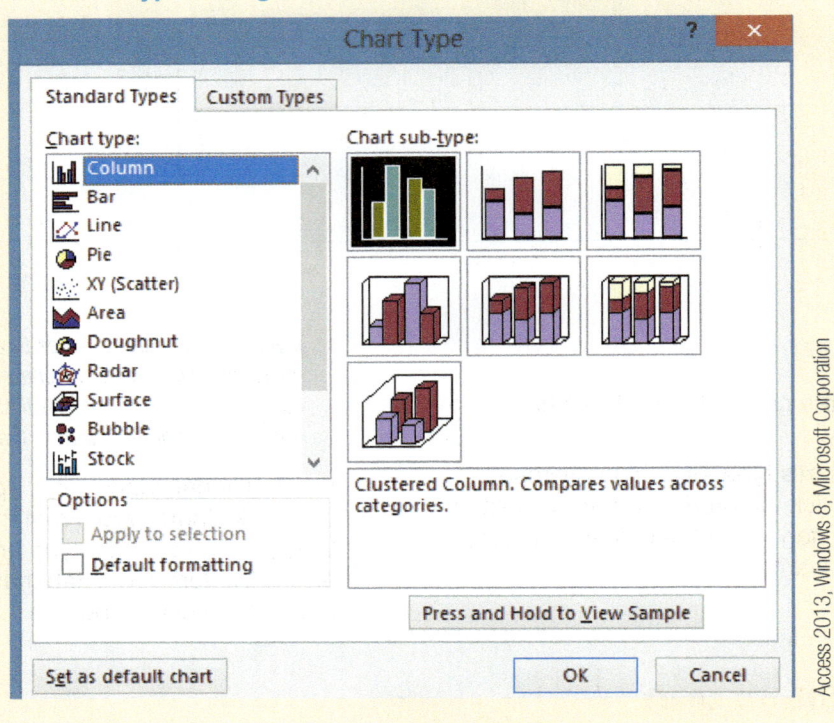

Changing Chart Options

- Sometimes a chart can convey a different message if you display its data by row versus by column. To switch between the two on a two-axis chart such as a bar, line, column, or area chart, use the By Row and By Column buttons on the Standard toolbar.

  ✓ *This is not applicable to pie charts.*

- You can toggle certain optional elements on/off the chart by clicking the buttons on the Standard toolbar. Some of these buttons are available only for certain chart types. See Figure 41-2 on the next page.

Figure 41-2

View Datasheet | Value Axis Grid | Legend | Category Axis Grid

Access 2013, Windows 8, Microsoft Corporation

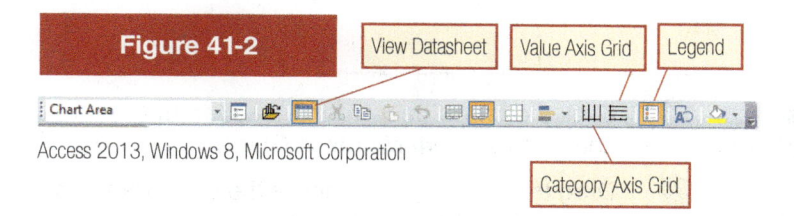

- Many other chart features can be controlled from the Chart Options dialog box. You can control the axis scale, legend, gridlines, titles, data labels, and data table from here. See Figure 41-3.

Figure 41-3

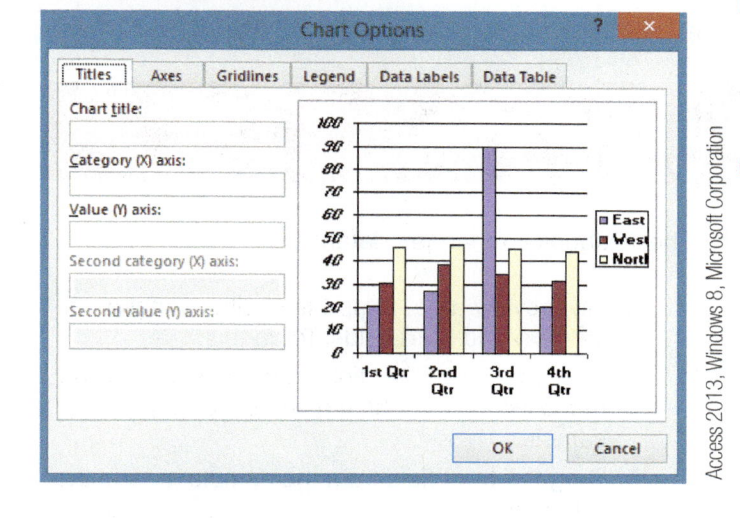

Chart Options dialog with tabs: Titles, Axes, Gridlines, Legend, Data Labels, Data Table. Fields: Chart title, Category (X) axis, Value (Y) axis, Second category (X) axis, Second value (Y) axis. Preview chart showing East, West, North series across 1st Qtr, 2nd Qtr, 3rd Qtr, 4th Qtr.

Access 2013, Windows 8, Microsoft Corporation

- You can use the character formatting buttons on the Formatting toolbar to format any of the text objects on the chart, such as the title, legend, and axes. Select any of these and then choose a different font, font size, attributes (such as bold and italic), and so on. These work just like they do in any other Office application. See Figure 41-4.

- There are also buttons on the Formatting toolbar for applying formatting to numbers, such as making numbers appear as currency or percentages and changing the number of decimal places. These work just like in Excel. See Figure 41-5.

- There are also buttons on the Formatting toolbar for aligning the text horizontally within its text box and slanting the text diagonally. See Figure 41-5.

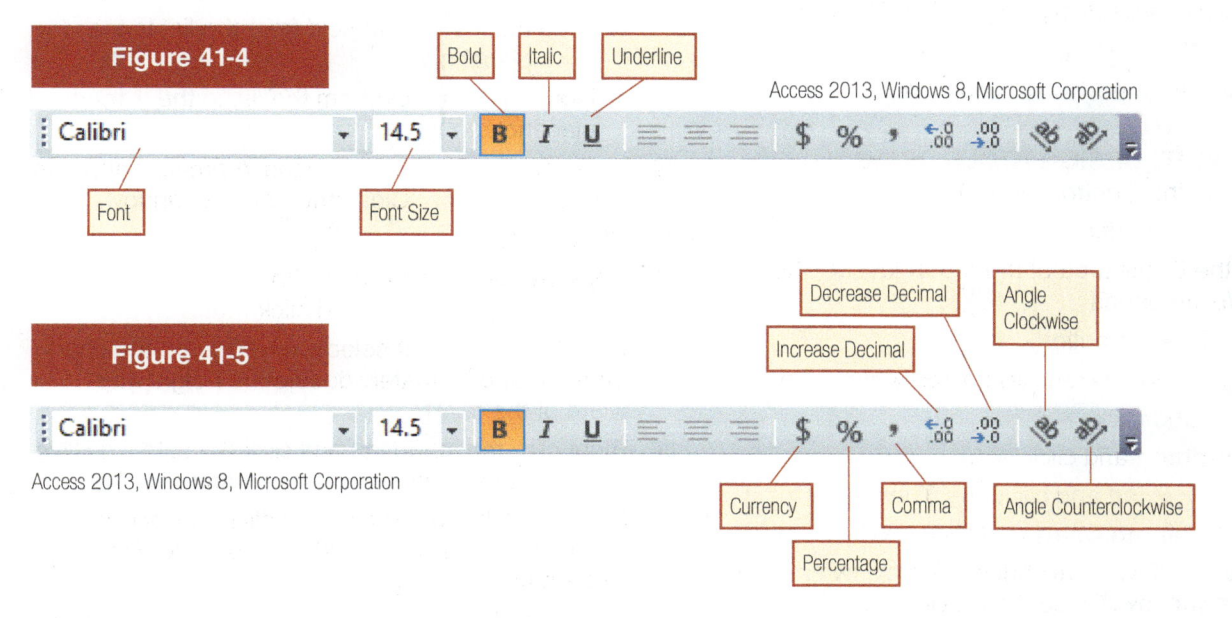

Figure 41-4

Calibri | 14.5 | Bold | Italic | Underline

Font | Font Size

Access 2013, Windows 8, Microsoft Corporation

Figure 41-5

Calibri | 14.5 | B I U | $ % , | Increase Decimal | Decrease Decimal | Angle Clockwise | Angle Counterclockwise

Currency | Percentage | Comma

Access 2013, Windows 8, Microsoft Corporation

Adding File Locations to Trusted Locations

- Depending on where the data files are stored for this course and how the system has been set up, you may have seen a security warning when previously opening data files. You may have had to click Enable Content in the information bar each time you opened a file. See Figure 44-1.

- You can avoid this message by adding the folder where you store your data files to the Trusted Locations list in Access.
  - ✓ This may have already been done for the computers in your location.

- You can also add any other locations to Trusted Locations, exempting files in those locations from the security warning.

Figure 44-1

SECURITY WARNING Some active content has been disabled. Click for more details.   Enable Content

Access 2013, Windows 8, Microsoft Corporation

Try It!   Adding a Folder to the Trusted Locations List

1. Click FILE > Options. The Access Options dialog box opens.
2. Click Trust Center.
3. Click Trust Center Settings. The Trust Center dialog box opens.
4. Click Trusted Locations.
5. Click Add new location. The Microsoft Office Trusted Location dialog box opens.
6. In the Path box, type the full path to the location where the data files are stored for this class.
   - ✓ Ask your teacher what the path is if you are not sure. You can also locate the folder by clicking Browse and browsing for it.
7. Click the Subfolders of this location are also trusted check box.
8. Click OK to set up the new location.
9. Click OK to close the Trust Center dialog box.
10. Click OK to close the Access Options dialog box.
11. Close the database, and exit Access.

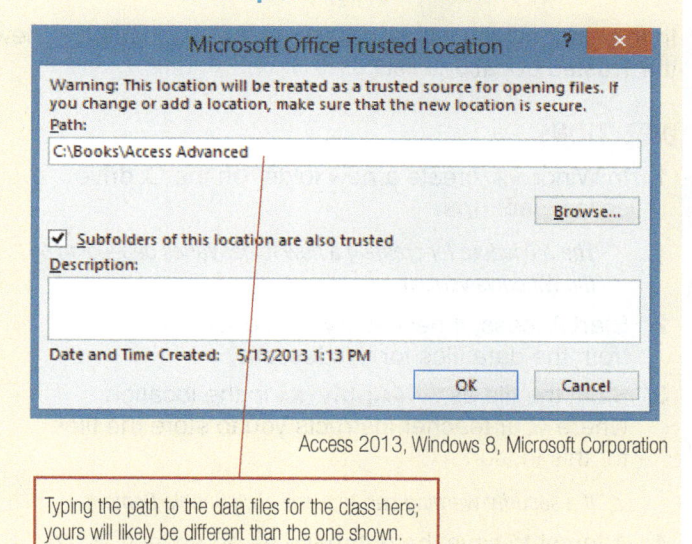

Set up a trusted location

Typing the path to the data files for the class here; yours will likely be different than the one shown.

Access 2013, Windows 8, Microsoft Corporation

Lesson 44—Practice

The Green Designs database will be shared with users who do not have Access 2013. In this project, you will compact and repair the database and save it in the Access 2000 database format.

DIRECTIONS
1. Start Access, if necessary, and open **A44Practice** from the data files for this lesson.
2. Click **FILE** > **Info**.
3. Click **Compact & Repair Database**.
4. Click **FILE** > **Save As**.
5. Click **Save Database As**.
6. Click **Access 2000 Database (.mdb)**.
7. Click **Save As**.
8. In the Save As dialog box, change the entry in the File name dialog box to **A44Practice_xx**. Navigate to the location where your teacher instructs you to store the files for this lesson.
9. Click **Save**. If a warning appears, click **OK**.
10. Close the database, and exit Access. If instructed, submit this database to your teacher for grading.

Lesson 44—Apply

In this project, you will also back up the database to a new folder that you create, and you will add that folder to the Trusted Locations list.

DIRECTIONS
1. In Windows, create a new folder on the C: drive called **Backups**.
   - ✓ *The procedure for creating a new folder varies depending on the Windows version.*
2. Start Access, if necessary, and open **A44Apply** from the data files for this lesson.
3. Save the file as **A44Apply_xx** in the location where your teacher instructs you to store the files for this lesson.
   - ✓ *If a security warning bar appears, click Enable Content.*
4. Attempt to save the database as an Access 2002-2003 database. An error message appears.
5. Click **OK**.
6. In the Access Options dialog box, on the General tab, set the new database sort order to General (Legacy):
   a. Click **FILE** > **Options** > **General**.
   b. Open the **New database sort order** drop-down list and click **General – Legacy** if it is not already selected.
   c. Click **OK**.
7. Compact and repair the database.
8. Save the database as an Access 2002-2003 database called **A44Apply-2003_xx**.
9. Add the **C:\Backups** folder to the Trusted Locations list.
10. Save a backup copy of the database, in 2013 format, to the **C:\Backups** folder created in step 1. Name the copy **A44Apply-backup_xx**. A dialog box opens saying the file is being saved in the 2007 format.
11. Click **OK**.
12. Close the database, and exit Access. If instructed, submit this database to your teacher for grading.

Lesson 45

Sharing Data with Word and Other Text Applications

➤ What You Will Learn

Merging an Access Table with a Word Document
Importing Data from a Word Table
Exporting Data to a Text File
Exporting Data to a Word Document
Publishing in PDF or XPS Format

Software Skills Microsoft Word is the most popular component of Office and the program that most people turn to for text-based tasks such as mail merge. Some people even use the tables feature in Word to create simple database lists. In this lesson, you will learn how to exchange data between Word and Access.

What You Can Do

Merging an Access Table with a Word Document

- Access works well as a data source for a Word mail merge. Because of the nature of Access tables, the fields are clearly and consistently defined.
- To use Access as a mail merge data source, set up the main document in Word, and then select the Access file as the data source in Word.
- In order to merge an Access table with a Word document, Word needs to know which of the fields in your recipient list match the fields that are required for the address field component. Use the Match Fields dialog box to distinguish which fields in the recipient list match the required fields.
- Word includes an **address block** code that inserts all the information needed for a mailing address with a single command. You will use this code in the following Try It rather than inserting each field individually.

    ✓ The following Try It starts the mail merge from Word. You can also initiate the merge from within Access with the EXTERNAL DATA > Word Merge command.

WORDS TO KNOW

Address block
A merge code in Word that inserts all the fields needed for a mailing address in a single code.

Delimited text
Text that has been separated into discrete pieces for use in a database. Each row is separated from other rows by a paragraph break. Each column is separated from other columns by a delimiter character.

Delimiter character
A consistently used character in a text file, such as a tab or a comma, that marks a break between fields.

Try It! Performing a Mail Merge in Word with Data from Access

1. Start Word, and open **A45Try.docx** from the data files for this lesson.
2. Save the document as **A45Try_xx** in the location where your teacher instructs you to store the files for this lesson.
3. Click MAILINGS > Select Recipients > Use an Existing List.
4. Navigate to the folder where the data files for this lesson are stored.
5. Click **A45TryA.accdb** and click Open.
6. A list of tables appears. Click Employees and click OK.
7. Delete Insert address here, and leave the insertion point in the box from which it was deleted.
8. Click MAILINGS > Address Block. The Insert Address Block dialog box opens.
9. Click the Match Fields button. The Match Fields dialog box opens.
10. Open the Courtesy Title drop-down list, which currently shows Position as its setting, and click (not matched). Then, click OK. Click Yes to confirm.
11. Click OK to close the Insert Address Block dialog box and insert the address block code.
12. Click MAILINGS > Finish & Merge > Edit Individual Documents. Click OK to accept the default of including all records.

    ✓ A new document is created.

13. Save the new document as **A45TryA_xx** and close it.
14. Save and close **A45Try_xx**.
15. Leave Word open to use in the next Try It.

Set the Courtesy Title field to (not matched)

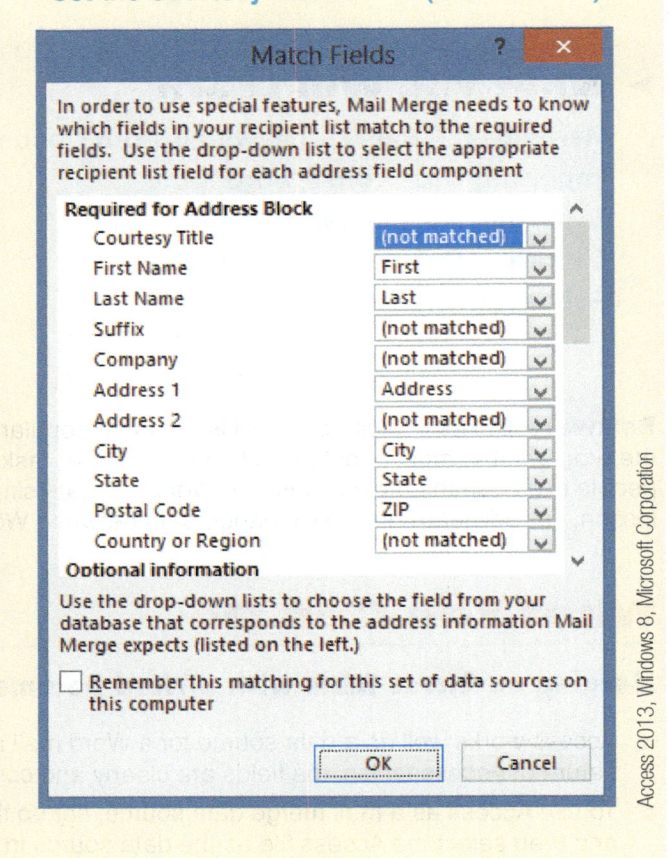

Importing Data from a Word Table

- You cannot directly import from a Word table into Access; Access does not accept Word as a valid file format for importing.
- You must perform an interim step of saving the Word table data to a format that Access accepts (such as plain text), and then import from that file into Access.
- Because plain text files do not support the Word tables feature, you must convert the table to regular **delimited text** before you save it in plain text format. The table columns are changed to tab **delimiter characters**, and the end of each table row is changed to a paragraph break.

Business Information Management II | Access | Chapter 7   729

Try It! Exporting a Word Table to a Delimited Text File

1. In Word, open **A45TryB.docx** from the data files for this lesson.
2. Select the entire table.
3. Click TABLE TOOLS LAYOUT > Convert to Text. Click OK to accept the default delimiter character (Tabs).
4. Click FILE > Save As > Computer > Browse.
5. Open the Save as type drop-down list and click Plain Text.
6. Navigate to the location where your teacher instructs you to store the files for this lesson.
7. In the File name text box, type **A45TryB_xx**.
   - ✓ If you do not add the .txt extension, Word adds it for you when you save.
8. Click Save.
9. Click OK to accept the default export settings.
10. Exit Word.

Try It! Importing a Delimited Text File to Access

1. Start Access, if necessary, and open **A45TryA** from the data files for this lesson.
2. Save the file as **A45TryA_xx** in the location where your teacher instructs you to store the files for this lesson. Click Enable Content if the information bar appears.
3. Click EXTERNAL DATA > Text File. The Get External Data – Text File dialog box opens.
4. Click Browse. Browse to the location where you stored the text file in the previous exercise.
5. Click **A45TryB_xx** and click Open.
6. Click OK. The Import Text Wizard runs.
7. Click Next to accept Delimited as the data type.
8. Click the First Row Contains Field Names check box. Then, click Next.
9. Click Next to accept the default field data types.
10. Click Choose my own primary key. Accept the default of Part # that appears.
11. Click Next.
12. In the Import to Table text box, replace the default name with **Parts**.
13. Click Finish.
14. Click OK to bypass the message that the index or primary key cannot contain a null value. (We'll fix this next.)
15. Click Close to close the Wizard.
16. Double-click the Parts table to open it in Datasheet view.
17. Select the blank record at the bottom of the table and press DEL to remove it. Click Yes to confirm.
18. Right-click the Parts tab and click Close.
19. Leave the database open to use in the next Try It.

Exporting Data to a Text File

- You can export data from any table or query to a delimited text file. This file can then be imported into almost any database program, regardless of its native format.

| Try It! | **Exporting Data to a Text File** |

1. In Access, with the **A45TryA_xx** file open, click the Duties table in the Navigation pane.
2. Click the EXTERNAL DATA tab. In the Export group, click Text File. The Export – Text File dialog box opens.
3. Click Browse and navigate to the location where your teacher instructs you to store the files for this lesson.
4. Change the file name to **A45TryC_xx**.
5. Click Save to accept the location.
6. Click OK. The Export Text Wizard dialog box opens.
7. Click Next to accept Delimited as the export type.
8. Click Tab as the delimiter character to use. Then, click Next.
9. Click Finish. The export completes.
10. Click Close.
11. Close the Duties table, and leave the database open to use in the next Try It.

Exporting Data to a Word Document

- You can export from Access to a Word document in Rich Text Format (RTF). Unlike exporting to plain text, exporting to Word in RTF allows you to keep any formatting that has been applied to the data.

- An RTF file is not really a Word document in that it is not in Word's native format. However, Word easily opens an RTF file—as easily as it does native Word files. Other word processing programs can also open RTF files.

| Try It! | **Exporting Data to a Word Document** |

1. In Access, with the **A45TryA_xx** file open, click the Employees table in the Navigation pane.
2. Click the EXTERNAL DATA tab. In the Export group, click More > Word. The Export – RTF File dialog box opens.
3. Click Browse and navigate to the location where your teacher instructs you to store the files for this lesson.
4. Change the file name to **A45TryD_xx**.
5. Click Save to accept the location.
6. Click OK. The Export RTF File dialog box appears.
   ✓ *There are no options you can set for the export.*
7. Click Close.
8. Leave the database open to use in the next Try It.

Publishing in PDF or XPS Format

- If you want to export data in a format that the recipients cannot easily edit, PDF and XPS are both excellent choices.

- Both are page description languages, which are encoding schemes that result in pages that look the same when viewed and printed on any computer system, regardless of the operating system or hardware.

- PDF is a format created by Adobe. It has been around for many years and is very popular. To read PDF files you need a free program called Adobe Reader or some other application that reads PDF files, such as Adobe Acrobat.

- XPS is the Microsoft equivalent of PDF. XPS files can be read using a built-in reader in Windows 7 and 8, and a free reader is available for download for earlier Windows versions.

Business Information Management II | Access | Chapter 7   731

Try It! Publishing a Table in XPS Format

1. In Access, with the **A45TryA_xx** file open, double-click the Employees table in the Navigation pane. It opens in Datasheet view.
2. Click **FILE > Save As**.
3. Click **Save Object As**.
4. Under Save the current database object, click **PDF or XPS**.
5. Click **Save As**. The Save As dialog box opens.
6. Open the Save as type drop-down list and click **XPS Document**.
7. Navigate to the folder where your teacher has instructed you to store the files for this lesson.
8. In the File name box, type **A45TryE_xx**.
9. Click **Publish**. The XPS file opens in the XPS Viewer, or in Internet Explorer, depending on your system settings.
   ✓ *You may need to execute additional steps to get to the XPS Viewer, depending on your system settings.*
10. Close the XPS Viewer window.
11. Return to Access. Close the database, and exit Access.

Lesson 45—Practice

The owner of Green Designs wants to reward clients with a gift certificate. You can use a table in Access as the data source for a mailing to clients. In this project, you will merge the Access table into a Word document. You will then add merge fields to the document and complete the merge.

DIRECTIONS

1. Start Access, if necessary, and open **A45Practice** from the data files for this lesson.
2. Save the file as **A45Practice_xx** in the location where your teacher instructs you to store the files for this lesson.
   ✓ *If a security warning bar appears, click Enable Content.*
3. Click the Clients table in the Navigation pane, and then click **EXTERNAL DATA > Word Merge**. Click **OK** to accept the default setting in the Mail Merge Wizard (Link your data to an existing Microsoft Word document).
4. Navigate to the folder where the data files are stored for this lesson, select **A45PracticeA.docx**, and click **Open**. Microsoft Word opens the specified document, with your Access database as the merge data source.
5. In Word, click **FILE > Save As** and save the file as **A45Practice_xx** in the folder where your teacher instructs you to store the files for this lesson.
6. Click immediately before the colon (:) in the greeting line to move the insertion point there.
7. On the **MAILINGS** tab, click the down arrow under **Insert Merge Field** and click **Client_First_Name**.
8. Click two lines above the greeting line to move the insertion point there.
9. Click **Address Block**. The Insert Address Block dialog box opens.
10. Click **Match Fields** and match the **Client First Name** and **Client Last Name** fields with the **First Name** and **Last Name** fields, respectively. Then, click **OK** to close the Match Fields dialog box.
11. Click **OK** to close the Insert Address Block dialog box.
12. Click **MAILINGS > Finish & Merge > Edit Individual Documents**.
13. Click **OK** to accept the default of All.
14. Save the new document as **A45PracticeB_xx**.
15. Save and close both documents, and exit Word.
16. In Access, close the database, and exit Access. If instructed, submit this database to your teacher for grading.

Lesson 45—Apply

One of the workers at Green Designs has created a couple of files that he wants to convert. First you will help him save a query as a PDF file and export the Clients table to a text file. Then, you will convert a Word file into a text file and import it into the Access database.

DIRECTIONS

1. Start Access, if necessary, and open **A45Apply** from the data files for this lesson.
2. Save the file as **A45Apply_xx** in the location where your teacher instructs you to store the files for this lesson.
   - ✓ If a security warning bar appears, click Enable Content.
3. Save the **Service Summary** query as a PDF file called **A45ApplyA_xx**.
4. Export the Clients table to a comma-delimited text file called **A45ApplyB_xx.**
5. Open **A45ApplyC** in Word, and convert the table to tab-delimited text.
6. Save the document as a text file called **A45ApplyC_xx.txt**. Then, exit Word.
7. Switch back to Access, and import **A45ApplyC_xx.txt** into a new table called **Products**.
   - ✓ Make sure you mark the First row contains field names check box, so the field names will import properly. Use the Product# field as the primary key.
8. Delete the blank record from the **Products** table.
9. Close the database, and exit Access. If instructed, submit this database to your teacher for grading.

Business Information Management II | Access | Chapter 7   733

Lesson 46

Sharing Data with Excel and Access

➤ What You Will Learn

Inserting an Excel Chart into an Access Report
Exporting Data to Excel
Copying Selected Records to Excel
Importing Data from Another Access Database
Exporting Data to Another Access Database
Saving and Running Export Specifications

Software Skills   Excel and Access are closely related; often data that is created in one application needs to be shared with the other. In this lesson, you will learn how to use Excel charts within Access and how to export Access records to Excel. You'll also learn how to share data with other Access databases and how to save your export specifications for later reuse.

WORDS TO KNOW

Import
To take data from one file and place the information in another file.

What You Can Do

Inserting an Excel Chart into an Access Report

- Because Access's charting features are not as robust as those in Excel, you may sometimes want to create a chart in Excel and then **import** it into Access for use in a report.
- Because the chart has no relationship to any of the data in the Access database, it is not affected by any changes made to any of the tables in Access.
- If you want to edit the chart later, you can double-click it in Report Design view and use the Excel charting tools.

Try It! Importing an Excel Chart into Access

1. Start Access, and open **A46Try** from the data files for this lesson.
2. Save the database as **A46Try_xx** in the location where your teacher instructs you to store the files for this lesson. Click Enable Content if the information bar appears.
3. Click CREATE > Blank Report.
4. Right-click the report's tab, and click Design View.
5. Open **A46TryA.xlsx** in Excel from the data files for this lesson.
6. Click the chart to select it.
7. Press CTRL + C to copy the chart to the Clipboard.
8. Switch to Access, and click the Detail section header on the report.
9. Press CTRL + V to paste the chart into the Detail area of the report.
10. Click REPORT DESIGN TOOLS DESIGN > View to view the report in Report view.
11. Click the Save button on the Quick Access toolbar.
12. In the Save As dialog box, type **Imported Chart** and click OK. Close and save changes to the Excel document.
13. Leave the report open to use in the next Try It.

Place the chart in the Detail area of the report

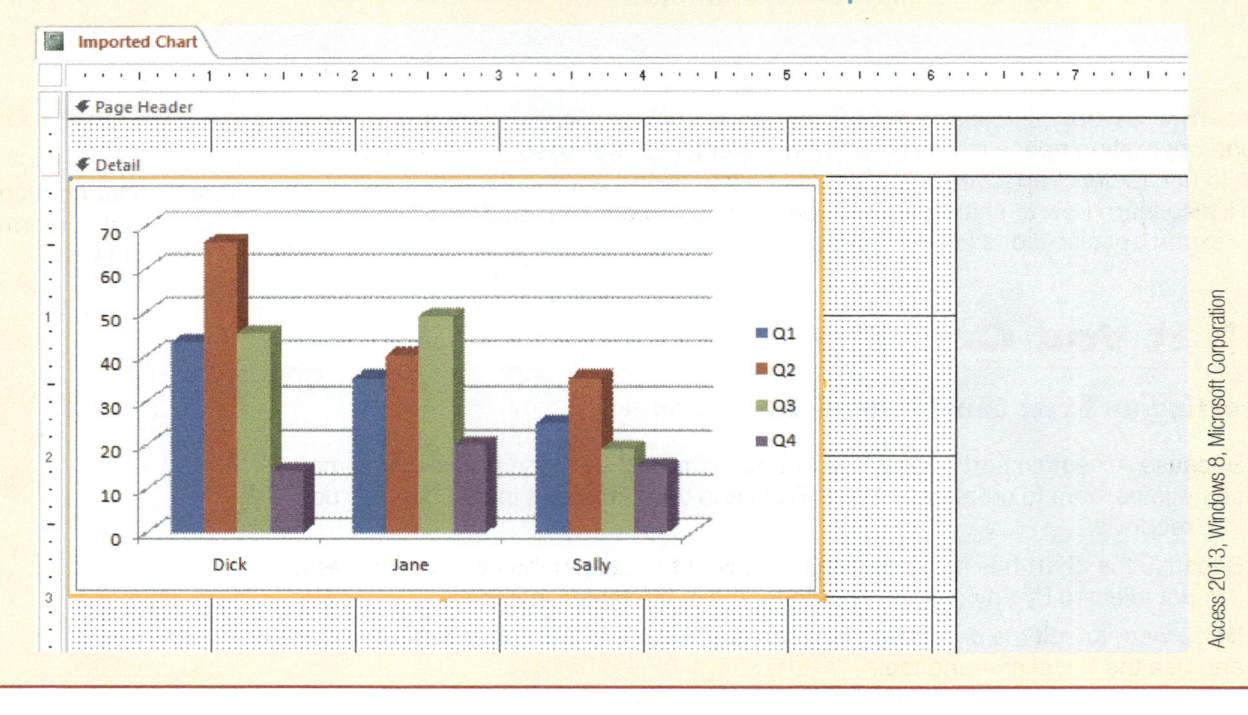

Try It! Editing an Imported Excel Chart

1. In the **A46Try_xx** file, right-click the Imported Chart report's tab, and click Design View .
2. Double-click the chart.
   ✓ Excel tools appear on the Ribbon for working with the chart. Multiple tabs appear below the chart, for access to the data.
3. Click the Sheet1 tab below the chart. The original chart data appears.
4. In cell A4, change the name *Sally* to **Lisa**.
5. Click the Chart1 tab to switch back to the chart.
6. Click the background of the report away from the chart to return to Access Report Design view.
7. Right-click the report tab and click Close. Click Yes when prompted to save changes.
8. Leave the database open to use in the next Try It.

Exporting Data to Excel

- You can move data from Access to Excel. This may be useful when you want to perform more complex calculations on data, for example, because Excel's number-manipulating functions are more robust than those in Access.
- You can export an entire table to Excel, or you can export selected records only.
- You can use the Export feature to export to a new Excel file, or you can simply copy and paste into Excel from Datasheet view in an existing Excel file.
- To export an entire table, use the Export Spreadsheet Wizard. When you use this method, you are prompted to specify a name for a new Excel workbook into which to place the data.

Try It! Exporting an Entire Table to Excel

1. In the **A46Try_xx** file, in the Navigation pane, click Employees.
2. On the EXTERNAL DATA tab, click the Excel button in the Export group.
3. Click the Browse button, and navigate to the location where your teacher has instructed you to store the files for this lesson.
4. In the File name box, type **A46TryA_xx**.
5. Click Save.
6. Click OK.
7. Click Close.
8. Leave the database open to use in the next Try It.

Copying Selected Records to Excel

- When you copy records to Excel, you don't have to go through a Wizard; you can use the Clipboard, which is faster and easier.
- You must already have an Excel workbook open into which you can paste. This can be a blank workbook or one that already contains data.

Try It! Copying Records to Excel

1. Start Excel, and open a new blank workbook.
2. Switch to Access.
3. In the **A46Try_xx** file, in the Navigation pane, double-click Employees. It opens in Datasheet view.
4. Select the three records in the table.
    - ✓ To select a record, click the record selector to the left of the first field. Drag across multiple record selectors to select multiple records.
5. Press CTRL + C to copy the records to the Clipboard.
6. Switch to Excel.
7. Click in cell A1.
8. Press CTRL + V to paste the records.
9. Exit Excel without saving the changes.
10. Close the Employees table.
11. Leave the database open to use in the next Try It.

Select the records to copy

Record Selector

ID	First	Last	Address	City	State	ZIP	Phone
1	Jan	Smith	233 W. 38th Street	Indianapolis	IN	46242	317-555-8822
2	Lashonda	Emerson	5211 E. State Street	Noblesville	IN	46060	317-555-1498
3	Lois	Lowe	720 E. Warren	Macon	IL	62544	217-555-5576

Access 2013, Windows 8, Microsoft Corporation

Importing Data from Another Access Database

- You can copy tables from other Access databases. This can save a lot of development time if you need the same table structures in multiple databases.
- You aren't limited to copying tables; you can copy any object type from any other Access database. However, only tables carry data with them when copied.
- Copying a report, for example, copies only the report definition; if the destination database does not have a table by the same name as the one referenced in the report, the report will not work.

Try It! Importing Data from Another Database

1. In the **A46Try_xx** file, on the EXTERNAL DATA tab, click the Access button in the Import & Link group.
2. Click the Browse button, and navigate to the location of the data files for this lesson.
3. Click **A46TryB** and click Open.
4. Click OK. The Import Objects dialog box opens, listing all the objects in the database by type.
    - ✓ Each type is on a different tab. The Tables tab appears by default.
5. Click tblMembershipType and click OK.
6. Click Close. The table appears in the Navigation pane.
7. Leave the database open to use in the next Try It.

Select the table to be imported

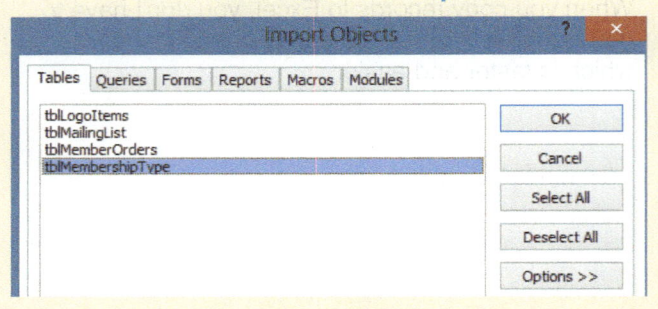

Access 2013, Windows 8, Microsoft Corporation

Exporting Data to Another Access Database

- You can export objects to other Access databases.
- To share objects between databases, you can initiate the process from either side, importing from one or exporting from the other. The result is the same.

Try It! Exporting Data to Another Access Database

1. Open **A46TryB** from the data files for this lesson.
2. Save the database as **A46TryB_xx** in the location where your teacher instructs you to store the files for this lesson.
3. Close **A46TryB_xx**, and reopen **A46Try_xx**.
4. In the Navigation pane, click Parts.
5. Click the EXTERNAL DATA tab.
6. In the Export group, click Access.
7. Click the Browse button, and navigate to the location where you stored the database file in step 2.
8. Click **A46TryB_xx** and click Save.
9. Click OK. The Export dialog box opens.
10. Click OK to accept the defaults.
11. Click Close.
12. Leave the database open to use in the next Try It.

Saving and Running Export Specifications

- If you frequently repeat the same import or export operation on the same data files, you may want to save the specifications so that you can re-run the import or export quickly without having to work through the Wizard each time.
- The following Try Its show how to save an export; saving an import works the same way when performing an import.

Try It! Saving Export Specifications

1. In the **A46Try_xx** file, in the Navigation pane, click the Assignments table.
2. On the EXTERNAL DATA tab, in the Export group, click Excel.
3. Click the Browse button, and navigate to the location where your teacher instructs you to store the files for this lesson.
4. In the File name box, type **A46TryC_xx** and click Save.
5. Click OK.
6. Click the Save export steps check box. Additional options appear in the dialog box.
7. Click Save Export. The export is saved.
8. Leave the database open to use in the next Try It.

(continued)

Lesson 33

Customizing Themes and Effects

➤ What You Will Learn
Applying a Theme to Selected Slides
Customizing Effects

Software Skills To add visual interest to a presentation using themes, you can apply a theme to selected slides. Choose the slides to which you want to apply the theme, or apply a theme to an entire section. Choose a different set of effects to customize the appearance of graphics in a presentation.

What You Can Do

Applying a Theme to Selected Slides

- One way to add visual interest to a presentation is to add a second slide master so that you have a number of different layouts to choose among when formatting slides.
- If you want to apply a different theme to only a few slides, however, you can do so in Normal view using one of these options:
  - Select the slides you want to format with a different theme and then use the Apply to Selected Slides command to apply the new theme only to those slides.
  - Select a section in the presentation and then apply a theme. The theme will automatically apply only to the slides in the section.
- When applying a different theme to selected slides in a presentation, try to make sure that the new theme coordinates with the existing theme, and do not apply more than two or three themes to avoid a loss of consistency among the presentation's slides.

Try It! Applying a Theme to Selected Slides

1. Start PowerPoint, and open **P33Try** from the data files for this lesson.
2. Save the presentation as **P33Try_xx** in the location where your teacher instructs you to store the files for this lesson.
3. Click slide 2.
4. Click DESIGN > Themes More button ⏷ and right-click the Basis theme.
5. Click Apply to Selected Slides.
6. Click the second variant from the right, the variant with the orange border.
7. Click the Who Needs Help section name to select the three slides in this section.
8. Click DESIGN > Themes More button ⏷ and click the Metropolitan theme. The theme is applied only to the slides in the selected section.
9. Save the **P33Try_xx** file, and leave it open to use in the next Try It.

Customizing Effects

- When you customize a theme for a particular presentation, you can change colors, fonts, and background styles, either in Normal view or on the slide master.
- You can also choose a different scheme of effects. Effects control the appearance of objects to which you have applied Quick Styles, such as placeholders, text boxes, or shapes.
- Each theme supplies a set of effects that you can see applied to sample shapes in the Shape Styles gallery.
- To further customize a theme, you can select a different effects scheme by clicking Effects on the Variants drop-down menu. Choosing a different scheme applies that scheme to the current presentation.
- You can also apply a different group of effects in Slide Master view to customize a shape or placeholder on the slide master.

Try It! Customizing Effects

1. In the **P33Try_xx** file, display slide 1.
2. Click DESIGN > Variants More button ⏷ > Effects to display the Effects gallery. The default effects scheme for the current theme is Subtle Solids.
3. Watch the two shapes on the slide as you move the pointer over some of the different effects schemes.
4. Click the Top Shadow effects scheme.
5. Click VIEW > Slide Master and select the slide master at the top of the Thumbnail pane.
6. Click the turquoise rectangle behind the Master title style placeholder to select it.
7. Click DRAWING TOOLS FORMAT > Shape Styles More button ⏷ and then select the Moderate Effect – Turquoise, Accent 1 style.
8. Click SLIDE MASTER > Effects and then click the Inset effect.
9. Click SLIDE MASTER > Close Master View ✖.
10. Display slide 6 to see the change in effects to the placeholder rectangle as well as the shapes on the slide.
    ✓ *Because you applied the Inset effects scheme in Slide Master view, the effects are applied globally throughout the presentation.*
11. Close the **P33Try_xx** file, saving changes, and exit PowerPoint.

(continued)

Try It! Customizing Effects (continued)

Effects gallery

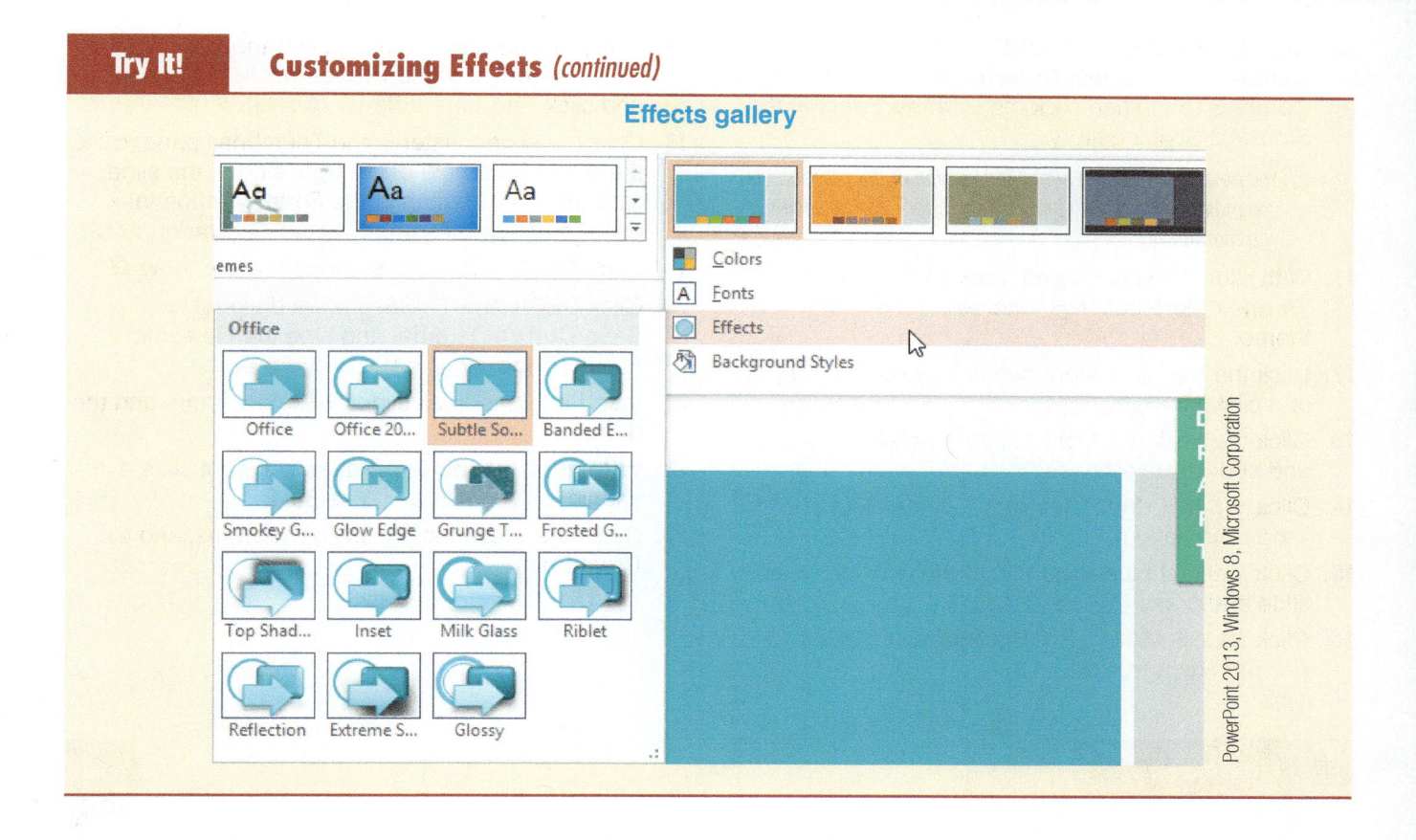

Lesson 33—Practice

Restoration Architecture wants you to customize the appearance of a presentation to give it a bit more visual interest. You begin that task in this project by creating a simplified version of the presentation from a Word outline. You apply and modify a theme by changing colors, background styles, and effects. You then save the theme so that you can apply it to Restoration Architecture's presentation in the next exercise.

DIRECTIONS

1. Start PowerPoint, and click **Open Other Presentations** to display the Open tab in Backstage view.
2. Navigate to the location where the data files for this lesson are stored, and choose to display All Files.
3. Select **P33Practice.docx** and click **Open**.
4. Save the presentation as **P33Practice_xx** in the location where your teacher instructs you to store the files for this lesson.
5. Click **VIEW** > **Outline View** to display the Outline pane.
6. Right-click *Design for Life—Design That Lasts* and click **Demote** to move this slide title back to slide 1 as a subtitle.
7. Click **VIEW** > **Normal** to return to Normal view.
8. Display each slide and click **HOME** > **Reset** to reset the slide formats. Apply the **Title Slide** layout to slide 1 and **Title and Content** to the remaining slides.
9. On slide 4, click the **Insert a SmartArt Graphic** icon in the content placeholder, click **Hierarchy**, and click the **Organization Chart** layout. Click **OK**.

10. Click **SMARTART TOOLS DESIGN** > **Change Colors** and select **Colorful Range – Accent Colors 5 to 6**. Then click the **Intense Effect** in the SmartArt Styles gallery.

    ✓ You have now set up a simplified version of the presentation you intend to modify so that you can check appearance as you format.

11. With slide 4 still displayed, click **DESIGN** > **Themes** More button and select the **View** theme.
12. Click the **Variants** More button, click **Colors**, and click **Median**.
13. Click the **Variants** More button, click **Effects**, and click **Smoky Glass**.
14. Click **VIEW** > **Slide Master**, and select the **Title Slide** layout.
15. Click the light blue rectangle at the left side of the slide and press DEL to remove it.
16. Click **SLIDE MASTER** > **Background Styles** > **Format Background**.
17. In the Format Background task pane, click **Gradient fill**, click the **Preset gradients** button, and click **Radial Gradient – Accent 2**.
18. Click the slide master in the Thumbnail pane, click the brown rectangle at the right side of the slide, click the **Color** button in the Format Shape task pane, and select **Orange, Accent 2, Darker 25%**.
19. Click **SLIDE MASTER** > **Close Master View**.
20. Click **DESIGN** > **Themes** More button > **Save Current Theme**, and type the file name **P33Practice_xx_theme**. Click **Save**.
21. Insert a footer on all slides with your name and the date.
22. **With your teacher's permission**, print slide 4. It should look similar to Figure 33-1.
23. Close the presentation, saving changes, and exit PowerPoint.

Figure 33-1

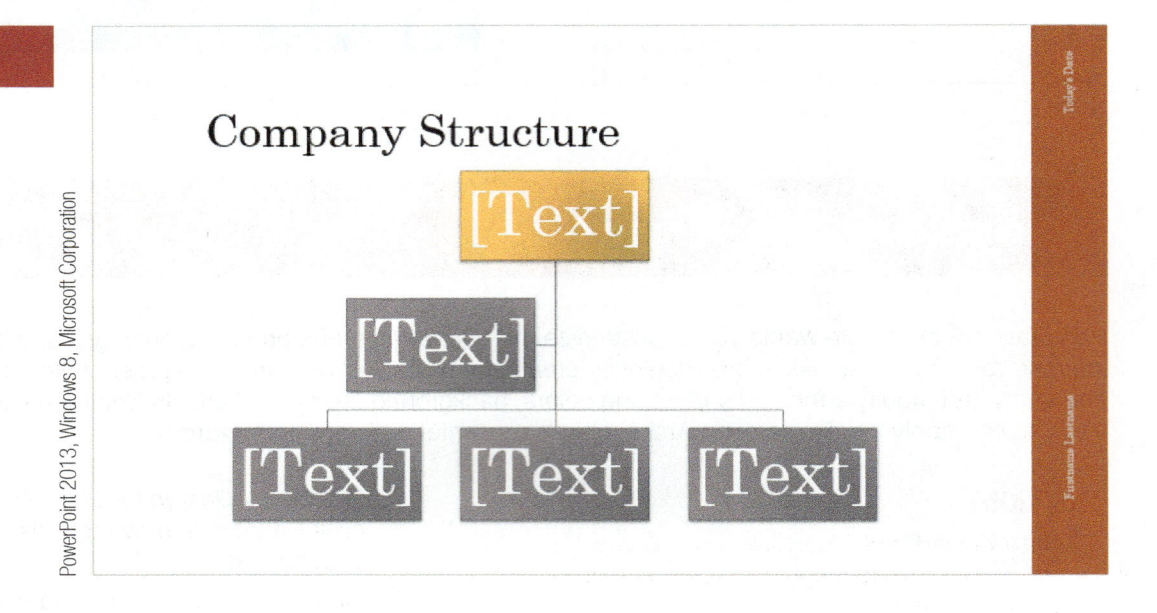

Company Structure

Lesson 33—Apply

In this project, you apply the theme you created in the practice exercise to selected portions of the existing Restoration Architecture presentation.

DIRECTIONS

1. Start PowerPoint, if necessary, and open **P33Apply** from the data files for this lesson.
2. Save the presentation as **P33Apply_xx** in the location where your teacher instructs you to store the files for this lesson.
3. With slide 1 displayed, on the DESIGN tab, right-click the custom theme you created in the practice exercise, **P33Practice_xx_theme**, and apply the theme to the selected slide.
4. Click the Company Graphics section name and apply **P33Practice_xx_theme** to the slides in that section. Note the change in colors and effects for the SmartArt diagrams and the charts.
5. Display slide 4 and click the text box to the right of the picture.
6. Apply the **Smoky Glass** effects scheme so this object will match the effect appearance of the other objects in the presentation.
7. Preview the entire presentation to see the changes you have made.
8. Insert a footer with your name and the date on all slides.
9. **With your teacher's permission,** print slide 5. It should look similar to Figure 33-2.
10. Save changes, close the file, and exit PowerPoint.

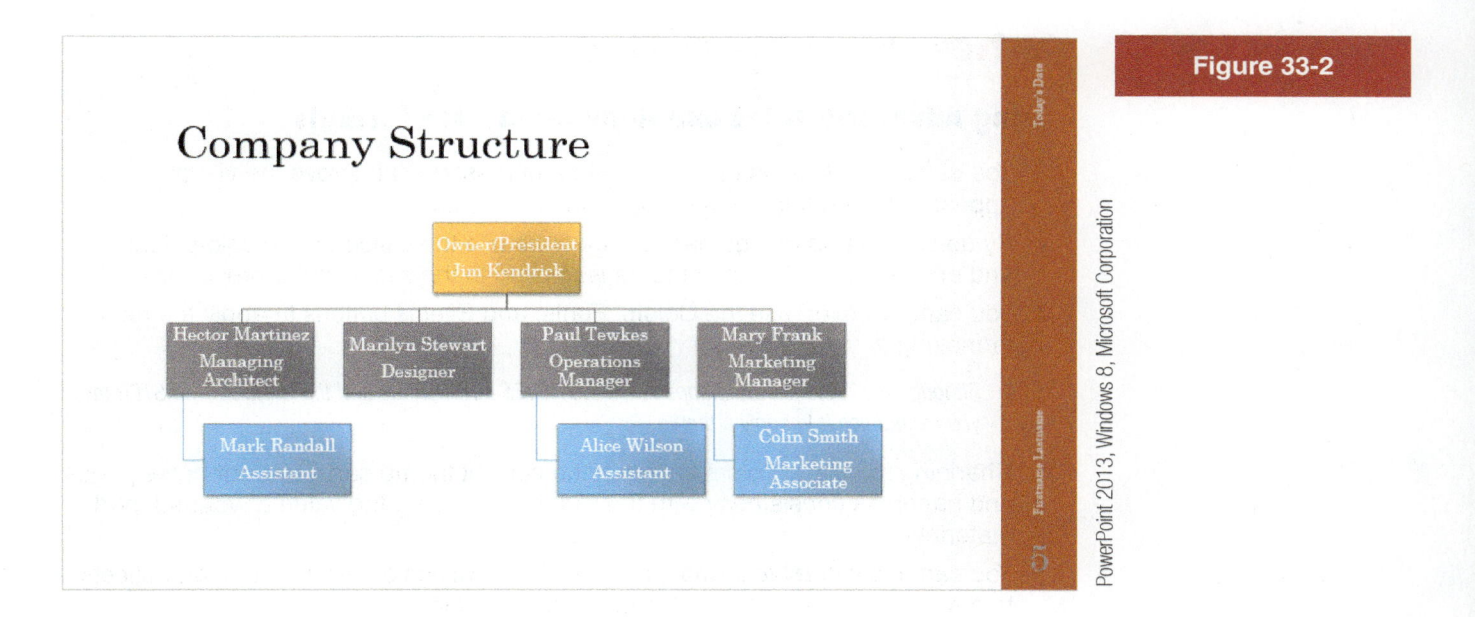

Figure 33-2

Lesson 34

Working with Notes and Handouts

> ### What You Will Learn
>
> Using Advanced Notes and Handout Master Formats
> Working with Linked Notes (OneNote 2013)

Software Skills You can customize your notes and handouts by making changes to the notes and handout masters. You can also use the Linked Notes feature to take notes on a presentation and share your notes with others.

What You Can Do

Using Advanced Notes and Handout Master Formats

- You can customize the notes and handout masters to improve the visual appearance of printed notes pages and handouts.
- By default, the notes and handout masters use the Office theme colors, fonts, and effects, no matter what theme is applied to the slides in the presentation.
- You can, however, use the Colors, Fonts, and Effects buttons to apply theme formatting to your masters.
  - ✓ *Although the Themes button appears on the NOTES MASTER tab and the HANDOUT MASTER tab, you cannot use it to apply a theme.*
- Changing fonts and colors to match the current theme can give your notes pages and handouts consistency with the slides, enhancing the value of your support materials.
- You can apply graphic formats such as Quick Styles or fills, borders, and effects to any placeholder on the notes or handout master.
- Use the Background Styles option in the Background group to apply a background that fills the entire notes page or handout. Background colors are controlled by the theme colors you have applied to the master.
- You can also add content, such as a new text box or a graphic, to the handout master. The content will appear on all pages.

- When adding content such as a text box to the handout master, be sure to position the content so it doesn't interfere with slide image placeholders for other layouts.

- If you insert a text box above the slide image on the one-slide-per-page layout, for example, it will obscure the slide images for other handout layouts.

Try It! Applying Notes Master Formats

1. Start PowerPoint, and open **P34Try** from the data files for this lesson.

2. Save the presentation as **P34Try_xx** in the location where your teacher instructs you to store the files for this lesson.

3. Click slide 10.

4. Click VIEW > Notes Master.

5. Click NOTES MASTER > Fonts and select the Corbel font scheme to match the fonts used on the slides.

6. Click the Notes placeholder, then click DRAWING TOOLS FORMAT > Shape Styles > Colored Outline – Blue, Accent 1.

7. Click NOTES MASTER > Background Styles and select Style 6.

8. Click NOTES MASTER > Close Master View.

9. Click VIEW > Notes Page to display the presentation in Notes Page view. Scroll through the pages to see the formats you added to the master.

10. Click VIEW > Normal to return to Normal view.

11. Save the **P34Try_xx** file, and leave it open to use in the next Try It.

Applying custom formats to the notes master

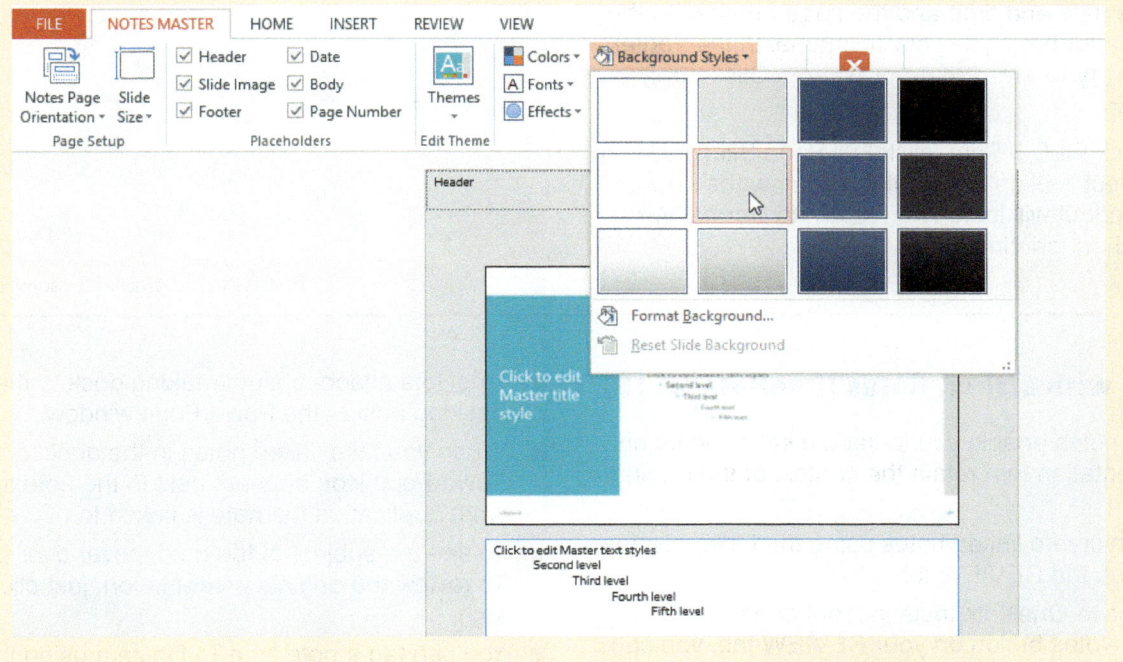

Try It! Applying Handout Master Formats

1. In the **P34Try_xx** file, click VIEW > Handout Master.
2. Click HANDOUT MASTER > Theme Colors.
3. Select the Blue Green theme colors.
4. Click HANDOUT MASTER > Background Styles and select Style 9.
5. Click INSERT > Shapes > Rectangle.
6. Draw a rectangle that covers the top of the page, as shown in the figure.
7. Right-click the shape, click the Outline shortcut button, and click No Outline.
8. Right-click the shape and select Send to Back.
9. Select the Header and Date placeholders, then click HOME > Font Color and select White.
10. Click HANDOUT MASTER > Close Master View.
11. Click INSERT > Header & Footer. On the Notes and Handouts tab, choose to display the date and time and the page number. In the Header box, type your full name. In the Footer box, type **The Power of Giving**. Click Apply to All.
12. Click FILE > Print, click Full Page Slides and select 1 Slide Handout to see how the new handout will look. Then return to Normal view without printing.
13. Save the **P34Try_xx** file, and leave it open to use in the next Try It.

A formatted handout

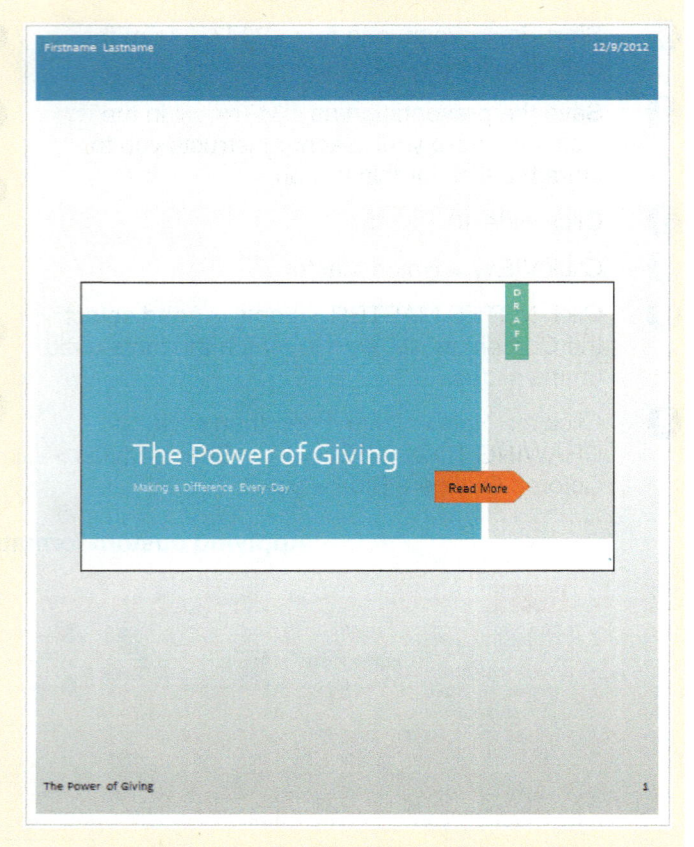

PowerPoint 2013, Windows 8, Microsoft Corporation

Working with Linked Notes (OneNote 2013)

- Linked notes enable you to keep a set of notes on a presentation that retain the context of the original slides.
- You can create linked notes using the Linked Notes button on the REVIEW tab.
- If you have OneNote installed, but don't see the Linked Notes button on your REVIEW tab, you can add it using the PowerPoint Options dialog box.
    - ✓ You will need to start OneNote to set up the application before you can begin working with it. You may also need to dock a OneNote window to your desktop before the Linked Notes button can be added to the REVIEW tab.
- OneNote attaches a note-taking dock to the desktop beside the PowerPoint window.
- When you take linked notes in the dock, a PowerPoint icon appears next to the note to show what application the note is linked to.
- To see the subject of the note, hover over the icon. To review the original presentation, just click the icon.
- You can tag a note as a To Do item using the keyboard shortcut CTRL + 1.
- When you use shared OneNote notebooks to store your Linked Notes, team members can see and respond to each other's notes.

Business Information Management II | PowerPoint | Chapter 5

Try It! Adding the Linked Notes Button to the Ribbon

1. In the **P34Try_xx** file, click FILE > Options > Customize Ribbon.
   - ✓ Remember that OneNote 2013 must be installed on your computer in order to use this feature.
2. On the Customize Ribbon page, select Main Tabs in the Choose commands from drop-down menu.
3. Click the button next to Review in the Main Tabs list on the left to expand the Review tab options and select OneNote.
   - ✓ If you do not see the OneNote option on the Review tab, start OneNote, choose Dock to Desktop on the VIEW tab, close OneNote, and close PowerPoint. After you restart PowerPoint, you should then see the OneNote option on the Review tab.
4. Select the Review tab in the Main Tabs list on the right as the location for the button.
5. Click the Add button and click OK.
6. Save the **P34Try_xx** file, and leave it open to use in the next Try It.

Try It! Working with Linked Notes (OneNote 2013)

1. In the **P34Try_xx** file, select slide 8.
2. Click REVIEW > Linked Notes.
3. Select any section or page, such as Quick Notes under your notebook, in the All Notebooks area and click OK.
   - ✓ Click the three dots at the top of the docked OneNote pane, if necessary, to display the Ribbon, and click New Page on the PAGES tab.
4. In the header area above the date, type your name and press ENTER.
5. In the note area, type **Find out when the MS Walk and AIDS Awareness Week will take place.**
   - ✓ If you receive a message about the linked note, click OK.
6. Display slide 10.
7. In the docked OneNote panel, click on the note box to select it. Hover your mouse over the PowerPoint icon next to the note box to see the original slide.
8. Close the OneNote dock. Close the **P34Try_xx** file, saving changes, and exit PowerPoint.

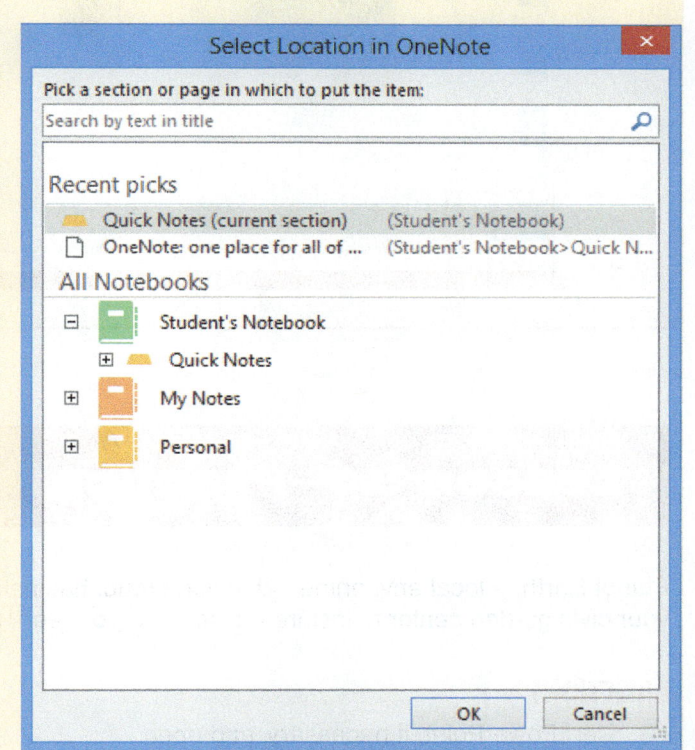

Select Location in OneNote dialog box

PowerPoint 2013, Windows 8, Microsoft Corporation

(continued)

> **Try It!** **Working with Linked Notes (OneNote 2013)** *(continued)*

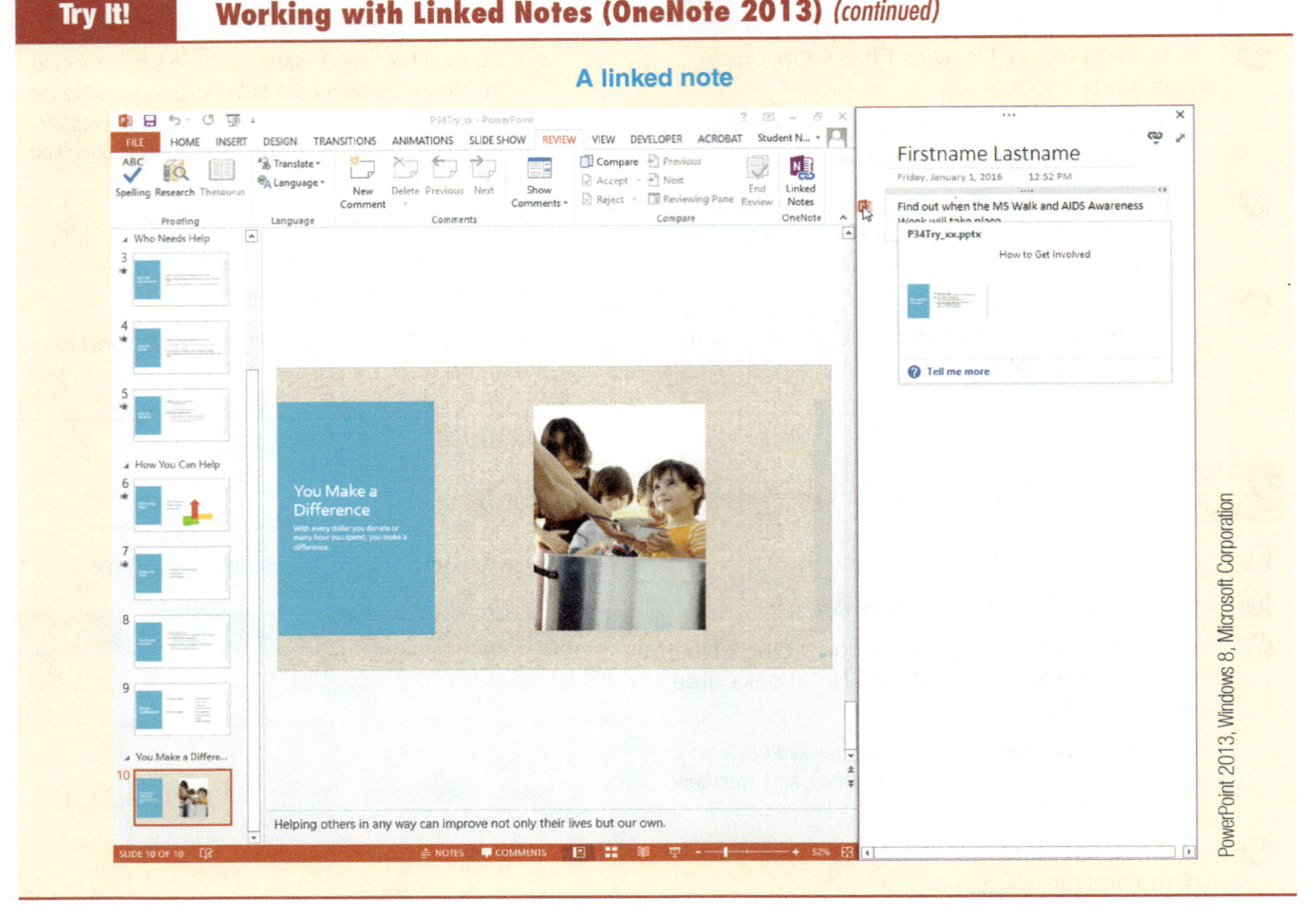

A linked note

Lesson 34—Practice

Planet Earth, a local environmental action group, has asked you to prepare a presentation that can be shown at your civic garden center to inspire residents to go green. In this project, you customize the notes master.

DIRECTIONS

1. Start PowerPoint, if necessary, and open **P34Practice** from the data files for this lesson.
2. Save the presentation as **P34Practice_xx** in the location where your teacher instructs you to store the files for this lesson.
3. Click **VIEW** > **Notes Master**.
4. Click **NOTES MASTER** > **Colors** and select **Green**.
5. Click **NOTES MASTER** > **Background Styles** > **Format Background** to open the Format Background task pane.
6. In the Format Background task pane, click **Gradient fill**.
7. Click the **Preset gradients** button and click **Top Spotlight – Accent 2**. Close the Format Background task pane.

8. Click **NOTES MASTER** > **Close Master View** ⊠.
9. Click **INSERT** > **Header & Footer** and insert a header on the Notes and Handouts tab that includes your full name and today's date.
10. Click **VIEW** > **Notes Page** to see the formats you added to the notes master. Your notes page should look similar to Figure 34-1.
11. Close the presentation, saving changes, and exit PowerPoint.

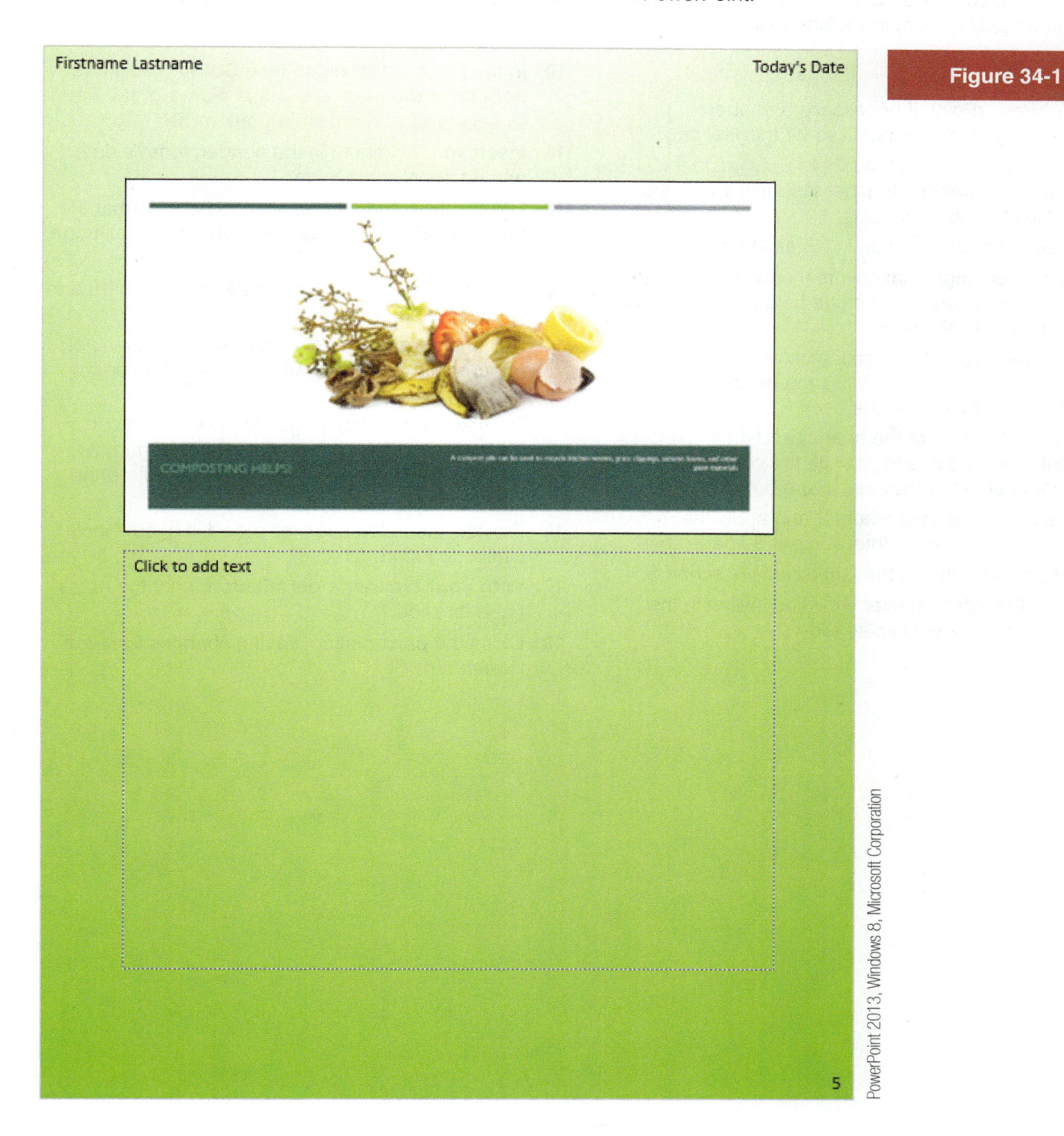

Figure 34-1

Lesson 34—Apply

In this project, you continue to work on the Planet Earth presentation. You complete the formatting of the notes pages and apply custom formatting to the handout master.

DIRECTIONS

1. Start PowerPoint, if necessary, and open **P34Apply** from the data files for this lesson.
2. Save the presentation as **P34Apply_xx** in the location where your teacher instructs you to store the files for this lesson.
3. Display the presentation in Notes Master view.
4. Draw a rectangle that covers the top of the page; make the rectangle the same height as the header and date placeholders.
5. Use the Shape Styles gallery to apply **Intense Effect – Green, Accent 1** to the rectangle, and send the rectangle to the back.
6. Change the size of the header and date text to 14 point, apply bold, and change the color if desired to contrast better with the shape behind the text.
7. Select the notes placeholder and apply the **Colored Outline – Lime, Accent 3** shape style.
8. Change the fonts to the **Gill Sans MT** scheme.
9. Close the Notes Master view and switch to the Notes Page view. Display slide 1.
10. In the notes placeholder, type **Going green can help save the planet, but it is also a great way to save you real green in your wallet!**
11. Insert your full name in the header, today's date, and an appropriate footer.
12. Display the handout master, choose to format the background, and choose to insert an online image as the page background.
13. Search for an image using the keyword **Earth**, and select an appropriate image.
14. Adjust the transparency to make the picture light enough that the slides will be easy to see on the handout.
15. Preview the handout pages to make sure your inserted picture is formatted correctly. Figure 34-2 on the next page shows one way that your page might look.
16. Preview the notes page for slide 1. It should look similar to Figure 34-3.
17. **With your teacher's permission**, print the notes page for slide 1.
18. Close the presentation, saving changes, and exit PowerPoint.

Figure 34-2

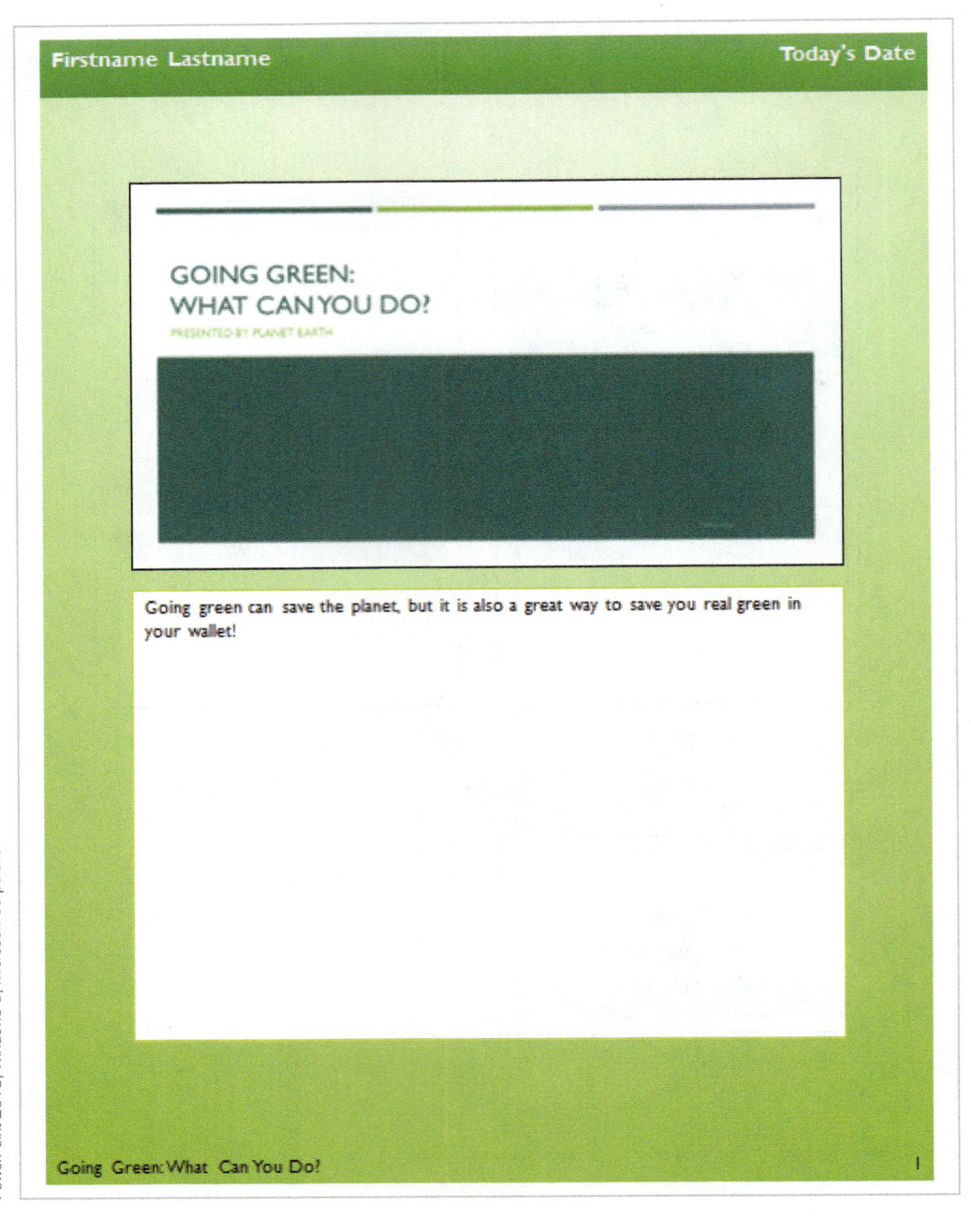

Figure 34-3

Firstname Lastname — Today's Date

GOING GREEN:
WHAT CAN YOU DO?
PRESENTED BY PLANET EARTH

Going green can save the planet, but it is also a great way to save you real green in your wallet!

Going Green: What Can You Do? 1

PowerPoint 2013, Windows 8, Microsoft Corporation

Lesson 35

Integrating PowerPoint with Word

➤ What You Will Learn

Exporting Handouts to Word
Linking Presentations to Word
Communicating with Others

Software Skills   Send presentation materials to Microsoft Word to take advantage of Word's formatting options. You can also choose to link the presentation materials to a Word document. Handouts linked to a presentation will change automatically when the presentation is updated.

What You Can Do

Exporting Handouts to Word

- When you are preparing a presentation, one aspect you should consider carefully is identifying and creating supporting materials that will enhance the presentation for your audience.
- Having handouts that include thumbnails of each slide will help your audience stay focused on and engaged with your presentation.
- Besides simply printing handouts from PowerPoint, you can send presentation data to Microsoft Word to create handouts or an outline. Exporting a presentation to Microsoft Word gives you the option of using Word's tools to format the handouts.
- You can modify the size of the slide images, format text, and add new text as desired to customize your handouts.
- Use the Create Handouts command on the Export tab in Backstage view to begin the process of sending materials to Word.
- The Send to Microsoft Word dialog box opens to allow you to select an export option.
- You have two options for positioning slide notes relative to the slide pictures and two options for placing blank lines that your audience can use to take their own notes.

WORDS TO KNOW

Active listening
Paying attention to a message, hearing it, and interpreting it correctly.

Communication
The exchange of information between a sender and a receiver.

Nonverbal communication
The exchange of information without using words.

Verbal communication
The exchange of information by speaking or writing.

- Slide thumbnails in the Word document usually display a border on three sides. You can delete this partial border, if desired, using the Borders tab in the Borders dialog box.

- You can also choose to send only the outline. The exported outline retains the font used in the presentation and displays at a large point size. You can then, if desired, apply Word heading styles to create a more useful document.

Try It! Exporting Handouts to Word

1. Start PowerPoint, and open **P35Try** from the data files for this lesson.
2. Save the presentation as **P35TryA_xx** in the location where your teacher instructs you to store the files for this lesson.
3. Click FILE > Export.
4. Click Create Handouts in the Export list, and click Create Handouts in the right pane.
5. Select Blank lines next to slides and Paste under Add slides to Microsoft Word document.
6. Click OK.
7. Click the Word icon on the taskbar to display the newly created Word document to see how the handouts look. Close Microsoft Word without saving changes.
8. Save the **P35TryA_xx** file, and leave it open to use in the next Try It.

The Send to Microsoft Word dialog box

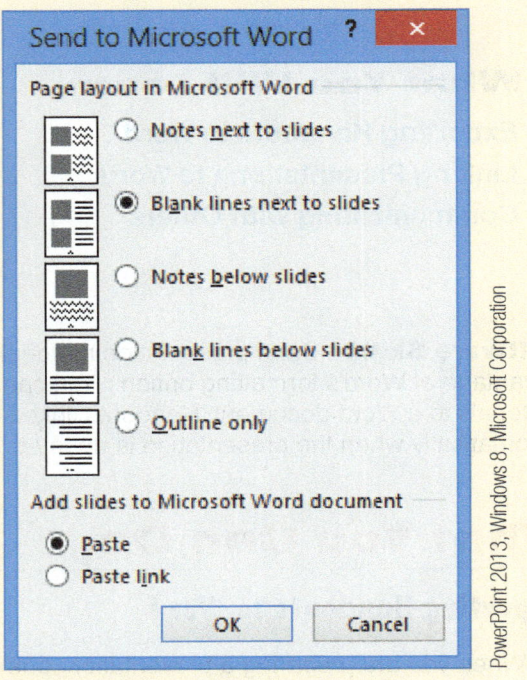

Linking Presentations to Word

- If the presentation might change over time, the best option is to maintain a link between the handouts in Word and the material displayed on a slide.

- When you choose the Paste link option in the Send to Microsoft Word dialog box, you create a link between the Word document and the PowerPoint presentation. Any changes you save to the slides in PowerPoint will appear in the Word document.

    ✓ You do not have the paste/paste link options when exporting an outline.

Business Information Management II | PowerPoint | Chapter 5

Try It! Linking Presentations to Word

1. In the **P35TryA_xx** file, click FILE > Export.
2. Click Create Handouts under Export, and click Create Handouts in the right pane.
3. Select Notes next to slides, if necessary, and Paste link under Add slides to Microsoft Word document.
4. Click OK.
5. View the newly created Microsoft Word document to see how the handouts look.
6. Return to **P35TryA_xx**, click DESIGN, and change the variant to the second variant from the right.
7. Save the changes, close **P35TryA_xx**, and exit PowerPoint.
8. Return to the Microsoft Word document and note that the slide thumbnails show the new variant you applied in PowerPoint.
9. Save the file as **P35TryB_xx** in the location where your teacher instructs you to store the files for this lesson.
10. Close the document, and exit Microsoft Word.

Updated linked handouts

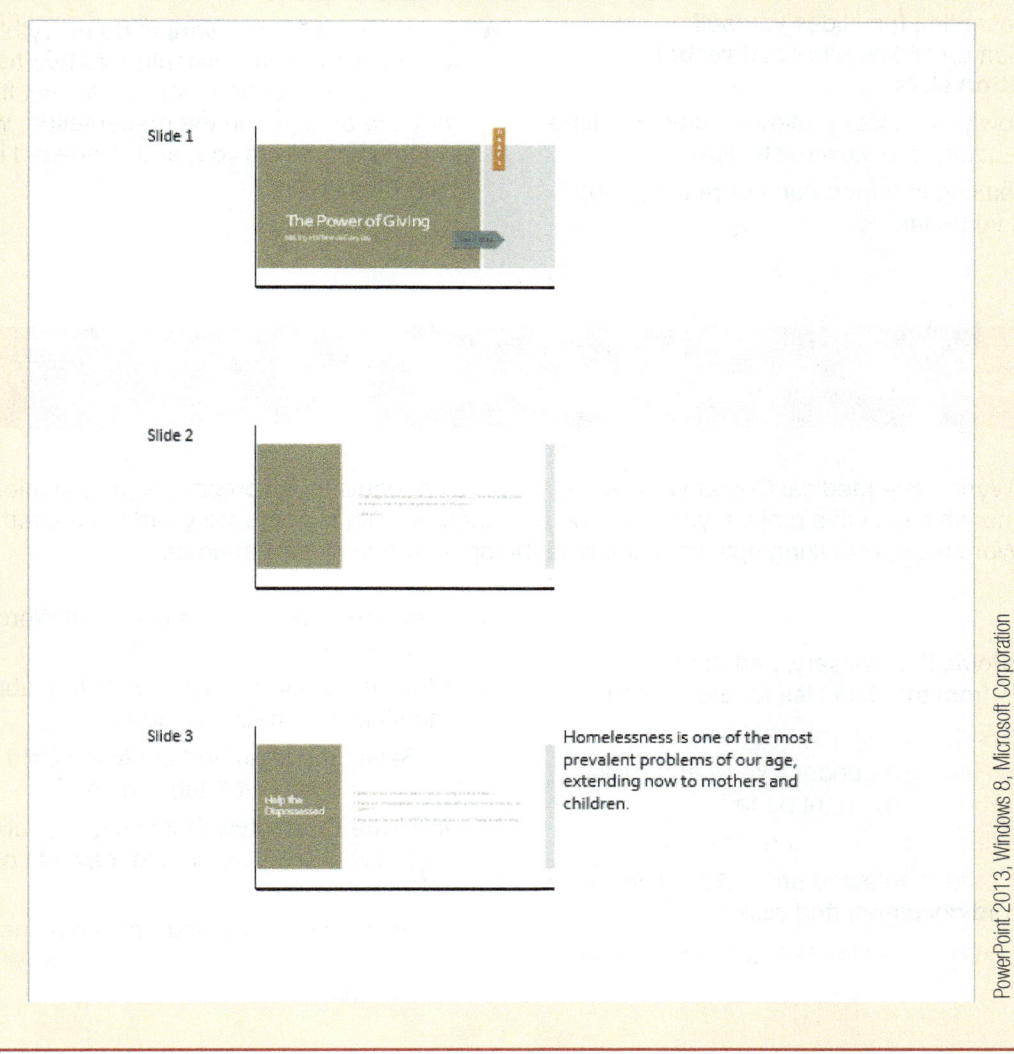

PowerPoint 2013, Windows 8, Microsoft Corporation

Communicating with Others

- When you prepare a presentation, you should always remember that the presentation is a form of **communication** and you should strive to make it as effective as possible.
- You communicate effectively when your audience interprets the information in the presentation in the way you intended it to be interpreted.
- As you prepare the presentation and its supporting materials, choose options that contribute to effective communication:
  - Make sure the slides are visually interesting.
  - Make sure text is easy to read and understand.
  - Use charts and tables to organize information for improved comprehension.
- A presentation's effectiveness also depends on how it is delivered.
- If you are presenting the slides yourself or using narration on slides, use good **verbal communication** skills:
  - Speak slowly and clearly, allowing plenty of time for your audience to view each slide.
  - Avoid speaking in a monotone or reading the slide text verbatim.
- Ask the audience if they have questions or encourage them to participate in the discussion, if appropriate, to foster communication between audience members and the speaker.
- Remember that you also deliver a message using **nonverbal communication** cues. Being at ease on the podium, smiling, and making eye contact with your audience are nonverbal ways to foster effective communication with others.
- You can ensure effective communication with your audience even if you are setting up a presentation to be browsed by an individual. Make sure the slides are displayed long enough that the content can be viewed and absorbed by people with all levels of reading skills.
- If the presentation does not loop automatically, make sure a viewer can easily navigate the presentation by including action buttons, links, and other prompts.
- As a presenter, you want to do everything you can to encourage active listening. **Active listening** is a sign of respect from your audience. It shows that they are engaged in the presentation, willing to communicate with you, and interested in you and your message.

Lesson 35—Practice

Surgeons from Wynnedale Medical Center want you to prepare handouts to accompany a presentation they will be making at a health fair. In this project, you send the presentation data to Microsoft Word to create handouts. You use some Word table formatting options to improve the appearance of the handouts.

DIRECTIONS

1. Start PowerPoint, if necessary, and open **P35Practice** from the data files for this lesson.
2. Click **FILE > Export**.
3. Click **Create Handouts** under Export and click **Create Handouts** in the right pane.
4. Select **Notes next to slides**, if necessary.
5. Make sure **Paste** is selected under Add slides to Microsoft Word document and click **OK**.
6. Close **P35Practice** without saving any changes.
7. View the newly created Microsoft Word document, and save it as **P35Practice_xx**.
8. Make the following changes to the table in which the slide information is stored:
    a. Select the table and apply the **Grid Table 1 Light – Accent 1** table style.
    b. In the Table Style Options group, click **First Column** to apply bold to the first column of the table.
    c. Select the center and right columns and click **TABLE TOOLS LAYOUT > Align Center Left**.

9. Insert a header with your name and today's date.
10. **With your teacher's permission,** print the document. It should look similar to Figure 35-1.
11. Close the document, saving changes, and exit Word.

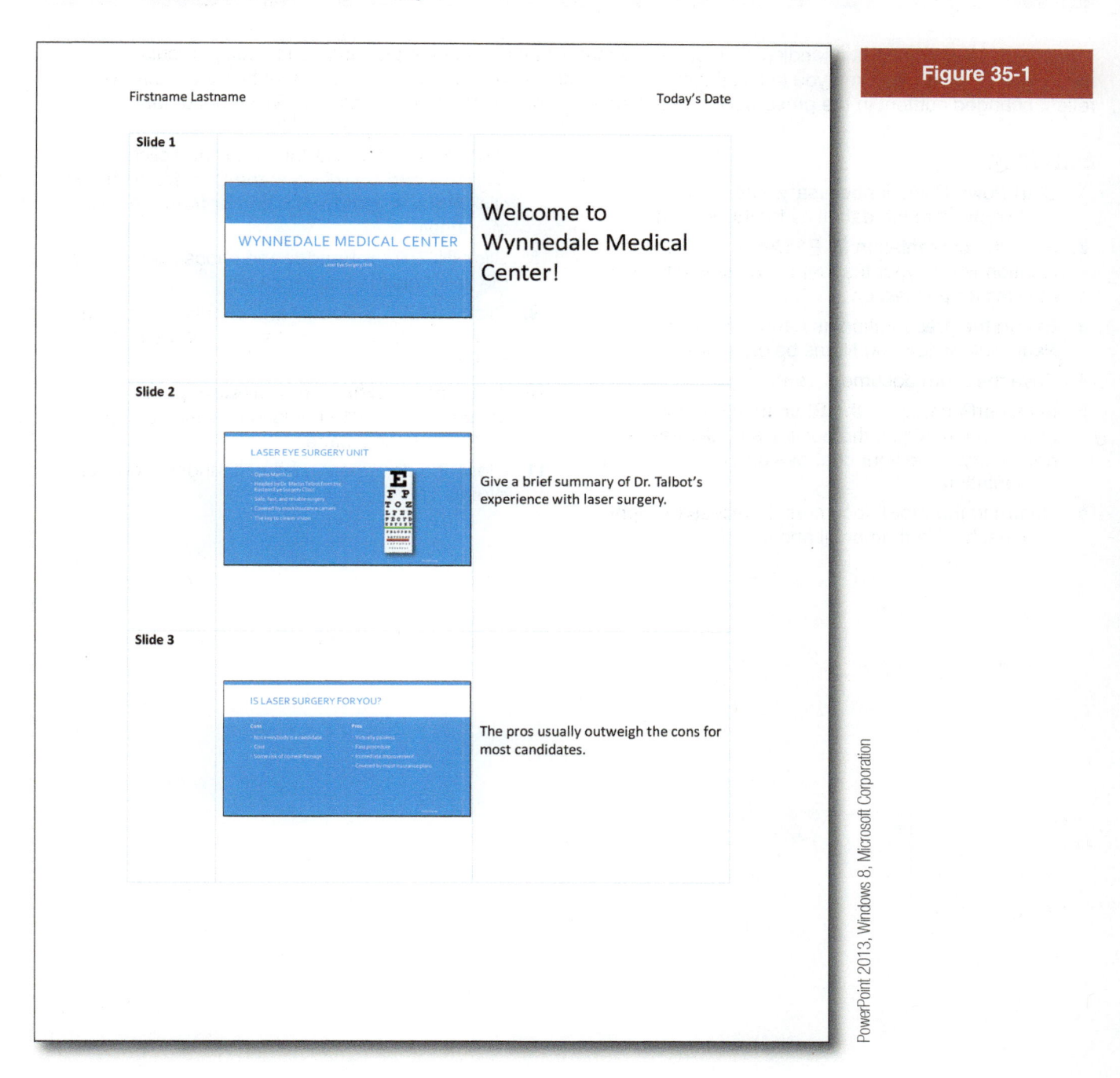

Figure 35-1

Lesson 35—Apply

The surgeons at Wynnedale Medical Center plan to make changes to their presentation to suit particular audiences. They have asked you to link the slides to handouts so that they can easily print handouts that will reflect changed content in the presentation. In this project, you link the presentation to a Word document.

DIRECTIONS

1. Start PowerPoint, if necessary, and open **P35Apply** from the data files for this lesson.
2. Save the presentation as **P35ApplyA_xx** in the location where your teacher instructs you to store the files for this lesson.
3. Export the presentation as handouts. Select the Paste link option and Notes below slides.
4. Save the Word document as **P35ApplyB_xx**.
5. In PowerPoint, apply the **Slice** theme to the presentation. Adjust the positions of pictures as necessary. Save your changes and close the presentation.
6. Return to the Word document. If necessary, right-click each slide thumbnail and click **Update Link**.
7. Right-click each slide thumbnail and click **Borders and Shading**. In the Borders dialog box, click **None** to remove the border from the slide thumbnail.
8. Click **INSERT** > **Header** and choose **Slice 2** from the list of built-in header styles.
9. Click **INSERT** > **Footer** and choose **Slice**. Your name should be inserted automatically in the footer.
10. **With your teacher's permission,** print the document. Page 1 should look similar to Figure 35-2 on the next page.
11. Close the document, saving changes, and exit Word.

Lesson 40

Applying Advanced Animations

➤ What You Will Learn

Applying More Than One Animation to an Object
Adjusting a Motion Path Animation
Applying Advanced Effect Options
Controlling an Animation with a Trigger
Working with the Animation Timeline

Software Skills Using custom animation options, you can fine-tune the way objects enter, exit, and move on slides. Use advanced features to trigger animations, and use the timeline to control when animations start and how long they last.

What You Can Do

Applying More Than One Animation to an Object

- You can apply more than one animation effect to any object on a slide.
- For example, apply an entrance effect to display an object and then an exit effect to remove the object from the slide.
- Use the Add Animation button on the ANIMATIONS tab to add another animation to an object.

WORDS TO KNOW

Trigger
An object you click to start the animation of another object.

Try It! Applying More Than One Animation to an Object

1. Start PowerPoint, and open **P40Try** from the data files for this lesson.

2. Save the presentation as **P40Try_xx** in the location where your teacher instructs you to store the files for this lesson.

3. Display slide 7 and click the Profit text box to select it.

4. Select Fly In from the Entrance gallery.

5. With the Profit text box still selected, click ANIMATIONS > Add Animation ⭐ to display a gallery of animation effects.

6. In the Emphasis section of the gallery, click Pulse.

7. Click ANIMATIONS > Preview ⭐ to view the added animation on the Profit text box.

8. Display slide 8 and click the pointing arrow shape to select it.

9. Click ANIMATIONS > Add Animation ⭐ and select Wipe.

10. Click ANIMATIONS > Effect Options ↑ > From Right.

11. Click ANIMATIONS > Add Animation ⭐ and select Shrink & Turn from the Exit gallery.

12. Click ANIMATIONS > Preview ⭐ to view the animations on the arrow.

13. Save the **P40Try_xx** file, and leave it open to use in the next Try It.

Choose an Exit effect for an object

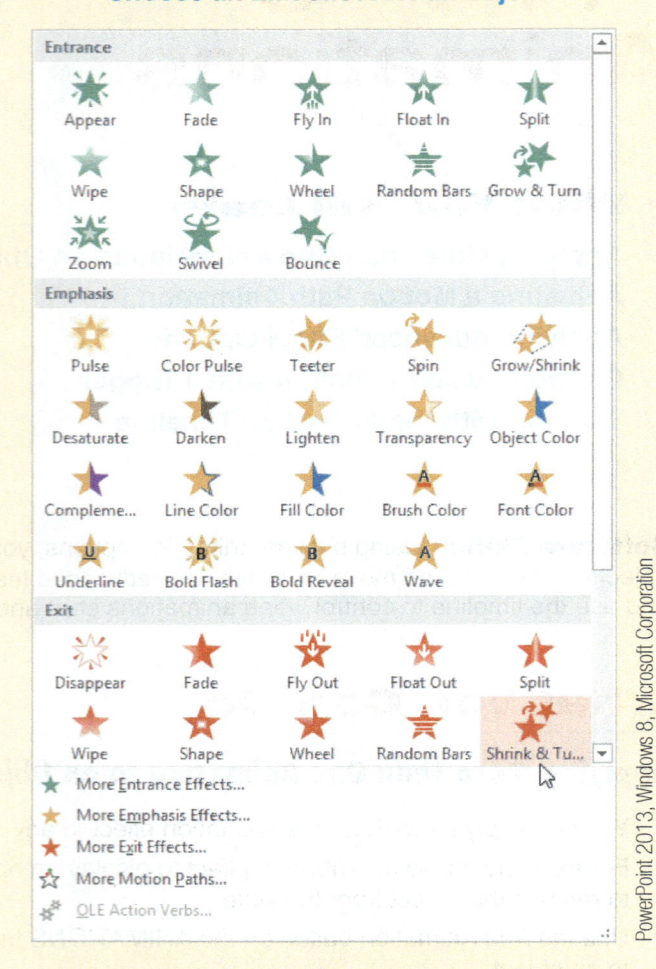

Adjusting a Motion Path Animation

- PowerPoint offers many options for setting objects in motion on your slides. You can choose among lines, turns, arcs, and special shapes.
- If you cannot find a default motion path that suits your needs, you can adjust any motion path to specify exactly where you want an object to be at the beginning and the end of the animation.
- A green handle or pointer marks the beginning of a motion path, and a red handle or pointer marks the end of the path. You can drag these handles as desired to reposition the path.
- You will see a shaded version of the object at the end of the motion path to help you position it correctly at the end of the path.
- You may also want to edit curve points along the path or use the Effect Options gallery to change the direction of the motion.

Try It!   Adjusting a Motion Path Animation

1. In the **P40Try_xx** file, display slide 1 and click the Planet Earth object in the upper-right corner. (Click the outside border to select the entire group.)
2. Click ANIMATIONS > Add Animation ⭐ and scroll down to display the Motion Paths effects.
3. Click Lines to apply a straight-line motion path to the object.
4. Click the red handle in the center of the shaded object as shown in the illustration and drag to the lower-left of the slide to position the end of the path below the words *Planet Earth*.
5. Release the mouse button when you are satisfied with the position of the object.
6. Click the Start down arrow and select After Previous. Set the Duration to 3:00.
7. Click ANIMATIONS > Preview ⭐ to view the adjusted motion path.
8. Save the **P40Try_xx** file, and leave it open to use in the next Try It.

Drag the handle at the end of the path to adjust the path

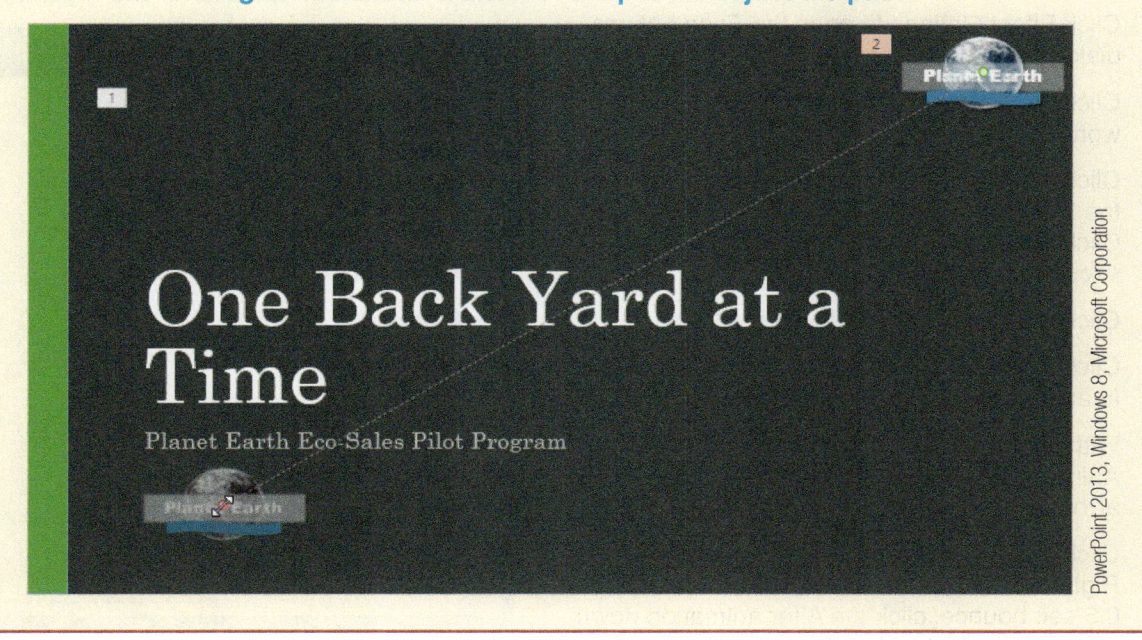

Applying Advanced Effect Options

- When you select an animation in the Animation Pane, a down arrow appears containing a number of options that you can use to modify an effect.
- Selecting Effect Options from the content list opens a dialog box for the currently selected effect. The Effect tab offers a number of special effects that you can apply to an object, depending on the type of object being animated.
- You can adjust the direction of the animation and choose Smooth start and Smooth end to control how the object starts and stops during the animation.
- All animation types enable you to select a sound effect from the Sound list to accompany the effect.
  - ✓ Use sound effects sparingly; it can be distracting to hear the same sound effect over and over when multiple parts of an object are animated.
- The After animation menu gives you a number of options for emphasizing or deemphasizing an object after the animation ends. You can hide the object after the animation, hide it the next time you click the mouse, or change its color.
- If the animated object contains text, the Animate text settings become active, enabling you to animate the text all at once, by word, or by letter, and set the delay between words or letters.

Try It! Applying Advanced Effect Options

1. In the **P40Try_xx** file, display slide 9.
2. Click ANIMATIONS > Animation Pane to display the Animation Pane.
3. Select the Title 1 animation and then click Fade in the Animation gallery to change the animation effect from Split to Fade.
4. Select the Title 1 animation again in the Animation Pane, if necessary, and click the down arrow to the right of the animation title.
5. Click Effect Options to open the Fade options dialog box.
6. Click the Animate text down arrow and click By word.
7. Click the Timing tab in the Fade dialog box, click the Start down arrow and select With Previous. Click the Duration down arrow and select 5 seconds (Very Slow).
8. Click OK to apply the animation effects.
9. Click the subtitle on the slide, and apply the Fly In animation.
10. With the subtitle animation selected in the Animation Pane, click the animation's down arrow and click Effect Options.
11. Click the Direction down arrow and select From Right; click the Bounce end up arrow to apply a 0.5 sec bounce; click the After animation down arrow and select Hide After Animation.
12. Click the Timing tab, set the Start to After Previous and the Duration to 5 seconds (Very Slow).
13. Click OK to apply the animation effects.
14. Preview the effects on the slide.
15. Save the **P40Try_xx** file, and leave it open to use in the next Try It.

Advanced effect options for the Fly In animation

PowerPoint 2013, Windows 8, Microsoft Corporation

Controlling an Animation with a Trigger

- You can specify that an animation will begin when you click an object called a **trigger**.
- Using triggers is one way to make a slide show interactive. A presenter can click one object during the presentation to start the animation of another object.
- Use the Trigger button in the Advanced Animation group to set the trigger that will start an animation sequence. You can also set a trigger from within an effect's options dialog box.

Try It! Controlling an Animation with a Trigger

1. In the **P40Try_xx** file, display slide 7.
2. Select the chart and the three text boxes at the bottom of slide 7.
   ✓ Hint: Press CTRL to enable you to select multiple objects.
3. Click ANIMATIONS > Float In.
4. Click ANIMATIONS > Trigger ⚡ > On Click of > TextBox 7.
5. Click Slide Show on the status bar to display the current slide in Slide Show view. The first two text boxes animate automatically. Click the slide to display the Profit box. Click to display the Pulse animation effect.
6. Point to the Profit box, which is the trigger for the next animation. Click the Profit box to display the chart and the remaining text boxes.
7. Click ESC to end the slide show.
8. Save the **P40Try_xx** file, and leave it open to use in the next Try It.

Working with the Animation Timeline

- The easiest way to fine-tune animation timing is to use the timeline feature in the Animation Pane.
- The bar next to an effect in the Animation Pane indicates the duration of the effect and when it starts relative to other effects.
- The timeline includes a seconds gauge at the bottom of the Animation Pane. You can use this gauge to see the duration of each effect as well as the overall duration of all animations on the slide.
- You can use the timeline to set a delay or adjust the length of an effect.
- You can double-click a timeline bar to open the Timing dialog box for further adjustments.
- Before you use the timeline to adjust animations, you may need to change the order in which the animations play. You can drag animations in the Animation Pane to change their order or use the Reorder Animation buttons Move Earlier and Move Later to change animation order.

Try It! Working with the Animation Timeline

1. In the **P40Try_xx** file, display slide 6.
2. Click ANIMATIONS > Preview to see how the objects are currently animated.
3. In the Animation Pane, click the Title 2 animation, which has a green star indicating an entrance effect.
4. In the Timing group, click the Move Earlier button ▲ to move the animation to the top of the Animation Pane.
5. Click the Group 12 animation, which has a red star indicating an exit effect, and then click the Move Later button ▼ twice to move the animation to the bottom of the list.
6. Click the Seconds down arrow at the bottom of the Animation Pane and select Zoom Out.
7. Click the Picture 11 animation in the Animation Pane, and position the pointer on the right edge of the green timeline box until the pointer changes to a double-headed arrow pointer. A ScreenTip indicates the start time and end time.
8. Drag the right edge of the timeline box to the right until the ScreenTip indicates 2.5s.

   ✓ To make it easier to adjust the timeline, you can increase the width of the Animation Pane by dragging its left border to the left.

9. Click the expand contents arrow ⋁ below the Content Placeholder effect in the Animation Pane to see both list items.
10. Use the left and right edges of the first effect's timeline box to adjust the timing on the first paragraph to Start 2s, End 3s.

Using the timeline to change the duration of an effect

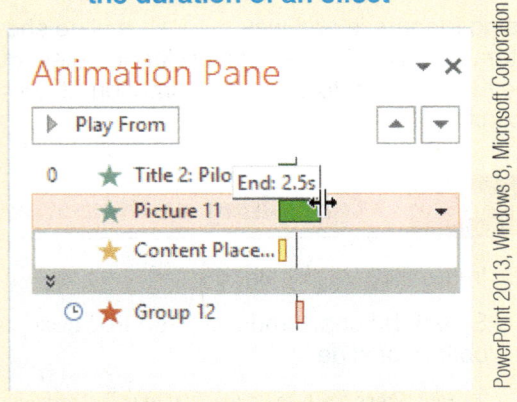

11. Adjust the timing of the second paragraph to Start 3s, End 4s.
12. Click the Seconds down arrow and click Zoom In.
13. Position the pointer on the Group 12 exit effect's timeline so that it becomes a horizontal two-headed arrow. Click and drag the entire timeline box to the right until the ScreenTip shows Start: 4.5s.

Setting a delay by dragging a timeline box

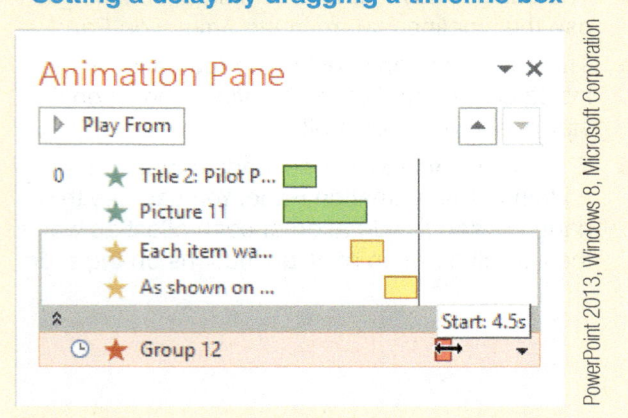

14. Preview the animations on the slide to see how timeline adjustments have changed duration and delay.
15. Close the **P40Try_xx** file, saving changes, and exit PowerPoint.

Lesson 40—Practice

Natural Light has asked you to add animations to a presentation that will be available in the showroom for visitors to browse. In this project, you work with a number of custom animation options.

DIRECTIONS

1. Start PowerPoint, if necessary, and open **P40Practice** from the data files for this lesson.
2. Save the file as **P40Practice_xx** in the location where your teacher instructs you to store the files for this lesson.
3. On slide 1, select the Star object.
4. Click **ANIMATIONS** > **Add Animation** ★ > **Color Pulse** in the Emphasis section of the gallery.
5. Click **ANIMATIONS** > **Effect Options** and select the last color on the top row.
6. Click **ANIMATIONS** > **Start** > **After Previous**.
7. Click **ANIMATIONS** > **Animation Pane** .
8. In the Animation Pane, click the Star animation's down arrow and select **Timing** from the menu.
9. In the dialog box, click the **Repeat** down arrow and select **Until Next Click**. Click **OK**.
10. Select the title and subtitle placeholders on slide 1 and click **ANIMATIONS** > **Add Animation** ★ > **More Entrance Effects**.
11. Select **Dissolve In** and click **OK**.
12. Select the subtitle placeholder and click **ANIMATIONS** > **Start** > **After Previous**.
13. In the Animation Pane, click the title animation down arrow and select **Effect Options**.
14. On the Effect tab, click the **After animation** down arrow and select the pale yellow-green square at the far right.
15. Click the **Animate text** down arrow and select **By word**.
16. On the Timing tab, click the **Start** down arrow and select **With Previous**.
17. Click **OK**.
18. Select the timeline box for the title animation and drag the right edge to the right until the ScreenTip reads **By Word: 4.0s**.
19. Drag the right edge of the subtitle animation to end the animation at **7.0s**.
20. Close the Animation Pane and click the **Slide Show** button on the status bar to view your animations in Slide Show view. Click [ESC] to end the slide show.
21. Insert a footer with your name and the date on all slides except the first slide.
22. Close the presentation, saving changes, and exit PowerPoint.

Lesson 40—Apply

In this project, you continue to work on the Natural Light presentation. You add and adjust animations to complete the presentation.

DIRECTIONS

1. Start PowerPoint, if necessary, and open **P40Apply** from the data files for this lesson.
2. Save the presentation as **P40Apply_xx** in the location where your teacher instructs you to store the files for this lesson.
3. Display slide 4 and apply animation effects as follows:
   a. Set the **Sales** placeholder to **Fade**, **After Previous**, **Fast**.
   b. Select the content placeholder below the Sales object and fade the text into view **After Previous**.
   c. Select the **Sales** placeholder and then click **ANIMATIONS** > **Animation Painter**.
   d. Click the **Service** placeholder to apply the same settings to the Service placeholder that you applied to the Sales placeholder.
   e. Delay the start of the Service placeholder by 1.5 seconds.
   f. Use the Animation Painter to apply the settings from the left content placeholder to the right one under Service. (You may need to reapply After Previous timing to the second bullet in this placeholder.)
4. Display slide 5 and apply a **Fly In** entrance animation to the SmartArt graphic, **After Previous**, **Fast From Left**. Then modify the animation effects as follows:
   a. Change the SmartArt Animation option in the Effect Options dialog box to **One by one**, then expand the effect to see all the shapes that make up the diagram. (You may need to apply After Previous timing to shapes after the first one.)
   b. Using the timeline, adjust the duration and delay of each shape so that a viewer has time to read the Step 1 shape before the first list shape appears, read the text in this shape before the Step 2 shape appears, and so on.
   c. Use the **Play From** button in the Animation Pane and the **Slide Show** button to test your delays until you are satisfied with the results.
5. On slide 6, set a trigger to animate the picture with a **Wipe** entrance effect, **From Top**, **Fast**, when the slide title is clicked. Then animate the picture description with a **Fade** effect so it appears after the picture.
   ✓ Hint: You might need to reorder the effects to get the animation right.
6. On slide 7, apply to the WordArt object the **Fade** entrance effect, the **Grow/Shrink** emphasis effect, and the **Fade** exit effect. Apply the following settings:
   a. Apply **After Previous** to all of the effects.
   b. Change the timing of the entrance effect to **Slow**.
   c. Make sure the timing of the emphasis effect is **Medium**.
   d. Change the timing of the exit effect to **Slow**.
7. On slide 7, add a motion path to the Star object so that it moves to the center of the slide after the WordArt object exits. Then apply a **Grow/Shrink** emphasis effect and use the Effect Options dialog box to increase the size of the object **200%**. Apply **After Previous** to both effects. The motion path should look similar to Figure 40-1.
8. View the slide show to see the effects. Make any adjustments necessary.
9. Insert your name and the date in a footer on all slides except the first slide.
10. Close the presentation, saving changes, and exit PowerPoint.

Figure 40-1

PowerPoint 2013, Windows 8, Microsoft Corporation

Lesson 41

Drawing and Adjusting Tables

➤ What You Will Learn

Drawing a Table
Using the Eraser to Merge Cells
Adjusting Column Width and Row Height
Adjusting Cell and Table Size
Changing Text Alignment and Direction

Software Skills Tables can help you present information clearly and succinctly by displaying information in a column-and-row format. You can customize tables by drawing the structure and adjusting the size of rows and columns, cells, and the table itself. Change the text direction and alignment for a final, expert touch.

What You Can Do

Drawing a Table

- You can create a new table using the Insert Table dialog box to specify the number of columns or rows. Or, you can click the Table button on the INSERT tab and then drag the pointer over the table grid to select rows and columns.
- To create a table that may not consist of a regular column-and-row grid, you can use the Draw Table option on the Table menu.
- After you click Draw Table, the pointer changes to a pencil, indicating that you can draw the table you want on the screen.
- Click and drag the outline of the table. Then select Draw Table in the Draw Borders group on the TABLE TOOLS DESIGN tab to activate the Draw Table pointer so you can create the table's columns and rows.
- You can change the color, style, and thickness of the lines you draw by using the Pen Style, Pen Weight, and Pen Color tools, also in the Draw Borders group.
- You can also use the Draw Table tool to change border formats on existing tables. Just choose the desired formats (pen style, pen weight, and pen color) and then drag the Draw Table pointer over existing borders to apply the new formats.

Business Information Management II | PowerPoint | Chapter 6   825

Try It! Drawing a Table

1. Start PowerPoint, and begin a new presentation using the Retrospect design.
2. Save the presentation as **P41Try_xx** in the location where your teacher instructs you to store the files for this lesson.
3. Click HOME > Layout and select Title Only.
4. Click INSERT > Table.
5. Click Draw Table.
6. Drag the pencil to draw the table outline in the content area of the slide. Release the mouse button when the outline is as large as you want it.
7. Save the **P41Try_xx** file, and leave it open to use in the next Try It.

Drag the pencil to draw the outline of the table

Click to add title

PowerPoint 2013, Windows 8, Microsoft Corporation

Try It! Adding Rows and Columns

1. In the **P41Try_xx** file, click TABLE TOOLS DESIGN > Draw Table.
2. Click on the left side of the new table about one-quarter of the way down from the top border and drag the pencil to the right border.
   ✓ Click slightly inside the border of the table to begin drawing; otherwise, PowerPoint may create a table within a table. If you accidentally insert a new table by clicking in the wrong place, simply press CTRL + Z to undo the error and try again.
3. Repeat until you have created four rows.
4. Click just inside the top border about halfway across the table and drag the pencil down to the bottom border.
5. Repeat to create a third column.
6. Save the **P41Try_xx** file, and leave it open to use in the next Try It.

Try It! Changing Border Formats As You Draw

1. In the **P41Try_xx** file, click TABLE TOOLS DESIGN > Pen Style down arrow. Select one of the dotted line styles.
2. Click TABLE TOOLS DESIGN > Pen Weight down arrow and select 3 pt.
3. Click TABLE TOOLS DESIGN > Pen Color and select Blue from the Standard Colors palette.
4. Click just inside the top table border to the right of the existing column lines, and draw a new line in the new style, weight, and color that extends to the bottom table border.
5. Choose a new Pen Style, Weight, and Color and draw a fourth line, similar to the third.
6. Save the **P41Try_xx** file, and leave it open to use in the next Try It.

Drawing new table lines with various styles

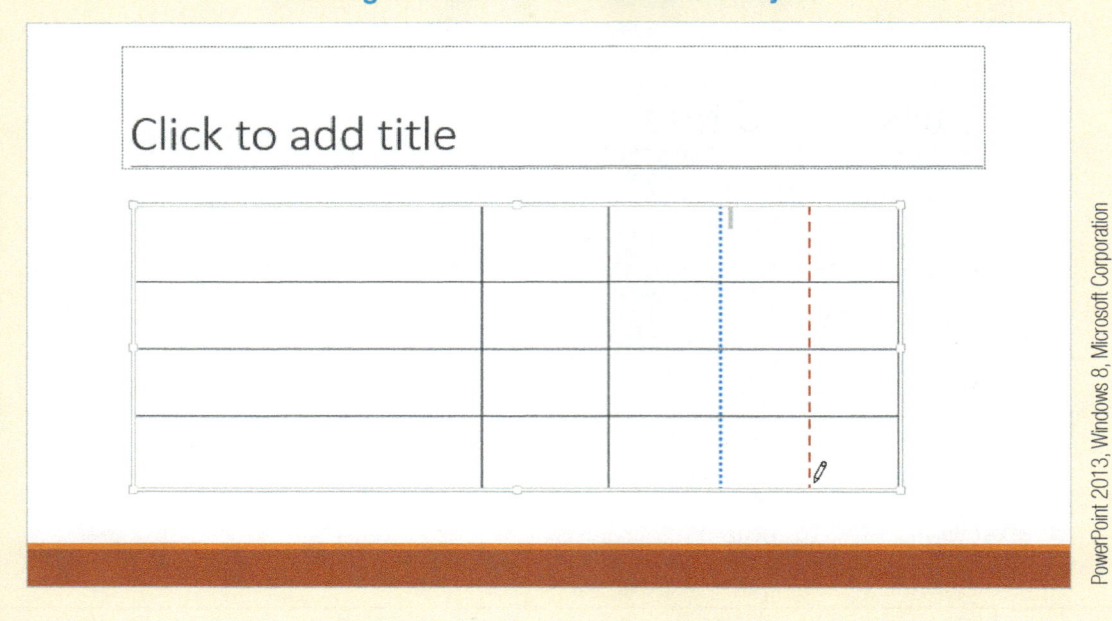

PowerPoint 2013, Windows 8, Microsoft Corporation

Using the Eraser to Merge Cells

- In some cases, you may want to merge cells to create a larger area.
- You might do this, for example, when you want to create a table heading that spans the width of the table, or when you want to create one cell for a column header that spans two subheads.
- One way to combine cells is to use the Merge Cells button on the TABLE TOOLS LAYOUT tab. Another way is to use the Eraser tool to remove cell borders.
- The Eraser tool is available in the Draw Borders group of the TABLE TOOLS DESIGN tab.
- To erase a line, select the Eraser tool and then click the line segment you want to erase. You can also drag the eraser over the line to erase several segments.
- When you erase a row or column line, the cells in the affected row or column merge to make a larger cell.
- The Eraser tool remains selected until you click Eraser again or click a different tool.

Lesson 44
Making a Presentation Accessible to Everyone

- Adding Narration to a Presentation
- Working with Advanced Accessibility Options

Lesson 45
Saving a Presentation in Other Formats

- Saving Slides As Pictures
- Creating a Picture Presentation
- Saving a Presentation in PDF or XPS Format

Lesson 46
Working with Links and Actions

- Using Advanced Link Settings
- Working with Advanced Action Settings

Lesson 47
Working with Online Presentations

- Working in the OneDrive
- Editing a Presentation in PowerPoint Online
- Sharing Online Files
- Working with Co-authors
- Supporting and Maintaining Web-Based Presentations

End-of-Chapter Activities

Lesson 44

Making a Presentation Accessible to Everyone

➤ What You Will Learn

Adding Narration to a Presentation
Working with Advanced Accessibility Options

WORDS TO KNOW

Alternative text
Text associated with a picture or other object that conveys in words what can be seen in the object.

Software Skills Add narration to a presentation to allow people with visual challenges to hear your content. Supplying accessibility information such as alternative text descriptions of pictures and other objects can also help a viewer to understand your presentation.

What You Can Do

Adding Narration to a Presentation

- One way to ensure that your presentation is accessible is to add narration to the presentation. Narration can help those who have visual impairments to understand your points.
- Narration can also be helpful in a self-running slide show to explain or emphasize your points to viewers. Narration takes precedence over all other sounds on a slide.
- To record narration, your computer must have a microphone, speakers, and sound card.
- Before you begin adding narration to slides, make sure your microphone is working correctly.
- To record narration, use the Record Slide Show button on the SLIDE SHOW tab.
- When you select whether to start at the beginning of the presentation or at the current slide, the presentation begins in Slide Show view so you can match your narration to each slide.
- You also have the option to record timings and narration or just narration.

- You will see that each slide to which you added narration has a sound icon displayed in the lower-right corner. Viewers can click the icons to hear your narration, or you can use the AUDIO TOOLS PLAYBACK tab to specify that the narration will play automatically.

- Before you begin, remember these tips.
  - Click through the entire presentation at least once, reading each slide's content.
  - Don't begin reading until the timer indicates 0:00:01.
  - If you make a mistake, keep reading (especially if you're also recording timings). Remember you can always go back and redo a single slide.

Try It! Adding Narration to a Presentation

1. Start PowerPoint, and open **P44Try** from the data files for this lesson.
2. Save the presentation as **P44Try_xx** in the location where your teacher instructs you to store the files for this lesson.
3. On the SLIDE SHOW tab, click the Record Slide Show down arrow.
4. Click Start Recording from Beginning.
5. If you have a microphone attached to your computer, select both options in the Record Slide Show box. If you don't have a microphone set up, you may not have the option of selecting Narrations and laser pointer. Click Start Recording.
6. When the slide show opens, read the text on the slide as clearly as possible. Be sure to time your reading with the way the text appears on screen.
7. When you've finished with slide 1, click the screen to move to the next slide.
8. Continue recording the slide text until the end of the presentation.
9. Save the **P44Try_xx** file, and leave it open to use in the next Try It.

Record Slide Show dialog box

PowerPoint 2013, Windows 8, Microsoft Corporation

Working with Advanced Accessibility Options

- Ensuring that presentations are accessible to all viewers can require you to do some behind-the-scenes work.
- Use the Accessibility Checker to identify issues that could make the presentation difficult to understand for persons with disabilities.
- You will remember that the Accessibility Checker task pane divides issues into three categories.
  - Errors are issues you should definitely fix if you want all viewers to be able to understand content.
  - Warnings are issues you do not necessarily have to fix but could fix for best comprehension by all viewers.
  - Tips give you suggestions for ways to improve content.

- Use the instructions in the Accessibility Checker task pane to help you make the necessary corrections.
- Missing Alt Text is a very common accessibility error, especially in presentations that contain pictures and other graphics. You provide **alternative text** to describe images for viewers who cannot see them.
- The Accessibility Checker will also always prompt you to check reading order—to make sure a screen reader will read content in the order you want. You will usually want the slide title to be read first, followed by text in the content placeholder.
- If you have added sounds or narration to a presentation, you may also be prompted to supply captions for the audio content to meet the needs of those with hearing challenges.

Try It! Working with Advanced Accessibility Options

1. In the **P44Try_xx** file, display slide 1.

2. Click FILE > Check for Issues > Check Accessibility. The Accessibility Checker task pane opens with a list of issues to check and correct.

3. View the Missing Alt Text errors. You do not need to supply alternative text for the Audio objects, but you should supply alternative text for the images and the table.

4. On slide 3, right-click the butterfly image, and then click Format Picture. In the Format Picture task pane, click the Size & Properties icon.

5. Scroll down, if necessary, and expand the ALT TEXT heading.

6. In the Title box, type **Butterfly Image 1**. In the Description box, type **Butterfly shape filled with a picture of a red flower**.

   ✓ Notice that as you supply alternative text, the error is removed from the Accessibility Checker list.

7. Display slide 4 and select the butterfly image. Supply the alternative text title **Butterfly Image 2** and the description **Butterfly shape with a green floral fill**.

8. Display slide 5 and select the table. Supply the alternative text title **Thorn Hill Workshops** and the description **Information about workshops at Thorn Hill Gardens, including programs for water features, perennial gardening, annuals, pruning, and shrubs and trees**.

9. In the Accessibility Checker task pane, view the suggestions under TIPS. You do not need to supply captions for the audio files, because they consist of narration you read directly from the slides. Under Check Reading Order, click Slide 1 to go to that slide.

10. To check reading order, click HOME > Select > Selection Pane. Objects are read from the bottom of this pane to the top. Content on slide 1 is in the correct order, with the title at the bottom, the subtitle next, and then the narration audio object.

11. Check the reading order for the remaining slides. On slide 4, move the TextBox 4 object to be the third object from the bottom of the list. Then close the Selection and the Accessibility Checker task panes.

12. Close the **P44Try_xx** file, saving changes, and exit PowerPoint.

Checking reading order for slide content

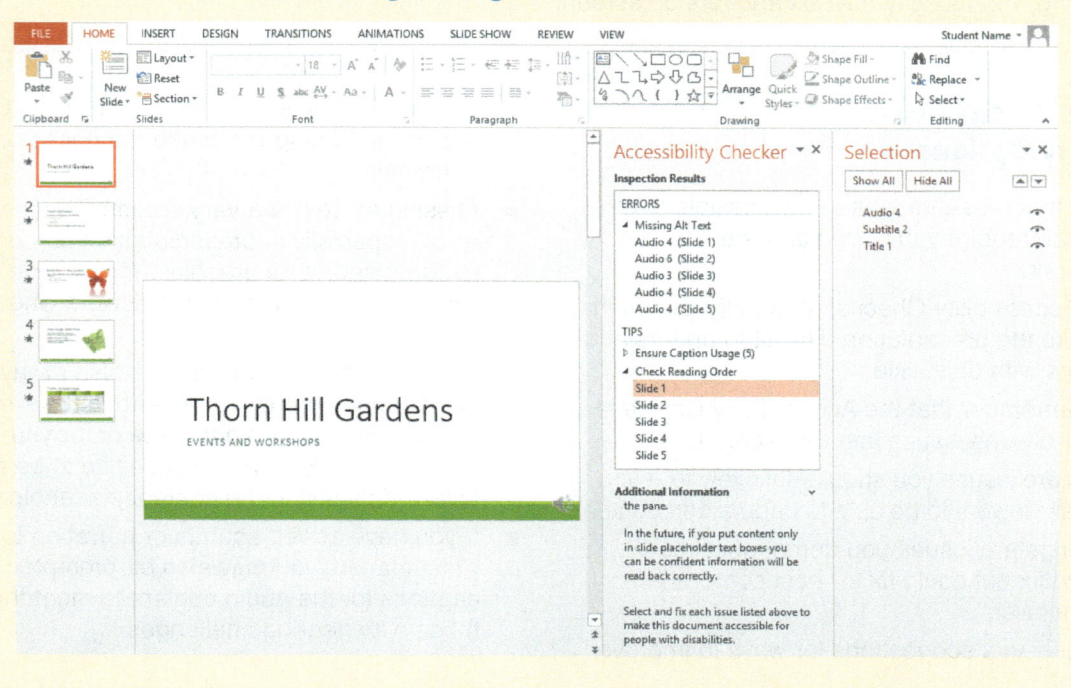

PowerPoint 2013, Windows 8, Microsoft Corporation

Business Information Management II | *PowerPoint* | *Chapter 7*   859

Lesson 44—Practice

Peterson Home Healthcare is preparing information for its annual board meeting. Several of the board members have physical challenges that you need to address as you are preparing presentations. In this project, you add narration to a presentation about options for upgrading IT equipment throughout the company.

DIRECTIONS

1. Start PowerPoint, if necessary, and open **P44Practice** from the data files for this lesson.
2. Save the presentation as **P44Practice_xx** in the location where your teacher instructs you to store the files for this lesson.
3. Create a footer with your name in it.
4. Click **SLIDE SHOW** > **Record Slide Show** > **Start Recording from Beginning**.
5. If you have a microphone attached to your computer, select both options in the Record Slide Show box.
6. Click **Start Recording** to begin.
7. Read the contents of each slide until you reach the end of the presentation.
8. Click **SLIDE SHOW** > **From Beginning** to listen to your narration.
9. Select slide 4 and in the Stage 2 box, place the insertion point at the beginning of the bullet point. Type **Hire a contractor** and press ENTER.
10. Click **SLIDE SHOW** > **Record Slide Show** > **Start Recording from Current Slide**.
11. Select the same options in the Record Slide Show box that you chose for the initial recording and click **Start Recording**.
12. Read the entire slide and then close the recording box.
13. **With your teacher's permission**, print slide 4. It should look like Figure 44-1.
14. Close the presentation, saving changes, and exit PowerPoint.

Figure 44-1

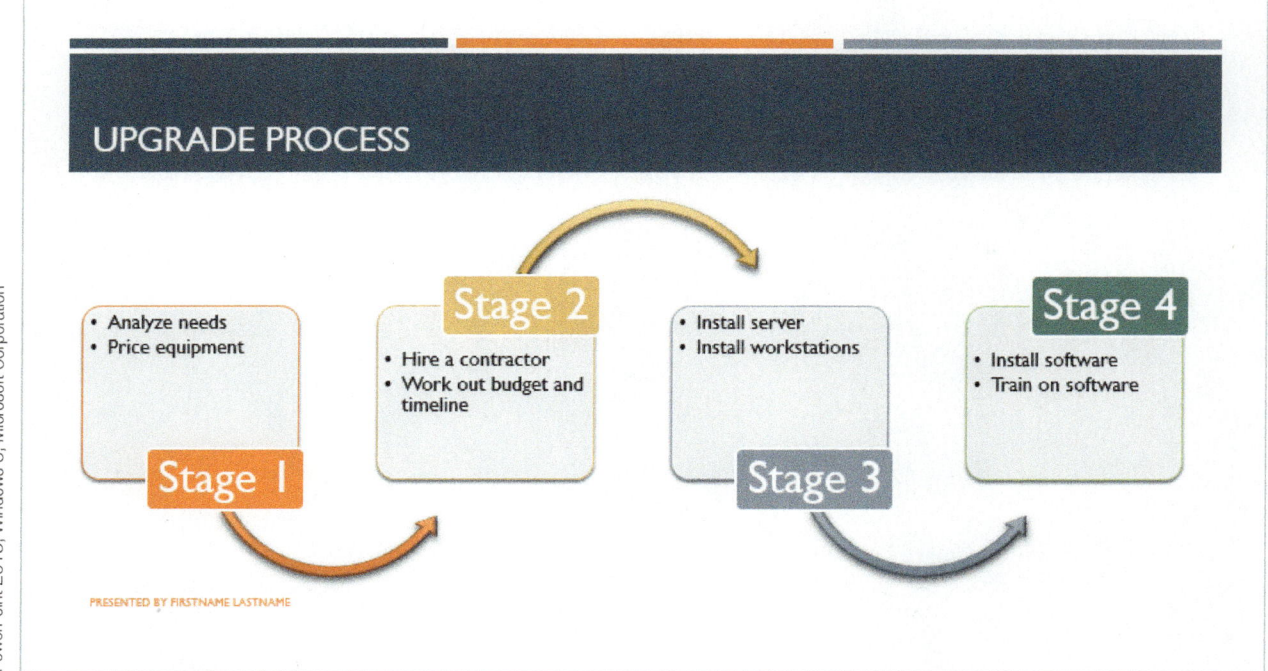

Lesson 44—Apply

In this project, you continue to work on the presentation for Peterson Home Healthcare. You check accessibility for the slides and make the necessary corrections to ensure that all viewers will be able to understand the presentation.

DIRECTIONS

1. Start PowerPoint, if necessary, and open **P44Apply** from the data files for this lesson.
2. Save the presentation as **P44Apply_xx** in the location where your teacher instructs you to store the files for this lesson.
3. Create a footer with your name in it.
4. Run the Accessibility Checker, and review the errors and tips listed in the Accessibility Checker task pane.
5. On slide 1, provide alternative text for the clip art image, supplying both a title and a description.
6. On slide 2, provide alternative text for the photo, supplying both a title and a description.
7. On slides 3 and 4, provide alternative text for the SmartArt diagrams.
8. Check the reading order on each slide and correct the order if necessary. Make sure the narration always appears just below the footer placeholder in the list of items that will be read.
9. Close the presentation, saving changes, and exit PowerPoint.

Lesson 45

Saving a Presentation in Other Formats

➤ What You Will Learn

Saving Slides As Pictures
Creating a Picture Presentation
Saving a Presentation in PDF or XPS Format

Software Skills Save slides or a presentation in a picture format so the slides can be used in other applications. You can save a presentation in other formats that make it easy to share the presentation with colleagues or clients.

What You Can Do

Saving Slides As Pictures

- You can save a single slide or an entire presentation in a graphic file format that allows you to insert the slides as pictures in other applications, such as Word documents.
- By saving a slide or presentation as a picture, you can ensure that it is viewable by anyone with a computer regardless of whether they have a Mac or PC computer or what version of software they are using.
- Use the Change File Type option on the Export tab in Backstage view to save a slide or presentation as a picture.
- You can choose among four picture file formats.
  - PNG and JPEG are listed on the Change File Type tab.
  - If you prefer GIF or TIFF, you can use the Save As button at the bottom of the tab and choose either option in the Save as type list.
- Once you have provided a name for the new file, selected a format, and issued the Save command, PowerPoint displays a dialog box to ask if you want to save only the current slide or every slide in the current presentation.
- The resulting files can be used just like any other picture file.

Try It! Saving Slides As Pictures

1. Start PowerPoint, and open **P45TryA** from the data files for this lesson.
2. Save the presentation as **P45TryA_xx** in the location where your teacher instructs you to store the files for this lesson.
3. Display slide 3.
4. Click FILE > Export > Change File Type.
5. Click JPEG File Interchange Format and then click Save As.
6. Change the file name to **P45TryB_xx** and make sure the file location is the folder where you are storing files for this lesson.
7. Click Save.
8. Select Just This One at the prompt.
9. In Word, open **P45TryC** from the data files for this lesson.
10. Position the insertion point on the blank line following the first paragraph of the memo, and then click INSERT > Pictures.
11. Navigate to the location where you are storing files for this lesson, click **P45TryB_xx.jpg**, and click Insert.
12. Resize the inserted picture to 5" wide, center it, and use PICTURE TOOLS FORMAT > Picture Border to apply a Lime, Accent 1 border.
13. Save the document as **P45TryC_xx** in the location where your teacher instructs you to store the files for this lesson.
14. Close the document and Word. Leave the **P45TryA_xx** file open in PowerPoint for the next Try It.

A slide used as an illustration in a document

Creating a Picture Presentation

- When you save slides as pictures using a picture file type, you create separate graphic files. This is the option to use if you need to insert a picture of a slide in a standard graphic format.
- You have another option for saving a presentation so that its slides become pictures.
- The PowerPoint Picture Presentation format, which can be selected from the Save as type list, transforms each slide in the presentation to a picture.
- You might use this option if you want to share a presentation but you do not want the recipient to be able to edit the presentation.
- Because all objects on a slide become part of a single picture, the presentation's file size may be smaller than the presentation from which it was created. This is often helpful when you are sharing a presentation via e-mail.
- A picture presentation uses the same .pptx extension as a default PowerPoint presentation.

Try It! Creating a Picture Presentation

1. In the **P45TryA_xx** file, click FILE > Export > Change File Type > Save as Another File Type, and then click Save As.
2. Change the file name to **P45TryD_xx**.
3. Click the Save as type down arrow and select PowerPoint Picture Presentation.
4. Click Save, and then click OK when you see the information box about how the presentation has been saved.
5. In File Explorer, navigate to the location where you are saving files for this lesson.
6. Position the pointer over the **P45TryA_xx** file to see a ScreenTip with properties, including the file size.
7. Now point to the **P45TryD_xx** file and compare the size of the file to that of the original PowerPoint presentation.
8. Double-click **P45TryD_xx** to open it.
9. Click on the first slide to see the selection box that surrounds the entire slide, indicating that it is a single picture.
10. Close the **P45TryD_xx** file. Leave the **P45TryA_xx** file open to use in the next Try It.

Saving a Presentation in PDF or XPS Format

- Another way you can prepare a presentation for sharing with others is to save it in PDF or XPS format.
- PDF, or Portable Document Format, is a format that preserves the look of a page or a slide so that a viewer can see the content without being able to edit it.
- XPS, or XML Paper Specification, is a Microsoft document format that preserves page content as PDF does.
- When you choose to save as PDF or XPS, by default PowerPoint will save the presentation as slides, with the slides proceeding one after another in the document.
- If you choose the Options button in the Publish as PDF or XPS dialog box, you can choose to save the presentation as handouts or notes pages, or in outline view. You can choose which slides to publish and choose among other options such as whether to apply a frame to slides or include comments and markup.
- Your PDF or XPS reader opens by default after you publish the presentation to enable you to review the presentation in its new format.

Try It! Saving a Presentation in PDF or XPS Format

1. In the **P45TryA_xx** file, click FILE > Export > Create PDF/XPS Document, and then click the Create PDF/XPS button.

2. In the Publish as PDF or XPS dialog box, change the file name to **P45TryE_xx**, and then click the Options button.

3. In the Options dialog box, in the Publish options area, click the Publish what down arrow and select Handouts. Then click the Frame slides check box.

4. Click OK, and then click Publish.

5. Your PDF or XPS reader opens to display the published handouts.

6. Navigate back to the presentation.

7. Close the **P45TryA_xx** file, saving changes, and exit PowerPoint.

Handouts published to PDF

Business Information Management II | PowerPoint | Chapter 7

Lesson 45—Practice

Planet Earth is preparing materials for a presentation at the Civic Garden Center on what every homeowner can do to promote a healthy natural environment. In this project, you save a slide as a picture and then insert it in an Excel worksheet. Then you save the presentation in picture format to archive the presentation in a smaller file size.

DIRECTIONS

1. Start PowerPoint, if necessary, and open **P45PracticeA** from the data files for this lesson.
2. Save the presentation as **P45PracticeA_xx** in the location where your teacher instructs you to store the files for this lesson.
3. Display slide 4.
4. Click **FILE** > **Export** > **Change File Type** > **JPEG File Interchange Format**, and then click **Save As**.
5. Navigate to the location where you are storing files for this lesson, and change the file name to **P45PracticeB_xx**.
6. Click **Save**.
7. Click **Just This One**.
8. Start Excel, and open **P45PracticeC** from the data files for this lesson.
9. Save the worksheet as **P45PracticeC_xx** in the location where your teacher instructs you to store the files for this lesson.
10. Click cell A3, and then click **INSERT** > **Pictures**.
11. Navigate to the location where you are storing files for this lesson, click **P45PracticeB_xx**, and then click **Insert**.
12. Resize the picture to **5"** wide, and adjust its position to fit in the blank rows between the *Compost Initiative* heading and the worksheet data.
13. With the picture still selected, click **PICTURE TOOLS FORMAT** > **Picture Border** and select **Green, Accent 1**.
14. **With your teacher's permission,** print the worksheet. Your printout should look similar to Figure 45-1.
15. Close the **P45PracticeC_xx** file, saving changes, and exit Excel.
16. In the **P45PracticeA_xx** file, click **FILE** > **Export** > **Change File Type** > **Save as Another File Type**, and then click **Save As**.
17. Change the file name to **P45PracticeD_xx**, click the **Save as type** down arrow, and click **PowerPoint Picture Presentation**.
18. Click **Save**, and then click **OK**.
19. Close the presentation, saving changes, and exit PowerPoint.

Figure 45-1

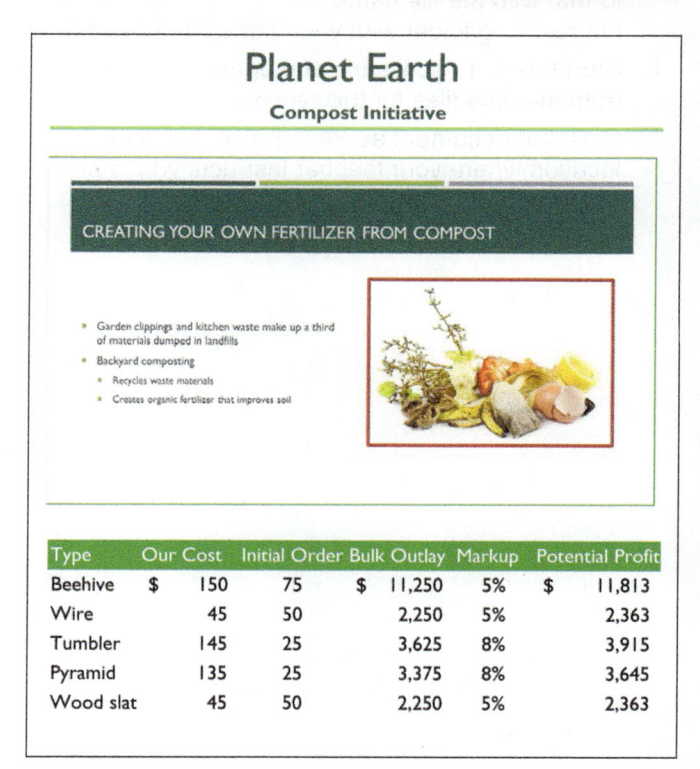

Planet Earth
Compost Initiative

CREATING YOUR OWN FERTILIZER FROM COMPOST

- Garden clippings and kitchen waste make up a third of materials dumped in landfills
- Backyard composting
  - Recycles waste materials
  - Creates organic fertilizer that improves soil

Type	Our Cost	Initial Order	Bulk Outlay	Markup	Potential Profit
Beehive	$ 150	75	$ 11,250	5%	$ 11,813
Wire	45	50	2,250	5%	2,363
Tumbler	145	25	3,625	8%	3,915
Pyramid	135	25	3,375	8%	3,645
Wood slat	45	50	2,250	5%	2,363

PowerPoint 2013, Windows 8, Microsoft Corporation

Lesson 45—Apply

In this project, you continue working with the Planet Earth presentation. You save all slides as pictures so that you can insert them in a Word document you have prepared to help you deliver the presentation. Then you save the presentation as a PDF so that you can easily e-mail it to the Planet Earth communications coordinator for approval.

DIRECTIONS

1. Start PowerPoint, if necessary, and open **P45ApplyA** from the data files for this lesson.
2. Save the presentation as **P45ApplyA_xx** in the location where your teacher instructs you to store the files for this lesson.
3. Insert your name and the date on all slides. For notes and handouts, insert your name and the date in the header.
4. Export all slides in the presentation in JPEG format with the file name **P45ApplyB_xx**, storing the resulting folder with your files for this lesson.
5. Start Word, if necessary, and open **P45ApplyC** from the data files for this lesson.
6. Save the document as **P45ApplyC_xx** in the location where your teacher instructs you to store the files for this lesson.
7. Click in the first cell under the Image heading, and then choose to insert pictures and navigate to the **P45ApplyB_xx** folder. Open the folder and select **Slide1.JPG**.
8. Resize the picture to **3.5"** wide.
9. Insert the remaining three slides in the appropriate table cells.
10. **With your teacher's permission,** print the Word document. The first page should look similar to Figure 45-2 on the next page.
11. Close the **P45ApplyC_xx** document, saving changes, and exit Word.
12. In the **P45ApplyA_xx** file, save the presentation in PDF format with the name **P45ApplyD_xx** as handouts with 4 slides per page, and frames around the slides.
13. Close the presentation, saving changes, and exit PowerPoint.

Business Information Management II | PowerPoint | Chapter 7   867

Figure 45-2

Saving the Earth:
What Can You Do in Your Own Back Yard?

Presentation Script

Slide	Remarks	Image
1	Introduce Planet Earth and the topic of the current presentation: what every homeowner can do at his or her residence to promote green initiatives and a healthy ecosystem.	 SAVING THE EARTH: WHAT CAN YOU DO IN YOUR OWN BACK YARD? PRESENTED BY PLANET EARTH
2	Discuss landscaping and point out how healthy and attractive plantings can not only add value to a home but can also provide important habitat areas for wildlife. Define hardscaping and point out that paths should be in good repair and in scale with both the garden and the house.	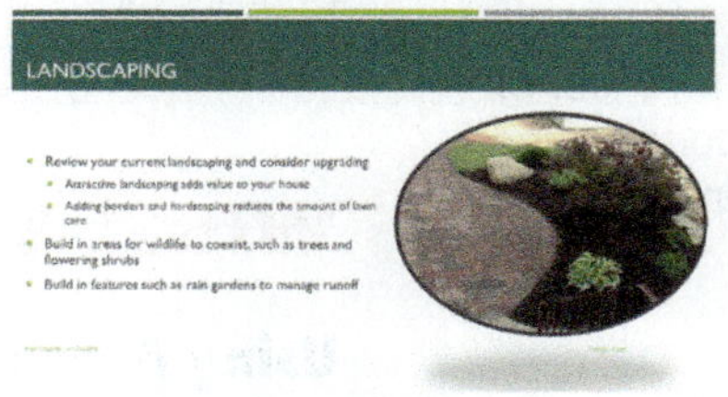 LANDSCAPING
3	Why plant native species? Point out that they have had a very long time to adapt to the climate and can thus be hardy and untroubled by pests. Organic fertilizing and pest control is particularly important for homes with pets and children who spend time on the lawn.	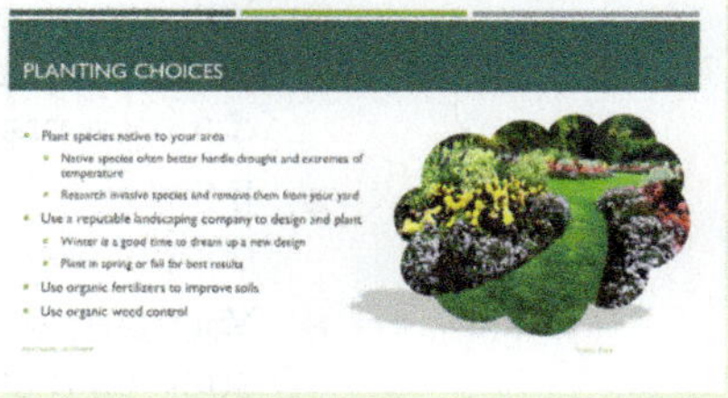 PLANTING CHOICES

PowerPoint 2013, Windows 8, Microsoft Corporation

Lesson 46

Working with Links and Actions

> ### ➤ What You Will Learn
> **Using Advanced Link Settings**
> **Working with Advanced Action Settings**

WORDS TO KNOW

Target
The slide, show, file, or page that appears when you click a link on a slide.

Software Skills Links and action settings can be used to create interactive presentations that allow viewers to jump to different locations in the presentation, open other files, run programs, or interact with objects on the slide.

What You Can Do

Using Advanced Link Settings

- You can use links to move from a presentation to another application to view data in that application. For example, you could link to a Microsoft Excel worksheet during a presentation.
- If the computer on which you are presenting the slides has an active Internet connection, you can also use a link to jump from a slide to any site on the Web.
- You can set up a link using text from a text placeholder or any object on the slide, such as a shape or picture.
- You have four **target** options to choose from.
  - Existing File or Web Page lets you locate a file on your system or network. Use the Browse the Web button to start your browser so you can locate the page you want to use as a target.
  - Place in This Document lets you select a slide or custom show from the current presentation. When you click a slide for the target, it appears in the Slide preview area.
  - Create New Document allows you to specify the name of a new document and link to it at the same time. If you create a file with the name Results.xlsx, for example, Excel opens so you can enter data in the Results workbook.
  - E-mail Address lets you set up a link that will open a new e-mail message to send to the address you specify.
- If you want to provide a little extra help to a viewer about what will happen when a link is clicked, you can provide a ScreenTip. The ScreenTip will appear when the presenter or viewer moves the mouse pointer over the link.

Try It! Creating Links to External Documents

1. Start PowerPoint, and open **P46TryA** from the data files for this lesson.

2. Save the presentation as **P46TryA_xx** in the location where your teacher instructs you to store the files for this lesson.

3. Start Word, and open **P46TryB** from the data files for this lesson.

4. Save the document as **P46TryB_xx** in the location where your teacher instructs you to store the files for this lesson. Close the document and exit Word.

5. Start Excel, and open **P46TryC** from the data files for this lesson.

6. Save the workbook as **P46TryC_xx** in the location where your teacher instructs you to store the files for this lesson. Close the workbook, and exit Excel.

7. On slide 1, click the earth in the Planet Earth logo.

8. Click INSERT > Hyperlink.

9. In the Insert Hyperlink dialog box, make sure Existing File or Web Page is selected.

10. In the Look in box, navigate to the location where you are storing files for this lesson, select **P46TryB_xx**, and click OK.

11. Display slide 10 and click the Discussion shape to select it.

12. Click INSERT > Hyperlink.

13. In the Current Folder list, scroll down and select **P46TryC_xx**, then click OK.

14. Save the **P46TryA_xx** file, and leave it open to use in the next Try It.

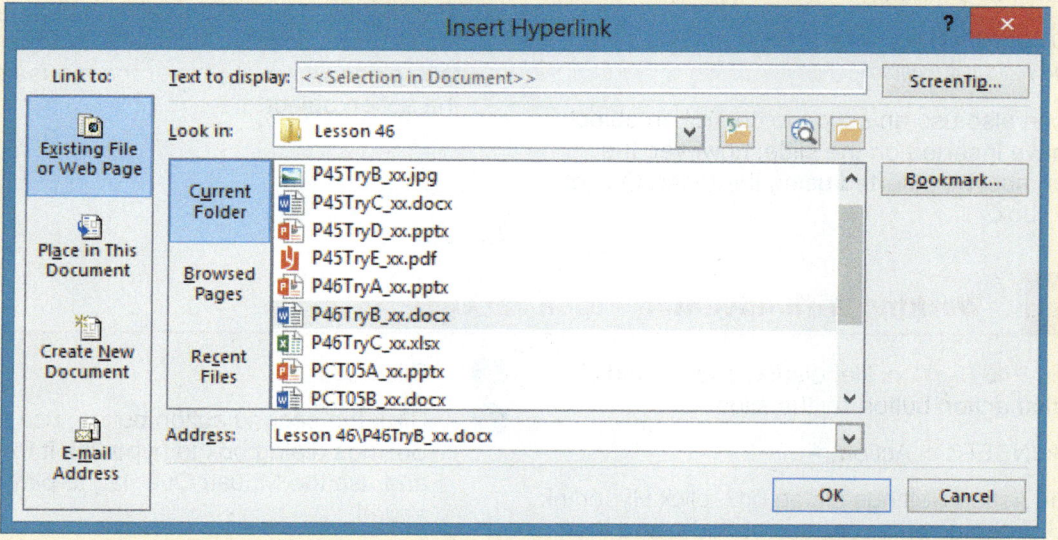

Insert Hyperlink dialog box

Try It!   Creating a ScreenTip for a Link

1. In the **P46TryA_xx** file, display slide 1 and right-click the earth in the Planet Earth logo.
2. Click Edit Hyperlink to open the Edit Hyperlink dialog box.
3. Click the ScreenTip button.
4. In the Set Hyperlink ScreenTip dialog box, click in the ScreenTip text box and type **Click here to learn more about Planet Earth**.
5. Click OK twice.
6. Save the **P46TryA_xx** file, and leave it open to use in the next Try It.

Working with Advanced Action Settings

- Like links, actions allow you to link to a slide in the current presentation, a custom show, another presentation, a Web page URL, or another file.
- Actions are most commonly associated with action buttons, shapes you select from the Shapes gallery and draw on a slide to perform specific tasks.
- You have a number of other options for applying actions, however.
  - You can use an action to run a program, such as Excel, or a macro.
    - ✓ You may have to respond to a security warning the first time you run a program.
  - You can also use an action to control an object you have inserted on the slide; however, the object must be inserted using the Insert Object dialog box.
    - ✓ If you use an existing file, you can choose in the Insert Object dialog box to display the object as an icon on the slide.
  - You can use an action setting to play a sound effect or sound file.
- Use the action options, such as Hyperlink to, Run program, or Play sound, in the Action Settings dialog box to set the target for the action.
- By default, you set actions on the Mouse Click tab, which means that the action takes place when you click on the action object during the presentation.
- The Mouse Over tab contains the same options as the Mouse Click tab. Actions you set on this tab will take place when you hover the mouse pointer over the action object.

Try It!   Working with Advanced Action Settings

1. In the **P46TryA_xx** file, display slide 2 and click the first action button on the slide.
2. Click INSERT > Action.
3. In the Action Settings dialog box, click Hyperlink to, click the down arrow, select Slide, and then select 3. Project Overview.
4. Click OK.
5. In the Action Settings dialog box, click the Mouse Over tab, click the Play sound check box, click the down arrow, and click Chime.
6. Click OK.
7. Click the second action button, use the Action Settings dialog box to hyperlink it to slide 7, and use the Mouse Over tab to play the Chime sound.
8. Continue setting actions for the next two buttons, linking to slide 12 and slide 16, and playing the Chime sound.
9. Display slide 9 and click the action button in the lower-right corner.

(continued)

Try It! **Working with Advanced Action Settings** *(continued)*

Specify actions in the Action Settings dialog box

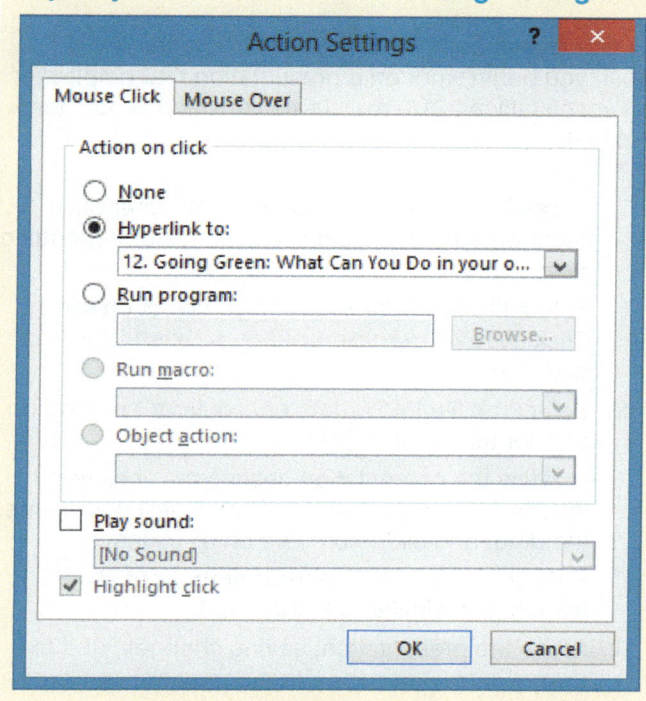

[Action Settings dialog box screenshot]

PowerPoint 2013, Windows 8, Microsoft Corporation

10. Click Insert > Action.
11. Click Run program and then click Browse.
12. Click Desktop in the left pane and select one of the shortcuts on the Desktop.
13. Click OK twice.
14. Click SLIDE SHOW > From Beginning and watch the slide show, clicking all the links and action buttons as they appear. On slide 2, move the mouse pointer over the action buttons to hear the chimes and then click the button to jump to a new slide. When you jump to an external document, view the content, then close the document and its application and return to the presentation.

    ✓ *If you receive a security warning when you click the action button on slide 9 to run a program, click Enable.*

15. Close the **P46TryA_xx** file, saving changes, and exit PowerPoint.

Lesson 46—Practice

Peterson Home Healthcare is starting the process of training employees on Microsoft Office 2013 after the installation of the new network and workstations. In this project, you begin work on a presentation that employees can access from their own computers to learn more about Microsoft Office 2013. You create links and action items to make it easy for employees to interact with the training materials.

DIRECTIONS

1. Start PowerPoint, if necessary, and open **P46PracticeA** from the data files for this lesson.
2. Save the presentation as **P46PracticeA_xx** in the location where your teacher instructs you to store the files for this lesson.
3. Start Word, if necessary, and open **P46PracticeB** from the data files for this lesson.
4. Save the file as **P46PracticeB_xx** in the location where your teacher instructs you to store the files for this lesson.
5. Display slide 2 and select the first bullet item.
6. Click **INSERT** > **Hyperlink** > **Place in This Document** and select the **Introduction** slide. Click **OK**.
7. Repeat this process for each of the other bullet items on slide 2, linking them to the corresponding slide.
8. Select the *Test Your Knowledge* object on slide 6. Click **INSERT** > **Hyperlink** > **Existing File or Web Page**.
9. Select the file **P46PracticeB_xx** from the solution files for this lesson. Click **OK**.
10. Preview the presentation, testing the links you inserted on slides 2 and 6. Then insert your name, the date, and slide numbers on all slides.
11. **With your teacher's permission,** print slide 2. It should look similar to Figure 46-1.
12. Close the presentation, saving changes, and exit PowerPoint. Close the Word document and exit Word.

Figure 46-1

Contents

- Introduction
- Ribbon Interface
- FILE Tab—Backstage View
- Quick Access Toolbar
- Mini Toolbar

Firstname Lastname   Today's Date   2

Lesson 46—Apply

In this project, you continue to work on the Peterson Home Healthcare interactive presentation. You add action settings to allow viewers to open other applications and links to make it easy to navigate the materials.

DIRECTIONS

1. Start PowerPoint, if necessary, and open **P46ApplyA** from the data files for this lesson.
2. Save the presentation as **P46ApplyA_xx** in the location where your teacher instructs you to store the files for this lesson.
3. Insert your name, slide numbers, and the date on all slides.
4. Open **P46ApplyB** from the data files for this lesson.
5. Save the presentation as **P46ApplyB_xx** in the location where your teacher instructs you to store the files for this lesson.
6. Select the shape at the upper-right corner of the first slide in **P46ApplyB_xx** and create a hyperlink to **P46ApplyA_xx**. Then save and close **P46ApplyB_xx**.
7. Select the word *here* in the last bullet item on slide 8 and link it to **P46ApplyB_xx**.
8. Open Slide Master view. On the Title and Content layout (not the slide master), select the **Questions** text box and create a link to an e-mail address. Use the following address: **jpeterson@petersonhomehealth.com**
   ✓ *This e-mail address is a dummy for setup purposes only.*
9. Select the **More Info** box and create a link to the Office Online home page at **http://office.microsoft.com/en-us**.
10. Add the following ScreenTip to the More Info link: **Visit Microsoft Office Online**.
11. Insert a Custom action button from the Shapes gallery below the More Info box and link the button to slide 2. Type **Contents** on the action button, and format the button with the same Quick Style as the text boxes but a different color, as shown in Figure 46-2 on the next page.
12. Make sure all three boxes are the same shape, width, and height. Align left and distribute the three boxes vertically. Then select the boxes, copy them, and paste them on all slide layouts except the title layout, section header layout, and picture layouts. Exit Slide Master view.
13. Display slide 4 and select the *Open Word* shape. Apply an action setting that will run Microsoft Word: Click **Browse** and navigate to the location where Office 15 program files are stored.
    ✓ *On a Windows 8 computer, your path may be similar to C:\Program Files\Microsoft Office 15\root\office15\WINWORD.EXE.*
14. Select the *Open Excel* shape and browse to the same location, but select **EXCEL.EXE** in the office15 folder.
15. You are ready to test your interactive presentation. Follow these steps in Slide Show view:
    a. On slide 2, test each of the links to slides, using the **Contents** action button to return each time to slide 2.
    b. Test the **Questions** and **More Info** buttons. Close the e-mail message window without creating a message, and close the Web page after you are done viewing it.
    c. On slide 4, click the **Open Word** shape, and then click **Enable** when alerted to the potential security risk. Close Word. Click the **Open Excel** shape, click **Enable** if necessary, and close Excel.
    d. On slide 6, click the **Test Your Knowledge** object to open the Word document with three questions. For extra credit, answer the questions and then save the document with a new name such as **P46ApplyC_xx**. Close the document to return to the presentation.
       ✓ *If you get an error message when you click this link, adjust the link target in Normal view and then return to the slide show.*
    e. On slide 8, click the link that takes you to **P46ApplyB_xx**. Use the link to navigate to the information on customizing the Quick Access Toolbar, then use the action button to return to the first slide. Use the button at the upper-right corner of the slide to return to **P46ApplyA_xx**.
16. **With your teacher's permission,** print slide 8. It should look similar to Figure 46-2 on the next page.
17. Close the presentation, saving changes, and exit PowerPoint.

Index

Symbols and Numbers
####, 461
#DIV/0!, 461
#N/A, 462
#NAME?, 461
#NULL!, 462
#NUM, 462
#REF!, 462
#VALUE!, 461
1NF (first normal form), 592, 593, 596
2NF (second normal form), 592, 593, 596–597
3-D effects, 398
3NF (third normal form), 592, 593

A
absolute recording, 420, 423
absolute reference, 439–441
   creating, 441
   using, 439–440
acceptable use policy, 228, 329
Access
   charts, 697–704
      editing, 698–700
      inserting in report, 697–698
      options, changing, 700–702
      types, changing, 699
   controls, 666–676
      bound, 669–670
      check boxes, inserting, 673
      combo box, inserting on form, 671
      formatting, 677–683
         concatenating fields, 681
         conditional, 678–680
         on forms and reports, 678
      labels, inserting, 672
      list box, inserting on form, 671
      option button groups, inserting, 674–675
      renaming, 673
      text box controls, inserting, 667–668
      unbinding, 670
      understanding, 666–667
   creating PivotTables from database, 515
   data, 727
      copying records to Excel, 735–736
      editing imported Excel chart, 735
      export specifications, saving, 737–738
      exporting entire table to Excel, 735
      exporting to another Access database, 737
      exporting to Excel, 735
      exporting to text file, 729–730
      exporting to Word document, 730
      exporting Word table to delimited text file, 729
      importing data from Word table, 728
      importing delimited text file to Access, 729
      importing from another Access database, 736
      importing from Word table, 728
      inserting Excel chart into Access report, 733–734
      linking to data sources, 740–743
         changing linked table, 741
         linking to table in another database, 740–741
         refreshing or updating link, 741
         removing linked table, 741
      merging Access table with Word document, 727
      performing mail merge in Word with data from Access, 728
      publishing in PDF format, 730
      publishing in XPS format, 730–731
   database, 722–726
      adding file locations to Trusted Locations, 725
      adding folder to Trusted Locations, 725
      backing up, 722–723
      compacting, 723
      converting to different database format, 724
      directory merge with, 261
      documenting, 746–747
      properties, setting, 744
      properties, viewing, 745–746
      repairing, 723
      saving in Access 2003, 724
   forms, 684–688
      creating with Form Wizard, 690–691
      default view, setting, 687
      displaying in Continuous Forms view, 684
      displaying in split view, 686
      multi-item, 684–685
      navigation, 712–716
         adding command button to, 713
         creating, 712–713
         tying into Switchboard, 714
      split, 686–687

navigation pane, customizing, 748
options, modifying, 747
queries, 626–654
    action, 643–646
        delete query, creating, 644–645
        understanding, 643
        update query, creating, 644
    crosstab query, 626–632
        creating in Design View, 629–630
        Crosstab Query Wizard, 626–628
    options, 647–652
    prompting for input, 637–642
    unmatched or duplicate records, 633–636
        Find Duplicates Query Wizard, 634–635
        Find Unmatched Query Wizard, 633–634
Quick Access toolbar, customizing, 748
report layouts, 658–665
    control margins, adjusting, 661
    control padding, adjusting, 661
    fields, 661
    layout types, switching between, 659–660
    Layout view, viewing in, 658–659
    page setup, changing, 662
    statistics, adding, 663–664
reports, 658
subforms, 689–696
    creating with Form Wizard, 690–691
    creating with Subform Wizard, 692
    editing, 694
    understanding, 689–690
subreports, 689–696
    creating with drag-and-drop, 693
    editing, 694
    understanding, 689–690
Switchboard, 705–711
    activating, 709
    creating, 706
    deactivating, 709
    formatting, 708–709
    pages, 706–708
        adding link that returns to main Switchboard, 708
        adding link to another page, 707
        adding link to form, 708
        default, changing, 707
        deleting, 707
        editing, 707
        testing Switchboard, 708
    Switchboard Manager
        adding to Quick Access Toolbar, 706
        opening, 705–706
tables
    copying, 592–593
    deleting, 598
    entries, 602–603
        Allow Zero Length, 602–603
        required, 602–603
    fields, 604–606
    formatting, 610–611
    hyperlinks, adding, 608
    macros, 614–620
        embedded, 617–618
        printing macro details, 618
        standalone, 614–616
    merging with Word document, 727
    normalizing table structure, 593–595
        for 1NF, 596
        for 2NF, 596–597
        example, 595
    object dependencies, identifying, 599–600
    properties, 607
    spelling, checking, 611–612
    splitting, using Table Analyzer, 598–599
    title, inserting, 662
Access 2003, saving Access database in, 724
accessibility
    Excel, 575, 576–577
        Accessibility Checker, 577
        adding alternative text (Alt Text), 577
        issues, 576–577
    PowerPoint, 857–858
    Word, 48, 50–51
Accessibility Checker, 48, 51, 575, 577
action query, 643–646
    delete query, creating, 644–645
    understanding, 643
    update query, creating, 644
action settings in PowerPoint, 870–871
active listening, 48, 49, 775, 778
active window, 228
ActiveX Settings, 324
address block, 727
ad-hoc join, 647
adjustment handle, 137, 140, 385, 387
agenda, 79
Allow Zero Length, 602–603
alternative text (alt text)
    Excel, 575, 577
    PowerPoint, 856, 858
    Word, 49, 50
anchor, 137, 139
animations in PowerPoint, 816–823
    controlling with trigger, 819–820
    effect options, 818–819
    more than one animation applied to object, 816–817
    motion path, adjusting, 817–818
    timeline, working with, 820–821

Index

893

Append Only, 605
argument, 488, 493
array, 430
aspect ratio, 137, 138–139
attachment fields, 602, 606
    creating and using, 606
    saving and removing, 606
authenticated, 107
AutoComplete, turning off, 554–555
AutoMark file, 202–203
AutoText, 67, 68
AVERAGEIF function, 430, 433
AVERAGEIFS function, 430, 434

B

banded columns, 480
banded rows, 480
bias, 58
bibliography, 208, 210
bitmap image, 802
blank file, inserting in Word, 5–6
body text, 168
bookmark, 191, 193–194
bound control, 666, 667
    binding record source to form, 669
        assigning entire table as record source, 669
        editing record source for form, 669
    binding to field, 670
break-even point, 446, 449
building blocks, 67–72
    Building Blocks Organizer, 68–69
    custom, creating, 68
    inserting built-in, 67

C

callout, 396–397
caption, 118, 121
case, 329
categories, 354, 356
change history, 544, 547
character style, 18
chart floor, 370, 371–372
chart object, 35
chart title, 35, 37
chart wall, 370, 371–372
charts, 35
    Access, 697–704
        chart options, changing, 700–702
        chart types, changing, 699
        editing, 698–700
        inserting in report, 697–698
    Excel, 354–384
        elements, 354–360
        inserting into Access report, 733–734
        shapes, 385–403
            3-D effects, 398
            aligning, 387–388
            arranging, 387–388
            drawing, 385–386
            effects, adding, 393–394
            formatting, 391–392
            grouping, 387–388
            resizing, 387–388
            rotating shapes, 399
            screen capture, inserting, 399–400
            text, adding, 396–397
        sparklines, 378–380
            column, inserting, 378–379
            formatting, 379–380
            line, inserting, 378–379
            Win/Loss, inserting, 378–379
        stacked area charts, 370–377
        templates, 403–412
            chart template, creating, 407–408
            other graphics, adding, 403–404
            watermarks, adding, 403–404
            workbook template, creating, 405–406
            workbook template, deleting, 406
            worksheet background, formatting, 404–405
        trendlines, 380–381
            inserting, 380–381
            using to predict, 381
        value axis, 361–369
            data markers, formatting, 364
            legend, formatting, 365
            modifying, 362–363
            secondary, adding, 365–366
            stock chart, creating, 361–362
    PowerPoint, 841–849
        appearance, fine-tuning, 844–846
        error bars, adding, 843
        text, formatting, 843–844
        trendlines, adding and modifying, 841–842
    Word, 35–41
        formatting, 37–38
        inserting, 35–36
        modifying, 37
circular reference, 439, 442, 460
citation, 208, 214–215
co-authoring, 875, 879
collapse, 168, 169
column heading, 626
combo box, 666, 671
command button, 712, 713
comment, 91, 544, 548
communication, 775

active listening, 48, 49
  nonverbal, 48–49
  in PowerPoint presentations, 775, 778
  verbal, 48, 49
composite key, 592, 593
compress, 146, 148
concatenate, 677, 681
conditional formatting, 677, 678–680
  expression in, 680
conflict, 58
consolidation by category, 499, 501
consolidation by position, 499, 501
Continuous Forms view, 684
controls, 666–676
  binding to field, 670
  bound, 669–670
  check boxes, inserting, 673
  combo box, inserting on form, 671
  formatting, 677–683
    concatenating fields, 681
    conditional, 678–680
    on forms and reports, 678
  labels, inserting, 672
  list box, inserting on form, 671
  option button groups, inserting, 674–675
  renaming, 673
  text box controls, inserting, 667–668
  unbinding, 670
  understanding, 666–667
COUNTIF function, 430, 434
COUNTIFS function, 430, 434
coupled, 522–523
cover page, 4, 5–6
criteria, defined, 248
criteria range, 488, 493
crop, 137, 141
cross-reference, 191, 194–195
crosstab query, 626–632
  creating in Design View, 629–630
  Crosstab Query Wizard, 626–628
Crosstab Query Wizard, 626–628

D

data axis, 35, 37
data label, 35, 37
data marker, 361, 364
data model, 514–515
Data Model, 532
data range, 35
data series, 35, 354, 358
data source, 474
data table, 354, 357

database
  Access, 474, 722–726
    adding file locations to Trusted Locations, 725
    adding folder to Trusted Locations, 725
    backing up, 722–723
    compacting, 723
    converting to different database format, 724
    documenting, 746–747
    properties, setting, 744
    properties, viewing, 745–746
    repairing, 723
    saving in Access 2003, 724
  Excel, 337, 338, 493–494, 514
database function, 337, 338, 493–494
database range, 488, 493
datasheet, 474
dates in Excel, 296–297
  with custom format, 297
  with standard format, 297
decoupled, 522
delete query, 643, 644–645
delimited, 474, 476–477
delimited text, 727, 728–729
delimiter character, 475, 476–477, 727, 728
demote, 168
dependents, 460, 464
Design View, crosstab query created in, 629–630
destination file, 228, 229
DEVELOPER tab
  Excel, 420–421
  Word, 269–272
dictionary
  adding word to, in Access tables, 612
  in Research task pane, 792
digital signature, 107, 575–576
direct formatting, 10, 12–13
directory, defined, 260
directory mail merge, 260–268
  adding formatting to field code, 262
  customizing fields in address list, 265–266
  inserting merge fields, 261
  merging, 261
  overview, 260–261
  previewing, 261
  selecting specific records, 264
  sorting records in data source, 263
  starting with Access database, 261
diversity, 58
document gridlines, 137–138
Document Inspector, 570–571
document Map, 10, 14
Document Panel in Word, 54

Index

documents, Word, 98–106
    combining, 101–102
    comparing, 100–101
    restricting access to, 107–111
    viewing side by side, 98–99
duplicate, 633, 634–635

E

effects, Excel, 391
    3-D effects, 398
    adding, 393–394
    rotating shapes, 399
    screen capture, inserting, 399–400
electronic portfolio, 4, 6
e-mail merge, 253–255
embedded macros, 614, 617–618
    creating, 618
    editing, 617
embedding, 228, 229–231
    editing embedded objects, 230–231
    objects, 229–230
employment package, 73, 75
employment portfolio, 4, 6
encryption
    Excel, 570, 571–572, 575
        with password, 572, 578
    Word, 107
entries
    Access tables, 602–603
        Allow Zero Length, 602–603
        required, 602–603
    index, 200–202
envelopes, 250–251
error bars, 841
Error Checking, 460–461
error messages, 461–462
    ####, 461
    #DIV/0!, 461
    #N/A, 462
    #NAME?, 461
    #NULL!, 462
    #NUM, 462
    #REF!, 462
    #VALUE!, 461
    circular reference, 462
errors, Excel
    correcting, 462
    turning off, 557
    turning on, 558
evaluate, 460, 463
Excel
    absolute reference, 439–441

cells, 296–303
    clearing formatting from, 299–300
    dates, 296–297
    numbers, 298–299
    style, 314–316
    time, 296–297
charts, 354–384
    elements, 354–360
    imported from Access, 735
    inserting into Access report, 733–734
    shapes, 385–403
        3-D effects, 398
        aligning, 387–388
        arranging, 387–388
        drawing, 385–386
        effects, adding, 393–394
        formatting, 391–392
        grouping, 387–388
        resizing, 387–388
        rotating shapes, 399
        screen capture, inserting, 399–400
        text, adding, 396–397
    sparklines, 378–380
        column, inserting, 378–379
        formatting, 379–380
        line, inserting, 378–379
        Win/Loss, inserting, 378–379
    stacked area chart
        chart floor, formatting, 371–372
        chart walls, formatting, 371–372
        creating, 370–371
        gridlines, displaying, 372
        layout, applying, 373–374
        styles, applying, 373–374
    stacked area charts, 370–377
    templates, 403–412
        chart template, creating, 407–408
        other graphics, adding, 403–404
        watermarks, adding, 403–404
        workbook template, creating, 405–406
        workbook template, deleting, 406
        worksheet background, formatting, 404–405
    trendlines, 380–381
    value axis, 361–369
        data markers, formatting, 364
        legend, formatting, 365
        modifying, 362–363
        secondary, adding, 365–366
        stock chart, creating, 361–362
consolidated/consolidating data, 502
copying Access records to, 735–736
copying data to Word, 130–131

creating PivotTables from, 515
customizing, 288–291
    cell style, 314–316
    data entry, 322–328
    options, 290–291
    Quick Access Toolbar, 288–289
    ribbon, 290
    table style, 316–318
    themes, 312–314
data entry, customizing, 322–328
    form controls, 324–325
    fractions, 323–324
    labels on multiple lines, 322–323
    mixed numbers, 323–324
database functions, 493–494
exporting Access data to, 735
exporting Access table to, 735
filters, advanced, 488–490
    with comparison operator, 490
    to extract records, 489
    to filter in-place, 490
financial statements, 446–452
    Analysis ToolPak Add-On, loading, 446–447
    charting break-even point with line chart, 449
    Goal Seek, 450
    moving average, calculating, 447–449
formulas, 460–467
    dependents, tracing, 464
    error messages, understanding, 461–462
    errors, correcting, 462
    evaluating, 463
    Formula Error Checking, 460–461
    precedents, tracing, 464
    showing, 463
    Watch Window, 464
functions, 430–438
    AVERAGEIF, 433
    AVERAGEIFS, 434
    COUNTIF, 433
    COUNTIFS, 434
    financial, 442–443
    IF Function, 432
    Insert Function, 430–431
    SUMIF, 433
    SUMIFS, 434
    TODAY, 434–435
    TRANSPOSE, 435
imported data, charts from Access, 735
importing data, 474–480
    from Access database, 474–475
    from text file, 476–477
    from Web page, 475–476
    from XML file, 477

iterative calculations, enabling, 442
macros, 420–429
    adding DEVELOPER tab to Ribbon, 420–421
    adding to Quick Access Toolbar, 425
    copying between workbooks, 426–427
    deleting, 426
    editing, 425
    recording, 423–424
    running, 424–425
    saving workbook that contains, 423
    security level, setting, 421–422
    trusted locations, setting, 422
mixed reference, 439, 441
PivotCharts, 522–529
    formatting, 526
PivotTables, 514–521
    creating, 515
    fields, 516–518
    formatting, 518
    working with, 514–515
Power View, 533–535
    fields, 534
    report, 535
    report, creating, 533
PowerPivot, 530–532
    adding data to Data Model, 532
    adding to Ribbon, 531
    to manage data, 531
relative reference, 439
replacing text, 332–333
    using REPLACE Function, 333
    using SUBSTITUTE Function, 332
scenario, 453–459
    ranges, naming, 455
    Scenario Manager used to create, 453–454
    summary, creating, 455–456
slicers, 491–493
    applying styles to, 492
    clearing slicer filter, 492
    deleting, 493
    inserting multiple, 491
styles
    cell, 314–316
    table, 316–318
subtotals, 337–346
    adding manually, 342
    creating, 338–339
    details, hiding and displaying, 341
    nested, creating, 340
    outlining manually, 342
    removing, 341
    using Go To and Go To Special, 337–338
tables, 480–487

Index

converting ranges to, 480–481
icon definitions, editing, 484
icon sets, applying, 483–484
showing Totals row in, 481–482
style, customizing, 316–318
viewing two tables side-by-side, 482–483
text, converting to columns, 292
   delimited text, 292
   fixed-width text, 292
text with formulas, 329–331
   using LOWER Function, 331
   using PROPER Function, 330
   using UPPER Function, 331
worksheet, inserting in Word document, 129–130
Excel Web App, 581, 582–583
Excel workbooks, 507–513
   data integrity, 554–562
      AutoComplete, turning off, 554–555
      duplicate data, removing, 559
      errors, notification of, 557–558
      validation, 555–560
         calculation options, changing, 560
         controlling data entry with, 555
         custom validation, setting up, 556–557
         duplicate data, removing, 559
         invalid data, circling, 557–558
         notification errors, turning off, 557
         recalculation, controlling, 559
         simple validation rule, setting up, 556
         validation rules, copying, 558
   elements, 304–311
      custom views, 308–309
      hiding data temporarily, 304–307
         hiding and redisplaying cell contents, 305
         hiding and unhiding workbooks, 306
         hiding and unhiding worksheets, 307
         hiding rows or columns, 305
         hiding zeros for worksheet, 305
         unhiding rows or columns, 306
      hiding row and column headings, 307
      hiding worksheet gridlines, 307
      printing worksheet gridlines, 307
   finalizing, 575–580
      Accessibility Checker, 577
      accessibility issues, 576–577
      adding alternative text (Alt Text), 577
      digital signature, adding, 575–576
      marking as final, 578
      versions, managing, 578
   linking, 507–509
   manually updating link, 509
   modifying linked, 509
   protecting data, 563–569
      cells in worksheet, locking/unlocking, 563–564
      range, 564–565
      workbook, 566–567
      worksheet, 566
   securing, 570–574
      Document Inspector, 570–571
      encrypting, 571–572
      identifying workbooks using key words, 572
   sending, 581–586
      margins for printing, setting, 581–582
      uploading to Live SkyDrive, 582–583
   shared, 544–553
      comments in, 548
      creating, 544–546
      margins for printing, setting, 581–582
      merging changes, 548–549
      modifying, 544–546
      removing workbook sharing, 549–550
      tracking changes in, 546–547
      uploading to Live SkyDrive, 582–583
      working in Excel Web App, 582–583
   themes, customizing, 312–314
      colors, 313
      fonts, 314
      saving and deleting, 314
expand, 168, 169
export, 243
   Access
      to another Access database, 737
      entire table to Excel, 735
      to Excel, 735
      specifications, saving, 737–738
      to text file, 729–730
      to Word document, 730
      Word table to delimited text file, 729
   Excel
      Access data to, 735
      Access table to, 735
   PowerPoint
      handouts to Word, 775–776
      notes to Word document, 244–245
      slides to Word document, 244–245
      text to Word document, 245–246
   Word
      Access data to, 730
      table to delimited text file, 729
expression, 677, 678
extension point, 396
extract, 488, 489

F

field code, 73, 74
field value, 73

fields
- Access
  - adding report layouts, 661
  - deleting report layouts, 661
  - field prompt, creating, 640
  - indexing tables, 604
  - long text fields in tables, 604–605
  - in Query Design View, changing, 649
  - reordering report layouts, 661
  - table attachment, 606
- attachment
  - creating and using, 606
  - saving and removing, 606
- Excel, 475, 514
  - PivotTable, 516–518
  - Power View, 534
- Word, 73–78
  - display options, setting, 74–75
  - employment packages, analyzing, 75
  - inserting from Quick Parts, 73–74

filter, 248, 480
find and replace
- formatting, 60–61
- images and text from multiple documents, collecting, 59
- Navigation task pane, 60
- wildcard characters in, 61–62

Find Duplicates Query Wizard, 634–635
Find Unmatched Query Wizard, 633–634
first-line indent, 782
Flash Fill, 499–500
fonts
- Excel, 314
- Word, 20

footers, 191–193
form controls, 324–325
Form Wizard, 690–691
forms, Access, 684–688
- creating with Form Wizard, 690–691
- default view, setting, 687
- displaying in Continuous Forms view, 684
- displaying in split view, 686
- multi-item, 684–685
  - creating new, 685
- navigation, 712–716
  - adding command button to, 713
  - creating, 712–713
  - tying into Switchboard, 714
- split, 686–687

Formula Error Checking, 460–461
formulas, Excel, 460–467
- dependents, tracing, 464
- error messages, understanding, 461–462
- errors, correcting, 462
- evaluating, 463
- Formula Error Checking, 460–461
- precedents, tracing, 464
- showing, 463
- Watch Window, 464

functions, 337, 430–438
- AVERAGEIF, 433
- AVERAGEIFS, 434
- COUNTIF, 433
- COUNTIFS, 434
- financial, 442–443
- IF Function, 432
- Insert Function, 430–431
- SUMIF, 433
- SUMIFS, 434
- TODAY, 434–435
- TRANSPOSE, 435

FV (Future Value function), 439

G

Goal Seek, 446, 450
gradient, 754, 755
gradient stop, 754, 755–756
graphics
- Excel, 403–404
- PowerPoint, 243, 754–755
- Word
  - cropping picture, 141
  - document gridlines, 137–138
  - inserting into tables, 126–127
  - objects, adjusting, 140
  - position features, 139–140
  - sizing features, 138–139

gridlines, 304, 307, 370, 372
group, 385, 387

H

Handout Master formats, 766–767, 768
handouts
- exporting to Word, 775–776
- Handout Master formats, 766–767, 768
- linking presentations to Word, 776–777

hanging indent, 782
headers, 191–193
headings, 304, 307
hide, 304
- hiding data temporarily, 304–307
  - hiding and redisplaying cell contents, 305
  - hiding and unhiding workbooks, 306
  - hiding and unhiding worksheets, 307
  - hiding rows or columns, 305
  - hiding zeros for worksheet, 305
  - unhiding rows or columns, 306

Index

hiding row and column headings, 307
hiding worksheet gridlines, 307
hyperlinks, adding to Access tables, 608

I

icon definitions, editing, 484
icon sets, 480, 483–484
If... condition, in mail merge, 256
IF function, 430, 432
import, 733
    Access
        from another Access database, 736
        data from Word table, 728
        delimited text file to Access, 729
        editing imported Excel chart, 735
        from Word table, 728
    Excel, 474–480
        from Access database, 474–475
        charts from Access, 735
        from text file, 476–477
        from Web page, 475–476
        from XML file, 477
    Word, 728
indents, 782, 783
independent scrolling, 98
index
    Access, 602, 604
    Word, 200–207
        AutoMark file, 202–203
        generating, 203–204
        marking entries, 200–202
        modifying, 204
ink annotations, 91
inner join, 647
input message, 554
Insert Function, 430–431
iterative calculation, 439, 442

K

kerning, 18, 20, 176, 180

L

labels, mailing, 251–253
labels in Access controls, 672
legacy, 722, 724
legend, 35, 37, 361, 365, 697
legend key, 354, 356
letters, merging, 249–250
line breaks, 322–323
linked notes (OneNote 2013), 768–770
    adding linked notes button to Ribbon, 769
    working with, 769–770

links
    Access, 740–743
        changing linked table, 741
        linking to table in another database, 740–741
        refreshing or updating link, 741
        removing linked table, 741
    Excel, 507–509
        manually updating, 509
        modifying, 509
        to PowerPoint presentation, 508
    PowerPoint, 868–870
        to external documents, creating, 869
        linking handouts to Word, 776–777
        ScreenTip for, creating, 870
    Switchboard pages
        adding link that returns to main Switchboard, 708
        adding link to another page, 707
        adding link to form, 708
    Word, 237–242
        breaking, 240
        linked object, editing, 238
        linking files, 237–238
        text boxes, 146, 147–148
        updating, 239–240
list box, 666, 671
lock, 563–564
logical function, 430, 432
long text fields in Access tables, 604–605
    Append Only, experimenting with, 605
    rich text formatting in, 605
lossless compression, 802, 803
lossy compression, 802, 803

M

macro security, 420, 421–422
macros
    Access, 614–620
        embedded, 617–618
        printing macro details, 618
        standalone, 614–616
    Excel, 420–429
        adding DEVELOPER tab to Ribbon, 420–421
        adding to Quick Access Toolbar, 425
        copying between workbooks, 426–427
        deleting, 426
        editing, 425
        recording, 423–424
        running, 424–425
        saving workbook that contains, 423
        security level, setting, 421–422
        trusted locations, setting, 422
    Word
        assigning shortcut key to, 275–276

copying, 277
deleting, 273
editing with VBA, 275
recording, 269–272
re-recording, 274
running, 272–273, 274
security of, 277
mail merge
  applying rules to, 255–256
  directory, 260–268
    adding formatting to field code, 262
    customizing fields in address list, 265–266
    inserting merge fields, 261
    merging, 261
    overview, 260–261
    previewing, 261
    selecting specific records, 264
    sorting records in data source, 263
    starting with Access database, 261
  e-mail merge, 253–255
  envelopes, 250–251
  If... condition, 256
  labels, 251–253
  letters, merging, 249–250
  overview, 248
  prompting user for input in, 255–256
main form, 689
MAPI, 248
markup language, 475, 477
master documents, 184–190
  creating, 184–185
  managing, 186
  revising, 186–187
metadata, 744
Microsoft graph, 697
mixed reference, 439
  creating, 441
  using, 439
module, 421, 426–427
moving average, 446
  calculating, 447–449
  growth based on, 448–449
multi-item form, 684–685
  new, creating, 685
multilevel lists, 29–34
  creating, 31–32
  customizing, 30–31
  deleting, 31–32
  formatting, 29–30
multimedia presentations, 810–815
  audio options, setting, 813
  supported video formats, 812
  understanding, 810–811

video options, setting, 811–812
Web video inserted in, 811

N
narration, 856–857
navigation forms, 712–716
  adding command button to, 713
  creating, 712–713
  tying into Switchboard, 714
navigation pane, 748
nested table, 126, 127–128
nonverbal communication, 48–49, 775, 778
normalized, 592
normalizing Access table structure, 593–595
  for 1NF, 596
  for 2NF, 596–597
  example, 595
notes
  advanced, 766–767
  linked (OneNote 2013), 768–770
    adding linked notes button to Ribbon, 769
    working with, 769–770
NPER (Number of Periods function), 440, 442

O
objects
  Access, 599–600
  PowerPoint, 816–817
  Word
    adjusting, 140
    aligning with another object, 146–147
    chart, 35
    embedding/embedded objects, 229–231
OneNote 2013 (linked notes), 768–770
order, 385, 387
Organizer, 18, 23–24
outcrop, 138, 141
outer join, 647
outlines, 168–175
  creating, 168–169
  managing, 169–170
  numbering, 170–171

P
page size, 176
paper size, 176–177
paragraph style, 18, 21
paragraphs in PowerPoint, 782–783
parameter, 637–642
  records with no parameter entered, showing, 639
  understanding, 637
passim, 208, 215

Index

password
   Excel, 572, 578
   Word, 107, 109–111
Paste Special, 554, 558
PDF format
   publishing Access data in, 730
   saving PowerPoint presentations in, 863–864
pictures
   PowerPoint, 802–809
      cropping techniques, 805–806
      for different types of pictures, 803–804
      picture used as fill, 804–805
      supported file types, 803
      understanding, 802
   Word
      background, removing, 149
      compressing, 148
      cropping, 141
PivotChart, 522
PivotTable, 514–521
   creating from Access database, 515
   creating from Excel worksheet data, 515
   fields, 516–518
      adding, 516–517
      custom sort for, creating, 518
      sorting, 517–518
      working with, 516–517
   formatting, 518
   working with, 514–515
pixel, 802
plot area, 35, 37, 354
PMT (Payment function), 440, 442
Power View, 530, 533–535
   fields, 534
   report, creating, 533
   report, formatting, 535
PowerPivot, 530–532
   adding data to Data Model, 532
   adding to Ribbon, 531
   to manage data, 531
PowerPoint
   action settings, 870–871
   animations, 816–823
      controlling with trigger, 819–820
      effect options, 818–819
      more than one animation applied to object, 816–817
      motion path, adjusting, 817–818
      timeline, working with, 820–821
   charts, 841–849
      appearance, fine-tuning, 844–846
      error bars, adding, 843
      text, formatting, 843–844
      trendlines, adding and modifying, 841–842

   effects, customizing, 762–763
   handouts
      exporting to Word, 775–776
      Handout Master formats, 766–767, 768
      linking presentations to Word, 776–777
   integrating with Word, 243–247
      PowerPoint notes, exporting to Word document, 244–245
      PowerPoint presentation, Word outline used to create, 246
      PowerPoint slides
         embedding in Word document, 244
         exporting to Word document, 244–245
         pasting as graphics, 243
      PowerPoint text, exporting to Word document, 245–246
   links, 868–870
      to external documents, creating, 869
      ScreenTip for, creating, 870
   multimedia presentations, 810–815
      audio options, 813
      understanding, 810–811
      video formats, 812
      video options, 811–812
      Web video, 811
   notes
      advanced, 766–767
      exporting to Word document, 244–245
      linked (OneNote 2013), 768–770
   picture formats, 802–809
      cropping techniques, 805–806
      for different types of pictures, 803–804
      picture used as fill, 804–805
      supported file types, 803
      understanding, 802
   presentations
      accessibility options, working with, 857–858
      communicating with others, 778
      narration, adding, 856–857
      online, 875–885
      picture presentation, creating, 863
      saving, 861–863
      Word outline used to create, 246
   research tools, 790–795
      Research task pane, 790–792
      translating text, 792
   slide master, 754–760
      background, customizing, 755–756
      slide layouts, customizing placeholders on, 757
      slide layouts, graphics added to, 754–755
   slides
      embedding in Word document, 244
      exporting to Word document, 244–245

pasting as graphics, 243
tables, 824
   border, 835–836
   cell, 826–828, 835–837
   columns, 825–828
   drawing, 824–825
   effects, modifying, 835–836
   eraser used to merge cells, 826–827
   formatting, 834–840
   image added to, 837–838
   resizing, 829
   rows, 825–828
   style, customizing, 834–835
   text, 829–830
text formats, 782–789
   advanced, applying, 786
   indents, 783
   paragraphs, applying, 782
   tab stops, 784–785
   text box margins, controlling, 785
themes, applying, 761–762
PowerPoint Web App, 877–882
  co-authors, working with, 880–882
  editing, 877–879
  sharing online files, 879–880
precedent, 460, 464
prejudice, 58, 59
primary key, 592, 593
print layout, 658
problem, 59
project, 58, 63
project management, 59, 63
project manager, 59, 63
promote, 168
protect, 563–569
PV (Present Value function), 440, 442

Q
Query Design View, 649
Quick Access Toolbar, customizing, 51–52, 748

R
recalculation, 554, 559
records, in Excel, 475
reflection, 4, 6
relative recording, 421, 423
relative reference, 440
REPLACE Function, 333
report filter, 514
report layouts, 658–665
  control margins, adjusting, 661
  control padding, adjusting, 661
  fields, 661

layout types, switching between, 659–660
Layout view, viewing in, 658–659
page setup, changing, 662
statistics, adding, 663–664
required, 602–603
Research task pane, 790–792
  dictionary in, 792
research tools, 790–795
  Research task pane, 790–792
    dictionary in, 792
  translating text, 792
revision marks, 91, 93
Ribbon
  Excel, 531
    customizing, 290
    DEVELOPER tab, 420–421
    PowerPivot, 531
  PowerPoint, 769
  Word, 52
rich text formatting, 602, 605
rotating shapes, 399
rotation handle, 396, 399
row heading, 626
rules, applying to mail merge, 255–256

S
scale, 138, 139
scenario, 453–459
  ranges, naming, 455
  Scenario Manager used to create, 453–454
  summary, creating, 455–456
Scenario Manager, 453–454
screen capture, 399–400
screenshot, 396, 399
separator character, 126, 130
shapes, 385–403
  3-D effects, 398
  aligning, 387–388
  arranging, 387–388
  drawing, 385–386
  effects, adding, 393–394
  formatting, 391–392
  grouping, 387–388
  resizing, 387–388
  rotating shapes, 399
  screen capture, inserting, 399–400
  text, adding
    to callout, 396–397
    to other shape, 396–397
    to text box, 396–397
shared workbook, 544–553
  comments in, 548
  creating, 544–546